Pvt. William C. "Billie" Crytz The Shady Grove Rangers-Company E[1]

---

[1] Photo Courtesy of Valerie Bowles and Tim Hamilton

Tight Ranks

The Fighting Record of the 34th North Carolina Infantry in the Civil War

A History and Roster

Donald E. Hazelwood

Table of Contents

Preface 7

Chapter 1

Home and Hearth 11

Chapter 2

Playing War 27

Chapter 3

Surviving the Seven Days 39

Chapter 4

Wounds of War 65

Chapter 5

Second Manassas 71

Chapter 6

Crisis at Sharpsburg 89

Chapter 7

Mutiny at Fredericksburg, Aurora Borealis, and a Pig War Veteran 99

Chapter 8

Camp Gregg and Marching With Stonewall Jackson at Chancellorsville 111

Chapter 9

The Crimson Plains of Gettysburg 135

Chapter 10

The Agony of Retreat 165

Chapter 11

To Fight Another Day – Recovering From Gettysburg and the Winter of 1863-64 181

Chapter 12

    A Long Bloody Trail – The Overland Campaign 201

Chapter 13

    Hard Times.. 219

Chapter 14

    The Bitter End 245

Chapter 15

    Appomattox – Duty Faithfully Performed 265

Chapter 16

    The End of the Beginning - The War's Closing Chapter.......... 283

Chapter 17

    Tar Heels in Yankeedom – The Galvanized Yankees 295

Chapter 18

    Reverend Lowrance Speaks... 305

Roster.. 309

Index.. 417

Bibliography.. 437

About The Author... 443

Lieutenant Thomas D. Lattimore, The Floyd Rifles – Company F

Thomas D. Lattimore enlisted as a Private in 1861, at age 17 and was promoted to Second Lieutenant on July 25, 1862. He served the entire war and wrote a history of the regiment which is referred to several times in this book.[2]

---

[2] Photo courtesy of Robin S. Lattimore

Preface

Studying census records can be about as exciting as watching paint dry. But the historical and genealogical information is invaluable. A census is a snapshot of America at one point in time. For the serious student of the Civil War, the 1860 census is crucial, and the long tedious hours spent pouring through these records had its rewards.

Take for example Rutherford County's oldest living citizen in 1860, Cornelius Clements, who was 103 years old. Think of it; Cornelius was older than America. Cornelius was a patriot soldier in the Revolution. As a young man, he fought in the Battle of King's Mountain, an important victory on our way to independence that occurred close to his home. His census taker was so impressed with him that he wrote an inscription in the margin of his ledger, "C Clements was born May 20, 1757. Served one year in the Revolutionary War. Was in the battle of King's Mountain. Died July 28, 1860 being 103 years, 2 months and 8 days old." It was a census-taker's tribute.

Then, there was eastern Mecklenburg County's oldest resident. Her name was Flora, and she was one year older than Cornelius. Flora had eighteen children, the youngest of which was a 58-year-old son who lived with her. We don't know her last name, and ordinarily we wouldn't know her first name. She was a slave. She had been on every census our country had ever taken, but only as a number, property on a slave schedule. She was never listed by name. This time, the census taker wanted her to be remembered, and recorded her by name, a rare honor for a slave. These two great old North Carolinians had grown up in America before it was America. One was a patriot who fought for our independence, the other a slave. Cornelius fought for the freedom that Flora never knew.

Everyone has their opinion of what place the Confederate soldier has in history. Our aim here is merely to show that they were human beings. They were someone's son, father, husband, or sweetheart who found themselves caught up in the most perilous time in America's history and were forced to make choices that none of us today would ever want to make. We do not attempt to glorify them, though the story is told in a positive light. Here, we just tell their story.

The late Senator John McCain once said, "War is wretched beyond description, and only a fool or a fraud could sentimentalize it's cruel reality." We will try here to remember the men, our ancestors, not a cause or the war, but the men and their families and the difficult time they lived through.

If we could make any generality about the men in the 34th North Carolina, we would say that they were uncommonly common. Most were yeoman, subsistent farmers, tillers of the ground. Some were tradesmen, very few were professionals. Their educations mostly came from the fields and blacksmith shops in which they toiled. They were not philosophers or moral trailblazers, just farmers and mechanics, the common men of their day. They were taught and influenced by their families and people in their communities; the roots of their customs went back generations. Loyalty was a matter of blood, and blood ran deep. They were also patriotic and proud of their history. Their grandfathers had fought in the Revolution. Though living in rural areas, they were well-aware of the national political debate over slavery and the subsequent secession crisis. They took the matter seriously.

The backbone of this report is the service records of the 1,535 men who served in the 34th NC. Each one's record is summarized in the roster at the end of the book. Lt. Thomas D. Lattimore wrote a history of the regiment years after the war. Lattimore wrote that he regretted not having access to records from which to give the names of the casualties of each battle they were engaged in. Having that access today, we have tried to fulfill Mr. Lattimore's wish. Naturally, analyzing this number of records is challenging. Records often contain incomplete, inaccurate, or conflicting data. Transcribing these records opens the likelihood for errors, any of which are entirely the author's mistakes. Truthfully, this book barely scratches the surface of the experience of our Civil War ancestors. Full justice for all the men of the 34th NC and their families would require several volumes, but this study helps us begin to understand the men and the hardships they endured.

This narrative will not give the entire summary of the battles they fought in, only their specific roles in those battles. Volumes have been written about these engagements, so recreating those accounts is unnecessary. General summaries are provided to provide context, but the focus is on their part of the battles. Keep in mind that the regiment almost always fought with the rest of the brigade it belonged to. As T. D. Lattimore noted, the history of the brigade was the history of the regiment, so following the one tells us about the other. Sometimes they had a minor part in a major battle, other times they had a large part in a small battle. But no matter where they fought, they did their duty and paid their share of the price in blood.

    Many sources were used to create this narrative including numerous books, articles, and online resources. We also reached out to many helpful individuals and organizations who enriched this narrative. We especially thank the Rutherford County Historical Society and Robin Lattimore for the work they do and contributions to this effort. Jason Harpe and Tina Guffey of The Lincoln County Historical Association were very helpful, as was the Mecklenburg County Historical Association. Our friends in Rowan County were helpful, including the folks at the Rowan County Library. Individuals in Ashe, Montgomery, and Cleveland Counties were also helpful. We are grateful to Ed Guy and his fellow guides at the Gettysburg National Military Park. They are all so knowledgeable and kind. Mr. Van A. Hoyle, Sr. of Shelby, NC shared an abundance of Hoyle family history and photographs. Van served ten years in the U. S. Army, one of which was in Vietnam. He is the Chaplain for the Lt. William Corbitt SCV Camp #525 in Rutherford County. Van's passion for history is apparent and greatly appreciated. Mr. Mike Stroupe generously shared many letters, photos, and information on the Stroupe and Dellinger families. Compliments to Mike for his dedication to preserving history. Much of his information was used.

    Many descendants of men from the regiment contributed photos, stories, and letters of their ancestors. All the photos are used with permission. We thank our friend from Texas, Mr. Will Lowrance. Mr. Lowrance loves history and enhanced this narrative with previously unseen material about Col. Lowrance that is deeply appreciated. Patti Martin provided a photo and memoirs of Pvt. Charles S. Martin that was remarkably interesting. We used much of that information. Valerie Bowles provided the photo of Billie Crytz which was used on the cover. Many others gave permission for photos, all warmly appreciated.

A special thanks to Michael C. Hardy, one of the finest historians around. You would be hard-pressed to find anyone more knowledgeable about North Carolina Civil War history. Having him read the manuscript was an honor. Michael's critiques provided invaluable improvement to this project. His help was very much appreciated.

Robert E. Lee once said, "What a cruel thing is war: to separate and destroy families and friends and mar the purest joys and happiness God has granted us in this world; to fill our hearts with hatred instead of love for our neighbors, and to devastate the fair face of this beautiful world."

For those who lived through the war, on both sides, and for the families of those who did not, this war was devastating. The Civil War was the great crucible through which our young republic had to pass in order to become the nation it is today, a nation of freedom and prosperity that is the envy of the world. Lee also said, "We failed, but in the good providence of God apparent failure often proves a blessing." May the adversities endured by our ancestors stand as a reminder of the blessings of peace and liberty to all generations, and may God continue to bless America.

Chapter 1.
Home and Hearth

It was late October 1861. The leaves were falling, the air was turning crisp, and the sun was shining beautifully in Rowan County. A large crowd gathered at the home of Dr. Sam Carr, a wealthy bachelor. Carmi McNeely was there. He was 25 years old from the Salisbury area. He had spent the past few summers working in Mississippi as an overseer on a plantation. This summer, he cut his stay short returning home in June. North Carolina had seceded from the Union, and he wanted to be with his people. The atmosphere that evening was festive. It was a close community where everyone knew each other. Every prominent family in the area was there. Seventy-four young men in fresh gray uniforms circulated among the crowd. Their parents and grandparents were there, brothers and sisters, whole families turned out, all dressed in their Sunday best. Food was everywhere; fried chicken, mashed potatoes, pies, and cakes. There was laughter and smiles, music, and dancing, on into the evening. The next day, folks brought wagons to take the men to Salisbury. Fathers offered parting words, and mothers, wives, and sweethearts bade tearful farewell as the community's best and brightest sons climbed on the wagons and slowly pulled away.[3]

Only a few weeks earlier, these young men came together at Miranda, a small community near there, and formed a company called the Oakland Guards led by Captain William Houck, a 35-year-old farmer. His First Lieutenant was William Lee Joshua Lowrance, a 25-year-old teacher and 1860 graduate of Davidson College. It was a good group. Carmi knew many of them, the Atwells, Ellers, and McLaughlins, along with the McNeely, Miller, and Overcash families. They came in small groups of friends and family from all over the county to join this company. They had grown up together, played together as children, and attended church together. They hunted the same woods and fished the same holes. They had no military experience but attempted some clumsy drill. The youngest was George Foster at 16. The oldest was 52-year-old John Williford who enlisted

---

[3] (McNeely 1907) NC digital Collections State Library of NC.

with his son James. Most farmed, a few tradesmen were among them. Francis Miller was a cooper (barrel-maker). The popular John Parks was a merchant, as was James Basinger. There were a few mechanics among them like Frank Stirewalt and John Hodgins. Green Eller worked in a mill. Most of them were yeoman farmers who worked their own patch of land for a living. Only one in five in this company came from families who had slaves. Half of those had three or less.

They laughed and bantered, the way young men do, as the wagons creaked and jostled along the winding bumpy road to Salisbury where they hopped a train bound for High Point. They carried their trusty squirrel guns and knapsacks. They had plenty of food, extra socks, blankets, and shirts. It was the adventure of a lifetime. Their clean-shaven faces betrayed the innocence of youth. Their hands were calloused, and their skin was tanned. They knew nothing of war. They had no idea that half of them would never see Rowan County again.

"If war is to come, I prefer to be with my own people."

Governor John Ellis was a Rowan County native. His initial opinion reflected much of North Carolina's attitude. He felt that Lincoln's election alone was not grounds for secession and adopted a wait and see policy. Many saw South Carolina's secession as rash, even reckless. Cooler heads prevailed in the Old North State. Many were conditional Unionists; so long as Lincoln did not threaten force against the south, they would remain in the Union. But the state was sharply divided. The eastern part of the state was flatter and had larger farms with numerous slaves. They were far more supportive of South Carolina's decision. The mountainous western part of the state featured smaller farms and far fewer slaves. Many there opposed secession. Thomas Crumpler, from Ashe County, declared he was no "submissionist" by opposing secession, arguing that their rights, including slavery, were best protected by staying in the Union. There were also religious groups who opposed secession, and slavery on religious grounds. Many of these were in the Quaker Belt areas in the Piedmont section of the state.

On February 18, 1862, Jefferson Davis was sworn in as President of the Confederate States of America with seven states forming the Confederacy. On February 28, North Carolina's citizens voted on whether to hold a secession convention. At the same time, voters elected delegates to represent them if the convention passed. With over 90,000 votes cast, the convention failed by a razor-thin margin of less than 700 votes. All the western counties but two voted against it by convincing margins. Ashe County voters rejected the measure by a vote of 758 to 144. Cleveland County voted for the convention overwhelmingly, as did Mecklenburg. In Montgomery County, voters strongly rejected the convention with 92% against it. Lincoln and Rutherford County voters favored the convention convincingly. Voting was closer in Rowan with a small majority opposed.[4] The fact that the state-wide vote was so close was not necessarily an indication that the state was so evenly divided on the issue. As author William T. Auman points out, many Unionists supported holding the convention believing that most of the delegates would be Unionists and would vote down secession at the convention.[5] They were right. There were 91 Unionist delegates elected versus 39 Secessionists. Had the convention passed, secession would surely have been soundly defeated.

"We are devotedly attached to the Union and opposed to secession."

Even in early April, Unionist loyalty remained surprisingly strong. On April 3, 1861, a meeting was held in Troy, Montgomery County.[6] The chairman was E. G. L. Barringer, Esq. The secretary at that meeting was Jesse S. Spencer, a merchant and future Lieutenant in the 34th North Carolina. Also attending was Martin Rush, a prominent farmer, slaveholder, and father of a young soldier who later served under Jesse Spencer. Among the resolutions unanimously passed was one that read, "That we heartily approve the course of our representative, the Hon. John A. Gilmer…and hope he will consent to be a candidate to represent this district in the next congress." They also resolved, "That we are devotedly attached to the Union and opposed to secession and will support for a seat in Congress any fit man who may

---

[4] These results per the Fayetteville Observer dated March 7, 1861. They do not appear to be the final numbers. The Observer had the convention voted down by 1,857 votes with 74,000 votes counted, but the final count was a margin of only about 700 with over 90,000 votes cast.
[5] (Auman 2014) Page 30.
[6] The Fayetteville Observer / April 8, 1861, (digitalnc.org)

be nominated by said District Convention who is a Union man, irrespective of his former party associations."

"You can get no troops from North Carolina."

Only days the meeting in Troy, on April 12th, Confederate forces opened fire on Fort Sumpter. Three days later, President Lincoln called for 75,000 volunteers to stop the rebellion. Two days after that, Virginia approved an ordinance of secession. Overnight, North Carolina's attitude changed. Lincoln was using force against the south. Conditional Unionists became secessionists. One of the state's leading Unionists was Zebulan Vance who was serving his first term in Congress. When Lincoln called for volunteers, Vance was in western North Carolina. He later wrote, "For myself…I was canvassing for the Union with all my strength. I was addressing a large and excited crowd, and had my arm extended upward, pleading for peace and for the Union of our fathers, when the telegraphed news was announced on Fort Sumpter and the President's call for 75,000 volunteers. When my hand came down from that impassioned gesticulation, it fell slowly and sadly by the side of a secessionist. I immediately with altered voice and manner called for the assembled multitude to volunteer, not to fight against, but for, South Carolina. I said: 'If war is to come, I prefer to be with my own people.'" In an instant, Vance changed from a Unionist to a Secessionist.

Lincoln's call for troops and Virginia's secession forced North Carolina to act. It proved the case of the secessionists and converted the conditional Unionists. Virginia's secession made it impossible for North Carolina to stay in the Union, as they would have been both geographically and politically isolated. When Governor Ellis received the telegram from the Secretary of War calling for two regiments to answer Lincoln's call for troops, he replied:

"Your dispatch is received, and if genuine, which its extraordinary character leads me to doubt, I have to say in reply that I regard the levy of troops made by the administration for the purpose of subjugating the states of the South, as in violation of the constitution, and as a gross usurpation of power. I can be no party to this wicked violation of the laws of the country, and to this war upon the liberties of a free people. You can get no troops from North Carolina."

Governor Ellis called a special session of the legislature for the first of May and ordered the seizure of federal property. The Assembly voted to have delegates elected for a convention to convene in Raleigh. On May 20, 1861, North Carolina's secession convention took place in Raleigh. Delegates voted unanimously in favor of secession. At Gov. Ellis's request, they also voted to not put the secession ordinance to a popular vote as other states had done. Ellis either feared it could still fail or believed that Lincoln's call for troops made the popular vote unnecessary. President Jefferson Davis declared North Carolina a Confederate state the next day. North Carolina's fate was cast with the southern Confederacy.

There is no neutrality in a civil war. These men had to choose a side. Many felt the way Zeb Vance did. Whichever way they thought about secession, their entire identity was with the south, an identity born of kinship, customs, and culture, not slavery or politics. How could they ever side with northern states and go to war against South Carolina, Georgia, and Alabama? How could they fight against their own people? Slavery was the key political debate that led to the secession of the southern states. The war wouldn't have happened without it. But slavery was not what inspired the men to volunteer to fight. These farmers and mechanics were sternly independent. They thought for themselves. At the end of the failed political debate stood these common men who had to decide the matter on the field of battle. When the issue was finally placed into their hands, a different cause emerged. For them, loyalty surpassed every other issue. When the debate was about slavery and secession, North Carolina remained undecided, but when the Old North State was being invaded, they went to war. They fought for home and hearth. They fought for each other.

The 34th North Carolina State Troops

The 34th North Carolina formed at High Point in October of 1861. The ten companies came from the counties of Ashe, Rutherford, Cleveland, Rowan, Lincoln, Mecklenburg, and Montgomery. They came from every walk of life, but most were yeoman subsistent farmers. Their average age was twenty-six. Eighty-five percent of them were farmers. Among other occupations, the regiment had eleven blacksmiths, fourteen carpenters, nine millers, eight wagon makers, and eleven merchants. A few were teachers, doctors, lawyers, masons, ministers, shoemakers, and one deputy sheriff. Some were educated and prosperous. Most were simple farm boys who had never been away from home. Companies were typically organized by prominent men in the communities. The ideal company had 100 men led by a captain. Volunteering was often a family affair. Brothers, cousins, even fathers and sons enlisted together. Blood was thicker than water in these parts. It was the bond that would sustain them through the dark days of war to follow.

A study of slave holders in the regiment's original roster revealed noteworthy facts. As of the 1860 census, 23% of the families in these counties held slaves with Ashe the lowest at 6% and Mecklenburg the highest at 38%. In each company of this regiment, however, the percentage of slaveholders is far lower than their respective county averages. The massive patriotic wave that swept the state in the spring and summer months had already taken many of the slaveholders.[7] In the 34th North Carolina, the percentage of slave holders was roughly 12%, half the overall averages. Of the 136 men who lived in slave-holding households, half held three or less, and 35 had only one. Though they lived in counties that had substantial slave populations, the 34th NC was dominated by non-slave holders.

Laurel Springs Guards – Ashe County

Stephen N. Wilson was a 45-year-old farmer from Ashe County when the war started. He organized the Laurel Springs Guards on August 10, 1861, naming it for the area in the eastern part of the county where many of the men lived. Some were from neighboring Allegheny County. Ashe shared a border with eastern Tennessee where Unionist sentiment was strong. Much of that loyalty was seen in Ashe County residents. But like the rest of the state, opinions changed with Lincoln's call for troops, and most supported the south. Ninety-seven young men volunteered for service in the Laurel Springs Guards. Captain Wilson's Lieutenants were Nelson Woodie, Eli Chandler, and Hiram Cox. The First Sergeant was Edwin Austin.

---

[7] The same study was done on companies D and G from the 16th North Carolina; both companies were from Rutherford County, and both organized in May of 1861. The percentage of slaveholders in this group was about equal the county average.

Ashe County was mountainous and had few slaves, only 391 in 1860. Few counties in the state had less. Only three Ashe County men in the company could be identified as members of slave holding households. Each of those held a single slave as of the 1860 census, and all three of those slaves were fugitives. Many men in the company came from the same families. Merideth and Thomas Anders were brothers. The Bare family had five members in the company, the Cox family had four. The Poe and Sheets families contributed several men to the company. Nearly all were farmers. The Laurel Springs Guards became Company A of the 34th North Carolina.

The Sandy Run Yellow Jackets
Rutherford and Cleveland Counties

From Rutherford County came a band of volunteers called the Sandy Run Yellow Jackets, formed on September 2, 1861, at the Philadelphia Primitive Baptist Church. They later became Company B of the 34th North Carolina and were the first of three companies from Rutherford County. They were organized by Captain John Edwards, a respected Baptist minister. At age 62, Edwards was the oldest man in the regiment, but he had no trouble raising ninety-six eager volunteers. He made his 22-year-old son, John N. Edwards, a sergeant. Captain Edwards was described as, "resolute, strong-willed with a highly developed sense of right and wrong." Joseph C. Byers was a popular 29-year-old from Cleveland County. He helped raise the company by bringing 25 friends with him.[8] Familiar names in the company were Beam, Bedford, Bridges, Dobbins, Edwards, Harrill, and Hamrick. Several sets of brothers were among them. There were five members of the Hamrick family, including Doctor N "Doc" Hamrick, so named because he was the seventh son of a seventh son, which some believed gave him healing ability.[9] Few of these men made a living outside of farming. Joel Daily was a tanner, and Jim Wilson was a blacksmith. About everyone else scratched their living out of the ground. The company's Lieutenants were Joseph C. Byers, William D. Edwards, and David B. Harrill. Their First Sergeant was William H. Harrill. They were mostly from the Sandy Run Creek area near Colfax.

---

[8] This is according to an article in the Forest City Courier dated December 19, 1929 by James C. Elliott. (digitalnc.org)
[9] (Tisdale 1997) Page 5.

Rutherford Rebels – Rutherford County

The Rutherford Rebels also formed on September 2, 1861, later designated Company C. At 108 strong, they were the largest company in the regiment. They were led by 48-year-old Captain Marcus O. Dickerson, the Clerk of the Court for Rutherford County. With him was his son, Robert Dickerson, whom he appointed a sergeant. Robert had enlisted in the 16th NC in May but transferred to his father's company. The Lieutenants were Francis Twitty, Alfred Weaver, and Alexander H. Shotwell. Nearly all were tillers of the ground. Joseph B. Carrier was a merchant, a skill that led to his position as regimental quartermaster. This company had one carpenter, one miller, and a painter. Silas Sorrells and Lorenzo Wilkie were carriage makers. The Nanney family contributed six men to this company led by 55-year-old James Nanney.

Oakland Guards – Rowan County

The Oakland Guards were formed in the Piedmont county of Rowan on September 9, 1861 and was designated Company D when the 34th NC was formed. With 74 members, they were a little understrength. Captain William Houck initially led them, with Lieutenants William L. J. Lowrance, John Graham, and John P. Parks. Houck was promoted to Lt. Colonel when the regiment was formed. His First Lieutenant William L. J. Lowrance was promoted to Captain and given command of the company. The Oakland Guards came from all over Rowan County with a few Iredell County men among them, including Lt. Lowrance. Their work force was a little more diversified. They had six merchants, two teachers, one miller, five mechanics, and one swamper, an unskilled laborer who would do any odd job to make a living. Francis Miller was a cooper (barrel maker). The Atwells, Ellers, McLaughlin, McNeely, and Overcash families were well-represented.

Shady Grove Rangers – Lincoln County

The Shady Grove Rangers, later Company E, hailed from Lincoln County and formed on September 11, 1861 led by Captain John F. Hill, a 44-year-old farmer. They were an ideal sized company of 100 men. Among their skilled laborers were two blacksmiths, two shoemakers, and a wagon maker named George Keever. Micah C. Davis was a minister. The company's Lieutenants were some of the best in the regiment, Hiram Abernathy, Charles J. Hammarskold, and David Rhodes. Hammarskold was from Sweden and 27 years old. He owned a large farm and operated an iron foundry. The First Sergeant was Adam R. Nesbit, a 26-year-old merchant. Familiar family names in this company included Abernathy, Baxter, Childers, Eaker, and Sane.

Floyd Rifles – Cleveland County

Cleveland County supplied two full companies to the regiment. The Floyd Rifles were formed on September 17, 1861, led by a well-regarded 31-year-old Lawyer named Captain Abraham G. Waters with Lieutenants David Hoyle and Pinkney Shufford. This company had 101 sturdy volunteers. Robert Fortenberry and Robert Shields were blacksmiths. John Lutz and David Peeler were tanners. Able Gannt and David Hoyle were millwrights, and George Elam was a miller. Eli Miller was a teacher, and his brother John was the regiment's surgeon. Several members of the Beam, Eaker, and Gantt families volunteered. The Hoyle family had four members in the company, the Lee family had five. The Lattimore, Shufford, and Wright families all had several young men in the company. This company was later designated Company F of the 34th NC.

Mecklenburg Boys – Mecklenburg County

The Mecklenburg Boys, later designated Company G, were formed on September 30, 1861, led by Captain William R. Myers, a lawyer, politician, and farmer. He was one of the wealthiest men in the regiment. Myers ran his farm near Charlotte with the labor of 19 slaves, making him one of the regiment's largest slave holders. Myers had been opposed to secession initially, but like many, he supported the southern cause when war came. His 71 volunteers were devoted and eager to serve. His Lieutenants were Anderson Cresswell and George Norment. Henderson Lucas was only 18 years old but was talented and capable enough to be appointed Ordinance Sergeant and later First Sergeant. Some of the well-known names in this company included Cathey, Abernathy, Mcgee, and Todd.

The Rough and Readys – Cleveland County

The second company to form in Cleveland County was the Rough and Readys. They were designated Company H once assigned to the 34th NC. They were formed on October 1, 1861, under the leadership of Captain Samuel H. Hoey, a 21-year-old druggist with a good reputation in the community. Hoey attended King's Mountain Military Academy in Yorkville before the war under the tutelage of Micah Jenkins.[10] Captain Hoey led the company's 79 volunteers with the help of Lieutenants John Roberts, Joseph Camp, James Wilson, and First Sergeant Clark Allen. The Allen family had six men in the company, the Camp family had five. The Dellinger, Earls, Revel, Roberts, Shields, and Wesson families were familiar names.

The Rutherford Band – Rutherford County

The third Rutherford County company was called the Rutherford Band, 79 volunteers under the leadership of Captain James O. Simmons, Lieutenants William McKinney and Asbury Simmons, and First Sergeant Jonas Watkins. They were formed on October 6, 1861. Very few did anything but farm for a living. John Goode and James Shehan were blacksmiths. Moses Simmons was a merchant. Everyone else farmed. The company became Company I in the 34th NC. Family names included Goode, Hester, Kimbrell, Morrow, Simmons, and Steadman. The Rutherford Band was later designated Company I.

Montgomery Boys – Montgomery County

Finally, from Troy in Montgomery County came the Montgomery Boys, Company K. The company started forming at a meeting in Bruton's District around the middle of August with some 300 people in attendance. The gathering was reported in the Fayetteville Observer, which stated, "Every lady in the section was present, with boxes, trunks, and baskets filled with the good things of life. Col. S. H. Christian delivered speeches, E. G. L. Barringer, Mr. Hurley Jordan, and others."[11] The article also stated, "Our crops are fine. We will make enough for two years, and everything we can spare is for the war. Our ladies, too, are doing their full duty in supplying socks, blankets and other comforts for the soldiers." Just four months

---

[10] The academy was established in 1855 by Citadel graduates Micah Jenkins and Asbury Coward. The academy closed when Jenkins and Coward joined the Confederate army. Brig. General Micah Jenkins was killed at the Battle of the Wilderness. Coward later reopened the school. Hoey mentioned the school in The Goldsboro Gazette on May 13, 1904. (digitalnc.org)

[11] The gathering was described in a letter to the Editor, The Fayetteville Observer September 2, 1861, (digitalnc.org)

prior, Barringer chaired the anti-secession meeting in the county, lending his influence to support the Union. Here, he spoke at a rally to recruit troops for the south.

The company officially formed on September 9, 1861 and elected 49-year-old David R. Cochran as Captain, Jesse S. Spencer and Jesse Sanders as Lieutenants, and Thomas C. Haltom the First Sergeant. Cochran resigned after only a month and was replaced by Jesse Spencer, another prominent member of Barringer's meeting. The Callicott family had five members in the company with two sets of brothers. The Coggin, Elliott, Haltom, Hurley, Reeves, and Sanders families all had several young men in the company.

High Point

By October 8th, six of the companies were at High Point with the rest on the way. One of the first orders of business was to elect a colonel to lead the regiment. The leading candidate was Collett Leventhorpe of Rutherford County. His friend from the county, Captain Marcus O. Dickerson, wrote to him from High Point saying that he was certain he would be elected. John F. Miller, the regiment's surgeon, also wrote to him, saying that he should have no opposition. An article in the Western Democrat endorsed Leventhorpe, noting his experience in the British army.[12] On October 25th, 1861, the 916 men of the 34th North Carolina Infantry Regiment stood in line and swore an oath of allegiance. Each company had its own identity that over time would be forged into one. These men had lived much like their fathers and grandfathers had lived. But everything was changing. The county had been torn in two, pulling these men away from homes and families into a world of uncertainty. Much like their grandfathers who fought in the revolution, they saw themselves as fighting for their independence.

As expected, the new regiment elected 46-year-old Collett Leventhorpe as its colonel. He learned of his election on October 28th while he was still in Rutherfordton. Leventhorpe wrote to Cpt. Dickerson with directions and appointments. He also wrote to Lt. Col. Houck with instructions for drill.[13] Leventhorpe was born in England and served ten years in the British army. He was stationed in Ireland and the British West Indies before transferring to Canada, rising to the

---

[12] The Western Democrat / October 15, 1861, (digitalnc.org)
[13] (Foley 2007) Page 62

rank of Captain of Grenadiers. In 1842, he sold his captaincy and went to work for a British company in Canada. On business, he travelled to South Carolina. In 1843, his travels took him to Asheville, NC where he met his future wife, Louisa Bryan, the daughter of General Edmund Bryan of Rutherford County. Leventhorpe enrolled in the Medical College of Charleston, South Carolina, graduating at the top of his class. In 1849 he and Louisa married and settled in Rutherfordton. He became a United States citizen that same year.

    Leventhorpe was an educated man with a pedigree, and he married into the right family, so he enjoyed a good standing in Rutherfordton. His friends were the influential people in the area, men like M. O. Dickerson. He loved the area and planned to make it his home for the rest of his life. He practiced medicine for a while but did not make medicine his life-long career.[14] He had a restless spirit and had many interests, including a try at gold mining in Rutherford County and Georgia.

    The new Colonel arrived in camp the first week of November. He was tall, slender, and had a commanding presence. His military bearing made an impression as a leader who demanded order and discipline. Having lived in Rutherford County for several years, he knew the men in his command. They were sturdy and devoted but had a fierce independent streak which could be both a benefit and a challenge. They were not accustomed to taking orders. They worked their own farms, made their own way, and lived by the sweat of their own brow. Very few of these men had worked for someone else, and almost none had prior military training. Men leading the companies were just as inexperienced as the men they led. Three of the junior officers were only 21 years old. Leventhorpe's second-in-command was Lt. Col. William Houck of Rowan County. Major Martin Shoffner served as the drillmaster. John F. Miller and John Lawing were the surgeons. Joseph J. Sloan of Rowan County was the Sergeant Major.[15] Rev. James S. Erwin served as chaplain starting in November.[16]

---

[14] Article in the Forest City Courier title Brig. Gen. Collett Leventhorpe-Outstanding Military Leader 12/19/1929. (digitalnc.org)
[15] Sloan enlisted as a Private, promoted to Sgt. Major Oct. 25, 1861, and reduced to private around Feb. of 1862, then discharged for disability in June.
[16] See North Carolina Troops, Vol. 9, page 253.

"We have fiddling, dancing, picking the banjo, cursing plenty..."

Camp Fisher at High Point was named after Col. Charles Fisher of Salisbury who was killed at Manassas. There, thousands of young men were eager to learn the soldier's trade. Camps were typically laid out in grid type patterns, after the regulation U.S. Army manner. Officers' quarters were at the head of each line, or street. The companies were arranged in the order they would take up in battle with their colors displayed outside their tents. Everyone was taught were to find the baggage trains, mess tents, and medical tents. Confederates typically used Sibley tents early in the war. They were large heavy canvas tents 18 feet in diameter and 12 feet tall with a heavy center pole and an opening at the top for ventilation. A small cone-shaped stove provided heat. Up to 20 men could sleep in the tent without much difficulty if a bit crowded.

Reveille was at five every morning. Roll call came first, then breakfast, then drill. This was the main method used to train the troops and Colonel Leventhorpe was an expert. A drill could last one to two hours and they had up six drills a day. They typically drilled first at the squad level, then by company, then as a full regiment. At first the men were eager for drill, but it soon became monotonous. But Leventhorpe was firm believer. There had several different drills. They practiced loading and firing their weapons, (a good man could fire three aimed shots a minute). They had extensive bayonet drills. Most of their drills, however, were marching, where they learned how to move from marching columns of four to line of battle and back. Leventhorpe taught them wheeling from the march and the halt, turning right and left, and breaking into platoons in preparation for battalion drill. Leventhorpe demanded precision. When the time came to do it in battle, they had to make these maneuvers quickly and smoothly. The only way to learn was repetition, and they got plenty of that. Between drills, there were many chores to be done. They had to gather fire wood, build roads, and dig trenches for latrines. The companies formed messes of 8-10 men each, supplied with a kettle and cooking utensils. Usually one man emerged as the designated cook for the mess. Many friendships were formed around these campfires. Some of them messed together the rest of the war.

Despite all the activity, the men still found time for mischief. Most were away from home for the first time and acted out at times. In a letter home, Sergeant George Huntley wrote, "There is a little of most everything carried on here, but more of evil than anything else. We have fiddling, dancing, picking the banjo, cursing plenty, preaching, praying, singing and other things that is as mean as any."[17]

Look away! Dixie Land!

Comradery and even some playful rivalries developed, but the regiment slowly came together. They even made up their own song to the tune of Dixie, with a verse for each company. A few verses survived the memories of the veterans:

When Dickerson's Rutherford Rebels come,
They'll make Abe wish he was home!
Look away, look away, look away in Dixie Land.
Chorus--
Then I wish I was in Dixie, hurrah, hurrah,
In Dixie Land I'll take my stand
To live and die in Dixie.
The brave Floyd Rifles led by Waters,
Will neither give nor ask for quarter!
Chorus--Look away, etc.
When the Sandy Run Yellow Jackets Spread their wings,
They'll scatter death with their wings!
Chorus—
And Hoey's boys from the Hornet's Nest
Will give the Yankee boys no rest!
Chorus—
And no less brave are the Cleveland Guards,
For when they meet the Yankees they'll hit them hard![18]

"Our mothers in their kindness and watchfulness…"

Early on, they began fighting their first deadly enemy of the war, disease. The most common diseases were typhoid fever, small pox, diarrhea, measles, pneumonia, and malaria. John Miller, the

---

[17] (Taylor 1994) Page 40, letter from Huntley dated December 3, 1861. Note: All letters of Huntly quoted in this book are from this source.
[18] Article titled "Old War Songs of '62 Submitted for Publication, The Forrest City Courier, May 19, 1927. digitalnc.org.

regiment's surgeon, was especially important to the men. Miller bonded right away with the regiment's Colonel. It was important that the surgeon have a good relationship with the officers. It helped that Leventhorpe had a medical background.

Despite their best efforts, disease began taking a toll. The first soldier to fall victim was 20-year-old Private William P. Davis from Rowan County who died on November 14th. He was the son of Richard and Deliah Davis. The disease that claimed his life was not recorded. The very next day, Private Aaron M Towry died. He was 21. Several others were hospitalized. T. D. Lattimore wrote, "We spent the winter of 1861, at High Point and Raleigh under rigid discipline, drilling hard, and having diseases which our mothers, in their kindness and watchfulness, had kept us from in our boyhood, to-wit, measles, mumps, whooping-cough, etc." Due to a shortage of medical personnel, Dr. Lawing was transferred less than a month after the regiment was formed. Dr. Miller would shoulder the burden of caring for the men with minimal assistance from here out. He had just turned 27 but proved to be a dedicated doctor with a tireless work ethic. During their stay at High Point, nine men from the 34th NC died.

Name	Age	Co.	Rank	Date of Death	Residence
William P Davis	21	D	Pvt.	Nov. 14, 1861,	Rowan
James M Dennis	20	K	Pvt.	Nov. 27, 1861,	Montgomery
William Lassiter	21	K	Pvt.	Nov. 26, 1861,	Montgomery
John J Lee	23	F	Pvt.	Nov. 26, 1861,	Cleveland
Henry W Morris	22	K	Pvt.	Dec. 4, 1861,	Montgomery
Joel J Overcash	29	D	Pvt.	Nov. 28, 1861,	Rowan
Washington Queen	21	E	Pvt.	Dec. 4, 1861,	Lincoln
Aaron M Towry	21	C	Pvt.	Nov. 15, 1861,	Rutherford
Willis G Wright	19	K	Pvt.	Nov. 27, 1861,	Montgomery

Colonel William Lee Joshua Lowrance[19]

---

[19] Photo courtesy of Will Lowrance, Michelle Muether, and Don Lowrance

Chapter 2.
Playing War

The 34th NC was ordered to Camp Mangum near Raleigh the fourth day of December. The camp was four miles from town on a ridge dominated by pine trees. Here, they continued Leventhorpe's regimen of drill. Since October they had shown much improvement. On December 23rd, Camp Mangum hosted a review for the Governor who commented that the 34th NC was the "best drilled regiment in North Carolina."[20] He was so impressed that Leventhorpe was given temporary command of three additional regiments.

On January 1, 1862, the regiment was officially transferred to Confederate service. Soon after, they received marching orders. Union General Ambrose Burnside was preparing his coastal expedition, and Roanoke Island was his first objective. On January 12th, the regiment was ordered to Wilmington. Sgt. Huntley describes the move in a detailed letter home, "We got orders last Sunday to have our tents tore down and ready for moving by daylight next morning. Early the next morning, on Monday morning, our baggage was all moved out to the railroad, which is distant from Camp Mangum one mile. When we reached the road, we found that there was only cars enough to carry the right wing of our regiment and the left wing, which is the wing that our company is in had to stay there in an old field till one hour after dark. On Monday night, the cars came up and the left wing crawled in. All the baggage of our company and all our men was put in one box. It was full from bottom to top. We just piled on top of one another and I thought from Raleigh to Goldsboro that our box would smash all to pieces."[21] Huntley's letter shows the logistical challenges they faced. The fact that they could get orders one day and execute the move the next day is remarkable, especially in cold January weather.

Their orders were changed on the way, and they halted at Goldsboro. The other regiments in Leventhorpe's temporary brigade were sent to other areas. Heading to Goldsboro and confrontation with Federal troops, Colonel Leventhorpe was concerned. The regiment was

---

[20] Governor John Ellis died in office on July 7, 1861. This was Henry Clark who finished Ellis's term.
[21] (Taylor 1994), page 51, Huntley letter from Goldsboro dated Jan. 17, 1862

still not properly armed. Not all his troops had weapons, and the guns they had were unreliable. Even the best drilled regiment needed arms to fight. Fortunately, within days of arriving at Goldsboro, they became fully armed. They even had proper uniforms. In a letter to his wife, the colonel wrote that the men "looked quite spicy in them."[22] On arrival at Goldsboro, the regiment reported 37 officers and 709 men present. Sickness was pulling their effective strength down fast. By the end of January, 34 men from the regiment had died. Eleven had been granted disability discharges. Over a hundred were absent because of sickness. Private Larkin Kendrick wrote to his wife of the death of Gilbert Webb on January 25th, "I helpt to put a man in his coffen this morning by the name of Gilbert Well [Webb] he was from Rutherford. He died in a ful triumph of a living faith."[23] Webb had a wife and five children.

"...we could sink all the gun-boats that could come up that river."

On February 8th, Union General Ambrose Burnside took control of Roanoke Island. The regiment left Goldsboro and moved 70 miles east to Williamston, arriving there around February 16th. They were ninety miles west of Roanoke Island. The coastal region was in a state of alarm. Troops in the area were spread thin. For the next month, their mission was to guard the vital Wilmington and Weldon Railroad and challenge Federal gunboats coming up the Roanoke River. The 34th NC was responsible for defending a large area with only a small company of local militia and one cavalry detachment in support.

A letter by Sgt. Huntley describes their movements during this time. "My last letter was wrote the day after we left Goldsboro, in that I stated to you that we was going down the Roanoke River on a steamboat. But being disappointed in getting a boat on the 13th of this month we were ordered to take up the line of march down the river. The evening we left Halifax Court House was fair and nice. We marched about eight miles that evening and took up camp. Next morning was cloudy and cold, and we had not marched far before it commenced raining. It rained on four days in succession. During them

---

[22] (Foley 2007), page 63, a quote from Leventhorpe to his wife, Louisa
[23] State Library of North Carolina Digital Collections (digital.ncdcr.gov)

four days we passed through the towns of Clarksville, Hamilton, and Williamston, all close on the river, and on the 17th of this month we reached Jamesville, a small town on the Roanoke River."[24]

By February 19th, the men were busy building defensive works. They could not block the river due to the depth of the water, and they had too few troops to challenge any big push by the enemy, so they built fortifications and constructed fire rafts to use against Federal gunboats. According to T.D. Lattimore, "The Spring of 1862, found us at Hamilton, N.C., on the Roanoke River, 'playing war.' Colonel Leventhorpe had us believing we could sink all the gun-boats that could come up that river." On the 20th of February, the regiment skirmished with a Federal gunboat near Gardner's Creek, twelve miles southeast of Williamston. It was a brief encounter with both sides withdrawing after a few shots. No casualties were reported. The next day, they were ordered back to Weldon, 65 miles to the northwest. The order was soon changed, sending them back to Hamilton by February 27th. For the first two weeks of March, they built new batteries designed to accommodate howitzers and large 12-pound cannons.

Shortly after they moved back to Hamilton, the regiment took its first official muster. Musters were supposed to occur every two months. This muster covered January and February 1862. Of the 916 men enrolled on October 25, 1861, 72 had been dropped, 49 of them due to death. Twenty disability discharges had been granted, two transferred to other regiments, and one officer had resigned. They did pick up 39 new recruits, giving them a total of 883 on the rolls. They reported 743 present, 79 absent due to sickness, 7 on leave, 3 Absent Without Leave (AWOL), and 2 on detached duty.[25]

Stolen Coffee

Discipline was not a major problem at this point. The most serious offence was the court martial of Private Willis Hurley of Montgomery County, held just before they left Goldsboro. The charge was conduct to the prejudice of good order and military discipline. The specification was, "In this, that the said Private Willis Hurley Company

---

[24] (Taylor 1994), page 61, letter by George J Huntley dated Feb. 25, 1862
[25] Official muster numbers could not be found. The muster summaries throughout the book are the numbers compiled from the muster cards of the soldiers' service records.

K, 34th Reg't. N.C. Troops, at some hour of the night of the 6th or 7th inst., being on sentry, did steal from the Commissary store room, one haversack full of coffee, and coffee sufficient in measure to fill half a haversack, which coffee was a part of the commissariat stores of the C.S. Army. This at or near the town of Goldsboro, N.C." Hurley entered a Not Guilty plea, but the court martial, presided over by Cpt. Stephen Wilson, found sufficient evidence to convict him. He was sentenced to hard labor on the fortifications on the coast for the remainder of his service.[26]

A soldier's life was not easy. In a March 3rd letter, Lt. Burwell T. Cotton of Montgomery County wrote, "I marched 40 miles with only two meals victuals except for a few roasted potatoes. I do not like our location. The water is not good and it is very swampy."[27] About a month later, he wrote, "I marched one day eighteen miles out about 10 OC had nothing for supper but a few roasted potatoes nothing next morning but a hog tongue marched 18 miles by 2 OC and had a very good dinner & good bed to sleep on at night. I had rather go in a battle than undertake such a march."[28]

Larkin Kendrick wrote home about Peter V. Beam, whose wife had given birth to their first child. "PV Beam is the proudest man that I ever saw since he got the news of the increase of is famley. I don't think the Col will keep him in the camp he is so proud."[29] Another letter written from Hamilton shows the confidence of soldiers not yet tested in battle. Nineteen-year-old James Freeland wrote to a friend, "I must acknowledge that I did not fully know the blessings of peace but now I know the blessings fighting or the fatigues of camp life….I hope that during the long absence of our many soldiers that you may fully learn to appreciate their company when an opportunity is offered."

On March 23rd, the regiment moved by train back to Goldsboro. On April 11th, Captain John Edwards passed away. The 62-year-old Baptist minister had formed Company B and watched his son

---

[26] Hurley age 47, was discharged in October of that year due to disability.
[27] (Taylor 1994), page 122, letter by Burwell Thomas Cotton March 3, 1862
[28] (Taylor 1994), page 123, letter by Burwell Thomas Cotton April 9, 1862
[29] State Library of North Carolina Digital Collections (digital.ncdcr.gov). The James Freeland letter was found as an offering on ebay.

die on March 1st. Not long after that, he was sent home on sick leave where he died in the presence of his wife, Margaret. The citizens of Rutherford County lost one of their most beloved leaders. The loss of Edwards and his son hit the community hard. The 34th NC had yet to face the enemy, yet 83 families back home were in mourning.

Shortly after coming back to Goldsboro, Colonel Leventhorpe's command of the 34th North Carolina ended. He was elected Colonel of the 11th North Carolina. Leventhorpe had taken men from the mountains and foothills of western North Carolina and drilled them into shape. He left the regiment confident they would do well when the time came to fight. When Leventhorpe left, he took with him 19-year-old Henderson Lucas to serve as his adjunct.

Colonel Richard H. Riddick

A few days after Leventhrope's departure, the regiment got a new colonel. He was 37-year-old Richard H. Riddick. Riddick was born in Gates County. His father died at an early age, and he was raised by his uncle, Benjamin Sumner, Esq. who was living in Rowan County. Riddick had a home in Lincolnton when the war started.[30] The family was prosperous and held a substantial number of slaves. As a young man, he volunteered for the Mexican War and earned a reputation as a reliable soldier. Later, he worked in the Department of the Interior. In 1855, he was appointed a lieutenant in the 1st US Cavalry and served in the 1857 expedition and Battle of Soloman's Fork.[31] After Fort Sumpter, he resigned his commission and offered his services to his native state. The Governor appointed him Assistant Adjunct General and Inspector General for the Department of North Carolina with the rank of Lt. Colonel. At first Manassas, he served as a volunteer aide to General James Longstreet who recognized him for gallantry. When Riddick learned of the threat against Newbern, he asked to return to North Carolina. In early 1862, he was headquartered in Goldsboro on the staff of General Gatlin. Riddick was respected and well connected. He was diligent in his administrative duties and brave under fire.[32]

---

[30] Most of Riddick's background information was found in his obituary in The Standard of Raleigh.

[31] (Chalafant 1989) Riddick is mentioned several times in this book.

[32] (Siniard 2007) Most of the biographical information comes from Riddick's obituary found on this web site.

Reorganization

On April 18th, the army was reorganized. This meant two things. First, there was a re-election of officers. Existing officers had to be re-elected to keep their positions. The election brought significant changes to the regiment's leadership. The highest-ranking officer who failed to be re-elected was Lt. Col. William Houck. He was replaced by Lt. Charles J. Hammarskold. Sgt. Eli Miller was elected Major to replace Martin Shoffner who had resigned in January. Lt. Joseph Byers was easily elected Captain in Company B to replace John Edwards. Two of Company G's three officers were defeated, Captain W. R. Myers, and Lt. Anderson Creswell. The company's 1st Sgt. Joseph McGee was elected captain. Pvt. Robert Ried and Sgt. Alexander Cathey were promoted to lieutenants. All three officers in Company I failed re-election including Captain James O. Simmons. Well-liked Sgt. John McDowell took his place. Joshua Camp was elected from civilian life as 1st Lieutenant. A physician by profession, he was the only man elected who was not already in the regiment.

Sometimes, a good officer might lose his position simply because he wasn't popular. Captain Hiram W. Abernathy was an example. He was a strict disciplinarian and was replaced with a more popular man. In all, the regiment's Lt. Col, two captains, and nine lieutenants were voted out and discharged. The rest were reelected. Lt. Hiram Cox was not re-elected but re-enlisted as a private.

The second part of the reorganization affected every man in the regiment. These men volunteered to serve one year, but the progress of the war showed that they would be needed much longer. By means of the recently passed Conscription Act, the men age 18-35 already serving were reenlisted to serve three years or the duration of the war. They were also given a $50 bounty. Those over 35 would be discharged when their year was up. T. D. Lattimore wrote, "Later we went to Goldsboro, where we re-enlisted for three years or "during the war," at the request of the Confederate Congress, under an act, called by some, "The Conscript Act." Up to this time we thought we had seen something of war, crossing swamps and streams where there were no bridges, but we found out later how little we knew of the actual hardships of long and continuous warfare."

Burnside's threat on North Carolina was subsiding, but things in Virginia were heating up. Shortly after the reorganization, the regiment was assigned, for the first time, to a brigade. They were assigned to the command of Brigadier General Joseph R. Anderson along with the 45th Georgia, 49th Georgia, 3rd Louisiana Battalion, 38th North Carolina, and the 1st South Carolina regiments. On April 23rd, the regiment boarded a train bound for Fredericksburg, Virginia. Many of these boys would never see the Old North State again.

Election of April 18, 1862

Failed Reelection	Co		New Officers elected	Co	Elected to
William A Houck		Lt. Col	Charles Hammarskold		Lt. Col
			Eli H Miller		Major
Hiram Cox	A	2Lt	Franklin Long	A	2Lt
			Joseph Byers	B	Captain
			William H Harrill	B	1Lt
John Graham	D	1Lt	John P Parks	D	1Lt
			Robert T Cowan	D	2Lt
			Samuel H Douglas	D	2Lt
Hiram W Abernathy	E	1Lt	William O Harrelson	E	1Lt
			Micah C Davis	E	2Lt
David H Peeler*	F	Lt	Jacob A Hogue	F	Lt
Anderson H Creswell	G	1Lt	Joseph B McGee	G	Captain
William R Myers	G	Captain	George W Norment	G	1Lt
			Alexander A Cathey	G	2Lt
			Robert S Ried	G	2Lt
William A McKinney	I	2Lt	John L McDowell	I	Captain
Asbury Simmons	I	2Lt	Joshua G Camp	I	1Lt
James O Simmons	I	Captain	Henry Jenkins	I	1Lt
			James Wood	I	2Lt
George M Clark	K	1Lt	Thomas C Haltom	K	1Lt
William Lewis	K	2Lt	Alfred H Hurley	K	2Lt

*David H Peeler was reelected but declined the position and resigned.

Virginia

Richmond faced a tough situation in the spring of 1862. Union General George B. McClellan had 100,000 men poised to move against the Confederate capital. Opposing him was General Joseph E. Johnston's 53,000 rebels. In addition to McClellan's heavy numerical advantage, his army was much better trained and equipped, and reinforcements were a telegram away. Johnston's plan was defensive. He had abandoned Yorktown without firing a shot and pulled his army back to the outskirts of Richmond. Johnston planned to concentrate his forces around the capital and wait for McClellan to attack. To make matters worse, Union General Irwin McDowell was at Fredericksburg with the Union First Corp. At the time of their choosing, McClellan could attack from the east and McDowell from the north, forcing the hopeless Confederates to spread their army out and be destroyed in detail.

One man in Richmond knew that Joe Johnston's strategy was doomed to fail. Robert E. Lee was virtually unknown at this point. At the time, he was Jefferson Davis's senior military advisor. Joe Johnston commanded the troops in the field. Lee saw that the army stood little chance in a head-to-head fight against McClellan's professional army. He felt that their only hope was to keep the Union forces from massing. McDowell at Fredericksburg had to be checked. But with the limited number of troops on hand and an uncooperative Joe Johnston in command, Lee had to pull strings behind the scenes. He used his contacts to draw troops from South Carolina, North Carolina, and Georgia to assemble a 12,000-man force and placed them under the command of Brig. General Joseph R. Anderson. Their job was to block McDowell. The 34th North Carolina became part of this force.

"We are now within sight of each other."

The trip to Fredericksburg by rail took two days and three nights, counting a short stop in Richmond along the way. They set up camp twelve miles from Fredericksburg and deployed pickets. The main body of McDowell's corps was twelve miles away with their pickets six or seven miles away. A few days after they arrived, they were reviewed by their new Brigadier General, Joseph Reid Anderson. Anderson was a West Point graduate and ran the Tredegar Iron Works in Richmond, a major source of munitions for the Confederacy.

The day of the review, Anderson ordered the brigade to move five miles closer to Fredericksburg. They camped in a piney field with access to good water. They were well satisfied with the camp site. General Anderson ordered their tents sent back to Richmond in case of an attack. The weather was improving, but the nights were still chilly, so the men pulled pine limbs around their blankets for extra warmth. The men came up with a new name for an old ailment. They called it the Virginia Quick Step. Many of them had it and there was nothing they could do about it.

Pvt. William B. Brown of Company H wrote to his wife saying, "Our armies have come out 10 miles this side the river. We expect to be in fight here before I am two weeks older and if I am killed I hope to meet you in heaven where the fighting we be no more." He also noted, "We march closer to the Yankees, 5 miles closer tomorrow morning. So must close, so write soon and give me all the news."[33] At this position, the opposing pickets were in sight of one another. In a letter home, Sgt. Huntley describes the situation: "We are now within sight of each other. Every day our pickets has taken some of the Yankies prisoners and the Yankies has taken some of ours. There is skirmishing every day between our pickets and the Yankies, though there has not been a man killed yet on neither side." General Anderson ordered them to have their clothes and equipment kept packed and ready to move with five minutes notice. They maintained this position for the next three weeks with no movement from the enemy.

"...we couldn't persuade the Yankees to fight us"

Near the end of May, they were ordered to strike camp and return to Richmond. Private Larkin Kendrick had been hospitalized and caught up to the regiment a few days before they left for Richmond. On arrival, he received a letter from his wife with the sad news that their young daughter had died. Before they moved, he penned a reply to express his sorrow, "I never heard that my child was ded till yesterday and tongue cant express my feeling about it my mind ran back home and I see in amagination all my famley but now I see them separated never to meet in this world.....I know the large river of simppath cant

---

[33] Letter from W. B. Brown dated 4/4/1862, letter courtesy of Mike Stroupe.

fetch my little Elizabeth back to me…I am satisfied that she is in Haven walking the golden streets of that upper and better world…"[34]

T.D. Lattimore wrote, "From Goldsboro we went to Fredericksburg, VA, and for the first time were attached to a brigade and had a "sure enough" General to command us and could really see the enemy from our picket posts. Well, we couldn't persuade the Yankees to fight us, and having no order to disturb them, we struck camp and marched back to Richmond." McDowell finally got orders to move toward Richmond, but his plans were changed. Shortly after he started his move, Stonewall Jackson delivered a crushing defeat to Union General Nathan Banks at Winchester. In 48 days, Jackson's 17,000 men marched 646 miles and fought several major battles against 52,000 union troops and bested them on every occasion. It was one of the war's most stunning feats of arms. Manassas made Jackson famous, but the Shenandoah Valley Campaign made him a legend. Banks marched his defeated troops north. As soon as Washington got word of Bank's defeat, Lincoln ordered McDowell back to Fredericksburg. By then his advanced units were already at Guiney's Station.

Farther south at Hanover Courthouse was 4,000 Tar Heels commanded by General Lawrence O'Bryan Branch. Johnston had posted them on his extreme left flank without adequate support. General McClellan learned of their presence and was concerned that they would interfere with McDowell's southward move. So, he dispatched Brigadier General Fitz John Porter and 12,000 men to dislodge them. Branch's men were routed, losing 200 men killed and over 700 captured.

Corporal Peter V. Beam

Corporal Peter Van Buren Beam of Cleveland County had been sick, and the weather made him worse. In early March, he was the happiest man in camp due to the birth of his son back home. He and his wife, Margaret, were married in November of 1860, and they were expecting when he enlisted. He never got to see his child. He died at Ashland on May 26th. He was 26 years old. The son he never saw was named David Cleveland Beam.

---

[34] State Library of North Carolina Digital Collections (digital.ncdcr.gov)

Richmond

The fifty-mile march back to Richmond was miserable. They marched day and night through rain and mud. The final leg of their march featured the ominous sounds of battle. Richmond knew that McDowell was as far south as Guiney's Station and considered his move connected with Porter's occupation of Hanover Courthouse. It was believed to be the advance they had been expecting. They didn't know that McDowell was being sent back to Fredericksburg and Porter's presence at Hanover was irrelevant. The moves were enough to prompt Joe Johnston to action. The men in the ranks became pawns in a giant chess match between generals. The 34th NC made camp three miles north of Richmond. The area was described as low swampy ground with standing water and mud everywhere.

On the last day of May, the men of the 34th NC listened all day to the sound of cannon fire. What they were hearing was the Battle of Seven Pines a few miles away. Mistaking the recent moves of Federal troops, Johnston decided to attack part of the Federal line before McDowell could arrive. Col. Riddick's men expected to be sent forward at any time, but the two days of battle passed with no orders for them to engage. Within earshot of the regiment, over 1,700 men on both sides had been killed and over 8,000 wounded in a battle that accomplished nothing. Their friends in 16th North Carolina did see action. The 16th was formed early in 1861. They were led by a dashing 35-year-old named Champ Davis of Rutherford County. Davis lost his life leading his regiment in the battle.

The most significant event from battle was on the second day when General Johnston himself was severely wounded. He would live to fight another day but not in Virginia. Due to his wound, President Davis replaced Johnston with Robert E Lee.

Pender's Brigade

Another important change at Seven Pines was the promotion of William Dorsey Pender to Brigadier General. President Davis personally promoted Pender on the Seven Pines battlefield. Davis liked to have regiments brigaded with men from the same state whenever possible, so some regiments were reassigned. Two of Anderson's North Carolina regiments, the 34th and the 38th, were assigned to General

Pender. His brigade was the 16th, 22nd, 34th, and 38th North Carolina regiments along with the 2nd Arkansas and the 22nd. Virginia.

Pender was a native of North Carolina, born in Edgecombe County. He was young, just 28, but was considered one of the most talented young leaders in the Confederate army. An 1854 West Point graduate, he resigned his commission at the start of the war. Pender was thought of as dark and intense. He was ambitious and unpredictable, qualities Lee and Hill liked. Unlike A. P. Hill, Pender was devoutly religious. He had earned a reputation of bravery while serving in the Indian Wars in the Washington territory. Pender's brigade was part of a newly formed division commanded by Ambrose Powell "A.P." Hill. General Hill called it the Light Division, a name reflected his intention to travel light and fast and hit the enemy hard. This assignment guaranteed that the regiment was sure to be in the thick of much fighting.

Sergeant Elisha Robbins, The Rutherford Band – Company I. Elisha was awarded a Badge of Distinction at the Battle of Chancellorsville[35]

---

[35] Photo courtesy of Robert Wilkins

Chapter 3.
Surviving the Seven Days

Robert E. Lee was 55 years old when he took field command of the forces in Virginia that he named The Army of Northern Virginia. At the start of the war, he was offered the rank of Major General in the U. S. Army but declined saying, "I look upon secession as anarchy. If I owned the four millions of slaves in the South I would sacrifice them all to the Union; but how can I draw my sword upon Virginia, my native state." Indeed, many of the men he led felt the same way.

Lee had about 60,000 troops who were not well prepared to face McClellan's vast professional army. McClellan had backed Johnston all the way to the outskirts of Richmond. Lee's challenge was enormous. McClellan could attack at the time of his choosing. Fortunately for Lee, McClellan was slow and cautious. For three weeks following Seven Pines, McClellan's army sat mostly motionless in their lines. McClellan grossly overestimated the number of rebel troops defending the city. Other than some repositioning, he sat passively and waited for reinforcements. This gave Lee the time he needed. In the latter part of June, the 34th NC was posted along the Chickahominy River. The enemy was on the other side.

The Chickahominy was described as docile and not very wide in most places, easy to cross except during periods of heavy rain such as they had experienced during the spring. When its banks overflowed, swamps formed nearly a mile wide in places. It was a good natural barrier. The weather was very agreeable by then with mild temperatures and less rainfall than the first half of the month. There were periodic skirmishes but no major action. From time to time, the enemy would throw harassing artillery fire across the river. On June 21, 1862, Company G 1st Sergeant John W. Davenport died of a wound he received a few days prior, likely from a random artillery shell. Davenport was 40 years old and left behind a wife, Mary. He was the first man from the regiment to die from enemy fire.

Ever since arriving in Virginia, the men experienced a mixture of anticipation, fear, and doubt. They wanted to experience battle. They wanted to know if they could withstand the test. At Fredericksburg, they had been within sight of the enemy, but nothing happened. They were bystanders at Seven Pines. For three weeks they had sat across the river from their lethargic enemy. The wait was agonizing, but it wouldn't be long. The new commanding general was nothing like Johnston. Despite facing an army that was far superior in number, he was unafraid to face them. He believed the best way to defend Richmond was to go on the offensive. Lee determined to seize the initiative from haughty McClellan.

Mechanicsville

On, June 24th, the men received orders from General A. P. Hill, "Brigade commanders will direct their commissaries tomorrow (Wednesday) to draw two days' rations (Hard Bread) to be issued cooked and put in haversacks. Each brigade will select one battery for service….no wagons will be taken along except one for each regt. And battery for ammunition, and the wagons mentioned for forage. Knapsacks will be left behind in the camp with the sick, Artillery as well as Infantry, the men taking but one blanket…. all men on extra or daily duty in and around the camp who can be spared must take their place in the ranks. Brigade commanders are urged to see that their men are in good fighting condition. These orders are precautionary and, as far as can be, confidential."[36]

The next day, General Pender briefed Colonel Riddick and the other commanders. The strategy was fraught with risk but was carefully planned. Late that afternoon, around 5:30, orders came to move out.[37] Near dark, the brigade was formed and ready. When they took up the march, the sixth brigade was led by the 34th North Carolina Infantry under Colonel Richard H. Riddick.[38] The sun was setting on a phase of their lives they would never again know. For many, it was their last sunset.

A. P. Hill's entire division, six brigades strong including Pender's, was moving. They had been positioned along the river to the left of the division of John B "Prince John" Magruder. Behind Magruder were the divisions of James Longstreet and D. H. (Harvey)

---

[36] (James I Robetson 1992) page 68.

[37] (War of the Rebellion Official Records) Report of Brig. Gen. William D Pender, page 898. Pender states leaving camp the afternoon of the 25th but does not state the time. Other reports state 5:00 pm.

[38] (Longacre 2001) Page 112.

Hill. Both of those divisions were also preparing to move. They had a shorter march and would not move out until sometime between two and three the next morning. The men in the ranks knew nothing of the plan. They marched when and where told. Even the officers were told only what they needed to know. Colonel Riddick surely must have noted that as the three divisions were marching north, the divisions of Magruder and Huger, about 25,000 men total, were the only troops between Richmond and 60,000 Union troops just across the river.
"If this battle is lost, Richmond must fall!"

Lee's first offensive of the war was a big one. His objective was the north flank of McClellan's army. If he could dislodge the enemy troops there, he could threaten the enemy's vital line of supply which was the nearby York River Railroad line from White House Landing, through which came the supplies for McClellan's 117,000 men. The divisions of Longstreet and Harvey Hill were to march north and stop along the river where Mechanicsville lie just opposite. There, they would wait. The Light Division would march farther north, past Richmond and stop at Meadow Bridges. Branch's brigade would then detach and move farther north. Branch was to wait for one other unit to arrive. A critical element in Lee's plan was Thomas J. "Stonewall" Jackson. Lee had ordered Jackson from the Valley to help with this offensive. He was to approach from Ashland. When Branch saw Jackson's approach, he would start south. That would signal A. P. Hill at Meadow Bridges to cross over the Chickahominy, clear the Union pickets, and then move south and clear the light Union garrison at Mechanicsville. This would allow the divisions of Longstreet and Harvey Hill to cross over. The Light Division would then turn east toward Beaver Dam Creek and assault the Federal positions there. Jackson would attack from the north and behind, a sort of pincer move that would force the Federals to abandon the position. The combined force would then drive the enemy south along the river and link back up with Magruder and Huger.

With Jackson on hand, the combined assault force numbered nearly 65,000 men of all arms to oppose the estimated 30,000 men on the Federal flank. The gamble was, for Lee to assemble such a force, over half of his total army, he had to weaken his line to the south. To compensate, the divisions of Magruder and Huger demonstrated in front of the Federal position across the river to make them think there was a larger force there. It was a sound plan but required very intricate execution. Everything must happen in the right order, and that was no easy task. With so many units spread out over several miles, coordination was a huge challenge. Jackson was expected to arrive by around seven in the morning. No one was to move before he was on the scene.

The Light Division marched as the sun became less conspicuous. They passed Richmond to their west and continued their trek. All up and down the line were officers leading men into battle for the first time. The 34th NC had several officers just elected in April, including Colonel Riddick. At the brigade level, Dorsey Pender was leading his men into battle for the first time. His superior, Ambrose Powell Hill, was leading his newly minted Light Division forward for the first time, and General Lee himself had been in field command less than a month. The men of the 34th NC had all the marks of troops new to battle; clean clothes, fresh faces, and a quick easy step. As planned, the Light Division halted at Meadow Bridges. While the men rested, General Pender summoned Colonel Riddick and the other regimental commanders. He told them they, "would be in a fight soon, and that he expected everyone to do his duty; the officers and men were to be informed that if this battle was lost Richmond would fall..."[39]

"...some of us had serious misgivings"

By 7:00 the next morning, the men were ready to move. By then, the divisions of Longstreet and Harvey Hill were moving up the Mechanicsville Turnpike approaching their destination along the river across from Mechanicsville. The bridge there had been burned by Federal troops, so the pioneers planned to install a bridge for them. Powell Hill's men were in position at Meadow Bridges and Branch's brigade was deployed and waiting for Jackson.[40] The deployments were going as planned. At Meadow Bridges near where the Virginia Central tracks crossed the river, the men of the 34th North Carolina waited with the rest of the Light Division. Hill moved the men into the nearby woods to conceal them and give them shade from the sun which was

---

[39] (Longacre 2001) Page 112.
[40] (Dowdey, The Seven Days 1978) Timeline of events for the morning of the 26th on page 172.

heating up fast. Soon, men were lounging under the trees and chatting. Hill did not expect the wait to be long. With Jackson's division nicknamed the Foot Cavalry, he expected to see Branch's brigade any time, the signal that Jackson had arrived. Hill was mounted on his horse, Prince, as he peered through his binoculars. The men liked him and often called him Little Powell. He was wearing a red calico shirt he often wore into battle, his battle shirt, as they called it. He wore a dark felt hat slouched forward and his sword hung at his side.

    An hour passed, then two, with no sign of Branch's brigade moving down the road from Half Sink. Jackson was running late and sent a message to General Branch saying that he was crossing the Virginia Central tracks six miles from Ashland. He was about six hours behind schedule. From this position, he had eight miles to go. Jackson's men had just completed their epic campaign in the valley and were making a long march to Richmond. The men were tired, and the area was unfamiliar to them. They had started moving at around 2:30 a.m., but the roads did not allow the kind of quick marches like they had made in the valley, and Federal cavalry hampered their movement. Jackson had underestimated how long it would take to get into position.

    Noon came, and the sun was bearing down hot. The temperature was around 80 degrees and the men were glad they were in the shade. They had gotten little sleep, so some were napping under the shade trees. Others nibbled on rations. Hill paced impatiently. Another hour passed and still another. By three in the afternoon, with no word from Jackson and no way to confer with Lee, Hill could wait no longer. With only a few hours of daylight left, Lee's entire plan was in danger. If he did not soon clear Mechanicsville, Longstreet and Harvey Hill's divisions could not cross the river by dark. Hill had a reputation for being impetuous at times, but a little impetuosity could sometimes be a good thing, and it served him well here. He sent the order, and soon the sounds of men moving and equipment clanging together replaced the relaxed sounds of the wooded area.

    The first to cross the river was the 2,000-man brigade of Charles Field, a Kentuckian who was considered one of Hills's best commanders. Field's enthusiastic Virginians stormed across the bridge with a loud yell and drove the Federal picket line away, pausing to fire a volley at the fleeing Yankees. After Field, came the Georgians commanded by Joseph R Anderson. Next came the brigade of the long-bearded Mexican War veteran James Archer. He was a native Marylander and a lawyer with a degree from Princeton University. He had a frail appearance but was a very professional soldier. After Archer came the brigade of Dorsey Pender, under whose command marched the 34th North Carolina. Last to cross was the brigade of Maxcy Gregg, a wealthy South Carolina lawyer and Mexican War veteran. Gregg was tough, aggressive, and fearless. No commander in Lee's army was braver than Maxcy Gregg and William Dorsey Pender The Light Division had a solid lineup of Brigadier Generals.

Being in the fourth brigade to cross, the men of the 34th NC could see the activity before them. They saw the Federal troops falling back as the gray columns approached. After crossing the bridge, the road ran in a northerly direction for a short distance parallel the Virginia Central before turning to the southeast. To ease congestion on the road, Pender's brigade took a shortcut across the open fields. Pender's brigade started taking artillery fire soon after crossing the bridge. Pender deployed them in line of battle and called up artillery to return fire. Soon, the Federal artillery withdrew, and the brigade advanced. Hill's column came to the road coming down from Half Sink and turned south toward Mechanicsville. Since Jackson was not yet on the scene, Branch was still north. Hill's columns marched toward Mechanicsville, joined by Pender's brigade. Mechanicsville was just a small collection of houses barely large enough to qualify as a village surrounded by open farm country. About three quarters of a mile from the village, the troops of the 34th North Carolina could see that the first brigade, Field's, was coming under artillery fire. Nearing Mechanicsville, the regiments spread out into the fields beside the road, in lines of battle.

The artillery fire continued and included bursting shells and solid shot. As Pender's brigade neared the village, the 16th North Carolina on the left became separated due to confusing roads and the bad advice of a guide and eventually had to join with another brigade.[41]

---

[41] According to Pender's official report, the 16th did not rejoin the rest of the brigade until after dark. They suffered some 200 casualties killed and wounded during the day and preformed bravely despite being separated from the brigade.

When Hill's column reached Mechanicsville, the Federal troops fell back toward Beaver Dam Creek one mile east. With Mechanicsville clear, the divisions of Longstreet and Harvey Hill were supposed to cross on bridges built by pioneers, but the pioneers did not have all the equipment they needed. Nearly 19,000 men in the two divisions waited while the pioneers scrambled to build an improvised bridge.

The first casualty at the Battle of Mechanicsville was Robert E. Lee's battle plan. Hill had crossed the river thinking that Jackson would surely be there, but he was not. Instead of four full divisions on the field, Hill's lone division was across the river while Longstreet and Harvey Hill waited for a bridge to be built, and no one knew where Jackson was. But Hill was committed. There was nothing he could do but forge ahead. Progress had been slow. It took Hill's 12,000-man division two hours to march two miles from the Meadow Bridges to Mechanicsville. By 5:00 p.m., only a single brigade of Harvey Hill's division had made it across the makeshift bridge at Mechanicsville. It was the brigade of Brig. General Roswell Ripley. Hill had but three hours of daylight left and could not wait for more reinforcements. He started deploying his brigades along a two-mile front toward Beaver Dam Creek.

Beaver Dam Creek and Ellerson's Mill

Federal troops were dug in on the bank across Beaver Dam Creek. They had a strong position bristling with artillery batteries and infantry protected by well-prepared works. They had twice the artillery Hill had on hand. Pender shifted his men to the east along Cold Harbor Road. Ripley's brigade was sent to their right in support. Pender was ordered to move in support of Field's brigade to the left. But as they neared the creek, Pender saw a Federal artillery battery obliquely to the right. He was concerned that keeping the original order exposed the flank to the battery, so he dispatched his two right-wing regiments to take it out. They were the 38th North Carolina and Col. Riddick's 34th North Carolina. The men moved on the battery. In trying to get into position, however, the 34th NC swung too far to the right and could not get into position quick enough. The 38th made a valiant charge on the battery. They got within 150 yards and were opened on with heavy artillery and musket fire. The 38th suffered severe casualties and was falling back as the 34th NC came up. The attack stalled.

Pender did not give up on the battery. He ordered the 34th NC farther right across Cold Harbor Road to try and find a way around the position. Col. Riddick led the men across the road as ordered but found a hundred-yard mill pond in their way. To make matters worse, the regiment was overlapped by the Federal left flank strongly fortified across the creek. A well-dug-in infantry brigade fired at the exposed 34th NC from across the creek, and the battery was still hurling ordinance unimpeded. They could do little more than take cover and return fire. To fall back would expose them to even more fire. Colonel Riddick directed them to a ravine along the creek where they could find refuge. He ordered them to stay there and withdraw after dark.[42]

T. D. Lattimore provides this first-hand account, "…we were ordered across the Chickahominy and at Mechanicsville, where we had our first experience in real war, we were very anxious to fight; but some of us had serious misgivings as to how we would act when the test came. After being formed into line of battle we marched in the direction of the enemy and came within sight of him just before dark. We had been taught that the proper thing to do was to raise the "rebel yell" and charge, which we proceeded to do, and found ourselves in a creek not far from the enemy's works."

They finally got support on their right when two regiments of Roswell Ripley's brigade arrived as the sun was starting down. Pender believed the Federal flank could still be turned. Ripley's regiments marched through heavy fire as they crossed the uneven ground leading around the mill pond near Ellerson's Mill. Federal troops threw a heavy barrage of shell and canister at them. The attack failed with heavy casualties. They too became stuck and waited for nightfall. Pender

---

[42] Historians disagree on who was to blame for the 34th NC's failure to support the 38th in the assault. Longacre says it was the "wayward leadership of Colonel Richard H. Riddick" that took them too far to the right. (Longacre 2001), page 114. Dr. Robertson was more forgiving, noting that "Pender made somewhat of a mess of his part of the attack." (Dr. James I Robertson 1987), page 74. Neither questioned why the 38th did not give the 34th more time to get in position. Pender did seem to take personal responsibility for the regiment's movement in his official report. In fact, the terrain seemed to be to blame. Neither Riddick nor Pender knew the area. The ground was marshy and brushy, making movement and communication difficult. No one knew about the mill pond. Beaver Dam Creek was a confusing mess for all.

brought up eight artillery pieces. Under cover of darkness and the guns, the weary troops crept out of their death trap on Beaver Dam Creek and marched back toward Mechanicsville. Around them, barns and buildings burned, and the ground was littered with battle debris. Wounded men were helped along. Occasionally a gray-clad form lay motionless on the side of the road.

The cannon fire continued until around 10:00 p.m. The men found a place to make camp for the night, rested, and reflected on the day's events. Though not successful in taking their objectives, they had stood the test. Seven men from the regiment perished in the fighting that day:

Killed in Action at Mechanicsville		
Drury Harrill	B	Pvt.
Weldon H Miller	C	Sgt.
Joab Moore	E	Pvt.
Soloman Carpenter	F	Pvt.
John Howell	H	Pvt.
Jason C Kennedy	I	Pvt.
Oran L Hurley	K	Pvt.

Drury Harrill was just 16 years old and had been with the regiment barely a month. The Rutherford County lad had been hired as a substitute soldier. According to T. D. Lattimore, at least fifteen were wounded.[43] The young regimental surgeon, John Miller, had his first battlefield experience and labored late into the night. With him was Dr. Richard Barr who had joined the regiment earlier in the month as assistant surgeon. Colonel Riddick led his men the best he could in the confusion at Beaver Dam Creek. He kept his men in place when emotion might have compelled them to fall back without the aid of darkness. He deserves credit for composure that saved the lives of many of his young troops. He himself had been wounded in the action but not severely. He received treatment and stayed with his men.

---

[43] One report stated six were wounded. That same report showed six killed in the action, but the search of service records revealed these seven. The wounded from this battle were particularly hard to identify, so only those killed are listed here.

Tactically, the battle had been a total loss for the Confederates. Other than clearing Mechanicsville and getting Harvey Hill and Longstreet's divisions across the river, which they did by dark, Lee's men had accomplished none of their objectives. Jackson had arrived but too late to deploy. He was bivouacked on the north flank. Many blamed Jackson for grossly underestimating the time he needed to get his men to the battlefield. Others blamed Hill for crossing the Chickahominy on his own initiative and making the attack without the rest of the army in place. Hill, in his official report, stated that the enemy works were too strong, and therefore he had not ordered a general attack. Lee endorsed Hill's account. The Light Division suffered 1,400 casualties. Nearly half came from the regiments in Ripley's bloody charge near Ellerson's Mill and the 38th NC's assault on the battery. A.P. Hill also noted in his report that "The 38th North Carolina...and the 34th North Carolina...of Pender's brigade made a gallant but abortive effort to force a crossing."

Lee graciously blamed neither Hill nor Jackson. While the battle was a tactical loss, it was not as bad as it may have seemed. Because of A.P. Hill's initiative, Lee's men were across the river and Jackson was in place. All were ready to renew the attack the next day. The men spent an uneasy night under the stars with little sleep.

Gaines's Mill

An hour and a half before dawn, the Union troops unleased a heavy artillery bombardment. For two hours, the men could do nothing but hunker down. Shortly after sunrise, the shelling stopped. Hill and Pender scouted the area carefully but could not determine exactly what they were facing. Around 8:00, Pender's brigade started forming as Maxcy Gregg's men marched by. Gregg's brigade was the freshest on the battlefield and was assigned the lead. Pender's men fell into line and began marching with trepidation back to Beaver Dam Creek. They passed through the area where they fought the night before, continuing to the part of Cold Harbor Road that turned and ran parallel the creek for a short distance. Unlike the day before, the bank on the other side was strangely silent, allowing them a peaceful march. They passed through the swampy area around the bridge at Ellerson's Mill which had been the scene of some of the heaviest fighting. Dead Confederates from Ripley's regiments were lying in the mud, and the earth still smoldered in places. At Ellerson's Mill, the enemy made a slight demonstration on the right but did not attack. Gregg's South Carolinians crossed Beaver Dam Creek and encountered only Federal skirmishers. The 34th North Carolina was the first from Pender's brigade to gain the enemy works, which were abandoned only minutes before.[44]

    The Confederates had accomplished more with yesterday's battle than they realized. On the northern end of the line, Stonewall Jackson had arrived at 5:00 p.m. the day before. It was too late for them to take part in that day's battle, but they were in position and the Federals knew it. Jackson's mere presence caused them to abandon their position during the night. The much-feared Beaver Dam Creek had become passive and allowed them an easy march. Hill's brigades marched down the curvy dusty road that ran toward Gaines's Mill on Powhite Creek. As they marched, they passed by deserted Federal camps. They kept going, not even stopping to police up the abandoned supplies. They marched by the most memorable landmark in the area, the Walnut Grove Church at the junction of Cold Harbor Road. Little Powell was seen galloping past the column and stopped at the church. General Lee and his staff rode up. Soon Stonewall Jackson and his staff arrived. The three generals conferred under a clump of shade trees outside the church. Some of Hill's men stopped to get a look at the fabled Stonewall Jackson. To the men in the ranks he was a heroic figure, and his presence caused a noticeable stir. At this point, Stonewall Jackson was far more famous than Lee.

    By noon, they had marched seven miles in the blistering sun in pursuit of the retreating Union soldiers. Hill's lead brigade, commanded by Maxcy Gregg, encountered Federal troops at Powhite Creek near Gaines's Mill. A brief skirmish ensued, and the enemy retreated across Cold Harbor Road to the wooded Boatswain's swamp area. Spoiling for a fight, Gregg's men pursued. When they crossed the swampy ravine, the ground sloped upward. Gregg halted at a line of pine trees so that he could get a look at the enemy position. As his regiments came up, the entire hillside erupted in fire from the main body of Federal troops that had retreated from Beaver Dam Creek. The

---

[44] Referenced in the official report of General Pender.

intrepid Maxcy Gregg had found where the enemy planned to make their stand. He pulled his men back to the shelter of the ravine and sent word back to General Hill.

Pender's brigade made tracks up Cold Harbor Road with the 34th North Carolina again in the lead. Once more, the fog of war dogged Colonel Riddick. As the brigade came up, Pender had not kept the regiments together, and Riddick misunderstood Pender's order of how far to go and led his men a mile too far up the road. The confusion may have been because there was an area called New Cold Harbor with Old Cold Harbor only a mile or so farther up the road. Hill's men were going into action at New Cold Harbor. When Hill ordered Pender to advance on Boatswain's Creek, the 34th NC was out of position. General Pender caught up with Riddick and his men at the forks of the road and directed him to the correct position. The regiment quickly moved back and deployed in line of battle.[45] The brigade was deployed between Powhite Creek and Boatswains' Creek. Riddick's men occupied a position near the center of the three quarters of a mile line. As they deployed, Pender called the men's attention to General Lee watching the deployments. General Pender said wryly, "The eyes of your chieftain are upon you!"[46] It was the first time many of them had gotten a good look at General Lee.

Across the creek on a range of hills, Federal troops waited. Hill had no idea of their strength. One man who was there wrote, "The enemy occupied a range of hills with his left on a wooded bluff, which arose abruptly from a deep ravine. The ravine was filled with Sharpshooters, to whom its banks gave protection. A second line of infantry was stationed on the side of the hill, behind a breastwork of trees, above the first. A third occupied the crest, strengthened with rifle trenches and crowned with artillery."[47] Union General Fitz John Porter's entire V Corps was there, some 35,000 strong. Hill held his

---

[45] Longacre is again critical of Riddick, perhaps more justified this time. The misunderstood order, however, shows how difficult communication was in the heat of battle. With orders sent by aides, sometimes verbally, such errors were not unusual. Note that Longacre states that Pender considered Lt. Col. R. H. Gray to be more level-headed than Riddick, incorrectly naming Gray as Riddick's executive officer. Gray was the executive officer of the 22nd NC.
[46] (Lattimore 1901)
[47] (James I Robetson 1992), page 82.

men in place while General Lee laid out his plan. Longstreet's men had been advancing on a road south of and roughly parallel Cold Harbor Road which Hill's column had taken. His troops were to Hill's right. Lee directed the divisions of Harvey Hill and Jackson to come up on Hill's left. Lee wanted his entire army to advance together. Gaines's Mill was important strategically because it was near the Chickahominy across from Magruder and Huger. If Lee could drive the enemy back, his divided army would be reunited. At 1:00, Hill and Longstreet were ordered to advance together. Hill's men were ready and waiting for Longstreet's division on their right. But Longstreet's men had difficult terrain to traverse and got bogged down trying to cross the creek with its steep banks, swampy ground, and trees felled by the Federals. An hour and a half passed, and Longstreet's division was still not in position. The oppressive heat made the wait more difficult. Hill would wait no longer. At 2:30, he ordered his artillery to open fire on the Federal lines. The roar of the guns told the men it was time. Men grasped their bayonetted muskets so hard their knuckles turned white. Young lieutenants and captains barely out of their teens were about to lead men in a massive assault.

  The terrain did not allow for an all-out advance, so the brigades went forward one at a time. Gregg's brigade stepped off first followed by Branch, Anderson, and Archer. The 34th NC with Pender's brigade waited. Gregg's brigade made a furious attack. The Palmetto brigade managed to reach the Federal line and fought hand to hand, using their bayonets and swinging rifles as clubs before falling back. Gregg rallied the men, and they stood and fired back at close range. Gregg's men were tangling with an artillery battery defended by Zouaves of the 5th New York. The 1st South Carolina Rifles lost a staggering 57% of their men, the most of any Confederate regiment that day. Next, Branch's brigade dashed forward. Two color bearers in the 7th North Carolina were shot down, and their Colonel picked up their flag and was himself shot down. Once again, A. P. Hill's division was fighting alone. The enemy was thus able to concentrate their fury on one lone division. The enemy fired at the advancing rebels from behind solid defensive works. They had put up logs from felled trees, rocks, and packed dirt into knapsacks sandbag style to rest their rifles on. This gave them the advantages of protection and well-aimed shots.

Pender then readied his brigade. Colonel Riddick stood tall and ordered them forward. Without hesitation, the regiment rose as one. The companies from old Rutherford were there. The men from Cleveland County, The Laurel Springs Guards of Ashe County, and The Montgomery Boys, all were ready. At Colonel Riddick's command, they went forward.

"...some of the bravest men that ever shouldered a musket or drew a sword."

From the cover of Boatswain's Creek, they formed an orderly line of battle. They cleared the safety of the tree line and dashed forward to the aid of their fellow Carolinians. Through intense heat, smoke, and dust, they advanced. Officers yelled orders to their men, and banners waved. As soon as they cleared the woods, the entire hillside in front of them erupted in gunfire and artillery. It was as if the hillside itself was firing at them as thousands of Federal muskets roared. Artillery caused the earth to shake like it was going to fly open and swallow them up. It was fierce and violent, and men fell fast. The brigade was forced back with too few men to break through. Pender regrouped and repeatedly battered the enemy line. They moved a few yards and dropped down to take cover catch their breath and moved forward again. They attacked in spurts, their line becoming thinner and losing cohesion with each effort. For two hours they struggled to continue the assault. Finally, Pender's regiments were too shot-up to make another coordinated effort.

Men from all over the brigade lay dead on the field. Riddick's men in the 34th North Carolina suffered severe losses. Riddick himself was badly wounded. Lt. Col. Hammarskold took command. Several officers were down. Captain Abraham Waters of Company F had been killed. Company K Lt. Alfred Hurley was mortally wounded. Several lieutenants and sergeants were down. Scores of men from the ranks were dead or wounded. They fought hard and died hard. After two brutal hours, the order came down the line to stop and lie down where they were. The Federal line had weakened but held. The troops hugged the ground and sought cover behind any rock or fallen tree they could find. Many trembled from the trauma of the attack. The battered Light Division troops could only hold their position and wait for support.

Elements of Richard Ewell's command had also attacked but fared no better.

Rebel artillery continued to pound the Federal line with some effectiveness, and despite the deplorable condition of Hill's line, the infantry mounted surprisingly effective counter fire. The sun was as merciless as the enemy guns. There was no shelter from the oppressive heat, and the exertion from the assault left them spent. All around, wounded men suffered with little aid available. Some wounded men made it back across Boatswains Creek. Around 5:00, word moved through the line that Jackson's men were to their left, as Lee slowly gained control of the separate commands on the field. For two more excruciating hours, the battered division clung to the bloody slopes. Longstreet on the right was finally into position. Behind Hill's troops formed the divisions of William Whiting and John Bell Hood's Texans. Jackson and Harvey Hill were to their left.

Then, at 7:00 p.m., after five horrendous hours on the field, the entire Confederate army began to attack for the first time in unison. Lee had coordinated 16 full brigades, some 32,000 men, in the largest combined single assault of the war. The beleaguered Light Division watched as one well-formed brigade after another advanced up the bloody hill. Facing the same challenges with terrain Hill's men faced, they could not advance in a solid line along the 2.25-mile front but in coordinated individual assaults. Eventually, the weakened Union lines began to break. The long hours spent fighting against Hill's men had forced them to expend an enormous amount of ammunition. Many rifles of the Union soldiers were fouled from hours of continued fire and were useless. First one line and then another began to break. With the sun going down, the Confederate troops reached the crest of the hill. Pender's casualty-laden brigade rose and lunged forward as well. The Federal troops fell back with Confederate units in full pursuit. A Union counterattack on the plateau failed, and the Confederates drove them from the field.

Union losses amounted to 6,837 killed, wounded, and captured. The price of the Confederate victory was 7,993, including 1,483 killed. Light Division casualties were 2,688, about 20 percent of its total strength. Though it was not the Light Division that broke the lines, their prolonged assault weakened the enemy for the final attack. T. D.

Lattimore provides this description of the battle: "The writer of this sketch witnessed every principal engagement of the Army of Northern Virginia from this time to the end of the war, but in no other battle in the long succession was the musketry to be compared to that of 27 June 1862, at Gaines's Mill....Among the killed were some of the bravest men that ever shouldered a musket or drew a sword. Here fell Captain Waters, one of nature's noblemen. At the same time 14 of his men were killed and 25 wounded." The 34th North Carolina suffered heavy losses, including 37 men killed in action, 84 wounded, and 9 taken prisoner. The following are the known casualties of the regiment's action of June 27, 1862:

Casualties from the Battle of Gaines's Mill

Killed in Action

Samuel Aikin	F	Pvt.	George R Keeter	C	Pvt.
John D Alexander	G	Pvt.	John R McNeely	D	Pvt.
Thomas J Anders	A	Pvt.	James K Means	G	Pvt.
Charles J Anderson	G	Pvt.	Daniel Perkins	E	Pvt.
Johnson E Beam	F	Pvt.	Leroy Putnam	H	Pvt.
James A Bryant	F	Pvt.	David Rhodes	E	2Lt.
Sansbury Cargal	I	Pvt.	Luther Roberts	H	Cpl.
William S Clay	F	Pvt.	Jacob Sellers	F	Pvt.
John H Eaker	E	Cpl.	Robert H Shields	F	Pvt.
George A Elam	F	Sgt.	Belton O Tanner	C	Pvt.
Otho W Felment	F	Pvt.	James A Todd	G	Cpl.
Elijah P Freeze	D	Pvt.	Alonzo G Wallace	C	Pvt.
Parham A Gold	H	Pvt.	Abraham G Waters	F	Cpt.
Pleasant G Green	K	Pvt.	John White	F	Pvt.
Harris C Hamilton	K	Pvt.	William D White	D	Pvt.
Benjamin K Hardin	F	Pvt.	David A Wilson	F	Pvt.
William L Hardin	F	Pvt.	Daniel Wise	E	Pvt.
Cephus Hartzog	E	Pvt.	Berry Wright	F	Pvt.
Nathan Hurley	K	Pvt.			

Mortally Wounded

Martin T Callicott	K	Pvt.	Soloman A Newton	F	Pvt.
Henderson Cody	E	Pvt.	Jonathan Pool	K	Pvt.
Abel H Gantt	F	Cpl.	Cyrus P Sparrow	F	Pvt.
James H Hill	E	Sgt.	Daniel M Stroup	F	Pvt.
Henry Hoyle	F	Pvt.	William B Wright	B	Pvt.
Alfred H Hurley	K	2Lt.			

Wounded[48]

Thomas W Abernathy	E	2Lt.	John Lemaster	E	Pvt.
James M Alle	B	Cpl.	William Long	H	Pvt.
James M Blanton	F	Pvt.	William L Lowrance	D	Cpt.
Abner Camp	H	Pvt.	Ahijah Oliver Lynch	C	Pvt.
John C Canipe	F	Pvt.	Allen M McInnes	K	Pvt.
Perry D Carpenter	E	2Lt.	David A Munn	K	Pvt.
William G Conner	C	Pvt.	John A Newton	F	Pvt.
Abraham H Davis	B	Pvt.	Presley Norman	F	Pvt.
William C Dennis	K	Pvt.	George W Norment	G	1Lt.
Jacob S Earls	F	Pvt.	Pinkney Parrish	A	Pvt.
Francis M Green	B	Pvt.	Allen Richardson	A	Pvt.
Marcus L Heavner	E	Pvt.	Richard H Riddick		Col.
George Hedgpeth	E	Pvt.	Martin Rush	K	Pvt.
William V Hopper	H	Pvt.	Elijah A Russell	K	Pvt.
Benjamin M Hoyle	F	Pvt.	Calvin Shoemaker	A	Pvt.
David R Hoyle	F	Lt.	Charles D Shull	E	Pvt.
George J Huntley	I	Sgt.	John H Wagoner	A	Pvt.
Freeman Hurley	K	Pvt.	Adolphus Withrow	B	Pvt.
Abram C Irvin	F	Pvt.			

---

[48] The list of wounded is incomplete. Many of the wounded from the first three battles are simply listed, "Wounded at Richmond" not stating which battle. Official records state the regiment suffered 84 wounded including those who later died of wounds.

Captured

William Crotts	F	Pvt.	William McK Mittag	H	2Lt.
William O Harrelson	E	Pvt.	Samuel Tallent	E	Pvt.
William Lyall	A	Cpl.	James D Wesson	H	Sgt.
Charles S Martin	E	Pvt.	Govan Williams	H	Pvt.
Alexander McCall	G	Pvt.			

Company F, the Floyd Rifles of Cleveland County, suffered the greatest loss including Captain Abraham G Waters and 1st Sergeant George Elam. From Company E, 30-year-old 1st Lt. David Rhodes was killed. He was described as, "A faithful, courteous, and attentive officer." Colonel Riddick, wounded slightly the day, was more seriously wounded at Gaines's Mill. General Pender noted that "Colonels Hoke and Riddick…were great losses to me."

Most of the wounds in this battle and throughout the war were gunshot wounds. Soldiers fired large caliber bullets that caused horrendous wounds. Privates Benjamin Hoyle and David A. Munn each lost a leg due to their gunshot wounds. Calvin Shoemaker of Ashe County lost 3 fingers from a painful gunshot wound. Private John A. Newton was admitted for treatment for "shock" but returned to duty the next day. Some wounds were minor allowing the men to return to duty quickly. Others never came back. Those captured were taken down the James River to Harrison's Landing and by boat to Fort Columbus in New York and were exchanged on August 5th. In those early days of the war, the two sides observed a system of prisoner exchange that kept prisoners from suffering long stays in the prisons.

The men spent the night on the plateau. They were dog-tired. Every muscle ached. Perspiration combined with the smoke and dust from the battlefield that left heavy grime on their faces. They had had little sleep for two nights and had been in two hard battles. Somewhere near 25% of the men in the 34th NC had been killed, wounded, or captured. They rested, splashed water on their dirty faces, and took some food and water. They listened to the sounds of gunfire and artillery as other Confederates pursued the retreating Yankees well after dark. Just 48 hours prior, they marched along the Chickahominy, never having fired a shot at the enemy. After this fight, they sat in the darkness on the blood-soaked battlefield with the full knowledge of war, its sights, sounds, death, and suffering. They were veterans.

During the night, men with lanterns combed the area for the wounded, Union and Confederate, and brought them in. Officers gathered up their scattered companies. Field hospitals worked through the night, as the worn-out men slept soundly. The next day, Saturday, they remained in place. Since they had borne the heaviest fighting, they were given a rest. In the daylight, they surveyed the appalling destruction of the battle. Hundreds of dead and dying horses lay around the battlefield. Pesky green flies swarmed. It was another extremely hot day, as grave details started their grim work. Others set about gathering up anything of value the enemy left behind. Mechanics repaired broken wagons, cannons, and caissons. They gathered guns, ammunition, and all types of camp equipment. All types of clothing were scattered for miles. Sounds of cannon fire were heard all day, growing faint as the enemy continued to retreat.

The field hospitals were busy throughout the day. Amputations were done on the spot when needed. The more seriously wounded were sent back to the hospitals in Richmond. Field surgeons like the 34th NC's John Miller did the best they could under difficult conditions. Stewards and nurses changed bandages and dispensed medicine. Wounded men suffered horribly with little medicine available to dull the pain. Some groaned and begged for help, others silently accepted their pain.

Field promotions were issued to replace fallen officers in the regiment. In the hard-hit Company F, Lt. David Ramsour Hoyle replaced Abraham Waters as Captain. Hoyle was a strong and intelligent man, a veracious reader, and deeply religious.[49] He had a substantial farm and was an excellent surveyor. Jacob Hogue and Nathan McGinnis were promoted to Lieutenants from the ranks. In Company E, Thomas Abernathy was promoted to Lieutenant to replace David Rhodes. The Light Division bivouacked one more night with orders to move out the next morning. At sundown, a thunderstorm moved through the area.

---

[49] After the war, he was a Magistrate and County Commissioner in Cleveland County. (Van A. Hoyle)

Frayser's Farm

As Col. Riddick recovered in a Richmond hospital, Lt. Col. Charles J. Hammarskold, the wealthy Swede, took command. Hammarskold enjoyed a prosperous life at his home on Beatty's Ford Road seven miles from Lincolnton. He had immigrated to America as a young man with his parents and sister. His father was the late C. W. Hammarskold who left an impressive estate for Charles to manage. They owned some 1,600 acres of land with several houses, a grist mill, an ore bank, saw mill, and other amenities.[50] He held eleven slaves as of the 1860 census. Some 250 acres of land were farmed, but the main source of income was the Spring Hill Iron Foundry. The forge had been in operation for many years and could produce 150 tons of iron per year. On the eve of the war, Hammarskold also served as postmaster, a position that made him a familiar man in the community. His mother still lived in the home, and his sister taught piano and led the Music Department at the Charlotte Female Institute.[51] Hammarskold was ready and willing to lead the regiment but questionably able. He had always been near-sighted, but weeks of exposure to the bright sun made his vision worse.

Hill's division moved south on Sunday, June 29th and crossed the Chickahominy. Ahead of them was James Longstreet's division. The two divisions numbered a little less than 20,000 men due to the casualties from the previous battles. Hill's men took on a forced march to catch up with Longstreet. Once again, the sun was blistering. The men marched one long hour after another with few breaks. The dust was terrible. The heat was insufferable. Scores of men fell out, incapable of keeping the relentless pace. They finally stopped about 9:00 that night near Atlee's Farm. As the weary foot-soldiers rested, another thunderstorm rolled through.

Early next morning, they were back on the march under a cloudless sky that promised another day of intense heat. They tramped down a long stretch of Darbytown Road and turned east on Long

---

[50] The various tracts of land owned by the family is described in The Western Democrat/September 9, 1862. (digitalnc.org)
[51] The Western Democrat September 9, 1861. The institute is now known as Queen's University of Charlotte, founded in 1857 as the Charlotte Female Institute.

Bridge Road. They headed toward the Quaker Road Junction, an area known as Glendale. The largest farm in the area was Frayser's Farm, and White Oak Swamp was two miles away. Longstreet's division stopped a half mile from the Quaker Road intersection. Hill's men stopped three-fourths of a mile behind them. Heat fatigue had caused Hill's line to be strung out, so his officers tightened up the ranks and gathered stragglers. The men waited in place as General Hill deployed skirmishers. Longstreet was not with his division, so A. P. Hill had temporary command of both divisions.

By noon, the enemy was in force and disposed to fight. Hill deployed the brigades. He planned for Longstreet's men to go in first with the Light Division close behind. Longstreet then came up and resumed command. As the senior division commander, Longstreet would have overall command of the field. Lee's plan was for Jackson to hit the Union position from the northeast near White Oak Swamp. He also wanted the divisions of Huger and Magruder in place and all Confederate units converging at once. The objective was to deliver a decisive blow by cutting McClellan off from the James River. By 4:30 in the afternoon, the men had been waiting in place for four sweltering hours. The divisions of Jackson, Huger, and Magruder were all delayed. Union troops had obstructed the roads with felled trees, and skirmishers sniped at them from the woods. Cavalry attacked parts of their columns which caused further delays. Once again, coordination was a problem. Lee, acting as impetuous as Hill, decided to attack with the two divisions on the field. Normally the attacking army tried to outnumber the enemy since the defenders had the advantage. Here, Lee was attacking an enemy twice his number in open country. It was audacious, but Lee believed his men could overcome the numbers.

Longstreet went forward at 5:00. A fierce battle quickly erupted. For two hours, the two sides attacked and counter-attacked. Finally, Union troops attacked both of Longstreet's flanks at once. Longstreet was in danger of being overwhelmed and ordered Hill's men forward. With the sun going down, the Light Division went in.
"This is my cannon!"

Field's brigade dashed up Long Bridge Road with Pender's men trailing. Maxcy Gregg led his men left. Archer moved right to cover Pender. Hill kept Anderson's brigade in reserve. Pender deployed his regiments in two lines. In the front were the 2nd Arkansas, the 16th NC, and the 22nd NC. Behind was the 38th NC and Hammarskold's 34th NC. The brigade raised the rebel yell and rushed forward. Pender kept a steady pace. Field's Virginians outran Pender's men, putting some distance between them. Suddenly, a lone enemy regiment appeared out of nowhere barely 75 yards away. Pender halted his men and ordered them to fire. The volley quickly scattered them. The delay put Field's men completely out of sight, so Pender quickened their pace. Field did not wait for Pender, and with bayonets fixed, charged the enemy line. A furious fight ensued as the Virginians dove into the Federal line. When Pender's men joined the fray, Field's men cheered. It was a ferocious fight with deafening volleys of gunfire combining with the roar of artillery. Solid shot from artillery crashed through trees and cut into tree trunks. Soldiers yelled, and the wounded cried out as the violent contest played out. Hill moved through the line shouting encouragement to the men. Branch's brigade faltered and started falling back. General Hill rallied them by grabbing the flag of the 7th North Carolina shouting, "Damn you, if you will not follow me, I'll die alone!"[52]

    The 34th NC found themselves in the hottest part of the field. They faced an artillery battery that was mauling the Confederates with canister rounds. This was an especially evil devise that fired canisters of one-inch iron balls. It was a giant shot gun that would shred a line of advancing infantry. It was up to the 34th North Carolina to put the guns out of business. The regiment charged aggressively. Young officers and sergeants stepped up and led a charge that no one from the regiment would ever forget. Second Lieutenant Alexander Shotwell of Company C was 22 years old from Rutherford County. When the color-bearer hesitated, Shotwell not only grabbed the colors but the color-bearer and surged forward. His bravery inspired the regiment. They blitzed the battery, overwhelming the Yankee gunners, who fled the position. Shotwell's reward for gallantry was a wound that proved fatal.[53] Twenty-seven-year-old Lieutenant John P. Parks of Company D ran up and placed his hand on the barrel of the first cannon and shouted, "This

---

[52] (James I Robetson 1992), page 92
[53] Alexander Shotwell died of his wounds on July 10, 1862.

is my cannon!" and was immediately shot dead. Another Company D Lieutenant, Robert T. Cowen, 22, was also slain.

At just the right moment, General Hill ordered Anderson forward. The Georgians charged, holding their fire until they got within seventy paces of the Union line and unleashed a devastating volley. Hill later wrote, "In less than five minutes, all firing ceased, and the enemy retired."[54] The fight ended around 8:30. It was an impressive feat of arms, but it was not the victory Lee wanted. Merely driving the enemy from the field accomplished nothing. He wanted them trapped, but the other divisions were not there to complete the victory. The divisions of Longstreet and Hill had beaten an enemy twice their number, but another 50,000 Confederates were within three miles of the battle. Had they come up as planned, Lee may have trapped the entire 40,000-man Union force, a large part of McClellan's army.

The regiment's performance was one of its best of the war. Lt. Colonel Hammarskold, despite his physical challenges, led well, as had all the officers in the regiment. Especially conspicuous were the junior officers and sergeants who led the regiment in one of the most daring charges ever made by the 34th NC. General Pender praised the regiment in his official report saying, "…the Thirty-fourth North Carolina on Friday behaved with great credit under a heavy and murderous cross-fire, and here let me mention that Lieutenant Shotwell…cannot be spoken of too highly for his gallant conduct; for he was not satisfied to take the colors, [but] seized the color-bearer and rushed him to the front, thus encouraging the regiment to move forward at a very critical moment." In the short but hard-fought battle, nine men from the regiment were dead on the field. At least twenty-two were wounded including seven who later died of their wounds.[55]

---

[54] (Dowdey, The Seven Days 1978)

[55] The nine killed in action agrees with the official numbers. Official records do not provide the number of the wounded. These are drawn entirely from the service records.

Casualties from the Battle of Frayser's Farm

Killed in Action

Greenberry Bridges	B	Sgt.	Wade H Putnam	H	Pvt.
Lorenzo D Bridges	B	Pvt.	William A Scott	G	Pvt.
Robert T Cowan	D	Lt.	James L Shelby	G	Sgt.
John Holaway	A	Pvt.	James Woods	A	Sgt.
John P Parks	D	1Lt.			

Mortally Wounded

James L Dobbins	B	Pvt.	Benjamin F Philbeck	F	Pvt.
John L Huntsinger	B	Pvt.	Thomas H Roberts	H	Pvt.
Martin P Miller	C	Cpl.	Alexander H Shotwell	C	2Lt.
Andrew Owens	B	Pvt.			

Wounded

Stanhope H Bagwell	C	Pvt.	Carmi K McNeely	D	Cpl.
William Bridges	B	Pvt.	James K McNeely	D	Sgt.
Samuel Brooks	B	Pvt.	Joshua A Queen	E	Pvt.
William P Burgess	I	Pvt.	David V Ried	E	Pvt.
Burwell T Cotton	K	Lt.	Richard T Stephens	G	Pvt.
Thomas C Haltom	G	1Lt.	Joseph S Willis	F	Pvt.
William L Jones	I	Pvt.	Street Wilson	B	Pvt.
Michael A Kimbrel	I	Pvt.			

The battle took all the strength they had. Many dropped to the ground as soon as the fight was over. Despite the horrors of the battlefield, some fell asleep within a half hour on the battlefield where the dead from both armies lay. Some could not distinguish the dead from the sleeping.

Malvern Hill

Just before dawn, the silence was broken by the footsteps of Magruder's fresh division arriving. Hill's men were so tired they barely acknowledge them. The generals met nearby and planned their next move. Lee decided to attack the enemy one last time at Malvern Hill. Longstreet and Hill would be held in reserve to rest their troops. Wearily, the Light Division rose and began moving. They made a short march of six or seven miles and halted south of Long Branch Road. They remained there for the balance of the day in reserve as the battle of Malvern Hill unfolded. Though in reserve, they were exposed to artillery fire for several hours, heavy at times. Private William Bradley, 24 of Rutherford County, was killed. Also killed was B. H. Ware of Company H, a 32-year-old millwright.[56] Lt. Romulas Hopper was slightly wounded.

    The Confederates were repulsed at Malvern Hill with heavy loss. McClellan's men made their way down the James River and left Virginia, ending the Seven Days Battles. Lee's men had beaten a much larger army and beaten them badly. Lee's unconventional and audacious moves convinced McClellan that the south had a much larger army in Virginia than Lee truly had. McClellan had looked to be on the verge of destroying Richmond. Instead, Lee had expelled him from the peninsula in impressive fashion. Generals get a lot of credit, and certainly their leadership was crucial. The main reason they won this victory, however, was the fighting spirit of the rank and file. Throughout the campaign, battle plans were hampered by poor coordination and lack of execution from the generals. But when it came time to fight, the soldiers rose to the challenge. They marched every mile, charged across every field, stormed every hill, and asked for more. They showed that fighting spirit can overcome numbers. They would need all the determination they could muster in the long days to come, but for now, they enjoyed the victory.

---

[56] Private Ware's record contains conflicting dates. The Roll of Honor card says he was killed June 30th, however other records including sworn affidavits say he was killed on July 1st. This is the day he is believed to have been killed, likely here while the regiment was in reserve under artillery fire.

Colonel Collett Leventhorpe

Chapter 4.
Wounds of War

After a week in the Malvern Hill area, the Light Division moved back and camped just south of Richmond. Doing chores again was welcomed. The 34th NC camped a short distance from the 16th NC in which many Rutherford County men served. Fellow Rutherfortonites got together every chance they got. Colonel Riddick was home recovering from his wounds. General Pender was wounded in the arm at Frayser's Farm. He was recovering. Over the next few weeks, the ranks were strengthened as more men returned.

"...I was so worn out that I had to leave the regiment."

    The Richmond citizens were immensely proud of their army. Six weeks prior, many thought they would have to abandon Richmond when the enemy attacked. In just seven days, their fortunes had changed. The men changed too. They now possessed that sense of pride that only those who had been in battle could know. Their pride extended beyond their company or regiment. They were part of A. P. Hill's Light Division and were proud of it. The division's prominent role in the Seven Days Battles spread its fame throughout the army. They also had a new hero in Robert E. Lee. His Army of Northern Virginia looked unbeatable.

    The men enjoyed reading newspaper accounts of their victories, in The Richmond Examiner. One account of the battle of Frayser's Farm inflated Hill's role, claiming that the victory was all his. Hill led his division well and displayed great personal courage, but the article diminished Longstreet's role. The brawny general's pride was injured, and a rivalry developed. Eventually, Longstreet placed Hill under arrest, confining him to quarters.

    The men watched what would become of their general and wrote letters home. They knew their families had heard of the battles and were eager to assure them they were well. George Huntley wrote a letter on July 16th. He barely mentioned the battles or his wound at Gaines's Mill beyond saying he was recovering and to complain about the price of food in Richmond, (butter was an astonishing $1.50 per pound).[57] He wrote a lengthy letter on July 24th. In this letter, he spoke entirely of matters back home, saying, "I have nothing that is interesting to you." He did mention the election coming up in September saying, "I am supporting Vance for Governor, Capt. Dickerson for the Senate, Capt. McDowell and B. Washburn for the Commons." Despite everything he had been through, he was much more interested in discussing the home front, a pattern in many soldiers' letters. Private Larkin Kendrick was scarcely more descriptive in his letter of July 10th. He summed up the entire Seven Days battles with one short paragraph, "We left camp on the 25th of June. On the next day, the fight began and continued for a week. I was in three desperate fights on Thursday on Friday and Monday. I came through all unhurt, but I was so worn out that I had to leave the regiment. I am now in camp resting and I think I will soon be well again." He wrote again on the 28th, "I have sent my blanket by lutenent P H Shufford [Pinkney H Shufford] To Shelby hit is a inglish blanket one side black and the other read hit wars taken off the battle field. Send to his house for hit and satisfie him for taken it."[58]

    Lt. Colonel Hammarskold provided solid leadership in Riddick's absence. He realized, however, that his vision was too bad to lead the men in battle should the need again arise, so he resigned his commission on July 17th. In his resignation letter he stated, "I have for many years been suffering from near sightedness and weak eyes which within the last few months by exposure in the sun increased so much as to disable me from fulfilling my duties in military service. I am now unable to know friend from foe at 50 yards and cannot tell any person's features at a distance of 20 yards." The regiment's surgeon John Miller vouched for his condition and recommended his resignation be accepted. Back at Lincolnton, Hammarskold served as a Justice of the Peace and a merchant for a time and then decided to move back to Sweden. He put his land and belongings up for sale.[59] When his property and remaining slaves were sold, he, his aging mother, and

---

[57] (Taylor 1994) Letter from Huntley dated 7/16/1862, page 91.
[58] State Library of North Carolina Digital Collections (digital.ncdcr.gov)
[59] (Carpenter 2016) Page 14.

sister left for Sweden where he spent the rest of his life.[60] Major Eli Miller assumed command of the regiment while Col. Riddick recovered at home in Lincolnton.

    The numerous hospitals in Richmond were full. Many men had wounds they should have survived but developed deadly infections. Many had limbs amputated by field surgeons and later died from infections or other complications such as pneumonia. Even a finger amputation could be fatal. Doctors did the best they could, but medical science could not compete with the science of war. In the weeks ahead, another 31 men from the 34th NC died from wounds they received in their first three battles. Some families around Richmond took in wounded men, mainly officers, to help them recover more comfortably. Alexander Shotwell, who led the inspirational charge at Frayser's Farm, was sent to a private home in the country where he was cared for until his death on July 10th. Before the war, Shotwell had been tutored for a future medical career by Collett Leventhorpe. He was 23 and left behind a young widow, Jennie, and a two-month-old son named John that he likely never saw.

    Cyrus Sparrow's wound was very severe. He suffered a compound fracture of the upper bone in his left arm. His pain was excruciating. The ghastly wound bled profusely on the Gaines's Mill battlefield, but the field surgeons did an amazing job under the circumstances and sent him to Richmond's General Hospital No. 9. He was in constant pain until a secondary hemorrhage ended his life of 18 years on August 8th, over a month after the battle.

    John Botts's wound was described as accidental. He died on July 12th. William Perry received a flesh wound to the knee, either at Mechanicsville or Gaines's Mill. An infection claimed his life. Burrett Atwell was sent home to Rowan County where he died in the tearful presence of his family. He was nineteen. Solomon Newton's gunshot wound was severe, but the details are not given in his records. The 21-year-old remained hospitalized for three months until his death on October 19th. He was a carpenter before the war, and his wife's name was Mary. The regiment listed him as "absent wounded" for a year before they learned of his death.

---

[60] Hammarskold died in 1884 in Stockholm, Sweden (Scandinavian Confederates 2017)

As the 34th NC rested in camp, disease returned with a vengeance. In the month of July, twenty men from the regiment died from disease including two First Sergeants and two Lieutenants.[61] The combined losses from disease and battle reduced the regiment. From the start of the Seven Days battles on June 25th through the end of July, 101 men from the 34th NC died. Many more were hospitalized.

Several promotions were issued to replace fallen officers in the regiment. In Company D, which suffered severely at Frayser's Farm, Monroe Gillon and James Basinger replaced their two slain lieutenants. In Company E, the Methodist minister Micah Davis was promoted to 1st Lieutenant. In Company I, Thomas Phillips was promoted to Lieutenant. The regiment's historian Thomas D. Lattimore was promoted to Lieutenant in Company F, and the prolific letter-writer Burwell Cotton was promoted from sergeant to Lieutenant.

Folks at home in the Piedmont and Western North Carolina were proud of their sons but were stunned at the casualties. Losses were expected, but the numbers were shocking. Families anxiously read letters from the soldiers and watched newspapers for casualty lists. War hit home as family after family got word that their son was among those killed, wounded, or missing. Severely injured young men came home, some without an arm or leg. Families began to see the sacrifice as more than they could bear. Proud as they were of their young men, it was a high price to pay.

The Conscription Act had been controversial from the start. These men had volunteered for one year, but the law obliged them to stay for the duration of the war, and men at home could be pressed into service. The communities were already suffering from the shortage of both farm labor and skilled laborers, such as mechanics, carpenters, and blacksmiths. At this point, the law was used to keep existing soldiers in the ranks. But volunteer enlistment was down sharply, and they had suffered staggering losses on the battlefields. Eventually they had little choice but to call more men up. North Carolinians were highly independent. Open resistance to conscription was being organized, prompting Governor Vance to issue a series of proclamations.[62] On September 23, 1862, The Western Democrat published Vance's first

---

[61] Five died of causes not stated. They were assumed to have died of disease.
[62] Zebulan B. Vance became Governor September 8, 1862.

proclamation which warned, "...all persons contemplating an armed resistance to the law...that they will commit the crime of treason..." Despite his strong statements, many still resisted. Much of that resistance came from the Quaker Belt areas of Moore, Randolph, Montgomery, and surrounding areas.

    Most of the men subject to the draft were from the families that suffered the most from their absence, the poorer families. They lacked the financial means and the labor to work the farms that the wealthier slaveholders possessed. In a war ignited by slavery, the non-slaveholders bore a disproportionate share of the sacrifice. These families would be asked to sacrifice much more in the days to come. For many, it was more than they could give.

[63]Private Frederick Washington "Wash" Dellinger, The Shady Grover Rangers – Company E

---

[63] Photo courtesy Mike Stroupe

Major General William Dorsey Pender
Pender was the 34th NC's brigade commander from the Seven Days to Chancellorsville. He was then promoted to command of the Light Division until his death on July 18, 1863.

Chapter 5.
Second Manassas

With General Hill still confined, newspapers reported another Union General making boasts of an invasion of Virginia. Brash Union General John Pope moved into Virginia with an army of 70,000 men bent on succeeding where McClellan had failed. The Richmond papers were filled with his bombastic claims. He was successful in the west and was confident he could win in Virginia. Robert E. Lee had about 55,000 men to fend off the verbose Union general. Once again, the odds were stacked against them. Lee immediately sent Jackson to Gordonsville with two divisions. He then intervened in the Longstreet-Hill quarrel and restored Hill to command, sending him to support Jackson. On July 28th, the 34th NC marched to Richmond to catch a train headed toward Gordonsville. The 70-mile trip by rail took about ten hours.

By August 3rd, they were camped five miles southeast of Gordonsville. Huntley wrote, "We left our tents and cooking utensils at Richmond and making up wheat dough on poplar board without grease or salt and baking it before the fire in an oak chip is the way we live."[64] Word circulated that two Federal divisions were moving toward Culpepper, so they didn't make themselves too comfortable. Jackson's combative mood was noticeable. A fight was coming.

While at Gordonsville, Captain Stephen Wilson of Company A resigned his commission. In his letter, he cited his age and declining health and included a statement from Dr. John Miller attesting to his health. He also noted that he was standing in the way of another officer's promotion to Major. The current Major, Eli Miller, was due to be promoted to Lt. Colonel. Many of the officers appeared to favor Captain Joseph McGee to replace Miller, but Wilson was the senior Captain. His resignation cleared the way for McGee's promotion. Wilson's resignation was accepted by Maj. Eli Miller, still in command in Col. Riddick's absence. The regiment left Gordonsville a few days later. Soon, Colonel Riddick returned to lead the regiment. His wounds were not entirely healed, but he wanted to be back with his men.

---

[64] (Taylor 1994) Page 95, Letter from Huntley dated August 2, 1862.

On August 6th, the men were heading north trailing Jackson's other two divisions. The sun rose hot and got hotter as the day wore on. When they stopped for lunch, the temperature was around 85 degrees. By 2:00 p.m. it was over 90. With the searing heat and dusty roads, the men could barely see. The sun mercifully set around 7:00. They marched another two hours with the temperature cooling only a few degrees. They consumed what meager rations they had and went to sleep under the stars. The next day's march started at around 8:00 to give them a little extra rest. The sun burned just as hot as the day before. Despite frequent rest breaks, straggling caused the line to stretch for miles. Any stream they passed invited men to fill canteens and refresh themselves. Men suffered heat exhaustion and dropped to the side of the road. Pender, normally a stickler for tight ranks, allowed the men some slack. When the sun went down, they kept going. The sweat-soaked men were relieved from the sun, but the night was still extremely hot. Tired, dirty, and hungry, they dropped beside the road and found a comfortable piece of ground to sleep on.

All day to March a Mile

The following morning, Thursday August 8th, the regiment was up before dawn with the rest of the brigade, ready to take up the march. Orders from the night before placed Hill's division second in line behind Ewell, so the men waited for Ewell's men to pass by. Jackson was strict about schedules, so the men were ready. Finally, one brigade after another filed past. Unfortunately, it wasn't Ewell's division. It was Jackson's own division, commanded by General John Winder, which was supposed to be last in line. General Hill learned that Jackson had altered the marching orders during the night without telling him. Jackson had sent Ewell on an alternate route to relieve congestion on the road. Hill's men should have been on the road ahead of Winder.

Hill's men couldn't move until Winder's division had passed. First the long line of infantry filed by. It took time for an entire division to move down the road. Then, they had to wait while hundreds of wagons carrying Winder's supplies rolled past. After several hours, the men fell into line and started marching, but progress was painfully slow. Several miles ahead, Ewell's division ran into Winder's, causing a huge traffic jam. Hill's division, last in line, made little progress. The temperature rose above 90 as the men did more standing than marching. The only thing worse than marching in the extreme heat, was standing still. By mid-afternoon, the sunbaked soldiers had moved only a mile or so. Tempers flared. The men swore at the generals and the hot sun. They cursed the war and the day they volunteered. The order finally came for them to turn around and return to Orange Courthouse. It was the most useless march they had ever attempted. During the day, or after dark back at Orange, George Baker and Ephraim Osborne from Ashe County deserted and were never heard from again. They had had enough. The 34th NC with the rest of the Light Division slept in the same area as the night before.

Cedar Mountain

At 2:00 a.m., they were back on their feet and tramping down the road. They got an early start to catch up to the rest of Jackson's command. Pender's men, including the 34th NC, were third in line as they moved out. As the sun rose, heat and dust again characterized the march, but without the roads jammed, they made good time. As they marched over the dry red clay roads, the air became clouded with reddish dust. It clogged their nostrils and covered their faces with sweaty and grungy red grime. Their skin was sunburned deep red and blistered. Even their beards changed color. On they marched, passing 1,200 supply-laden wagons beside the road. The train had been ordered to halt to allow Hill's division to pass. The men crossed the Rapidan River and kept moving. Early in the afternoon, as Hill's men were closing with the rest of Jackson's command, riders came down the line with word that Jackson's lead units were encountering resistance near Cedar Mountain. Hearing the muffled sounds of artillery, they forged ahead knowing that their march would terminate in a battle. By late afternoon, they could discern the unmistakable sounds of a full-scale battle. Their pace quickened. The fight had not gone well for Jackson, and Hill's men were needed. Around 6:00 in the evening, orders came, and the men prepared to go in.

"...the northern army had some brave men and the Confederates some poor marksmen..."

The leg-weary troops of the 34th NC dusted themselves off and moved straight to line of battle. Pender directed his men to the left on the double-quick. Sheer adrenalin propelled them through the choking dust and smoke. The men could tell little of what was happening beyond a few yards around them. They moved as ordered and braced themselves for whatever was ahead. Branch, Archer, and Pender's brigades were advancing together. Branch and Archer's brigades came under heavy fire, but slowly bent the Federal line back. Pender's men pressed ahead in support. The enemy fell back to an open wheat field where they were reinforced and refused the line. Pender had been seeking an opportunity to throw his men into the fight and found the chance. He sent his men, including the 34th NC, flying into the enemy's right flank. Immediately, the nature of the fight changed. For a few minutes, they tried to fend off Pender's gritty brigade, but the line broke and the blue-clad soldiers fled. As darkness fell, a brief charge across the wheat field by Yankee cavalry was quickly broken by rebel muskets. Jackson continued to push, so the Light Division took off in pursuit. They rapidly advanced a mile and a half before the gathering darkness slowed them down. Artillery screened their movement and allowed them to keep moving, taking some prisoners along the way.

After dark, a bizarre and memorable event occurred related by T.D. Lattimore. "After dark, the brigade, still being in line of battle in an open field, a mounted Federal rode up within a few steps of our line and inquired what troops we were. An officer stepped forward to receive him, and approaching near, the Federal fired at him with his pistol. He wheeled and putting spurs to his horse, dashed away. From three to five hundred shots were fired at the fleeing Yankee, but to no effect, so far as we could see. I mention this incident to show that the northern army had some brave men and the Confederates some poor marksmen, especially when shooting by starlight."

Sometime after 10:00, they were ordered to stop. The bone-weary troops trudged back to the original battlefield. It has been said that infantrymen learn to sleep on the march and surely, they must have that night. They had been up 24 hours, marched all day, and were in a running fight. It had taken a herculean effort to go the distance. One blessing in disguise was the previous day's bungled march. The mistake had placed the 34th NC in the back of the line instead of up front. Had they been where they were supposed to have been, the entire nature of the battle would have been different. As it was, they entered the battle late in the day, avoiding the worst of the fighting. Theirs had been a running fight that drove the enemy back with light loss. The troops slept peacefully on the battlefield where they may have died had it not been for the mix-up.

Official reports show no casualties from the 34th North Carolina during this battle, but Private Jesse Dobbins was admitted to the hospital in Richmond on August 14th with a gunshot wound to the shoulder, more than likely from this battle. There were likely other minor wounds not recorded. The march in the days leading up to the battle caused more losses to the regiment than the battle.

George Huntley referred to the battle in a letter, "I am very unwell at this time, caused, I suppose by so much hard marching and exposure…. there has been a power of rain and we have taken it all. Just lie down and lie in the rain all night without anything over us." He continued, "We have got orders now to cook two day's rations to move somewhere, I reckon, but I don't know where. On the 9th of this month…. we attacked the Yankees. The fight lasted till about two hours in the night. We whipped them with all ease and run them about one mile and taken about 500 prisoners."[65]

The sun rose hot again the next morning. By noon, rain brought some relief, growing to a steady downpour. Sporadic skirmishing occurred but no general engagement. They set to work burying the dead and caring for the wounded. By this time, the men had seen so much death that they became callous to it. Letters home mention the carnage of the battlefields as casual as if talking about the weather. They remained in place one more day and on the 12th of August marched back a few miles and set up camp. The men noticed that General Hill sported a new gray horse. He had acquired it from the battlefield and named it Champ. Hill found it difficult to get along with his superiors but had an exceptionally good relationship with his men.

The Grinding Marches With Stonewall Jackson

On August 14th, General Jackson ordered military operations to pause, and religious services were held to give thanks to God for their recent success and to pray for continued blessing.[66] The pious Jackson openly encouraged his men in spiritual matters. The next morning, they packed up. By afternoon, all three divisions were heading north, reaching Mountain Run near Clark's Mountain by dark. Longstreet was

---

[65] (Taylor 1994) Page 96, Letter from Huntley dated August 15th, 1862.
[66] (W. W. Hassler 1965) Page 168, letter from Pender to his wife Aug 14, 1862.

bringing up ten brigades, giving them enough men to face Pope. By August 19th, they had spent several grueling days under an unforgiving sun. That night, the weary troops went to sleep with orders to march at dawn. However, Jackson had once again changed the orders. He wanted the men on the road two hours sooner, but Hill did not get the order. Jackson rode into camp angry that they were not on the road. Jackson barked orders, and the men packed up and got in line.

The Light Division put in another hard day's march at the head of the long column, crossed the Rapidan, and continued north. Men grew numb to the pain after a while. In the middle of the 34th NC's line marched Pvt. Pinkney Etters with the Mecklenburg Boys. Pinkney didn't think anything about the cramps in his legs. Leg pain was nothing unusual after days in the heat. Every part of his body hurt. He couldn't get enough water and became dehydrated. His skin was red and searing hot. Curiously, the sweat that had poured from his forehead for days had stopped. His heart raced, and his head throbbed. He felt nauseated, but his stomach was empty. His friends noticed that he was mumbling and seemed confused. Eventually, they helped him to the side of the road, but it was too late. Pinkney died in the blistering August sun. He was 29 years old from Mecklenburg County. He survived the fighting in June but not the March to Manassas.

Marching under Stonewall Jackson could be a brutal experience. Pvt. Charles S. Martin recalled one experience while marching with Jackson, possibly this march.[67] They were in a forced march and not allowed to stop. The men were hungry and desperate for water. As they forded a small stream, the men quickly filled their canteens and took a drink. They continued along the trail and soon found themselves crossing back over several hundred yards upstream from where they had previously crossed. There, in the middle of the creek lay a dead horse in "an advanced state of decomposition."[68] Surely many canteens and some stomachs were quickly emptied.

---

[67] (Martin n.d.) Essay courtesy of Patti Martin.
[68] This is from a post war recollection by Pvt. Charles S. Martin. The account states that this happened just prior to the Seven Days Battles as part of Jackson's command. However, the 34th NC was not under Jackson's command until after the Seven Days. It seems more likely to have occurred around this time or later.

By the 22nd, they were camped near White Sulphur Springs. Late that afternoon, heavy rain came down. The generals found houses to set up in, but the men had no shelter. On the 23rd, Federal artillery fired into Hill's division. Confederate artillery answered, and for several hours the men amused themselves by watching an artillery duel which caused much noise but few casualties. When the firing stopped, a column of Federal infantry was seen heading their direction. Rebel artillery drove them off. The column was a mere probe. Two large armies were feeling one another out. All the signs of a looming large battle were present. The division stayed in place one more day. Lee had an audacious plan in mind, even more outlandish than his battle plan at Richmond. As he had done against McClellan, he would again divide his army. This time, however, he would spread them out over a greater distance against a more dangerous foe.

At sunrise, August 25th, the men were rushed into line and headed out. They traveled light as usual, with no knapsacks. Ewell's division was in the lead, Hill was second, and the Stonewall Division was last. The 34th NC was but a small cog in the huge marching machine under the command of Stonewall Jackson. The sun bore down hot, but the men marched all day. Some opted to take their shoes off and march through the dust in bare feet. As they passed through the Virginia farm country, they took anything they could find to supplement their lean rations. Among the delicacies were corn, apples, pears, and sweet potatoes. On the 26th they reached Thoroughfare Gap.

There, Jackson made an unexpected move, dividing his force into three parts, each with a specific objective. It was a risky but calculated strategy. Ewell's division moved on to Bristoe Station to burn an important railroad bridge and disrupt Pope's supply line. Jeb Stewart's cavalry and two regiments of infantry raced to Manassas Junction to take a stockpile of Yankee supplies. Hill's division went with Jackson to the railroad junction. Jackson tried to turn Hill's division into foot cavalry, forcing a blistering pace, at times three miles an hour. Food was in short supply, but even more troublesome was the lack of water. They stopped anywhere they could to fill canteens but there just wasn't enough. Dehydration and exhaustion caused many to fall from the line. By the time they reached Gainesville early on the 27th they had covered fifty-four miles in three foot-blistering days. The men in the ranks didn't know it, and they would have been too tired to care if they did, but they had accomplished one of the greatest flanking movements of the war. They were in the last place Pope expected them to be. They were behind Pope's army, only twenty-seven miles from Washington, D.C.

"...lobster salad, potted tongue, cream biscuit, and the like..."

Shortly after sunrise the 27th of August, the foot-sore men made it to the railhead. There they experienced something they would never forget. Sitting stationary on two train tracks were two lines of boxcars a half mile long full of Yankee supplies being guarded by the two infantry regiments that had accompanied Stewart. It was the sweetest sight they had ever seen. Despite the objection of the troops guarding the supplies, Hill's men stormed the trains as if it was an enemy battery. They found everything from vegetables and corned beef to coffee, whiskey, even champagne, and lobster. They had just begun to enjoy their opulent feast when they were ordered back into line.

It's a small wonder the famished men didn't revolt, but they obeyed. A Federal brigade was less than a mile away. Pender's brigade was sent ahead to support Hill's artillery which was deploying forward. A brief engagement ended with the Federal brigade falling back. The artillery scattered them with the infantry doing little work. After the skirmish, the men marched back to the junction ready to resume their assault on the supply trains. To their chagrin, Jackson made them wait. Finally, word was given. The men charged the trains, not with bayonets, but with forks. For several hours, the malnourished men filled their bellies with everything they could find. In the words of one delighted soldier, "it was more than funny to see the ragged, rough, dirty fellows who had been half living on roasted corn and green apples for days, now drinking Rhine wine, eating lobster salad, potted tongue, cream biscuit, pound cake, canned fruits, and the like; and filling pockets and haversacks with ground coffee, tooth-brushes, condensed milk, silk handkerchiefs."[69]

It was Christmas in August. The men drank whiskey, smoked "segars," and found fresh undergarments to replace the rags they wore. Never since the start of the war and never again until the war ended

---

[69] (James I Robetson 1992), Page 114,

would there be so many smiles. Though dust-covered, bone-weary, and sunbaked, the men felt almost human again. Jackson allowed them to consume all they could and carry away what they wanted. Without wagons to take the rest and not wanting to leave it to the Yankees, the cars were torched at midnight. The conflagration made quite a spectacle. At 1:00 in the morning, the men marched away. The Light Division travelled the heaviest they had since the start of the war with every pocket, haversack, and bag full of anything could tote away. Hill's division took the road to Centreville while the other two divisions moved to Groveton, west of Bull Run.

Second Manassas

Hill's division reached Centreville at daylight on August 28th. A heavy breeze made the heat more tolerable. The men stopped for a short rest, some dozing under shade trees. Back on their feet, they marched toward Bull Run to catch up with Jackson. The men could see large dust clouds in the distance resembling their own. It was Federal troops concentrating at Manassas Junction. Officers ordered the men to close ranks and step up the pace. "Tighten up! Push on!" they yelled up and down the dusty line. They crossed Bull Run, listening to the distant sounds of battle. Jackson's men were clashing with Federal troops at Groveton. Turning in the direction of Sudley Springs, they were ordered to a ridge a mile from the Warrenton Turnpike, a short march from Groveton. There, an unfinished railroad cut ran along a slope 500 yards from the top of Stony Ridge. It was a beautiful defensive position. All three of Jackson's divisions were compacted there, the entire line barely a mile and a half long.

Hill positioned his men in two lines. From left to right, the brigades of Gregg, Thomas, and Field were in the front near the cut. Behind them were Archer's, Pender's, and Branch's brigades. The 34th NC was center the entire division. Colonel Riddick positioned his men and set them to work. After sundown, they piled felled trees, rocks, and earth to set up defensive works. Behind them, artillery batteries rolled into position. Much of the area was covered in trees and brush, heavily in places. It was an ideal defensive position, but as the men rested for a few hours, an unknown danger existed. Between the brigades of Gregg and Thomas in the front row was a 175-yard gap that was somehow overlooked. Pender's brigade was straight behind the gap.

There was not a cloud in the sky on Friday, August 29th. The area was unnervingly quiet at sunrise. They sat waiting, daring the enemy to come. After an hour, they did. Through the woods, the dark-clothed mass of Yankee troops came up the hill, two brigades strong heading for Hill's position. The men of the 34th NC watched and listened. Gregg's brigade, obliquely to their front and left was the target. Hard-hitting Gregg ordered his men to counter attack. The 34th NC was just out of sight of Gregg's action but could hear how intense the fight was. At noon, Gregg's men still held their ground. Pender's men, untouched thus far, remained in place. Soon, four new Federal brigades, commanded by "Fighting" Joe Hooker, plunged through the brush, and struck Hill's other two brigades in the front line. The brigades of Field and Thomas made maximum use of their defensive position and poured lead into the attackers. Tree limbs fell, and bark flew from the trees. Dry grass caught fire in places, and smoke filled the area. Hooker's men went head-to-head with Field and Thomas. Men fought with bayonets and clubbed muskets. The Rebel line held.

At around 3:00 in the afternoon, the Confederates saw a fresh Yankee brigade moving through the smoky woods. Using the terrain to screen their movement, they disappeared for a time and then suddenly reappeared in front of the 175-yard gap between Gregg and Thomas. Raising their own version of the rebel yell, the Yankees stormed over the embankment like a tidal wave, paused to fire a volley, and then charged. One of Gregg's regiments rushed to meet the threat in a desperate effort to close the gap. Thomas sent another regiment from the other side. For an hour, the two sides threw everything they had at each other. Gregg's men ran out of ammunition but refused to leave, fighting with bayonets, and even throwing rocks at the enemy. Pender had waited patiently and found the opportunity to send his men in. Colonel Riddick drew his sword and at Pender's command, the men rose and dashed forward through the choking smoke, dust, and gun powder. Pender somehow found the perfect place to strike on the enemy's flank. Hooker's stunned troops fled in a rout leaving behind over 350 casualties. Pender pursued the fleeing enemy too far, flying through the woods and out into the open. There, they were turned back by heavy artillery fire. Pender fell wounded by a shell that cut a gash in the top of his head. They fought their way back to the railroad cut.

"Let us die here, my men!"

Pender's wound was not serious but required attention, so command of the brigade temporarily fell to Colonel Riddick. The brigade was pulled back in reserve near Gregg's severely damaged brigade. Many Light Division troops had little or no ammunition. Shortly after 5:00, distant Federal troops were spotted forming for one last assault. They came in three orderly lines of battle, smashing into the rebel line. The fighting came down to hand-to-hand combat. Men swung rifles as clubs, thrust bayonets, fists, and threw rocks. During the furious assault, General Gregg waived a Revolutionary War sword and yelled, "Let us die here, my men! Let us die here!" The rebel line slowly fell back from the railroad cut, but Jackson sent reinforcements in time to shore up the line, and the enemy retired. By day's end, the division had beaten back six separate Federal assaults. Federal artillery rained shells on the men as the sun set. The 34th NC was sent to the rear for rest and rations then came back to the line to prepare for the next day's fight. Riddick's regiment had been fortunate. Their reserve position at the battle's outset shielded them from the initial attacks. In the final assault, they were again positioned away from the heaviest fighting. Only one man from the regiment was killed the first day of the battle. Several were wounded. These casualties occurred when Pender made his over-zealous counter charge in the afternoon.

The next morning was again hot and dry as the two large armies waited. Longstreet was in position on the far right ready to finish the job. Federal troops made light stabs at Hill's line to test their strength, but no general assault. Pender, sporting bandages from his head wound, was back in command of the brigade. At two in the afternoon, the Federals launched an even larger attack than the day before. The main thrust was at Jackson's right, away from Hill's troops, but the fighting spread to parts of Hill's line. At the height of the fighting in Hill's area, he once again called up Pender's brigade. Pender shifted down the railroad cut to join with Field's brigade. Pender's North Carolinians and Field's Virginians sailed forward and threw the enemy back with great loss. With enough daylight for one more attempt, the Federal troops came again. Pope stayed fixated on Hill at the railroad cut and ignored his left flank, unaware that the other half of

Lee's army was in position. Pope paid the price for his negligence. Longstreet was ready to pounce.

Sensing victory, Lee ordered Jackson and Longstreet to attack. Jackson and Hill shifted their troops. Longstreet's men started forward at 4:00. They had to advance two miles through numerous natural barriers. Jackson's troops were exhausted from the heavy fighting, so it took two full hours to get into position. Pender was moved south of the cut and ordered into line of battle. Colonel Riddick formed his men with the rest of the brigade. They were positioned north of the Warrenton Pike and Henry Hill, west of the Sudley Springs Road. Once formed, the division advanced in echelon, a tricky maneuver in which each brigade advanced slightly behind and to the right of the other. The order left to right was: Branch, Archer, Thomas, Pender, Field, and Gregg's battered brigade last. The 34th NC, therefore, had three full brigades ahead and to their left. To make it more difficult, the huge formation was to move forward obliquely.

The complicated nature of the advance caused some problems when some of the brigades got tangled up with Longstreet's advancing men. The generals untangled the traffic jam, and the well-disciplined troops moved ahead. Finally, 50,000 rebels moved forward in a well-coordinated arching line spanning five miles. The men of the 34th NC dashed across the field overwhelming the enemy before them. Archer's men captured half a Federal battery in the rout, and Pender's men finished it off. When darkness fell, Pender was still pressing the attack. His head wound from the day before should have reminded him not to push too far, but his enthusiasm got the best of him. Again, the men had to shoot their way back to Hill's main line. By dark, the Confederates had completely driven Pope's men from the field in an impressive rout of a much larger enemy. A year ago, Stonewall Jackson has won his nickname on this same ground, where they remained undefeated. The Light Division had been conspicuous in this victory. Half of the Light Division casualties in the two-day battle came from Gregg's brigade who lost 613 men. Pender's men experienced lighter casualties. It rained hard for much of the night, washing the blood-stained battlefield. The men slept uncovered in the downpour.

Two men from the 34th NC died in the fighting. On the battle's first day fell a 24-year-old farmer from Troy, NC named John Dennis, the son of James and Mary Dennis. He had enlisted with his younger brother James who died of disease the past November. Sgt. Robert Crowder from Cleveland County fell on the second day. He was 30 years old, the son of Barlett and Mary Crowder. He married Eunice Jane Evans four years before the war. A son and a daughter were born to them before he went off to war. The regiment reported seventeen wounded, light casualties considering the scope of the battle.

Bloody Ox Hill

The weary 34th NC got little sleep and woke up soaking wet. But there was no time to rest. By noon they were marching. The Light Division set the pace with Stonewall Jackson's other two divisions trailing. Lee wanted Jackson to hunt Pope down and finish off his wounded army. It rained much of the day, as many had trouble keeping up with Jackson's ruthless pace. They were all tired, but the older men had the hardest time. Edwin Leach from Montgomery County was 42. He gave it all he had but just didn't have the legs. He fell out of the line and was never heard from again.[70]

Their weary legs carried them ten miles, and they camped near the Pleasant Valley Baptist Church on the Little River Turnpike. Once again, they slept under the stars with little to eat. The next day, September 1st, their march started at daylight with Hill's men again leading the way. They marched under a heavy cloud cover that looked sure to rain. Progress was even slower than the day before. By lunchtime, they had covered barely three miles. By two-thirty in the afternoon, the lead units were running into Federal troops near Ox Hill. The column stopped at Chantilly Plantation and fanned out into line of battle. Hill's division was on the right in a wooded area, Ewell in the center, with Jackson's division on the left.

Around three o'clock, the Federals attacked straight up the center. Pender's brigade was first ordered to stay in support, but Pender received orders from Gen. Jackson to reinforce Brockenbrough's brigade which was hard pressed.[71] Pender's brigade went forward. When they reached the rear of Brockenbrough's brigade, Pender's brigade was thrown out of order with the 34th NC and the 16th NC

---

[70] Leach was dropped from the rolls a year later, "supposed to be dead."
[71] This was Field's brigade. Field had been wounded at Manassas, so Brokenbrough led in his place.

bearing right and becoming separated. The thick woods added to the confusion. Eventually, the 34th and the 16th on the right supported Branch's brigade, while the rest of the brigade supported Thomas. Only the 34th and 16th were actively engaged in the fighting.[72] Just then, the clouds opened, and it started coming down in sheets. The Federal troops were first driven back into a corn field, but heavier fire developed as both sides committed more troops to the battle. As the fighting grew heavier, so did the rain. Most of their gun powder was soaked and useless. Then, a massive wave of Federal troops came charging through the downpour. The weather notwithstanding, the Federals would not give up, and the Confederates determined to hold. *"Go on! I am shot, but not conquered!"*

    Thunder and lightning added to the dreadful scene as the 34th and 16th were ordered to move in. Colonel Riddick led the 34th NC into the fray. Rain pelted their faces, reducing visibility. The thunder vied with the sound of artillery and the lightening with the flash of explosions. It was as if the gods of war were punishing them for daring to fight here. The battle devolved into an ugly confusing fight for survival. Muskets became clubs, bayonets were thrusted, rocks and even fists were used. It was hard to tell friend from foe. Men slipped and fell in the mud and were trampled. The men of the 34th NC found themselves in the middle of a nightmarish battle. Among the men who fell was Colonel Riddick who was wounded in the side and wrist.[73] When he went down, his men rushed to his assistance, but he shouted, "Go on! I am shot, but not conquered!" The Union troops finally ceded the field, and the savage clash ended. The short fight left eight men from the 34th NC lifeless on the muddy field. Twenty others were wounded. The regiment lost some of its best men in this terrible fight.

    Major Eli H. Miller was gravely wounded in his neck. He died two days later under the care of his brother, the regiment's surgeon Dr.

---

[72] O.R. Series 1-Volume 16, Aug. 16-Sept. 2, 1862-Campaign of Northern Virginia, No. 187-Report of Brig. Gen. William D. Pender, C. S. Army.
[73] The nature of his wounds is not described in his records. They were mentioned in a report in The Western Democrat dated September 23, 1862, Report of Casualties near Fairfax C. House, September 1st. The same article mentioned Major Eli Miller's wound. The list was provided to the paper by Dr. John Miller, the regiment's surgeon.

John F. Miller. Eli was a teacher before the war and was elected Major at the April 18th, 1861, election. The 24-year-old had a promising future ahead of him as a son of a wealthy Rutherford County physician. Henry D. Eaton had enlisted as a private. For distinguishing himself at Gaines's Mill, he was promoted to sergeant and given the honor of bearing the regiment's colors. He was later promoted to lieutenant in Company E. He was 6'3" tall and respected among the Lincoln County men. The 36-year-old farmer died on the brutal field of Ox Hill. His wife, Catherine, and their six children were left to grieve his loss.

Joseph Bedford was 21 years old. He and his younger brother Seth enlisted together in Rutherford County when the Sandy Run Yellow Jackets were formed. The fresh-faced young farm hands left home to fight together. Seth would march away from Ox Hill alone. Franklin Long was a 21-year-old lieutenant from Ashe County. Seven members of the Long family enlisted in the Laurel Springs Guards the year before. Franklin was the third man from the family to die when he fell at Ox Hill. Robert England suffered over a month before he died on October 18th. John Hendrick lived until November 21st three months after the battle. He was 18 years old.

Official records show four men captured in the battle, but only two were found in the search of service records. James and Michael Miller were both wounded and taken prisoner. The Ashe County men were father and son. They were held at Old Capital Prison and exchanged the following March. The 16th NC lost 1 man killed, 8 wounded, and 1 captured. The following are the 34th NC's known casualties from the Battle of Ox Hill:

Colonel Riddick's wound proved to be mortal. He lingered six days and died on September 7th, 1862, in a hospital near Fairfax. The men had come to respect him for his courage under fire. He was described as, "Modest, truthful, and possessed of an amiable disposition."[74] They followed wherever he led, even across that deadly field at Ox Hill.

---

[74] A quote from Colonel Riddick's obituary.

Casualties from the Battle of Ox Hill

Killed in Action

Joseph B Bedford	B	Pvt.	Jesse J Phillips[75]	G	Pvt.
Henry D Eaton	E	Lt.	William L Plaster	D	Pvt.
Elisha Haltom	K	Pvt.	George J Sweezy	B	Pvt.
Franklin Long	A	2Lt.	Aaron W Whiteside	C	Pvt.

Mortally Wounded

Robert A England	C	Pvt.	Richard H Riddick		Col.
John W Hendrick	F	Pvt.	Frank E Johnston	G	Pvt.
Eli H Miller	F	Maj.	Joseph U Whiteside	C	Cpl.

Wounded

Jacob Bare Sr	A	Pvt.	James C Miller*	A	Sgt.
Elijah Crotts	F	Pvt.	Michael D Miller*	A	Pvt.
George F Fulbright	E	Pvt.	James R Morrow	I	Cpl.
Levi Long	A	Pvt.	Moses P Petty	F	Pvt.
Daniel R Louder	D	Pvt.	James F Shehan	I	Pvt.
Ahijah Oliver Lynch	C	Pvt.	Isaac Smith	K	Pvt.

*Wounded and captured

---

[75] Some of the records for Phillips say he was killed at Manassas. However, a notarized affidavit specifically says he was killed at Ox Hill.

William Lee Charnock Cox

Private William Lee Charnock "Mr. Charn" Cox – The Mecklenburg Boys – Company G. Lost an arm at Gaines's Mill.[76]

---

[76] Photo courtesy Amber Kelly Crum

Captain William O. Harrelson, The Shady Grove Rangers – Company E[77]

---

[77] Photo courtesy Mike Stroupe

Chapter 6.
Crisis at Sharpsburg

The Manassas Campaign took a heavy toll but was an extraordinary victory. For the second time in two months, Lee's army had defeated a much larger enemy. Both times, Lee gambled by dividing his army in the face of superior numbers and emerged victorious. They not only defeated their opponents, they humiliated them. Lee was once called Old Granny by his men, but he was now called that wily gray fox by his enemies. The pace had been grueling, but the men had borne it well. On the heels of Second Manassas, Lee asked even more of his hardy troops. In an incredibly bold plan, he would take his army north and invade Maryland. Lee was a gambler, but he believed in his men, and they would follow him anywhere. Rations were slim, and feet were bleeding, but spirits were strong as they headed north.

    The 34th NC took its place in line and marched all day September 3rd, stopping for the night at Dranesville. Shortly after 4:00 the next morning, they were up and tramping down the road again. Hill was late getting the men moving and was reprimanded by Jackson. The Light Division set the pace for the day, and the contrary Hill pushed his men. Normally, they stopped at noon for lunch. This day, Hill kept going. The column eventually halted, and the men watched a very disgruntled A. P. Hill being marched to the rear under guard. Hill's failure to stop at noon led to a confrontation between the two stubborn generals, and Jackson placed the fiery Hill under arrest. The Light Division was temporarily led by Brigadier General Lawrence Branch. On September 5th, the men were treading Maryland soil. At Frederick, they got a well-deserved five-day rest. Green roasted corn was the main dish as the men sat around their campfires. During the break, the sad news of the death of Colonel Richard H. Riddick came to the 34th NC.

    Since the 34th NC did not have a field-grade officer, General Pender moved quickly to fill the positions. Under the circumstances, promoting from within was the logical choice, so Pender looked to the regiment's captains. On September 7th, Pender, with A. P. Hill's approval, promoted 26-year-old William Lee Joshua Lowrance to Colonel. He was the son of John and Jane Lowrance of Iredell, NC. Lowrance was an 1860 graduate of Davidson College and taught school briefly in Memphis, TN and Lebanon, MS. When North Carolina seceded, he put his teaching career on hold to volunteer for the 34th North Carolina as a lieutenant in Company D. He was a devout Presbyterian, a quality Pender liked. He wasn't loud or brash, but was intelligent, highly articulate, and a natural leader with a gift of influence. He was loyal to his duties. Though he had no military experience before the war, he had proved himself on the battlefield. No man in the regiment was more suited for the position. Captain John McDowell, an exceedingly popular officer in the regiment, was promoted to Lt. Colonel. Captain Joseph McGee was promoted to Major. Carmi McNeely and George Norment were both promoted to Captain. Nelson C. Woodie was promoted to Captain in Company A to replace Stephen Wilson. Alexander A. Cathey, Bartlett Martin, and William Edwards were promoted to 1st Lieutenants.

In promoting Lowrance to Colonel, General Pender caused a slight problem. The Confederate Army followed the U.S. Army practice of observing seniority among officers. If two officers held the same rank, the officer who had held that rank the longest was the senior officer. Only two of the regiment's original captains remained in service by this time, Sam Hoey of Company H and Lowrance of Company D. Hoey enlisted as captain on October 1, 1861, Lowrance enlisted as a lieutenant and was promoted to captain on October 25, 1861, giving Hoey three weeks seniority. General Pender felt the promotion board would agree that this was trivial. He picked Lowrence because he was the best man for the job. In addition, McDowell and McGee were both promoted ahead of Hoey. Sam Hoey was a man of good character, but Pender felt he just wasn't ready for higher command. Officers sometimes waived their seniority or resigned to allow others to be promoted. Hoey did not. Lowrance's field promotion stood, but Hoey would take his case to the Promotions Board in Richmond for the final say.

Pvt. Jacob Dellinger wrote to his father during the regiment's rest at Frederick. He wrote, "we have sen hard times for the last three months of marching and fighting and any other hardship that man can endure. There is about 150 to 180 men in our camp that is ready for duty. We have been in 5 different battles or fights, since the battle in front of Richmond, but we have been victorious in every battle, and now instead of them invading our land, we are invading theirs. And I hope that we may be crowned with success a while longer and I think peace will prevail. I must inform you that Lt. Eaton was killed on Monday last, the first day of this month, and there were 13 others in our camp wounded in Saturdays fight at Manassas."[78]

On September 10th, Colonel Lowrance and his men took their place in line with the Light Division and the rest of Jackson's command and embarked on a new mission. Federal troops occupied Harper's Ferry, but Lee thought the garrison would be drawn to Maryland as they marched north. The Union troops had stayed, however, and posed a problem. They could potentially block Lee's route back to Virginia, so Lee ordered Jackson and the Light Division to dislodge them. Once again, Lee showed no fear in dividing his army, but this time the stakes were even higher. Dividing his army in Maryland was dangerous. Any mistake could be disastrous. The fate of the war depended on the movements they would make in the days to come.

Harper's Ferry

Instead of taking the shorter direct path to Harper's Ferry, they took a longer 51-mile route to approach Harper's Ferry from the north. They bivouacked that evening near Williamsport. The next morning, the men were happy to see that General Hill had been restored to command. On the evening of the 11th, the column marched through the town of Martinsburg where they seized a large wagon train filled with supplies left behind by retreating Federals. The men filled their empty stomachs and carried away what they could. They paused, having marched but four miles that day. The next day, they marched a demanding seventeen miles. Nearing Harper's Ferry, the stragglers were loaded into wagons rather than being allowed to drift behind. During the long march, three men from the regiment deserted together never to be heard from again. They were all from Company K of Montgomery County, Robert and William Brewer, and Harvey Latham With their departure, the regiment had experienced 15 cases of desertion since the regiment was formed.

Around mid-morning on September 13th, lead brigades began arriving west of Harper's Ferry. Jackson and Hill deployed the troops.

---

[78] Letter from Jacob Dellinger dated 9/8/1862, at Frederick City, MD. Letter courtesy Mike Stroupe.

Pender guided his regiments to their place with the rest of Hill's division on Schoolhouse Ridge. They were just west of the Federal line on Bolivar Heights. Once in position, they waited as the rest of Jackson's deployments were made, which took time. All around were sounds of skirmishing but no general engagement. Across the Shenandoah River on Louden Heights, Confederate artillery was setting up. On Sunday morning, September 14th, the men expected a fight, but instead faced more waiting. They stayed in place until late afternoon when orders came to move forward. They were to advance north of the railroad and turn the Federal flank at the southern end of Bolivar Heights. Confederate artillery shelled the Federal position as the men inched forward. The Federals occupied the high ground on the left. Pender directed the brigade, including the 34th NC, to advance on the position. As the sun was starting down, they were within 150 yards of the enemy line. They paused while Confederate artillery fired. The artillery was accurate, and the Federal troops lost interest in holding the ground. When the infantry advanced, they met light resistance. By nightfall, they had easily turned the Federal flank.

  The checkmate was complete. The Federal garrison of 14,000 men was completely boxed in. To their south was the Shenandoah River with A. P. Hill's men poised at their flank. To their front, the Confederate line extended all the way from the Shenandoah to the Potomac to the north. To their rear, the two rivers converged with the bridges leading away from town blocked by Jackson's division. Jackson had used his knowledge of the area to trap the Federals. There was no way out. The next morning, September 15th, a heavy fog covered the area as rebel artillery lobbed shells into the helpless garrison. Federal guns answered, and the dual lasted an hour. Finally, the bugler sounded the advance, and Pender's men moved ahead. Artillery provided cover as the veterans advanced in excellent order. Just before 9:00, a mounted Federal officer rode out carrying a white flag. Union Colonel Dixon Miles had made the decision to surrender. He had made a critical mistake in failing to hold the heights away from town and placed his men in a trap. The quick decision to surrender saved many lives, but it would have consequences in the days to come.

  It was a clean victory with truly little loss. There were no casualties from the 34th NC. The sack of Harper's Ferry netted 12,419

Federal prisoners, 13,000 stands of arms, 73 cannons, 200 wagons, and a vast store of food and supplies, all of which were desperately needed.[79] The Federal prisoners taken at Harper's Ferry were the largest number of U.S. prisoners taken in battle until the WWII Battle of Bataan. Pender's brigade was placed in charge of the prisoners. Under the terms of surrender, the men were allowed keep overcoats, personal belongings, and were given two days' rations. They would then be paroled and allowed go home. Under the prisoner exchange system that then existed, the paroled Federal troops would be sent home with their parole papers and could not rejoin the Federal service until properly exchanged, meaning an equal number of Confederate prisoners were exchanged and allowed back into the service. Under this system, prison stays were kept short.

    Colonel Lowrance's 34th NC with the rest of the brigade started processing prisoners, recording the name, rank, and command of each man, issuing their paperwork and rations, taking their weapons, and getting them ready to leave. No one could miss the contrast between the Union and Confederate soldiers. The Union troops were well equipped and well fed, while their rebel captors were in rags without proper shoes and had obviously lived much harder. Federal troops remembered their treatment by Pender's men as being very civil. They remarked that the rebels used almost no profane language and treated them well. Many Union soldiers wanted to get a look at Stonewall Jackson. One m remarked, "Boys, he isn't much for looks, but if we'd had him we wouldn't have been caught in this trap."[80]

    Late that evening, Jackson left Hill's division behind and started his other two divisions back to rejoin Lee. The next day, the 34th NC went back to work paroling prisoners and indulging once again in the Federal supplies. They filled knapsacks with all the food they could carry and commandeered horses to haul supplies away. Many of Hill's men procured Federal shirts, pants, hats, jackets, shoes, anything they needed. Blue wasn't exactly their favorite color, but it beat the rags they wore. They hadn't seen their wagon train in six weeks, and their clothes were tattered. The men slept well that night,

---

[79] (James I Robetson 1992), page 138.
[80] Wikipedia – Account of the Battle of Harper's Ferry

finding shelter in town with light rain falling. Their stomachs were full, and they had accomplished their mission.

Sharpsburg

An out-of-breath courier rode hard into Harper's Ferry at 6:30 the next morning, Wednesday September 17th. Within 30 minutes, the men were marching away from the town. Hill pushed his men to move quickly. Many were clad in Yankee blue and carried captured Yankee guns. Hill led the column on a route a few miles longer than the 12-mile direct route from Harper's Ferry to Sharpsburg, giving them a 17-mile hike. The men were tired. Since September 1st, they had been on the march eleven of the seventeen days, but the looming battle motivated them. The day was hot and humid, and the pace was demanding. With very few brief pauses, the men kept moving. Younger legs could keep up, but older men had a tough time. The column moved swiftly. They understood the urgency of the situation. All along the line, officers admonished the men to keep moving. "Press on! Close up!" they barked. "General Lee needs you!"

Indeed, General Lee did need them. All day long, Lee's main body, then joined by Jackson's two divisions from Harper's Ferry, had been relentlessly attacked. They were holding onto a very tenuous north-south line east of Sharpsburg, but they were grossly outnumbered. By the afternoon hours, General Ambrose Burnside's men presented a grave threat. For three hours, Burnside had assaulted the bridge across Antietam Creek and had finally driven the Confederates back, allowing his men and wagons to pour across. Burnside was now poised to crush Lee's right flank on the southern end of his line. If Burnside was successful, Lee's bloodied army could be cut off from Virginia. Lee's gamble of dividing his army to take Harper's Ferry endangered his whole army. The fate of the war hung in the balance. If Hill's men did not arrive in time, the war could end right there. Lee had taken massive casualties and could be forced to surrender if his route back to Virginia was blocked by Burnside.

At 2:00 in the afternoon, the hard-marching Light Division started across the Potomac near Boteler's Ford. There was no time to build a bridge. They splashed across. The temperature was in the mid 70's and it was very humid. No doubt the men were glad to plunge into the water. They barely paused long enough to fill canteens and get a drink of water. To keep their gunpowder dry, they held their muskets and cartridge boxes over their heads and waded across the shallow portion of the river. As they hastened on, the sounds of the battle at Sharpsburg were clearly audible. Once across the river, the Light Division caught its second wind. The men had covered seventeen miles in seven hours of determined effort. Not counting the very few breaks they took, they had averaged close to three miles per hour in hot, humid, and dusty conditions. The Light Division had started the march with around 5,000 men. Barely 3,000 remained in line. Arriving on the field, the 34th NC was described by T. D. Lattimore as a "mere skeleton" with only four commissioned officers in the entire regiment.

The battle raging before them had gone badly. The Confederates had fought hard, but the division on the extreme right had been beaten down to barely 2,000 men to face Burnside's 12,000 eager Yankees. At 3:00 in the afternoon, the Federal onslaught started toward the horribly out-gunned rebels. They inched slowly forward as Confederates artillery fired. Hill's men were still perhaps a mile and a half away and stepped up their pace. Finally, some forty minutes after Burnside started his final attack on Lee's right flank, Hill's lead brigades came onto the field. The foot-sore troops came to the rescue in one of the most dramatic moments of the war. Marching on sheer adrenaline, the men ignored their pain and responded to the emergency. Without pause, battle lines were formed, and they went forward. Pender sent his men to the right along with Brockenbrough's brigade to guard against a flanking movement by the Federals. The rest of the Light Division went left. Archer's brigade to the far left stormed across a corn field and dove into the Federals. When the Federal troops saw Archer's men, they mistook them for Federal reinforcements because of the Yankee uniforms they had taken from Harper's Ferry. Taking the Federals troops in a cross-fire, an entire Yankee regiment was decimated in a matter of seconds. Almost 200 Federal troops lay on the field dead or wounded. The left side of Hill's division then engaged in a furious battle in an open field, crashing into Burnside's advancing line. The 34th NC with Pender's brigade was to the right of the heaviest of the fighting, guarding the flank. Barely an hour into the fight, Burnside's stunned troops fell back. The massive assault that had looked unstoppable broke apart, his troops retreating in disorder. The epic march and timely arrival of the Light Division saved the army and cemented their legendary status.

The 34th NC's casualties were light. Lincoln County native, First Sergeant John Stamey was killed. He was 21 years old, the son of John and Nelly Stamey. Four men were wounded. Ashe County native Pinkney Parish received his second injury of the war. He still limped slightly from the shrapnel that hit his knee at Mechanicsville. Manual Mooney, a 20-year-old from Lincoln County, died the next day of his wound. Cleveland County native, E. H. Revel survived his wound. Thirty-year-old James Basinger was one of only four commissioned officers in the regiment that made it to the field. He was wounded and was sent home where his wife Elizabeth cared for him. It was November 21st before the Rowan County merchant died, of complications from his wounds.[81] Private James Barrett of Company F was the only man captured by Union troops. He was exchanged ten days later. Dependable Brigadier General Lawrence Branch was killed in the battle. He had been a steady leader in the division.

Had the Light Division not arrived when they did, Burnside would surely have wrecked the Confederate right flank. Lee had no one from his mangled army to send to the rescue. Here, Harper's Ferry becomes critical. If the Federal garrison there had held out for only one more day, the Light Division would not have made it to Sharpsburg in time. With vastly superior numbers, McClellan and Burnside would have destroyed Lee's army in detail. An uneasy truce hung over the battlefield the next morning as burial details began their dreadful job. There was much work for them. It was the bloodiest single-day battle in American history with staggering combined losses of 23,000 men killed, wounded, or missing. In the afternoon, scattered rain showers pelted the area. That night, Lee began withdrawing his maimed but intact army. Hill's men were the last to the field and would be the last to leave, pulling into line at one in the morning to serve as the army's rear guard. They crossed the Potomac sometime around mid-morning the

---

[81] There is some confusion on Basinger's date of death. Elizabeth signed an affidavit in March of 1863 claiming his wages due. The affidavit states he died November 21, 1863, an obvious error. The final account by the Confederate Treasury Dept. in 1864 stated he was due wages up to November 21, 1862, the date of his death.

next day, relieved to be back on Virginia soil. They stopped for the night about miles south of Shepherdstown and slept under the stars.

Shepherdstown

Early next morning, word came that the Federals were giving chase. The Light Division was ordered back to block them. The men left before daylight back to Boteler's Ford. Shortly before nine in the morning, Hill's men deployed into two battle lines. Col. Lowrance's 34th NC stood in the front line with the rest of Pender's brigade. It became eerily quit as they stood in formation. The farm boys couldn't help but notice the beautiful farm country around them. They stood in a cornfield with a field of recently harvested wheat in front of that with wheat stacks scattered around. One thousand yards beyond was the Potomac. The only thing to remind them it was a battlefield was the row of Federal artillery on the banks on the other side of the river and the waiting Federal infantry. It was moments like this that Pvt. Charles S. Martin remembered as the most disconcerting parts of the battle, when the battle lines were drawn up and facing one another. Martin recalled one instance, (maybe this or another occasion), when, "an almost spent cannon ball came rolling along, apparently no faster than a man could walk. One of [Martin's] buddies set his foot down in front of the ball to stop it. The momentum of the ball broke the man's leg like snapping a match stick."[82]

The men started across the fields as Confederate artillery fired. The front line started forcing the Federal infantry backward. The Federals counter-attacked in Pender's area, but the rebel muskets scattered them. The Federal troops were Pennsylvanians who had never been in action and soon buckled before the steely Confederate veterans. Light Division troops chased them back to the river and fired on them as they dashed across. It was a complete rout that was over in less than two hours. The 34th NC lost only seven men wounded in the action. With 700 casualties on both sides, it was the bloodiest battle fought in what would later become the State of West Virginia.

---

[82] This story was found in an essay titled "Grandfather, CSA" by Cliford R. Martin, courtesy of Patti Martin.

Brigadier General Alfred Moore Scales was the 34th NC's brigade commander from the Gettysburg campaign through the end of the war. He represented North Carolina in the House of Representatives from 1875-1884 and was North Carolina's Governor from 1885-1889.

Chapter 7.
Mutiny at Fredericksburg, Aurora Borealis, and a Pig War Veteran

Rest finally came to the weary troops when they marched to Bunker Hill, Virginia.[83] Colonel Lowrance and his men busied themselves setting up camp. They hadn't changed clothes in the six weeks since leaving Orange Courthouse. They had lived outdoors with no proper camp equipment and nothing resembling a proper bath. Hair and beards were home to lice, tics, and fleas. Many were sick or recovering from wounds. The grinding marches, sickness, and fighting all took a terrible toll. It had been a year since the regiment was formed with nearly 1,000 eager young men unsullied by war. One year of field service had aged them beyond their years, inflicting the physical and emotional effects of war. In that first year, 245 had died from disease and wounds. Many had left the ranks with wounds that would never heal. Remarkably, only sixteen had deserted at that point. Life was hard, but the victories had buoyed their spirits. As Autumn air moved in, they gathered firewood and settled into what became a very tolerable camp. Men wrote letters and enjoyed the monotony of camp.

One Mother's Broken Heart

Alpheus Leroy Dancy joined Company D, the Oakland Guards, on May 15, 1862, three weeks after his eighteenth birthday. He was the greenest man in his company when the fighting started in late June, but he held up well, making it through the summer without any serious injuries. In camp, he became sick. He complained of a sore throat for several days and then developed a fever. Dr. Miller sent him to Chimborazo Hospital on August 11th. From there, he was transferred to Danville. When his mother, Mary, learned he was in Danville, she made the trip from the Miranda area of Rowan County to see her boy. Mary had been a widow for seventeen years. Her husband left her enough land to farm, and she raised her two sons and one daughter the best she could. She survived on determination and hard work.

In May of 1861, her older son Napthali, (she called him Nafter), joined the 6th North Carolina. He was wounded at Manassas

---

[83] Now West Virginia.

and sent to a private home near Louisa Courthouse. When Mary learned of his whereabouts, she went there and took care of him until he died on September 6, 1861. One a year later, Alpheus was extremely ill. He had developed Rheumatic Fever. Along with the fever came an itchy rash, some chest pain, and aching joints. His arms and legs twitched. For over a month, Mary sat by his bedside wiping his forehead and praying for him to recover, helpless as the fever ravaged her son. Mary was with Alpheus when he died September 24, 1862. Heartbroken, she took her son home to Rowan County and buried him at the Thyatira Presbyterian Church. Her two boys gone, she returned to her only child left, Margaret. Sadly, Margaret became ill and died two years later. Mary buried her in the same cemetery as Alpheus. When Mary died in 1880 at the age of 77, she too was buried there.

Conscription Controversy

The regiment organized on October 25, 1861, the men volunteering for one year's service. In April, the Conscription Act had extended their service to three years or the duration of the war for those 18-35 years old. Those outside that age range expected a discharge soon unless they chose to reenlist. The problem with the Conscription Act from the beginning was the way it was administered. Exemptions were allowed for men in certain occupations such as teachers, mail carriers, or druggists. Those who had the means could hire substitutes. Starting in October, exemptions were allowed for those from families who held twenty slaves or more. Very few men from the 34th NC qualified for this, and the exemption angered many. No exemptions existed for the farm boys who were needed back home. The rank and file detested these provisions since all the advantages favored the wealthy. Many complained that it was a rich man's war but a poor man's fight.

As the men rested at Bunker Hill, the Confederate Congress changed the law, raising the upper age limit from 35 to 45. This created an immediate problem in the 34th NC for those men age 35 to 45. Since April, these men had expected to be discharged after one year's service. Only one month before their discharge, they were told that the law had changed, and they had to remain in uniform. They immediately protested, starting a dispute that lasted for weeks. It became an administrative nightmare for the regiment's colonel. Lowrance sympathized with the men but was duty-bound to obey the law. There were 56 men in the regiment between 35 and 45 years old. Most were married with young children at home. Some were willing to stay, but most wanted to go home. They felt that it was unfair to ask them to remain in the army three more years when the law changed only one month before they were eligible for discharge. They had served a year and endured the hardships. Many had been wounded, some more than once. They had done their share, and their families back home had sacrificed in their absence.

Fifteen young men from the regiment who were under 18 at the time of their enlistment asked for and were granted discharges. The youngest was Martin Beam from Rutherford County who was just 14 when he joined the Sandy Run Yellow Jackets with David and William Beam, his older cousins. Those over age 45 were clearly exempted from the law and were discharged, but there were few of those left by this time. Most of these older men had already been discharged due to wounds or poor health. The regiment's officers did not know what to do with those 35-45. Colonel Lowrance was sympathetic but had trouble justifying their discharges. While he debated the issue, the men waited in camp. The 34th NC's dilemma was unique in the brigade. The 16th and 22nd North Carolina, sister regiments in the brigade, had formed in June and July of 1861. Because their year was up in July, their men over 35 had already been discharged. Because the 34th hadn't formed until October, their term expired one month after the September change in the law increasing the age limit. Elsewhere in the army, other regiments like the 34th that formed late in 1861, faced the same problem, and small-scale revolts were occurring.

In September, Zebulon Baird Vance was elected Governor of North Carolina. Vance strongly supported states' individual rights. Under Vance, North Carolina was the only state to observe the right of habeas corpus and kept the courts functioning. He also made sure North Carolinians received their fair share of supplies smuggled past the Union blockade before sending them to Confederate service. Vance was a former Colonel in the 26th North Carolina and saw action at New Bern and Richmond. As a soldier and western North Carolina native, he was popular with the men in the 34th NC. Vance understood the military necessity of conscription and urged the citizens to obey the law, but he opposed the Conscription Act's most oppressive provisions and became a thorn in the side to President Jefferson Davis. Conscription began to change the attitudes of many citizens back home. Many felt that they rebelled against one oppressive government only to replace it with another.

As the debate continued, the work went on. In late October, the division moved about twenty-five miles south to Berryville and went to work tearing up the B&O Railroad track to keep the Federals from using it. They destroyed twenty-five miles of track working their way north stopping four miles south of Harper's Ferry, which was then reoccupied by Federal troops. On November 7th, they saw the winter's first snowfall, a few inches of pristine snow covering the Virginia countryside. Many had no shoes and used strips of cloth or beef hides tied around their feet. On the November 9th, they occupied Snicker's Gap capturing some Federal prisoners and a store of supplies. Here, they learned that McClellan had finally been replaced. The new Union Army commander was Ambrose Burnside who was threatening Fredericksburg.

Bloody Footprints

In the early morning hours of November 22nd, the men began a forced march toward Fredericksburg. The temperature was in the 30's and the men lacked proper overcoats, gloves, shoes, anything to protect them from the cold. Jackson marched his men through Winchester, then south toward Madison and a slow difficult passage across the Blue Ridge Mountains at Fisher's Gap. For twelve straight days, they marched through miserable weather from 4:30 in the morning till 6:30 in the evening. It was cold every night with frost on the ground most mornings. The ground was often frozen solid, and the men left a trail of bloody footprints in the snow and ice.

On December 3rd, they arrived five miles south of Fredericksburg. The twelve-day cold-weather forced march covered roughly 175 miles, an average of 14 miles a day.[84] The march was memorable only for misery and pain. Vincent Avery, 36 from Lincoln County, was one of the men whose discharge was on hold because of the change in the conscription law. The day after arriving at

---

[84] (James I Robetson 1992) Page 158.

Fredericksburg, Vincent died in camp. He had been wounded in the Seven Days battles and returned to duty. He could survive the fighting and deprivation, but not the cruel winter march to Fredericksburg. He was 36 years old.

Discharged Illegally – A Mutiny

The next two days brought another 4" of fresh snow. They had few tents and barely one blanket for every three men. Burnside's army was threatening to cross the Rappahannock any day. Here in their dismal camp with a battle looming, the debate over discharges returned. For over a month, the men over 35 had been demanding discharges. They endured the forced march and were facing another battle. It was December, well beyond the end of their one-year term. It was neither the time nor the place for such an argument, but a decision was overdue, and the men asked for a resolution.[85] Twenty-three of the regiment's men over 35 had decided to stay by that time. Thirty-three demanded discharges.

Colonel Lowrence conferred with General Pender He then met with his company commanders, and the decision was made. On the 8th of December, 33 men from the regiment were given discharge papers and were sent to Richmond. Each discharge was signed by the soldiers' company commanders with Colonel Lowrance's full consent. He even signed at least one himself.[86] They were sent to the Paymaster in Richmond, Major John Ambler, to collect their pay and travel allowance for the trip home. Major Ambler was an attorney and worked in Richmond as Paymaster for the Army of Northern Virginia. He would have the final say on the legality of the discharges. When the men came in with their discharge papers on December 10th, he at once recognized that the discharges were improper. He paid them their wages due, but being under age 45, he marked their pay sheets "Discharged by mistake, returned to duty" and ordered them back to their companies. He did make some exceptions, for hardship or other reasons. Most, however, he ordered back to duty.

What occurred next could only be described as a small mutiny. Only five men obeyed Maj. Ambler's order and returned to duty for

---

[85] Surprisingly, only one man, Henry Perry, had deserted while awaiting the decision. He deserted on November 8th.
[86] See the papers of Levi Pethel.

fear of being arrested as deserters.[87] The rest took their cash and went home. They were through with the war. Twenty-eight men from the 34th NC went home with illegal discharges.[88]

At least one company commander falsified a soldier's age on the discharge to allow him to go home. When Pinkney Parrish enlisted in the Laurel Springs Guards in August of 1861, his original muster card clearly listed him as 40 years old, as does his Roll of Honor card. The census records for Ashe and Allegheny Counties agree with that age, but when Captain Nelson Woodie wrote Pinkney's discharge, he described Pinkney as 5'11" tall, dark complexion, black hair, black eyes, and all of 46 years old. Surely, Pinkney deserved to go home. He had served faithfully for the year he had promised. He took a piece of shrapnel to the knee at Mechanicsville, and a gunshot wound at Sharpsburg. Back home, his wife and five children needed him on the farm. Captain Woodie's kind act was one of the last official duties he would perform for the regiment.

Fredericksburg

Back in Fredericksburg, the Federal army was in motion. Burnside's artillery pounded Fredericksburg on December 11th trying to dislodge the Mississippians defending the town while their engineers worked under fire to build pontoon bridges. The next morning at dawn, the Light Division was ordered to a position along the railroad on Longstreet's right, south of town. As they moved into position, Burnside's troops made it across the Rappahannock and took control of Fredericksburg, fighting street to street and looting the town. The Light Division prepared to defend their position. That night, the shelter-deprived men got little sleep enduring an icy wind for several hours.

The wind died down at dawn and they woke to a heavy fog and a cold gray sky. Around 10:00 the fog lifted revealing 4,500 Pennsylvanians arrayed in three perfect lines of battle. Pender's men,

---

[87] Hugh Elliott, Scott Hutchison, Hiram Stamper, William Wesson, and Virgil Elliott returned to duty.

[88] Nine of them had been approved by Major Ambler, but his approval meant nothing. He had no authority as Paymaster to approve discharges that were contrary to the Conscription Act. These discharges were still technically illegal. Four of the 28 later reenlisted, probably under pressure from Conscription Agents.

including the 34th NC under Colonel Lowrance, stood ready on the left of Hill's line. Hill's division was Lee's right flank, south of Marye's Heights where the day's most brutal fighting would occur. They were positioned behind the railroad track. About a mile beyond the track was the Rappahannock River. Skirmishers had been deployed forward including parts of the 34th North Carolina.

The Pennsylvanians moved forward like they were on parade drill with the sun shining on their fixed bayonets. When the Yankees were 400 yards out, Confederate artillery started firing and the rebel infantry delivered long-range musket fire. Federal artillery answered. The Federal troops strove for over an hour and fell back. For the next hour, Federal artillery shelled the Confederate line. Around noon, the Federal troops came again advancing from 850 yards out. The southerners held their fire until the Federals had advanced about 200 yards and then opened fire with a heavy artillery barrage. The line withered, then surged again. The men in the 34th NC with the rest of Pender's brigade fired at the Federal troops who seemed to be concentrating at the center of Hill's line where a gap existed between the brigades of Lane and Archer south of Pender's position.

Reminiscent of Second Manassas, the Yankees found the gap and attacked. This time it was Maxcy Gregg's brigade stationed a quarter-mile back that had to rush to seal the breach. When General Gregg rode forward, the hard-of-hearing general mistook the Federal troops for retreating Confederates and ordered his troops to hold their fire. Realizing the mistake, he ordered his men forward. A Federal bullet found its mark in the general's spine and toppled him from his horse. Maxcy Gregg died two days later.

Pender's brigade, though north of the heavier fighting in the gap, was taking casualties. One was Pender himself who seemed to have developed a bad habit of being wounded. This time, his left arm was limp and covered in blood from a gun-shot wound, but he remained on the field. The Light Division sealed the breach and pushed the Federal troops back. By three in the afternoon, the fighting in their area settled down. Farther north, the sounds of one of the war's most furious and bloody battles raged, as Burnside sent wave after wave of blue-coated troops to their death on Marye's Heights. The slaughter there continued till dark. General Jackson sent an order for the Light

Division brigades to prepare to counter-attack after dark, but the attack was cancelled when a large Federal artillery bombardment rained down on the area. Under cover of darkness, the Light Division was relieved and marched to the rear.

They stayed on alert the following day, hearing scattered firing during the morning. That afternoon a cease fire was arranged so that Burnside's wounded could be taken from the field. That night, the men around the decimated battlefield gazed into the sky and saw the beautiful Aurora Borealis, or Northern Lights, a sight that brought some hope for the wounded, dying, and weary soldiers who had fought there. It was a sight many would always link to the battle. Over 12,600 Federal soldiers were killed, wounded, or captured in Burnside's foolhardy assault at Fredericksburg. Even Robert E. Lee felt badly for the Federal troops saying, "It is well that war is so terrible, or we should grow too fond of it."

Two men from the 34th NC were killed that cold December day. Lemuel Pendleton was 25 years old from Lincoln County. He had worked extra duty as a pioneer. Wilborn Hudson was 27 from Montgomery County. At least twelve were wounded including 19-year-old John J. London of Cleveland County who died thirteen days later.

Of great loss to the regiment was Captain Nelson C. Woodie of Company A from Ashe County. Ten days after over-stating Pinkney Parrish's age to allow him to go home, Nelson suffered a horrendous gunshot wound that led to the removal of the lower half of his jaw. He resigned his commission and returned home to Ashe County. His wound never healed, and he was unable to talk or eat solid food. He suffered nearly six months before he died on June 9, 1863. Nelson was the son of James and Margaret Woodie. His father died when he was young. Nelson was cared for by his mother and siblings. He was 32 years old. His mother died the following month.

Casualties from the Battle of Fredericksburg

Killed in Action

Wilborn Hudson	K	Pvt.	Lemuel Pendleton	E	Pvt.

Mortally Wounded

John Jefferson London	F	Pvt.	Nelson C Woodie	A	Cpt.

Wounded

Isham F Blake	K	Pvt.	Thomas J Stroud	B	Pvt.
James L Freeland	D	Pvt.	James F Henderson	C	Sgt.
Larkin S Kendrick	F	Pvt.	Jacob R Kurf	D	Cpl.
Richard T Stephens	G	Pvt.	George W Robinson	E	Pvt.
John H Davis	B	Pvt.	Elbert J Wiles	A	Pvt.

Larkin Kendrick received an excruciating gunshot wound to the left elbow that shattered the joint, a wound that never fully healed. His military career was over. In unusual detail, he wrote to his wife from the hospital in Richmond, "I was detailed in the morning to go on picket, E Hamrick John Hardin and myself. We remained together until evening when we were separated and I have not seen nor heard from them since. I remained on my post until I was wounded when I went into a ditch by the side of the rail road to shelter myself from the fire of enemie. I remained there until dark when I was assisted by a North Carolinian and taken to a camp and then the next morning he helped me to a hospital. This man was a stranger to me." He also wrote, "I am still confined to my bed. My arm is swolen a good deal and is very sore yet but is mending. It is not as sore as it has been and don't hurt me as bad as it did from first."[89]

James Henderson and Richard Stephenson were both wounded by artillery fire. James Freeland was shot in the chest, which disabled him until the following spring. Fredericksburg was a rare instance in which only part of the regiment was engaged. According to Burwell Cotton, "All our regiment were not engaged only those who went out on skirmish."[90]

Much of Fredericksburg was in ruins. Homes were burned and destroyed. Streets were littered with debris. Shallow graves were all over the area. Any building standing became temporary shelter for families whose homes were lost. Roads were impassable with deeps ruts left by wagons and thousands of marching soldiers. The Light

---

[89] State Library of North Carolina Digital Collections (digital.ncdcr.gov)
[90] This was found in a letter from Burwell T Cotton dated December 18, 1862. (Taylor 1994), supported by the letter of Larkin Kendrick referenced above.

Division found a suitable place for winter quarters eight miles south of town along the Rappahannock. They named it Camp Gregg in honor or General Maxcy Gregg who was lost at Fredericksburg. The 34th NC set to work building winter quarters. They built small shelters of pine logs and canvas roofs. Their crude shelters were of every shape and size, some more elaborate than others. They had small stoves and plenty of firewood. Crude as it was, they were glad to have it.

The men had changed much in their first year of the war. Gone were the inexperienced farm boys. They were now grim veterans with leather-like skin, shaggy beards, and battle scars. By the year's end, 287 men from the regiment were dead, 120 of battle-related injuries, the rest of disease. Barely over half of the original volunteers were still on the rolls. In the first half of 1862, forty-four new volunteers had joined the regiment. Volunteering dropped sharply after the fighting started. Only eight joined the second half of the year. On the first day of December, James Tiddy, a 21-year-old marble mason born in England, joined Company E. Tiddy was very bright, a former cadet at the North Carolina Military Institute in Charlotte under Major General Danial Harvey Hill. He enlisted as a private, but his training ensured he would later become an officer.

The Legendary George T. Gordon, Pig War Veteran

Yet another Englishman joined just before Christmas when Major George T. Gordon was assigned to the 34th NC. Like Leventhorpe before him, Gordon was said to have served in the British army. He was described as, "a big, soldierly-looking man with red whiskers, and with such beautiful manners that he was received as a constant visitor in many of the most refined southern homes."[91] He was married but was known as a lady's man. He also had a reputation as a fighter, gambler, and a heavy drinker in the saloons in Richmond. Gordon's swash-bucking reputation contrasted with Lowrance's reserved manner, but the two seemed to work well together.

Three years earlier, Gordon was involved in the so-called Pig War, an international incident between the United States and Great Britain that occurred at San Juan Island off the coast of the Washington Territory. The exact boundaries between the U.S. and Great Britain had

---

[91] (Lonn 1940) Page 175.

been in dispute for years. A few American settlers were there. An American farmer found a large black pig rooting around in his garden and eating his potatoes one day. He shot and killed the pig which belonged to a Canadian from a nearby farm. He offered compensation for the pig, but British authorities threatened to arrest the man. The incident escalated, and British troops made threats to invade the island, and U.S. troops commanded by George Pickett were sent to defend the area. Pickett famously said, "We'll make a Bunker Hill of it!" The incident was tense, but cooler heads prevailed with no shots fired. No one wanted to go to war over a pig. Gordon and Pickett became acquainted from serving in the area. This association may help explain how he got from there to Virginia and a commission in the Confederate army. Gordon's commission came at the recommendation of Generals Lee and Hill. Gordon had earlier served on Hill's staff. Hill noted that he was "possessed of ability, industry, and activity."

"A Brigade & Division that is second to none"

The hardships of army life had taken a lot out of everyone. Some officers sought more comfortable assignments if they could get them. Even the regiment's surgeon, John Miller, sought a new post. He wrote to Governor Vance asking for a commission in North Carolina. He noted that he had, "served in a Brigade & Division that is second to none…but the service is exceedingly hard & if the state service be any easier, I would much prefer it on account of my health & reasons of a domestic character."[92] Miller's "domestic" reason was a woman he planned to marry. Dr. Miller may have met young Sarah Borden when the regiment was in Goldsboro. Their nuptials had to wait. Dr. Miller did not get the commission he wanted and stayed with the regiment.

The year 1862, had been a year of victories. They defeated three powerful Union advances, all the while severely outnumbered and lacking every material necessity. Their string of victories was broken only by their venture into Maryland. But those wins came at a frightful cost. Many of their best soldiers were lost. At home, times were only getting harder, and there was no sign the north was giving up. The

---

[92] (Longacre 2001) Page 157. Longacre quotes a letter from Miller to Gov. Vance dated Dec. 20, 1862, found in the Vance Letterbooks and Papers NCSDA&H.

mettle of Lee's army was beyond question, but the following year would test their will.

Lieutenant Bartlett Yancey Martin, The Laurel Springs Guards-Company A[93]

---

[93] Photo Kimberly D'Anna-Farnam

Chapter 8.
Camp Gregg and Marching with Stonewall Jackson at Chancellorsville

As 1863, arrived, the Camp Gregg men witnessed a sobering event. They gathered in an open field and watched as a member of the 1st Virginia Infantry was shot for desertion. The army had seen desertion rates rise steadily through the summer months. The ultimate punishment was meted out to curb the problem. Court Martial sentences up to this point had often been light. Men would be listed Absent Without Leave for a few weeks and then return. They faced loss of rank, forfeiture of pay, and reimbursement for any equipment they took with them. They were sometimes kept in the guard house on bread and water for a time. To rein in the growing problem, sentences grew more severe. In January two 34th NC men from Rutherford County received 30 lashes for desertion. John and Thomas Kennedy deserted August 5, 1862, just before the regiment left Gordonsville heading to Cedar Mountain. Their sentence was carried out in front of the whole brigade.[94] It was a brutal punishment, the worst short of death. By the end of 1862, twenty men from the 34th had deserted. Eight were from Ashe County and five from Montgomery County. It was the counties with the fewest slaves that had the highest desertion and AWOL rates. The 34th NC's mix of soldiers reflected the complexities of the war in western North Carolina. Ashe County had few slaves and bordered eastern Tennessee where there was strong Unionist sentiment. Bitterness between Unionist and Confederate families sometimes turned violent. Problems also existed in Montgomery County where influential religious groups opposed both slavery and secession. Bands of Unionists and deserters formed, and violence was rising.

On January 6th, General Hill reviewed the division. He was enormously proud of the division's accomplishments, and they were proud to serve under him. The next day, the division collected money for the people of Fredericksburg. The entire division chipped in from their meager pay and raised an impressive $10,000. It was a life-saver

---

[94] The Kennedys went on to serve the rest of the war without another unauthorized absence.

for families who had lost their homes and were living in barns or crude shacks. The citizens had supported them, now they gave back.

Serving under Stonewall Jackson ensured that religious services were always available. In January, the regiment was assigned a new chaplain, Augustus Bennick.[95] Throughout the army, religious revivals were held during the winter. These men had grown up during the religious revivals of the mid-nineteenth century. Religion was a big part of their lives, and their faith was frequently seen in their letters.

The winter weather varied with periods of snow and bitter cold. There were some breaks in the weather. On January 15th, the temperature hit near 60 degrees. Two days later it was back in the teens. When the ground wasn't frozen, it was nothing but mud. When it wasn't snowing, it was raining. Men with no shoes tied green beef hides around their feet and insulated them with leaves or strips of cloth. Frost-bite was problem. Rations diminished in quantity and quality as the winter wore on. The men were somewhat cheered late in January when word came that General Ambrose Burnside had been replaced. For his failure at Fredericksburg and the recent embarrassing Mud March, Burnside became the third Union commander whose career was dashed by the Army of Northern Virginia. Joe Hooker replaced him.

Starting in January, the regiment saw new recruits coming into the ranks by means of conscription. Until then, volunteers were relied on to keep the ranks full, but with volunteering down, Richmond was forced to use conscription. The conscripts were not well regarded by the veterans. They were mostly older men, married with children. They were more worried about their families than the war effort.

The troops filled their time with chores, playing cards, snowballing, playing music, and writing letters home. Across the Rappahannock, Yankees did the same. Often, soldiers from the two armies bantered and bartered for coffee and tobacco. Pvt. Charles S. Martin remembered those times. It might be a Reb or a Yank who would initiate the meeting by calling out "Hey, Yank, or Hey, Reb, wanna do some trading?" The other side would say, "no, too risky" or "yeah, come on over. You have my word. Everything is safe." The Rebs would usually have tobacco. The Yanks would have coffee,

---

[95] James S. Erwin resigned on Oct. 1, 1862. See NC Troops, Vol. 9, page 253.

newspapers, or other items. Sometimes the Yanks would trade buckshot that the Rebs could use to shoot game for food. Sometimes an officer would come upon one of the trading sessions and order his man to arrest the soldier from the opposing side. The order was always protested since they had "given their word." If the officer was smart, he would turn and walk away.[96] Some soldiers made small boats to float across the river to ferry their trades back and forth. Sometimes the pickets felt saucy and taunted one other, but it was just soldier's banter. There existed a measure of respect among the fighting men of both sides. Though enemies, they were also comrades of sorts. They had all seen too much death and destruction. They understood each other in ways that folks back home could not.

Desertion continued to be a problem. Lt. Burwell Cotton wrote on February 25th, 1863, "I saw one man shot to death this week for desertion. Several have been branded in our reg. for desertion."[97] Cotton also described a large battle that occurred the day before the letter. This one was not with guns, but snowballs. The 34th North Carolina, with Pender's and Maxcy Gregg's brigades, engaged in a full-scale organized battle. The men formed lines of battle, and officers ordered flanking movements as the two sides fought it out. It was the largest snowball fight they had seen. Much laughter was heard, a rarity in those days. The battle was remembered for years to come.

"Tell me all about the outliers in Montgomery County..."

The same February 25th letter from Cotton also revealed something the Montgomery County men were concerned about, "I want you to write as soon as you get this and give me all the news. Tell me all about the outliers in Montgomery County & how they succeed in catching them. I have heard very exciting reports but do not know whether they are so or not." Cotton does not name the outliers, but he was certainly referring to Bill Owens and his band that was just then gaining notoriety.[98] The band originated in Randolph County which shared its southern border with Montgomery County. The band was

---

[96] (Martin n.d.)

[97] No record was found of men from the 34th being branded. Perhaps he meant the brigade.

[98] Bill Owen's exploits are detailed in Victoria E. Bynum's book, The Long Shadow of the Civil War and articles found in digitalnc.org.

made up of deserters and loyal Unionists. Owens organized them to emulate a military unit, calling himself Colonel Owens. His men took oaths of allegiance to the United States and observed standard military practices such as paroling captured militia officers. The band captured a militia captain named Peter Shamburger and "forced him to march through rain with them as they robbed, pillaged, and abused families of the area."[99] In early 1863, the band overtook the workshop of Pleasant Simmons, a 63-year-old slaveholder and silversmith in Montgomery County. They used his workshop to repair guns they had stolen. Simmons and his family supported the Confederacy. The militia officer captured by the band was Simmons's son-in-law. His nephew, Alexander Leach, was Captain of the Montgomery County Home Guards. In addition to bands like Owens,' the religious protest of the Quakers and Wesleyan Methodists in the area grew stronger as did resentment between impoverished non-slaveholding families and well-to-do slaveholding families. The strife sometimes turned violent.

Passing Muster

At the end of February, the regiment took a muster. In accordance with CS Regulations, regiments were to be mustered every two months, at the end of February, April, June, August, October, and December. After the rolls were complete, the men were paid and read the Articles of War. For all of 1862, only the first two musters of the year are recorded. With the activity of the summer campaigns, the musters might not have been done or were lost or destroyed. The first muster of 1863 shows the effects of the previous year's campaigns. The regiment listed 538 on the rolls including 45 new volunteers since the last muster in April of 1862. There were 372 men present in camp. They reported 202 deaths since last muster. Unauthorized absences were rising. Fifty-eight men were listed as AWOL, 31 from Ashe County's Company A, which had only 23 men present, the fewest in the regiment. The regiment had dropped seventeen from the rolls as deserters, six from Ashe County, the rest divided among the other companies. By far, Ashe County had the highest AWOL and desertion rates. The regiment's officers took steps to bring in their stray soldiers.

---

[99] (Bynum 2010) Page 29

Colonel Lowrance ran an ad in the Western Democrat on April 14, 1863, offering a reward for two of his absent men:

$60 REWARD

> The above reward ($30 for each of them) will be paid for the apprehension of John D Ewing and Thos. King, members of my company, when delivered at Camp, near Guinea Station, Va., or wherever the company may be stationed. The said Ewing and King left the camp near Guinea Station on the 28th of March last without leave. Ewing is about 26 or 27 years of age, about 5 feet 7 inches high, sandy hair, grey eyes and fair complexion—and is supposed to be lurking in the vicinity of Charlotte, N.C. King is about 18 years of age, 5 feet 7 inches high, dark hair, blue eyes, fair complexion—and is supposed to be lurking in the neighborhood of Steel Creek or the vicinity of Charlotte, N.C. By order of Col. W.L.J. Lowrance, G. M. Norment, Capt. Co. G, 34th N.C. Regt.[100]

To help improve discipline in Company A, Hiram Abernathy was appointed Captain in March of 1863. Abernathy was originally a lieutenant in Company E from Lincoln County. His style as a strict disciplinarian made him unpopular, and he failed to be reelected at the reorganization in April of 1862. Colonel Lowrance was a friend of the Abernathy family before the war. Abernathy replaced Nelson Woodie.

Lowrance issued promotions in to fill vacancies. Tilman Davis of Company D was promoted to 2nd Lieutenant for his skill and valor during the Seven Days battles. For gallantry at Fredericksburg, James Tiddy was promoted from Private to 2nd Lieutenant and became the regiment's drill master. William McKinley Mittag was promoted to 2nd Lt. in Company H for his general skill and valor. As the war progressed, promotions were earned by bravery in battle rather than election. In Lowrance's former company, H, Sam Hoey had resigned his commission in February after the promotion board having failed to

---

[100] The Western Democrat April 14, 1863 (digitalnc.org). Ewing returned to his company in July or August and served the rest of the war without another unauthorized absence. King did not return for another year and a half.

promote him. Lowrance promoted John Roberts to Captain,[101] Joe Camp to 1st Lt., and George Blanton to 2nd Lt.

In April, Col. Lowrance enlisted Theophilus Twitty from Rutherford County to serve as the Hospital Steward for Dr. John Miller, the regiment's surgeon and Dr. Richard Barr, the assistant surgeon. Hospital Stewards had to be intelligent and literate since they were responsible for many of the medical records. They also had to be honest, dependable, and temperate. Temperance was important since stewards dispensed medicinal whiskey. The Stewards' duties included assisting the surgeon in operations, supervising nurses, and even prescribing some medicine and performing minor procedures in times of emergency. The over-worked doctors were glad to have a dependable man to help them.

"I wish to know if my son is dead or alive"

Joseph Haltom was listed on the Jan/Feb 1863, muster as "at home sick." He was not. His mother had not heard from him in five months and neither had the regiment. They mistakenly believed he was home. Desperate, Sarah Haltom ran an ad in the Fayetteville Observer on March 26, 1863, saying, "I wish you to ask any and all persons in Virginia and North Carolina if they know anything of him. If any person knows I would be very grateful if they would write to me at Troy, Montgomery County, N. C. I wish to know if my son is dead or alive, as I have not heard from him in so long."[102] Joseph had not been with the regiment since September 6th. On the next muster, he was listed "absent in the hospital." Then finally in August, he was dropped from the rolls, "supposed to be dead." His Roll of Honor card states that he died in October of 1862, of disease.

The weeks passed, and spring was approaching. Disease was still a problem but seems to have been better controlled. Measles and mumps made their usual runs. Pneumonia and the Virginia quick-step were always a problem. The Light Division saw an outbreak of Small Pox in March, but medical staffs reacted quickly. At the first signs a soldier was infected, he was sent to a quarantine hospital. Brigadier

---

[101] Roberts was a Justice of the Peace and Mail carrier for Cleveland County, positions that could exempt him from Conscription. He earlier resigned but changed his mind. He served to the end of the war.

[102] The Fayetteville Observer March 26, 1863 (digitalnc.org)

Generals, Field and Gregg, who had been killed the past year, were replaced. Henry Heth took Field's place. Maxcy Gregg was replaced by Samuel McGowan. General Hill was as fiery as ever, threatening to "burn down Washington." As the weather faired and the trees budded, the gladness for the coming of spring was tempered with the realization that fighting would soon start. Union General Joe Hooker had a reputation as a fighter, as the 34th NC had seen firsthand at Second Manassas. Hooker had skillfully led his men into the gap on the railroad cut and nearly broke the Confederate line.

The war at home in 1863

At home, conscript agents were roaming the countryside picking up men to send off to war. They hit Cleveland County at the end of February, netting twenty-four men for the 34th NC. They then ran through Montgomery County, crossing the line into neighboring Gaston County, picking up thirty-seven men the first week of March. They grabbed at least eight more in Lincoln County. Nearly all were in their mid-to-late thirties, some over forty. Conscription was in full force draining the home-front of laborers needed to raise crops and keep farms going. Among Company K's new conscripts were brothers John A. Beaman and Andrew Jackson Beaman, ages 37 and 39. The Beaman men were part of a group of Wesleyan Unionist families who staunchly opposed slavery, the war, and conscription.[103] Another conscript from this family was Armistead Hurley.[104] He was married to Mary Ann Beaman. Armistead was 37 years old. His 22-year-old brother Nathan had volunteered in September of 1861 and was killed at Gaines's Mill.

To make matters worse, the Confederate Congress imposed the hated Tax-in-Kind in April of 1863. Each congressional district was assigned a quartermaster responsible for collecting material for the war effort. Ten percent of each farm's produce and livestock raised for slaughter was taken. Naturally, the poor families suffered the most. The smallest farms and the most impoverished families were exempted from the tax, however these families often depended on help from

---

[103] The roster states that they were enlisted in May, but family records indicate that was an error.
[104] Armistead's records show he enlisted March 5th, so he likely came in with the Beaman brothers.

neighbors who were subject to it, making it harder for them to provide help. The rich man's war was the poor family's fight to survive as the pernicious grip of war persisted.

Linville Price and the Red Strings

Incidents of violence at home continued. The problems were naturally greater in areas where the citizens were not unified in support of the southern cause. Choosing sides made them a hero to one side and an enemy and traitor to the other. In Ashe County, the family of Jesse Price worked their 2,000-acre spread in the southern part of the county, raising hogs. Before that, they had lived in Eastern Tennessee. Price's sympathies lay with the Union, and he was vocal in his opinion. Early in the war, he became a target of resentment with the southern loyalists in the area. The accounts of Jesse Price and his family vary in a highly partisan manner. Some called him a loyal patriot forced into hiding by Home Guardsmen who robbed him of everything he had and forced him into the mountains. A letter to the Raleigh Register described him as a "notorious tory" in Ashe County. The Fayetteville Observer called them a "band of bushwhackers…who have committed many acts both of murder and robbery."[105]

Jesse, his sons Hiram and Moses, and his nephew Solomon were arrested by men from the 37th North Carolina who were hunting deserters. They found the Price men sneaking into town for food and jailed them in Jefferson. Angry members of the community removed the Prices from the jail and without judge or jury proceeded to hang them all. Jesse was forced to witness his two sons and nephew hanged before the rope was placed around his neck. When the four bodies were taken down, Moses was found to be still alive. He was resuscitated and allowed to live if he joined the Confederate army. He did, but soon deserted and joined a Union regiment and fought for the Union the rest of the war. His nickname became "Scape Gallows" Price.

The story of the Price hangings was well-known to the Laurel Springs Guards in the regiment, at least one of whom was related to the family. Linville Price volunteered in August of 1861, at the age of 21. He deserted just before the regiment left for Manassas with Stonewall Jackson. His whereabouts at the time of the hanging of his cousins is

---

[105] The Fayetteville Observer / April 23, 1863 (digitalnc.org), article titled "Bushwhackers Hung."

unknown. Later, he was discovered to be a member of the secret society known as the Heroes of America, also called The Red Strings. The aim of this group was no less than the defeat of the southern Confederacy. They were highly clandestine. They used secret signs and handshakes and wore red threads on their shirts as identification. Some worked as spies and reported rebel troop positions and movements. They helped Union POW's who escaped from Salisbury and other prisons and worked with the Underground Railroad operating in Piedmont and western North Carolina.

Chancellorsville

In mid-April, rain set in for ten straight days. On the 25th, the sun came out and dried the roads. Across the river, Federal troops went in motion. The sounds of skirmishing were unmistakable signs a fight was coming. Officers issued rations and ammunition, and the 34th NC got their marching orders. On April 29th, the 34th NC marched away with the Light Division on a forced march to Hamilton's Crossing along the military road near the position they held during the Battle of Fredericksburg. It was a twenty-five mile, sixteen-hour march in a cold drizzle over a mud splattering road. Unfortunately, they would go to Chancellorsville without their Colonel. On April 30th, Colonel Lowrance was admitted to the Institute Hospital in Richmond with a severe case of Icterus, (Jaundice). He was transferred to General Hospital No. 4, and on May 8th, he was sent to Salisbury for a 30-day leave. In addition, Lt. Col. John McDowell was listed AWOL. It was up to Major George T. Gordon to lead the regiment to Chancellorsville.

The morning of May 1st was beautiful and spring-like. At four in the morning, the division left Hamilton's Crossing. Men noted clover in bloom bringing war-ravaged fields back to life. They halted four miles from Chancellorsville and waited for orders. Three brigades, Heth, Lane, and McGowan, were sent forward along the Orange Turnpike. The 34th NC and the rest of Pender's brigade waited. Soon they heard sounds of battle as Lee explored Hooker's position. By nightfall, the entire division was inside the area known aptly as The Wilderness. This area was twelve miles long and six miles wide, densely wooded with small pines and gnarly underbrush. They could scarcely see beyond twenty yards in most places. It was dark and foreboding with a few narrow roads and murky little streams hidden in the thickets. Being there gave off a sinister feeling. That evening, Sgt. Huntley and others from the regiment saw Generals Lee and Jackson seated by the road side quietly talking. Huntley couldn't hear the conversation, but the generals were planning a bold move. It was a fateful meeting, the last time these two generals would ever meet.[106] The Light Division spent an uneasy night listening to sounds of unseen animals, crickets, and frogs. They got little sleep.

Jackson's Great Flanking Movement

At 4:30 the next morning, a Saturday, the men rose and prepared to march. The drowsy foot soldiers had no idea they were making one of the war's most dramatic movements. Lee was again dividing his forces against an enormous Federal army. Jackson's entire corps was to march twelve miles to Hooker's right flank. Stuart's cavalry had found the flank, occupied by Oliver O. Howard's corps, in the air and unsupported. Expecting nothing to happen in the dense landscape, they hadn't even thrown up works. The movement left Lee with barely 14,000 men to face the bulk of the Federal army. If Hooker figured out what was happening, he could destroy Lee in detail. The dense forest would help screen the movement, but Jackson's fast-marching troops had to make the march before the Federals put the pieces of the puzzle together. If the gamble failed, all was lost.

The roads through the shadowy forest were barely wide enough for a column of four which impeded their progress. They also had to be careful not to make excessive noise, so the first units didn't get moving until around 7:00 a.m., much later than Jackson would have preferred. The Light Division was last in line and had to wait until almost eleven to fall in. Skirmishers nearby were firing, and an occasional bullet tore through the woods as the men formed up. The ground was perfect; damp enough to keep the dust down but not muddy. The men swung into line with a jaunty gait. Canteens were ordered to be either full or empty, and care was taken to keep equipment from clanging. No talking was allowed in the ranks, and straggling was tightly controlled. If one dawdler fell into enemy hands, the entire plan could be foiled. The only sound was the muffled footsteps of thousands of troops and

---

[106] Huntley mentions seeing the meeting in a letter dated May 10, 1863. (Taylor 1994)

some squeaky wagon wheels as the long column snaked its way through the dismal woodland.

    At Catharine Furnace, the intrepid column turned south. There, units from Hooker's center found and attacked a portion of the Light Division line. The attack was repulsed, and the march resumed. The skirmish could have doomed the operation, but the Federals assumed the Confederates were retreating and made no effort to alert their vulnerable flank. The Division marched several fast-paced miles before stopping for a two-hour afternoon rest then resumed their trek. At Orange Turnpike, they turned east, marched another mile, and stopped at around four in the afternoon. Jackson had marched seventy infantry regiments plus artillery and wagons across the line of three Federal corps. Other than one brief encounter, which the enemy misinterpreted, the movement was flawless. It was a taxing march, averaging over three miles per hour at times, but Jackson had 28,000 Confederate troops in place, and their foe had no idea they were there.

    The final challenge was the brushy terrain. Deploying troops there was difficult and time-consuming. Jackson's two lead divisions began forming two battle lines. Part of the Light Division deployed forward to form a third wave while the rest of the division was still stacked up on the road. Pender's brigade, including the 34th North Carolina, formed north of the turnpike to support Jackson's left. All the dispositions went smoothly enough but took too much time. There would be little daylight left if the advance delayed much longer. At 5:15, with trailing units still miles away, Jackson ordered the attack.

    The Federals had only a thin line of skirmishers to stand guard and were taken by complete surprise. Oliver O. Howard, a West Point classmate of General Dorsey Pender, was entirely unprepared. The sudden wave of screaming butternut-clad southerners struck as Howard's men were sipping coffee and preparing the evening meal. The shocked Yankees fled in nothing short of a complete rout. Jackson ordered his commanders to press the enemy hard. For three miles, panicked Federal troops ran for their lives. The Light Division was still coming up when the assault began. The first two waves of rebels raced ahead. The Federals retreated so swiftly that pursuing Confederate units became separated and confused in the brush-entangled woods. Control of the attack became impossible. After two hours, momentum was lost, and the routed Federals formed a defensive line. The Light Division finally came up in line of battle amid a setting sun, but the hour meant nothing to Jackson. He wanted to regain the initiative and ordered the division to advance into the twilight and cut off the Federal line of retreat across the Rappahannock at United States Ford. The objective was not to drive the Federal army from the ground; it was to trap them there and destroy them. At nine o'clock, the entire division was creeping through the woods, but the darkness slowed their efforts.

Friendly Fire

As the men of the 34th NC and the rest of the division struggled to maneuver in the dark shadows of the forest, only scattered firing was heard. They were close enough to the enemy to hear the axes and voices of the Yankee troops who were fortifying their positions. They peered through the darkness, ready to counter any movement. Suddenly the calm was broken by a volley of musket fire nearby. Shouts of soldiers hidden in the darkness were followed by a few rounds of artillery. Scattered musket fire continued for a few minutes. Another solid volley was fired from the Confederate line followed by frantic yells. Horses shrieked and fell. Such skirmishing was common in these situations and aroused little concern. Some Federal artillery shells fell into the 34th NCs position, wounding some. Sgt. Simon D. Davis of Rutherford County was hit by a shell which shattered his left leg. It was later amputated above the knee. Sgt. Tyrell Camp lost his right arm from his wound, and Cpl. Caleb Sparks was also wounded.

As they watched and listened, a rider came into the lines of the 34th North Carolina. It was Captain Benjamin Leigh of General Hill's staff who was urgently calling for a surgeon. On hand was Dr. Richard R. Barr, the 34th North Carolina's assistant surgeon. Without knowing the situation, Dr. Barr grabbed his field surgeon's kit and left with Captain Leigh. The captain led Dr. Barr through the darkness into the dangerous area between the lines, and when they stopped, Dr. Barr was astonished to find a badly wounded Lieutenant General Thomas J. "Stonewall" Jackson. Jackson and his party had ridden too far forward in the darkness and were fired on by members of the 18th North Carolina in Lane's brigade who mistook the group for Federal cavalry. Jackson was shot twice in the left arm and once in the right hand. As Dr. Barr administered aid, Jackson asked, "Is he a skilled surgeon?"

General Hill assured him that Barr stood high in his brigade. With bullets still flying through the woods, Barr quickly applied a tourniquet to Jackson's mangled arm. Nothing more could be done in these conditions. Litter bearers came and rushed the injured general away. Jackson was taken to his personal physician, and Dr. Barr returned to the regiment. At General Hill's request, the men were not told of Jackson's wounds until the battle was decided.

Edgy troops on both sides fired at any sound. Artillery shells exploded in places. General Hill rode up with a severely wounded leg dangling from his horse's stirrup. He had been hit with shrapnel from a shell after Jackson was taken away. Hill issued orders for Pender's brigade which was to the left of Lane's brigade, who's 18th North Carolina had mistakenly fired on Jackson's group. Thomas's brigade shifted to Pender's left to solidify the line. Soon after, Hill's wound required him to leave the field. General Jeb Stuart, the cavalry commander, took command of Jackson's corps. Hill's division would be led by Brigadier General Henry Heth for the remainder of the battle.

May 3, 1863

Sunday, May 3rd dawned cool and misty. The military situation was far different from the day before. Federal troops were fully prepared behind works of felled trees, rocks, and earth ready to redeem themselves. Though the flank had been pushed in, Lee's army was still perilously divided and outnumbered, and Generals Jackson and Hill were down. They did have one advantage. Union forces left the Confederates a gift by abandoning the high ground at Hazel Grove. Much of the nearby terrain rendered artillery useless. This was the best artillery position for miles around, and the rebels wasted no time mounting several batteries on the crest. Soon the pieces were firing. As the artillerists worked to soften the Federal line, the infantrymen steeled themselves. The Light Division's battle line was a mile and a quarter wide. Only 150 yards separated the opposing lines in Pender's sector.

At General Pender's order, the 34th NC rose and rushed forward with a high yell. Battling through the brush under heavy fire, they made it to the first line of works. They quickly carried the position, and the Federals dropped back to a second line. Heartened by the success, Pender formed his men for another push. He aggressively drove his men deeper into the thickets. The enemy proved more obstinate this time and threw a torrent of artillery and musketry at the North Carolinians. The 34th NC surged through the storm of lead that seemed as thick as the tree limbs hitting them in the face as they advanced. The line became more disjointed in the brush, and the Federals mounted a counter-charge. Terrain started hampering Confederate artillery, but the Federal troops had several pieces massed against the advancing rebels who were forced back to the first line of works. The 34th NC had lost several men, but they held firm.

Intense firing persisted all morning. Small trees were felled by musket and artillery fire. The Federal troops fought doggedly. Casualties were rising on both sides. Pender was determined to drive the enemy back and reformed the brigade. The 34th NC was ready when the wave of rebels plunged back into the thickets. Pender personally took charge and led them forward in dashing style. Fighting like a man possessed, he shouted and led his men by example. The battered 22nd North Carolina faltered, so Pender grabbed the colors and ordered everyone forward. Inspired by Pender's bravery, the plucky 34th North Carolina led by Lt. Col. Gordon, surged. In short order, the Federal line broke, and the brigade stood proudly in possession of the second line of works. By this time, the 34th NC's ranks were much thinner, but there was more work to be done.

Pender ordered the hardy men deeper into the war-torn woods, encountering enemy troops in a pine thicket. By this time, the entire brigade was low on ammunition and was forced to fall back. They were relieved by fresh troops coming up. All along the line, Confederates had fought aggressively and had driven the Federal troops back. They were unsuccessful in cutting them off from the United States Ford as Jackson had wanted but had mauled Hookers army. It was a hard, toe-to-toe fight. The terrain did not allow for fancy maneuvers, just smash-mouthed fighting. As darkness descended, fires ignited in places. The dry pine saplings were perfect fuel, and the flames spread fast. Wounded men on both sides became trapped. Sometimes soldiers from opposing sides worked together to rescue men from the fire, risking their own lives to save friend and foe alike. They couldn't save them all. Horrified men screamed as they were burned alive. Charred bodies were found clinging to trees with outstretched arms. The hellish, scene would live in the nightmares of the survivors for years to come.

Burwell Cotton wrote his sister saying, "My Dear Sister it was the most horrible sight I ever saw. The explosions of the shells fired the woods and burned a great many of the dead and wounded."[107]

"Three deserted since the fight."

The dense woods afforded an opportunity for some to desert. Burwell Cotton wrote, "Three deserted since the fight Joel Cranford, A. Hurley & John Beaman. I have not seen nor heard from Clay Morgan since the fight.[108] I saw him run & tried to stop him but could not. He & Jackson [Andrew J] Beamon are missing. I saw both of them run."[109] According to this and two subsequent Cotton letters, Morgan and both Beaman brothers deserted during the fighting on May 3rd. On June 8th he wrote, "I saw him [Clay Morgan] running and did my best to stop him but it was no use. I called him by name but he would not notice me. He was so badly frightened that he run among the yankees.[110] It was not his bravery that caused him to be taken prisoner. In our advance we cut off a yankee brigade and did not find it out that stayed in our rear some time but finally made their escape. They took a good many stragglers. It was them that captured Morgan and Beamon. During the fight General Pender sent me back after reinforcements. While I was going back John Beamon run by me without hat, gun, or anything in the way of accoutrements. I tried to stop him and get him to stay with me but he said he was afraid of getting killed."[111] Cotton's letter sheds light on how most of the regiment's prisoners were taken. The Beaman brothers spent the rest of the war at home in Montgomery County.[112] Armstead Hurley the kinsman of the Beaman brothers, deserted on May 20th.

"...doing no good at tall at home."

John Beaman and his wife, Malinda, had a tough time at home during the war. John wrote this letter to Gov. Vance to ask for help:

---

[107] (Taylor 1994) Letter from Cotton dated 5/9/1863, page 139. NOTE: All letters of Burwell Cotton are from this source.
[108] Clay Morgan returned to duty December 10, 1863.
[109] (Taylor 1994) Letter from Cotton dated 5/16/1863, page 140.
[110] In the same letter he wrote, "He did not stay in the fight ten minutes."
[111] (Taylor 1994) Letter from Cotton dated 6/8/1863, page 143.
[112] John was immediately listed as a deserter and removed from the rolls. Andrew was listed as AWOL for the remainder of the war. Why they were differently treatment is unknown. Clearly, they deserted together.

"Mr. Z. B. Vance, gov, I take the presant opertunity of droping you a few lines to inform you [of] the condition of my settlement and our county and the parciality of the conscript law [so] you know the rotnest of it and the men that is exempted by it; and unles it is repeald you can't think us conscrps will obey the call that is made. You know the farmer is the life of hour country and I want you to tell me one farmer exempted unles he has twenty slaves; and I want you to tell me one of them that has anything to sell tht will sell for confedrt money
I have trid [to buy from] them and also I hav trid [to buy from] the manufactors that is exempted; and corn or bacon they must have [for payment] or you cant buy cotn [cotten] yarn or shurtin [shirting]. Confedrit money they will not hav, and I want you to tell me hough hour family will liv if we leav to fight for such men as these. We air forced to revlutionize unles this roten conscript exemption law is put down, for they are laws wee don't intend to obey, for wee farmers had as well to be exempted as the slavholder and the manufactory for we air the life of the hole [country].
I hav made moor corn and mor wheat and more bacon than any slavholder in the confedret state for sale, and I hav dun more smithin than any smith in hour county–for nothin acordin to my fose [foes?]; and yet I must go to fight for the seeceders and all mechanics and men who air doing no good at tall at home.
Mr. Vance, I want you to send me some exemptions for I am doing no good at tall, for they want me to fight and I am bound not to go unless all the rest of the blacksmiths and manufactors do.
Gov, I will close."[113]

An impressive victory

For the next two days, the Light Division remained in the battle-ruined woods waiting to see what would happen next. On May 5th, in a drenching rain, Hooker's bloodied army retreated. As the Federals fell back, Private Henry Walls of Company B was killed by retreating skirmishers. The 22-year-old was the son of Kinchin Walls from Rutherford County. He was the 34th NC's final casualty of the action. Rain continued the following day as General Hill, still suffering

---

[113] https://renegadesouth.wordpress.com/2009/11/20/civil-war-letters-from-north-carolina-john-a-beaman-to-governor-vance/ by Victoria Bynum.

from wounds, pulled his men out of the forest back to Orange Turnpike. The next day, they marched back to camp near Fredericksburg. Once more, the Confederates had won a battle they should have lost. Again, they had gone against conventional wisdom by dividing the army in the face of superior numbers. As at the Seven Days and Second Manassas, they had taken a huge risk to overload the flank and outnumber the enemy at the most crucial point. The enemy had failed to see what was happening in plain sight.

As impressive as all their victories had been, Chancellorsville was something special. The flanking movement was spectacular. It gave them a pride unlike anything they had known in previous battles. Pender had been at his best, as was his entire brigade. All day long, they braved severe fire and never backed down. Major Gordon did his job leading the 34th NC through the fight. His horse was killed by Yankee cavalry pickets on the day before the battle, but he came through unhurt.[114] The regiment's performance was outstanding, but they paid dearly. One-fourth of the men from the 34th NC were killed, wounded, or captured. Eighteen were killed in action. Ninety-seven were listed wounded. Thirteen were taken prisoner or missing. Wounds in this battle seemed especially bad. At least twenty of the wounded later died of their wounds.

Casualties from the Battle of Chancellorsville
Killed in Action

Perry D Carpenter	E	2Lt.	Max Mahugh	H	Pvt.
David Cox	A	Sgt.	Levi W Pasour	E	Pvt.
Hiram Cox	A	Sgt.	Jefferson G Petty	F	Pvt.
James Hardester	K	Pvt.	Martin Roberts	H	Pvt.
Marion Honeycut	I	Pvt.	Joseph W Shields	H	Pvt.
Daniel Hovis	E	Pvt.	Thomas S Shuford	F	Sgt.
Daniel Johnson	A	Pvt.	James F Toms	C	Pvt.
Franklin A Lowrance	D	Sgt.	James Wilkerson	C	Pvt.
James A Lucas	B	Pvt.	Henry H Walls	B	Pvt.

---

[114] The horse was his personal property, so he was reimbursed $100 for the loss.

Mortally Wounded

James J Bain	G	Pvt.	William O Ledbetter	C	Pvt.
William P Camp	H	Pvt.	Eli C Long	A	Sgt.
Charles Callicott	K	Cpl.	Christopher Martin	F	Pvt.
Claiborn Callicott	K	Pvt.	Lorenzo N McBrayer	C	Sgt.
Monroe P Finger	E	Cpl.	Wilson Norman	F	Pvt.
Noah Freeman	K	Pvt.	David B Ray	D	Pvt.
Marcus A Gantt	F	Pvt.	James G Richardson	A	Sgt.
Lawson Greenhill	G	Pvt.	Moses Self	H	Pvt.
Archibald B Hogan	K	Pvt.	Daniel Sheets	A	Pvt.
George Kiser	E	Pvt.	Martin L Shittle	C	Pvt.

Wounded

Columbus Abernathy	G	Pvt.	Charles S Martin	E	Pvt.
Hiram W Abernathy[115]	A	Cpt.	John J Martin	F	Pvt.
James Allen	H	Sgt.	John C Mints	I	Pvt.
William Allen	H	Pvt.	Thomas J Mints	I	Pvt.
W Jackson Armstrong	E	Pvt.	Isaac Mooney	F	Pvt.
John R Asbury	G	Pvt.	John A Moore	B	Pvt.
Henry Atwood	A	Pvt.	James R Morrow	I	Cpl.
Stanhope H Bagwell	C	Pvt.	Calvin J Murchison	K	Pvt.
John Jr Bare	A	Pvt.	David C Peeler	F	Pvt.
John Beaty	G	Pvt.	John P Philbeck	B	Sgt.
Tyrell Camp	H	Sgt.	Jesse Reep	E	Pvt.
Noah Carpenter	E	Pvt.	Franklin E Reeves	K	Pvt.
Jacob L Clayton	I	Pvt.	Daniel Reinhardt	E	Pvt.
John Cook	C	Pvt.	Elisha Robbins	I	Sgt.
Simon D Davis	B	Sgt.	John W Robert	H	Pvt.
Samuel Dellinger	H	Pvt.	Samuel Rupp	I	Pvt.
John A Dobbins	C	Pvt.	William F Russell	K	Pvt.
John Eaker Sr	F	Pvt.	Phillip A Sloop	D	Sgt.
William H Elliott	C	Pvt.	Caleb L Sparks	B	Cpl.

[115] Hiram Abernathy's record only shows he was "sick" following the battle. In a letter dated May 14, 1863, Colonel Lowrance stated that he was twice wounded in the battle.

John W Ellis	D	Sgt.	Thomas J Stroud	B	Pvt.	
William Foster	C	Pvt.	James C Terres	G	Pvt.	
Cornelius C Gibbons	F	Pvt.	George C Todd	G	Cpl.	
William R Green	B	Pvt.	William A Turner	F	Pvt.	
Eli O Hamrick	B	Pvt.	Thomas C Weaver	C	Pvt.	
James B Hawkins	I	Pvt.	William Weeks	C	Pvt.	
Samuel L Hayes	G	Pvt.	Thomas H White	E	Pvt.	
Peter Heavner	E	Pvt.	William V White	F	1Sgt.	
Charles C Hensdale	I	Sgt.	Doctor F Williams	F	Pvt.	
Moses S Hovis	G	Pvt.	John M Williams	F	Pvt.	
Marcus M Hull	E	Pvt.	William W Williams	F	Pvt.	
William A Jones	B	Pvt.	James T Williford	D	Pvt.	
William A Kilpatrick	D	Sgt.	Lawson Wise	E	Pvt.	
John Kiser	E	Pvt.	Thompson J Wood	I	Pvt.	
Hamilton Koonce	A	Sgt.	Logens Woode	A	Pvt.	
George W Koone	C	Sgt.	George W Woods	A	2Lt.	
John F Linebarger	I	Pvt.				

Captured

W Jackson Armstrong	E	Pvt.	Abel C Hartzog	E	Pvt.	
John Bare Jr	A	Pvt.	Z Kane		Pvt.	
John F Bess	E	Pvt.	Aaron Lee B	F	Pvt.	
J R Coffman		Pvt.	John H Lee	F	Pvt.	
Jesse Eaker	E	Pvt.	Spencer Morgan	K	Pvt.	
James Early	C	Pvt.	Robert A Taylor	E	Pvt.	
David B Harrill	B	1Lt.	John Womack	B	Pvt.	

Among those killed were brothers Hiram and David Cox, both sergeants from Ashe County's Laurel Springs Guards. The brothers went off to war with a third brother Levi when the company was formed. Hiram enlisted as a lieutenant but failed in the re-election. Instead of going home, he re-enlisted as a private and was later promoted to sergeant. David's first child was born a month after they enlisted. The loss devastated their parents, William and Elizabeth Cox, as well as their brother Levi who was still in the company. Their captain, Hiram Abernathy, was wounded twice in the battle.

A second set of brothers lost their lives in the battle. Charles and Claiborne Callicott enlisted in Montgomery County together in September of 1861. It is said that one of them was shot and fell in a creek. When his brother stopped to help, he too was shot. Charles died of his wounds on May 13th, Claiborne two days later.[116] They were the last of the five Callicott men who enlisted together in Company K. Their older brother Martin was mortally wounded at Gaines's Mill. Their cousins Henry and John Callicott, themselves brothers, had both died of disease in the first few months of their service. No family in the regiment paid a higher sacrifice then the Callicotts. All five, including two sets of brothers were dead.

The regiment was given the honor of selecting men to recognize with a Badge of Distinction for gallantry in the battle.[117] There was no actual badge or medal, rather a formal recognition with their names published in a special Roll of Honor. Each company chose one man by vote who had especially distinguished himself. The following men from the regiment were so recognized for bravery at Chancellorsville:

Badge of Distinction for bravery at Chancellorsville

Matthias Brown	A	Pvt.	Elisha Robbins	I	Pvt.
Samuel Dellinger	H	Pvt.	Thomas S Shuford	F	Pvt.
Obediah Eller	D	Pvt.	David M Taylor	E	1Sgt.
Joseph Hogan	K	Pvt.	Charles B Todd	G	Pvt.
George W Koone	C	Sgt.	Wallace Winn	B	Pvt.

These men were listed in a special Roll of Honor published in the Western Democrat on December 1, 1863. Thomas Shuford's recognition came posthumously. He was killed on May 3rd. He and his brother Pinkney had served together until Pinkney resigned his commission as a 2nd Lt in Company F for health reasons the past July.

---

[116] Information on the death of Charles and Claiborne provided courtesy of Joe Callicutt corroborated by the official records. Claiborn's record states he "died of wounds received at Chancellorsville" on 4/15/63. It is believed that the date was incorrect and was probably 5/15/63.

[117] It was called a Medal of Honor in the records but is most often called the Badge of Distinction.

Wallace Winn was a 37-year-old conscript who had only been with the regiment since February. This was his first battle. He was the only conscript to receive this honor. The men were recognized in a formal dress parade. Others not voted to receive this distinction were recognized by their officers for bravery. Sgt. George Huntley was one of those. One could make the argument that Chancellorsville rather than Gettysburg was the high-water mark of the Confederacy. Their spirits and confidence soared to new heights. The esprit de corps they felt here was never again equaled. They could conquer the world.

Lt. Col. John L. McDowell was dropped from the rolls on May 6th for prolonged AWOL. McDowell was arrested, but Governor Vance personally intervened on his behalf. Instead of being sentenced for desertion, McDowell was permitted to reenlist in Company I as a private.[118] Despite the circumstances, McDowell remained a respected figure among the men. George Huntley wrote home saying that Col. McDowell was in the company as a private and, "is a fine man."[119] George T. Gordon was promoted to Lt. Colonel. George Clark was promoted to Major.

On Sunday, May 10th, the sad news came that Stonewall Jackson had died. He survived the amputation of his arm but fell victim to pneumonia. His last words were, "Let us cross over the river and rest under the shade of the trees." The men of the Light Division had had their grievances with Jackson but were proud to have served under him. Jackson's widow, Anna, was born at Cottage Home in Lincoln County near the Gaston County line. After her husband's death, she and her six-month-old daughter moved back to Cottage Home where her father still lived. She became known as the Widow of the Confederacy.

A Rigged Election

Some companies elected officers to fill vacancies left by the recent battle. A controversy flared in Company I from Rutherford County. George Huntly and John Crawford were nominated for the Lieutenancy. The company's Lieutenant Thomas P. Phillips oversaw the voting since Captain Wood was in the hospital. He wrote the names of the two candidates on a piece of paper and had the men line up and

---

[118] One record stated that McDowell resigned in December of 1862. Apparently, he departed without his resignation being formally accepted.
[119] (Taylor 1994) Page 94, footnote.

Phillips would mark their votes. Phillips wanted Crawford to have the spot, so he cheated and declared Crawford the winner. Suspicious, the men discussed the situation and discovered Phillips' trickery and went to the Colonel. A new vote was taken, and Huntley won by a count of 17 to 4. Phillips was reprimanded for his actions.[120]

The Third Corps

For two weeks while camped at Fredericksburg, the men waited to see who would take Jackson's place. On May 24th, General Lee formed a third corps for his army. He had long pondered the move. He felt the two-corps arrangement was difficult to manage. The new Third Corps would be commanded by A. P. Hill who was promoted to Lieutenant General. Richard Ewell assumed Jackson's position as commander of the Second Corp. Longstreet remained in command of his First Corps. The new Third Corps consisted of the Light Division, Richard H Anderson's division transferred from Longstreet's Corps, a new division to be organized, and five artillery battalions.

With Hill's promotion, command of the Light Division had to be filled. Hill had a special fondness for his Light Division and wanted it to have a strong leader. Hill's choice was William Dorsey Pender. Pender was a battle-tested leader who had repeatedly distinguished himself. Though just 29, he had shown his mettle and was a favorite of Hill from the beginning. Hill noted that Pender's brigade, including the 34th North Carolina, was the best drilled and disciplined brigade in the division. Hill felt the division would continue to perform brilliantly under Pender's unflinching leadership. Hill also elevated Henry Heth to division command. The brigades of Archer and Heth were combined with two other brigades to form Heth's division. Pender's Light Division was four strong brigades, Pender's former brigade, Lane, McGowan, and Thomas.

By early June, the army was recovering from the losses at Chancellorsville. Since January 1st, the 34th NC had picked up 102 new recruits, 76 of those were conscripts. The average age of the conscripts in this group was 34. The average volunteer was 26. Among the new recruits were two men hired as substitutes, Adam Clark and Drury Turner, who were 46 and 47 years old. Adam Clark received a

---

[120] The account of this election comes entirely from Hundley's letter dated 5/20/1863. (Taylor 1994)

black mark on his record for having "shamefully abandoned his colors at Chancellorsville." Clark made up for his shortcoming, going on to prove his worth despite his age. Turner would also prove to be a strong soldier. Substitutes and conscripts had to work hard to gain respect. Despite their reputation of being poor soldiers, many fought hard to prove otherwise. The 34th NC also welcomed back Colonel Lowrance who had recovered from his bout with jaundice. He was ready to lead the regiment on their next campaign.

Private Henry K. Dellinger, The Shady Grove Rangers – Company E[121]

---

[121] Photo Courtesy Mike Stroupe

Private Charles S. Martin, The Shady Grove Rangers - Company E[122]

---

[122] Photo courtesy Patti Martin

134

Chapter 9.
The Crimson Plains of Gettysburg

On June 3rd, General Lee put the army in motion for his most fateful campaign of the war. Ewell's corps started north first, marching through the Shenandoah Valley to cross the Potomac and travel through Maryland into Pennsylvania. Longstreet then moved northward from Culpepper. Hill would then move out, following in Ewell's footsteps. As Ewell began his trek, Hill's men remained at Fredericksburg guarding a 20-mile line to keep an eye on Joe Hooker. On June 13th, Hooker took out after Lee's north-marching columns, which had a ten-day head start. The next day, Hill's men started moving. Anderson's division moved out first followed by Heth the next day. Pender's division waited until Hooker was out of sight. On the 16th, Pender's division started marching.

They passed through the battlefield of Chancellorsville and viewed the torn and burnt woods and shallow graves. They shared the feeling of their commanding general who wanted the coming battle to be the last of the war. On May 18th, Pender's division reached Culpeper, a day behind the main body of Hill's corps. There, they stopped for a short rest. Culpeper was General Hill's hometown and was in a devastated condition. From Culpeper, the men marched through Chester's Gap to cross the beautiful Blue Ridge Mountains. The heat became oppressive. Day after day, they struggled on dealing with the usual straggling. By the 21st, they neared Berryville where General Lee was seen riding among the columns. Everywhere he went, troops cheered. On the 23rd, they crossed the Potomac near Shepherdstown where they recalled their victory following the Sharpsburg fight last September.

That day, Pender officially passed command of his old brigade to Alfred Moore Scales, an attorney, and former U.S. Congressman. Scales and Pender had served together in the 13th North Carolina. Scales succeeded Pender as Colonel of the 13th North Carolina when Pender was promoted to brigade command. Scales had shown great courage in battle. He collapsed after Malvern Hill and came near death. He took command of the brigade when Pender was wounded at Fredericksburg. At Chancellorsville he again displayed great gallantry, gaining Pender's praise in his official report. Scales was wounded in the thigh in the battle but had recovered in time for the current campaign. That evening, a band played for the new General who spoke to his troops expressing pleasure at having the honor of leading them. The 34th North Carolina marched for the first time as part of Scales' Brigade, Pender's Light Division of A. P. Hill's Third Corps.

The next two days brought rain as they entered Hagerstown, Maryland, whose citizens gathered and watched them march through. On the 26th, they crossed into Pennsylvania. Continuing north, they reached Chambersburg, turned east for another four miles, stopping near Fayetteville. They had covered 157 miles in twelve days and were due a rest. Here, they learned that Joe Hooker had been replaced as the Federal army commander. Lee had humbled the mighty McClellan, humiliated bombastic Pope, and crushed Burnside. Joe Hooker then joined the roster of defeated Union generals. That wily gray fox had ruined another Yankee general's career. George Meade replaced hooker, a capable but cautious general.

It was raining on Monday, June 29th as parts of Hill's corps resumed the march, moving through South Mountain and stopping near Cashtown. Eight miles to the east was the town of Gettysburg. Pender's men moved out the next day. Before they marched, they took a muster. The 34th North Carolina fielded 300 men and 37 officers present.

July 1, 1863

Wednesday July 1st, 1863 began hot and humid across the Pennsylvania countryside. Heth's division was in the lead and moved out at 5:00 in the morning heading toward Gettysburg where they hoped to find supplies. Pender's division left Cashtown at eight. As Pender's men started marching, distant battle sounds were heard as Heth's division ran into Federal cavalry under General John Buford. Though under orders not to force a major engagement, Heth believed they were just a small force and determined to push on, but Buford was reinforced by infantry. By 8:00 Heth had his hands full. The battle of Gettysburg had begun.

General Lee did not want a full-scale engagement since not all his army was up, so Pender advanced his division slowly, staying close enough to support Heth. McGowan's brigade was out front. McGowan commanded Maxcy Gregg's old brigade, but wounds from

Chancellorsville had him sidelined. Abner Perrin led in his place. Behind Perrin marched Alfred Moore Scales' brigade including the hard-fighting 34th North Carolina led by 27-year-old Colonel William L. J. Lowrance. The 34th NC felt as confident as any unit in the army after their performance at Chancellorsville. Behind them marched the brigades of Lane and Thomas.

Perrin's brigade reached Marsh Creek around 9:30 that morning with Scales not far behind. They were about two miles east of McPherson's Ridge where Heth was brawling with Buford. Pender ordered the men into line of battle. The brigades formed in the fields on both sides of Chambersburg Turnpike. Once formed, they moved up steadily. They arrived at Herr Ridge a little before noon as Heth was being repulsed. Pender halted on the ridge and surveyed the situation. His combative instinct would have urged him on, but he held back according to General Lee's orders. He rested the brigades until around 2:30. When Heth renewed his attack, Pender reformed his men, keeping in striking distance.

Lane's brigade was the left of the division with Scales in the center just south of the pike. Perrin's South Carolinians were to the right. Thomas's Georgians were left behind to guard the wagon trains and artillery. In this order, they advanced about a quarter of a mile taking only light fire. When they halted, Lane was sent to the far right to engage Federal cavalry, making Scales the division's left flank. Scales' left regiment was at the turnpike. With Lane and Thomas detached, Pender advanced with only Scales and Perrin. Artillery fire grew heavier when they resumed the advance. In the distance, Scales saw rebel troops heavily engaged and ordered his men to quicken their step, which caused the Federal troops to drop back. From there, Scales' advance was slowed by running into parts of Heth's division. The delays played havoc on the men's nerves.

"Press on to Victory!"

The veterans in the regiment could tell by the sounds how serious the battle ahead was. A pair of former members of the 34th NC was in the thick of the fighting including their former Colonel. Collett Leventhorpe had led the 11th NC since April of 1862. When he left the 34th to take command of the 11th NC, he took Henderson Lucas of Company G with him to serve as his adjunct. The two fought side by side as Leventhorpe led the 11th across Herr's Ridge, driving the enemy before them. When they crossed Willoughby Run, the Federals made a stand in Herbst Woods in front of McPherson's Ridge. Herbst Woods was a small area, and the fighting there was close and violent, and the 11th NC's casualties were heavy. Leventhorpe and his men faced the Iron Brigade whose fame for valor was well-known. As Leventhorpe led his men forward, he received a serious gunshot wound to the left fore-arm which disabled him. With several other officers and the color-bearer down, Henderson Lucas grabbed the regiment's colors and ran forward. His bravery rallied the men, but he was soon shot down. A letter in the Fayetteville Observer reported, "He rose again waving the colors and urging on the men. He was again brought down, but still supported the Old Bethel [11th NC] colors with his left arm until that arm was shot through."[123] When an officer in the 11th NC passed him, Henderson was still urging the men on crying, "Press on to victory!"

"Every discharge made sad havoc..."

At 4:00 p.m., Pender gave the order to attack the Federal line which had fallen back to Seminary Ridge. Crossing Willoughby Run, the 34th NC passed thorough Herbst Woods where the 11th NC and Pettigrew's brigade had fought. The men took note of the carnage left behind. Those new to war were shocked. The veterans took it in stride.

Author Don Ernsburger explains the problems caused by Pender's slow advance. First, the enemy had time to build robust defensive works. Second, Federal artillery shifted to high ground north of Chambersburg Turnpike, giving them perfect defilade on Scales' brigade. Scales' regiments were arranged north to south in this order: the 38th NC, just south of the pike, the 13th NC, the 34th NC, the 22nd NC, and the 16th NC. Union artillery on the northern end was sighted toward the valley, away from Scales' left flank held by the 38th NC. It was the center regiments that would face these guns as well as the artillery and infantry in their front. The 34th NC was the center of Scales' line.

It took courage to march into the face of such deadly fire, and they faced it like the veterans they were. But the destruction awaiting them was unlike anything they had faced before. Twenty Federal

---

[123] (Foley 2007)

artillery pieces stood hub to hub on elevated ground just north of the pike. They would be firing case, canister, and double-canister rounds. Pender's division was attacking at half-strength.

Scales' brigade went up and over McPherson's Ridge, passing through the last fragments of Heth's division. Coming out of the woods, they passed over the spot where Union General John Reynolds had been killed earlier. As they crested the ridge, the Cupola on top of the seminary building appeared. The Lutheran Theological Seminary came into full view fronted by a solid line of Yankee infantry. Without pause, they descended the gently sloping ground heading straight for the enemy line. Coming down the slope, Scales' brigade was separated by a fence with the 16th and 22nd to the right of the fence. The 34th NC was just left of the fence.[124] As soon as they started down the ridge, they came under heavy artillery fire. From the left they took canister and shell fire. From the front, they took canister and musket fire. The cross-fire was devastating. General Scales wrote in his official report, "…we pressed on at a double-quick until we reached the bottom [depression], a distance of about 75 yards from the ridge [rise] we had just crossed, and about the same distance from the college [Seminary] in our front." For artillery, it was point blank range. The area became a killing field, the valley of death for many southern men.

They never stood a chance. It seemed like every gun fired at once. Sheets of flame belched from the enemy guns, the double-shot canister wrecking the lines. Fire from the Federal muskets came in torrents. Smoke filled the area, shrouding their enemy. Colonel Lowrance tried in vain to keep his regiment together. In a few awful minutes, men from the regiment fell in clusters. The earth shook. Men became confused. Screams of the wounded and shouts of officers strove futilely with the deafening artillery and musket fire. Lowrance's proud regiment was reduced to fragmented squads. Soldiers he had served with since the beginning littered the ground, some writhing in agony, some silent and motionless. Lowrance could only watch in horror as his regiment was decimated. They had marched into a perfect storm of destruction. In twenty terrible minutes that must have seemed

---

[124] This fence does not appear on every map, but a map on display at the battlefield does show it and was explained by the battlefield guides. The fence is not there today.

like an eternity, the entire brigade was shot to pieces. General Scales wrote in his official report, "Every discharge made sad havoc in our line…our line had been broken up, and now only a squad here and there marked the place where regiments had rested."

General Scales fell with a severe leg wound from an exploding shell. Colonel Lowrance also fell wounded. Lowrance's wound was not severe but temporarily disabled him. For a few minutes it was unclear who was in command. Two of the 34th NC's officers were serving on General Scales' staff that day, Lt. John D. Young and Cpt. James Riddick. When the general fell, the two young officers braved the smoke and confusion to assess the situation. Cpt. Riddick fell wounded. Lt. Young somehow managed to escape injury. Only two field-grade officers in the entire brigade were still standing. One was the 34th NC's Lt. Col. George T. Gordon. With Colonel Lowrance and General Scales down, command of the brigade fell to Gordon. Scales' brigade was shattered, but to their right Perrin's men began to break through a weaker point in the Union line. Gordon took what was left of the brigade and moved in support of Perrin. The Union left had not been as strong and began to break apart. Perrin's brigade raced ahead and broke the Union line in front of the seminary with Scales' survivors in support. In a half hour, Seminary Ridge was under new ownership; Pender's Light Division of A. P. Hill's Third Corps. Parts of Perrin's brigade chased the fleeing Yankees through Gettysburg, capturing and killing many. A few of Scales' shell-shocked men joined the pursuit, but most stayed on the ridge. By nightfall, Pender brought up Thomas's brigade and the entire division occupied Seminary Ridge. General Lee established a HQ just north of the pike where the artillery battery had poured death and destruction at the rebels. Col. Lowrance wanted to know how many casualties his 34th NC had suffered but it was impossible to know. There were many men he could not account for.

The 34th NC's losses were shocking.[125] Over half of the regiment was dead, wounded, or missing. Among the casualties was Lt.

---

[125] Ernsburger relates in his Preface the research difficulties of studying the individual soldiers who were engaged on both the first and third days, as the 34th NC was. Service records recorded soldiers as "killed at Gettysburg July 1-3, 1863," or "captured at Gettysburg July 1-5, 1863," etc. It is thus impossible to know how many of the men were lost on the first day versus the third day.

George Job Huntley of Rutherford County. Huntley was promoted for bravery after Chancellorsville and was leading as an officer for the first time. He died of his wounds the next day. His last letter home was written two days before the fight that took his life. It was a short letter addressed to his sister. He spoke of the Pennsylvania countryside as some of the finest he had ever seen and said they were resting in a beautiful oak grove.

Lt. Nevin McLeod and 1st Sgt. Norman McLeod were brothers from Montgomery County serving in Company K. Nevin fell wounded with a gunshot wound to the right leg, and Norman was killed. First Lt. Alexander A. Cathey received a severe leg wound. He would have an exceedingly long road to recovery. George Clark, who was promoted to Major a few days after Chancellorsville, was killed in the action. He was a student before the war and a cousin to the McLeod brothers.

T. D. Lattimore witnessed the carnage. He wrote, "The brigade...was exposed to a deadly enfilading fire from artillery on the left and infantry in front, from behind breastworks. For the first time in its history, the brigade was repulsed by this thunderous fire." By dark the men bivouacked near Fairfield road just south of the seminary. Scales' wound would keep him out of action for the rest of the battle, so command of the brigade fell on the shoulders of Colonel Lowrance. Command of the 34th NC fell to Lt. Col. George T. Gordon, the flamboyant Englishman who joined the regiment the past December.

Mills A. Higgins

Rutherford County lost a steady and brave soldier when Mills A. Higgins fell in that field of death in front of the seminary. Mills was the son of John and Margaret Higgins. He married Mary Melissa Elliott on May 24, 1854. They had four children before he went off to war with Cpt. Dickerson's Rutherford Rebels in 1861, His youngest daughter was born only a few months before he left. His record shows no absence other than a hospital stay in November of 1862. He was detailed to bring home the body of one of his friends in April of 1862, to Rutherford County. It was a brief stay, the last time he saw his family. He survived many hard battles before he came to Gettysburg. His wife, children, and parents shed the bitter tears for the fallen that so

---

Even an overall accounting is impossible. To be sure, most of the casualties from the regiment and brigade came from the July 1st fight.

many had already shed. How much longer would the war go on, and how many more must die. Mills Higgins was 27 years old.[126]

Assessing the Damage

Colonel Lowrance wasted no time. While still tending to own minor wound, he began assessing the damage done to the brigade. He authorized battlefield promotions for the 34th NC. Henry Rickert was promoted to Sgt. Major. Lowrance also elevated Captain Francis L. Twitty to Major in the place of Clark, who was killed. Replacing Twitty was the reliable John D. Young. Both Young and Cpt. Riddick won praise in General Scales' Gettysburg report while serving on his staff that day. Young had served as an aide-de-camp for Scales, a role he had also performed for General Pender According to General Scales, Young and Riddick were, "cool, calm, and intelligent…" and acted, "with a gallantry that deserves this notice." While Colonel Lowrance led the brigade, Captain Young would serve as his aide-de-camp as well. Since Cpt. Riddick was wounded, Col. Lowrance asked David M. McIntire, the Adjunct of the 38th NC to also serve on his temporary staff.[127] After dark, the brigade was ordered to the right. At 1:00 a.m., the men stacked arms and rested.

July 2, 1863

At dawn, the brigade was moved to the right near the artillery. Concerned the enemy would attack, Lowrance deployed a strong line of skirmishers to guard the guns. He also continued to assess the condition of the brigade. The 34th NC looked more like an over-sized company. The brigade was less than a full-sized regiment. Barely 500 men were fit for duty in the entire brigade. Most of the field officers and many line officers were dead or wounded. Several companies didn't have a single officer.[128] Many in the ranks were walking wounded. Lowrance described the state of the brigade as, "depressed, dilapidated, and almost unorganized." He spent the day reorganizing the brigade and making sure the regiments were consolidated and officered. Longstreet was south of Hill's corps. Pender's division was strung out along

---

[126] Photo and family history from Elliott Family Heritage by Ivarea Flack and Genevieve Elliot Gassner, 1976.
[127] This was found in an article written by McIntire and published in the Weekly Star 9/14/1877. (digitalnc.org)
[128] See the official report of Col. William L. J. Lowrance

Seminary ridge. Pender's brigades of Perrin and Scales, (Lowrance), would remain inactive for this day, but part of the division would see action supporting Longstreet's attack on the right. Longstreet attacked the Union left through the Peach Orchard, the Wheat Field, and Devil's Den, culminating in the attack on Little Round Top, where Federal forces commanded by Joshua Chamberlain won the day. In one of the war's most inspiring stands, Chamberlain's men fended off repeated assaults. Running out of ammunition, he ordered a bayonet charge that finally ended the fighting there.

At one in the afternoon, Lowrance's brigade was relieved and ordered to rejoin the division. Upon reporting for duty, he was ordered to a two-brigade division being formed under the command of General Isaac Trimble. Lowrance's brigade was positioned to the right of Lane's brigade. They were posted at McMillan Woods. About a mile directly ahead was Cemetery Hill with the Federal line running from there down Cemetery Ridge parallel to the Confederate line on Seminary Ridge. Between Scales' brigade and Cemetery Hill was the Bliss barn and farmhouse. The barn was a huge building, 70x35 feet. The lower level was made of stone and had several windows and doors which could be used by Sharpshooters. One hundred men could occupy the building. The barn changed hands changed hands several times that day in sharp fighting. Some 800 men were killed or wounded there. The 34th NC and the rest of the brigade was just back from the crest of the ridge. They could view the fight from the ridgeline but were not involved in the action.

The most significant event that day was the wounding of their division commander, Maj. General William Dorsey Pender Pender was in front of McMillan's woods inspecting the lines when a shell exploded and cut a large gash in his thigh. It was his fourth wound of the war. One of the men who carried the wounded general from the field was Pvt. Jesse Lattimore of the 34th NC from Cleveland County.[129] It was said that it was the third time he had carried Pender from the field wounded.

---

[129] Related in an article titled "North Carolina Regiments in the War Between the States by James C. Elliott published in the Forest City Courier 2/27/1929 (digitalnc.org).

The Pickett-Pettigrew-Trimble Charge

Friday, July 3, 1863. Sunrise was 5:00 a.m. The men had breakfast and lined up for muster at 8:00. Under the command of Lt. Colonel George T. Gordon, just 150[130] men stood in the ranks of the proud but battered 34th NC, some wearing bandages to cover wounds from the battle's first day. Along with Lane's brigade, they were ordered farther to the right as the line of battle was organized. They were placed under the command of Maj. General Isaac R. Trimble who was seen riding through the lines of his patched-together division. He met with General Lane and Colonel Lowrance who commanded his two banged-up brigades. Colonel Lowrance was calm and steady, a reassuring presence in a brigade that had been badly shot-up less than 48 hours prior.

They should never have been there on July 3rd. The regiment and the brigade had lost too many men the first day. Nonetheless, they were needed on this final fateful day, so they lined up to do their duty, many for the last time. General Lee felt he had no choice. They were in enemy country where they could not stay much longer. There were no reinforcements coming. Retreating after fighting for two inconclusive days was not an option. If they stayed, they would fight. Lee felt the center was the weakest part of the Federal line. He had attacked both flanks, and the enemy had reinforced those areas. He believed they would break in the center if a concentrated attack was made there.

Many of the senior officers were killed or wounded in the first two days. Since Scales was disabled, Lowrance led the brigade in the assault, passing command of his regiment to George T. Gordon. With Pender wounded, the division was placed under the command of Maj.

---

[130] The regiment had 337 men present when the battle started a difference of 187. Only 64 were accounted as casualties from the first day, leaving 123 unaccounted for. They reported only 116 total casualties for both days combined. Those killed or captured were accounted for. The difference is the wounded. General Lee's policy was to only report men whose wounds would keep them out of action for an extended time. Any man who would return to duty in a week or two was not counted. The purpose was to not alarm folks at home with large casualty numbers. Though there could have been some "shirkers" hiding out to avoid the next fight, most of the missing were likely wounded. It can only be concluded that the numbers of the wounded were greatly understated.

General Isaac R. Trimble, then in command of Stonewall Jackson's old division. Trimble was a solid general but had never worked with the men of the Light Division. General Heth was also put out of action on July 1st. His division was led by Brig. General J. Johnston Pettigrew, a highly respected North Carolinian and Heth's senior brigade leader. Two brigades of Anderson's division of Hill's Corps were sent right to shore up Pickett's area of the field.

"Pickett, my men are not going up today."

By noon, the men were waiting in the woods in sweltering heat. Gordon, whom the men had started calling "English Gordon," was prepared to lead the remnants of the 34th NC into battle. General George Pickett was inspecting the lines of Armstead's brigade and came over to speak to his fellow Pig War veteran. Pickett introduced Gordon to his aide, Capt. Robert Bright, who later wrote of the encounter. According to Bright, Pickett said, "This is Colonel Gordon, once opposed to me in the San Juan affair, but now on our side."

Gordon said, "Pickett, my men are not going up today."

Pickett replied, "But Gordon, they must go up; you must make them go up."

Gordon answered, "You know, Pickett, I will go as far with you as any other man, if only for old acquaintance sake, but for the last day or two my men have lost heavily under infantry fire and are very sore, and they will not go up today."[131] Despite Gordon's protest, the men did go. When duty called, they went no matter the odds.

Around 1:00, the artillery bombardment began. For about an hour, the infantrymen watched the greatest artillery exhibition ever seen in North America.[132] For the rebel artillery, however, it was a lot of smoke and noise but minimal damage to the Federal line. Just prior to leaving for Pennsylvania, Lee's artillery received new fuses from South Carolina and Alabama since the Richmond arsenals did not have enough to supply them. They did not test the fuses before going north. The new fuses burned at a slower rate than the ones they had been using. As a result, their ordinance ranged up to 200 yards farther than

---

[131] (VIP 2013)

[132] Accounts vary on how long the artillery bombardment lasted, from 45 minutes to two hours. It is generally accepted to have lasted 45 minutes to an hour.

they intended. They were overshooting their target every time. In the smoke of the cannonade, the spotters could not see where their shots were hitting and had no idea that they needed to shorten their fuses. The Federals noticed and lessened their fire to conserve ordinance and deceive the rebels into thinking they were breaking up.

Dress to the colors!

When the firing stopped, the men clutched their weapons and got ready to go. The men of the 34th NC rose to do their duty once again:[133]

Captain Hiram Abernathy led the remaining eleven Laurel Springs Guards. Both his lieutenants, Bartlett Martin and George Woody, were wounded the first day of the battle.

Company B, the Sandy Run Yellow Jackets, was led by Captain Joseph Byers. Eleven men from this company went into battle on July 3rd.

After the death of Major George Clark on the first day, Company C's Captain Twitty was promoted to Major. First Lt. John D. Young was promoted to Captain to lead the eighteen Rutherford Rebels across the field.

Company D, the Oakland Guards, was led by Captain Carmi K. McNeely. Ten officers and men from this company were ready to march across the field.

The young Methodist minister Captain Micah C. Davis led Company E. Twenty-three officers and men reported for duty.

Company F, the Floyd Rifles, was led by Captain David Hoyle and Lt. Thomas D. Lattimore. Fourteen men from this company were present for duty at 8:00 the morning of July 3rd.

The only remaining officer from Company G was 24-year-old Lt. James Todd. Cpt. George Norment and Lt. Alexander Cathey were both wounded. Lt. John Abernathy was killed. Fourteen Mecklenburg Boys were present.

Company H, the Rough and Ready's, was led by Cpt. John Roberts and Lt. Joseph Camp with 23 ready for battle.

---

[133] (Ernsberger 2008) The following summary of the companies of the regiment comes from pages 114-116. Ernsberger did not mention Lt. Lattimore in Company F, but he was there and wrote about it.

Company I lost severely on July 1st including three of their four officers. Captain James Wood was wounded in the head and right arm. Lt. Henry Jenkins was wounded. Lt. George Huntly was killed. Nineteen-year-old Lt. Thomas Phillips led nine surviving Rutherford Band men into battle.

Company K, the Montgomery Boys, was led by Lt. Thomas Haltom. Haltom was 43 and one of the oldest men in the regiment. Lt. Nevin McLeod had been wounded and 1st Sgt. Norman McLeod was killed. Sixteen men from this company were present.

The companies were, as General Scales stated, reduced to mere squads. This regiment was typical of many going across the field that day who had also fought on July 1st. The 34th North Carolina marched into Pennsylvania with 337 officers and men, but on July 3rd only 150 plus a few Field and Staff officers remained. When the artillery barrage concluded, the rugged band summoned all the courage within them, and waited for the order to advance knowing that many of them had but minutes to live. They stood shoulder to shoulder with men they had left home with, men they had fought with from Gaines Mill to Second Manassas, Fredericksburg, Chancellorsville, all the way here. They knew that it was a defining moment for themselves and for the war. Col. Lowrance and Lt. Col. Gordon joined the chorus of officers barking orders. "Dress to the colors!" "Dress to the right!" They obeyed as if they had done it a thousand times. They were all veterans now, ready to do and to die. Banners were held high, men stood motionless, officers mounted on horses with swords drawn. For one long last moment they stood confident and orderly, with a pride that would never again be equaled.

At the simple command "Forward!" the men moved.
"We advanced across a wide, hot, and already crimson plain."

Three quarters of a mile ahead was their objective, the Federal line. Earlier that morning, Federal troops had fired the Bliss barn and farmhouse to keep them from falling back into rebel hands. Their smoldering ruins were at the center of the Pettigrew-Trimble assault.

Pettigrew's men formed in line of battle with Trimble's men behind. Pettigrew's longer line consisted of, from left to right the brigades of; Brockenbrough, Davis, Marshall, and Fry. Behind them, Trimble's two brigades were Lane on the left, and Scales, command by

Lowrance, on the right. Lowrance arranged his regiments the same as they had been on the battle's first day, left to right: the 38th, 13th, 34th, 22nd, and the 16th North Carolina regiments. The nearest brigade farther right was Lewis Armstead's men from Pickett's division.

The soldiers passed through the artillery batteries whose guns were still hot. For the first 1,500 yards, they marched over gently downward-sloping ground. They started receiving artillery fire almost immediately, but they marched steadily forward with rebel artillery firing back. Pettigrew's line was about 140 yards in front of Trimble. Colonel Lowrance kept a steady pace and a tight formation. The 34th NC with Lowrance's brigade advanced to the right of the still smoldering Bliss barn. As the lines neared the Bliss barn, Brockenbrough's brigade on the far left was hit by heavy artillery fire and a surprise attack by the 8th Ohio Infantry. Brockenbrough's men became demoralized and broke and fled to the rear. The Ohioans turned their attention to Davis's brigade inflicting some casualties and then retired. Pettigrew and Trimble shifted their lines to fill Brockenbrough's place.

The ground leveled at the Bliss farm. Nearby was an orchard and a few shade trees. Federal skirmishers in the area fired on the advancing rebels, wounding some before falling back. Two hundred yards farther, the ground again sloped slightly downhill. Artillery fire grew more intense. They came to a shallow waterway called Stevens Run which traversed their path, marked by a battle-ruined fence. In rainy weather, it was a small stream; on July 3rd, it was just a muddy ditch. Before crossing, Pettigrew's line paused to realign itself, causing Trimble's line to close the gap.[134] Resuming the march, they crossed over the muddy gully. Next, they had to cross a field of ripened grain 800 yards to the Emmitsburg Road.

Confusion began in the wheat field. Lane's brigade, marching left of Lowrance, began to split. The 7th NC and half of the 37th NC went straight ahead while the other half of the 37th went left with the 28th, 18th, and the 33rd, to fill the place vacated by Brokenbrough. It

---

[134] (Ernsberger 2008) page 153. Ernsburger cites several men who remembered the pause. An officer from the 11th NC believed it was due to the Marshall's brigade getting too far ahead of the rest of the line. Another such pause may have occurred before they reached Emmitsburg Road.

appears that General Lane tried to bring the fractured brigade back together, but General Trimble issued an order that drove the two wings farther apart.[135] Thus, the 7th NC and half of the 37th NC eventually supported Lowrance's troops, while the rest supported Davis's brigade in Pettigrew's line. Colonel Lowrence had kept his brigade together, but the splintering of Lane's line would greatly reduce the strength of the Trimble line.

As they moved through the wheat field, artillery found the range on Lowrance's men. The men dressed right to fill gaps when men fell. Private James South, one of the Ashe County men in the charge, was knocked unconscious by a shell. Nearing the Emmitsburg road, they came within range of Yankee muskets. A strong Federal skirmish line had extended in places nearly half-way to the Bliss farm. The skirmish line was so strong at the Emmitsburg Road that many thought it was the main Federal line. Some considered the road to be the advanced part of the enemy works, which would be a fitting description given its proximity to the Federal line.[136] A heated exchange occurred, until the Federal skirmishers fell back.

Colonel Lowrance later wrote in his official report, "We advanced across a wide, hot, and already crimson plain." He further noted, "Now their whole line of artillery was playing on us, which was on an eminence on our front, strongly fortified and supported by infantry." He also noted, "…ere we had advanced over two-thirds of the way, troops from the front came tearing through our ranks, which caused many of our men to break."

---

[135] (Ernsberger 2008) Page 160. Ernsberger cites a letter from the commander of the 37th NC who stated that the gap already existed, and Gen. Lane ordered a left wheel, evidently to bring the brigade back together, when General Trimble ordered a bayonet charge which widened the gap.

[136] The term "enemy works" on this day should be interpreted with caution. The literal "works" was the stone wall occupied by the Union soldiers. Because of the field's layout and the strong Federal skirmish line at the road, many of the veterans referred to the road as part of the "works." Maj. Joseph A. Engelhard wrote of the battle saying Scales' brigade occupied the *"advance works"* of the enemy. It appears that the area from the road to the stone wall was what many of the veterans were calling the works, or advance works. This would be understandable. The road here was much closer to the Federal line than it was for Pickett's division. It would be natural for the veterans to use it as a marker.

"I wish the ground would open up so I could fall in it."

Making it to the Emmitsburg Road was not easy. They struck the road to the left of the angle in the stone wall. They were roughly 175 yards from the stone wall.[137] The road was lined on both sides by strong rail fences well within enemy musket range. The rifle fire was intense. Federal troops stood four-deep in places, firing devastating massed volleys at the exposed rebels. The road slanted away from them, but the brigade struck the road at an angle; the men on the left side of the line hit the road first and were in the road by the time the right side crossed.[138] The scene became chaotic as men toppled over the fence under heavy fire. Many climbed up the fence and were shot dead before they hit the ground. To add to the confusion, many of Pettigrew's men were already falling back. Pettigrew's much stronger line ahead of them had tried to claw their way to the stone wall only to be turned back by a torrent of lead. All unit cohesion evaporated, making command and control difficult. The bulk of Lowrance's brigade stalled at the road, took cover, and fired. Pvt. Scott B. Hutchison of Company G was heard to say, "I wish the ground would open up so I could fall in it."

Those who made it to the road saw a grim future ahead if they pressed forward. Pettigrew's line was already badly shot up. What was left of Trimble's line was not enough. The Yankees reinforced and poured heavy musket and short ranged artillery fire into them. Considerable artillery fire came from their right near the angle. The rebels had no other troops coming, no reserve, no support. The fog of war hangs heavy at this point. From all accounts, the bulk of Lowrance's brigade and Trimble's line in general did not make it past the road. With so few men left and no reinforcements coming, there was little they could do. Documentation exists that some men from the

---

[137] The is an estimate based on the author's observation of the field with the help of a Gettysburg guide. The exact spot where they landed in the road is not marked.

[138] Since the road angled away from them on the left, and the left of the line hit the road first, their line was evidently slanted quite a bit. Lowrance noted that they advanced "in rather an oblique line." They may have been trying to wheel right toward the angle, though that was not stated in Lowrance's report.

brigade and the 34th NC did cross and got near or into the enemy lines, mixed in with other units.

"I thought you were dead."

Ernsberger relates the story of Malachi Hovis, a Corporal in Company E from Lincoln County. Hovis found cover in a gully about 100 yards from the enemy line and fired at the Union troops. Hovis later wrote, "I got down in a gully beside a wounded Yankee I took for dead. I loaded and took ten good shots at the Yankees who were but 100 yards away. When I loaded and raised up for the eleventh shot, the Yanks were gone. When I announced this to some of the other boys, the dead Yankee raised up and said, 'You've got me this time' I said, 'I thought you were dead.'" The Yankees were not gone, and Hovis took his prisoner with him to the rear where he found Lt. James Tiddy who had been wounded in the foot. Hovis asked the Yankee and Pvt. Levi Wacaster, also wounded, to carry Tiddy back to the litter bearers.[139]

"Some of the 34th were captured at the enemy's works."

Another Company E man who survived the attack was Benjamin Carpenter who wrote a letter to the Raleigh Observer published on November 12, 1877. It states, "We charged and went into the works. Some of the men were on the works with the colors of the 16th North Carolina when Pickett's men ran (what did not surrender). This allowed the enemy to flank us and we had to cut our way back."[140] Men from other units in the brigade stated that some of Lowrance's men did reach the enemy works. One was Captain Hugh Guerrant of the 13th NC[141] which advanced on the 34th NC's left. T. D. Lattimore wrote, "Our brigade was in the second line under General Trimble, marching into the struggle with magnificent appearance, but was repulsed and driven back in disorder, as was every other command engaged in that destructive charge. Some of the 34th were captured at the enemy's works."

A lieutenant in the 38th NC, which advanced at the 34th's far left, stated, "A large portion of my own command reached the enemy

---

[139] (Ernsberger 2008) Page 225. Ernsberger quotes the memoirs of Reverend John Malachi Hovis.
[140] (Ernsberger 2008) Pages 225-226. Ernsberger quotes from Carpenter's letter to the Raleigh Observer, 11/12/1877.
[141] (Ernsberger 2008) Page 226.

works…I lost a large portion of officers and men killed and captured inside the enemy's works."[142] Another officer in the 16th NC stated that the left side of Scales' brigade touched the enemy works and went forward until the right side of the brigade did the same.[143] Lowrance indicated in his official report that, "we went forward until the right of the brigade touched the enemy's line of breastworks, as we marched in rather an oblique line[144]…Here many were shot down, being then exposed to a heavy fire of grape and musketry upon our right flank. Now all apparently had forsaken us. The two brigades…not numbering in all 800 guns…were the only line to be seen upon that vast field, and no support in view."[145] Colonel Lowrance rallied the men to fire at the enemy works from the road.

Dying for the colors.

The attack was failing. They had suffered too many casualties and had no support coming. General Trimble was severely wounded leaving General Lane in command. Pettigrew's line was falling back, causing men from Trimble's line to do the same. Lt. Colonel Gordon fell wounded and was struggling to keep the 34th NC intact. Major Twitty was also wounded. Lowrance's regiments were tangled and confused. They saw no hope for piercing the Federal line. Colonel Lowrence did not even have to order the retreat. The survivors began falling back. Some chose to surrender rather than risk being killed in the retreat. Colonel Gordon, suffering from a gunshot wound to the left leg, looked to the north and saw Federal troops advancing on their position and ordered the men to fire a volley. The 8th Ohio Infantry, the

---

[142] (Ernsberger 2008) Page 227. Statement made by Lt. Col. Ashford of the 38th NC who was himself wounded at the road but bore witness to the command as they went forward.

[143] (Ernsberger 2008) Page 231. Quoting Lt. William J. Edney of the 16th NC.

[144] Here, Colonel Lowrance himself seems to refer to the road as the outer part of the enemy works.

[145] It is possible Lowrance expected support. According to Lt. Gen. James Longstreet's memoirs, "The general order required further assistance from the Third Corps if needed, but no support appeared. General Lee and the corps commander [A. P. Hill] were there but failed to order help." (Longstreet 1992), page 393. This is one of several places in Longstreet's memoirs in which he blames Lee for the loss at Gettysburg.

unit that had dispatched Brockenbrough's brigade, charged and sent Lowrance's fought-out brigade flying to the rear.

The 34th NC's color bearer became the target. According to author Phillip Thomas Tucker (Tucker 335), "A shell exploded above the band of men, knocking the dazed color-bearer to his knees. 'Covered with dust, the blood trickling from a gash on his forehead.' A young North Carolina officer, despite being wounded, grabbed the flag before it touched the ground to avoid the ultimate disgrace. The Ohio sergeant demanded the colors from the injured officer, who was alone with an empty revolver. The wounded officer refused, and then dodged a bayonet thrust 'with great dexterity.' Sergeant John Miller then demanded, 'Surrender or I'll shoot you.' Instead, the Tar Heel officer made his own thrust with his sabre that cut the sergeant's wrist. Now 'Miller had to shoot [and] The southern [er] fell backward upon his banner [and] So tight was his grasp on the staff that Miller had to tear off the flag."[146]

Col. Gordon's wound was quite severe, and he needed help getting to the rear. He called on D. M. McIntire, the adjunct of the 38th NC who was serving on Col. Lowrance's staff, to help him. After the war, McIntire wrote, "Lt. Col. Gordon of the 34th N. C. regiment, being badly wounded within twenty steps of the works, called to me after the line had broken, to assist him to the rear, which I did, and the enemy doing their best to kill us, while on the way to the rear. Gen. Lane came up to us, and we three left the field together."[147] Another man who helped Gordon off the field was Pvt. Eli Franklin Pasour of the 37th North Carolina. According to a post-war letter, "Col. Garden [Gordon] was also wounded at or near the Yankee lines. He was Col. [Lt.Col.] - 34th NC. I helped him off of the field, for which he thanks me very much. He told me he was a British subject and did not want the damn Yankees to get a hold of him."[148]

The men fell back amid relentless cannon and musket fire. Several were killed or wounded as they retreated. In the rear, General

---

[146] (Tucker 2016), page 335. Tucker quotes an article in the Carolina Watchman dated September 15, 1887.
[147] This was found in a letter to the editor by D. M. McIntire, The Weekly Star dated 9/14/1877. (digitalnc.org)
[148] (Thornburg 1913) Letter by Pasour.

Trimble passed by General A. P. Hill as he was being taken off the field and said, "If Hell can't be taken by the troops I had the honor to command today, it can't be done at all!" Trimble's leg wound eventually required amputation.[149] General Pettigrew was also wounded and had three horses shot out from under him. The retreating rebels limped to the rear hearing the chant, "Fredericksburg! Fredericksburg! Fredericksburg!" by Federal troops happy to avenge that battle.

An accurate accounting of the 34th NC's Gettysburg casualties is impossible. Most of their casualties occurred on first day but identifying which were from the first day and which were from the third day cannot be done in most cases. Official reports put the total number of casualties at 116 but the wounded were understated. Records show 15 killed in action and 55 wounded. The regiment reported 46 captured, but 53 were found. Most of those taken prisoner were wounded men who were left behind, but an unknown number were taken prisoner near the enemy works on the third day. Many men were listed as Missing in Action for several months, eventually accounted for as prisoners of war. One was never accounted for, 1st Sgt. A. J. Webb. He was likely killed in action. The following are the known casualties from the Battle of Gettysburg:

Casualties from the Battle of Gettysburg
Killed in Action

John Abernathy	G	2Lt.	Joseph H Huss	E	Sgt.	
Joseph Carpenter	G	Pvt.	Allen M McInnes	K	Pvt.	
Jesse J Carter	F	Pvt.	Norman J McLeod	K	1Sgt.	
George M Clark	K	Maj.	Ibsom A Miller	D	Pvt.	
Levi Costner[150]	E	Pvt.	William Moore	H	Pvt.	
Titus M Elliott	K	Pvt.	Jackson Robbins	I	Cpl.	
Andrew Fulenviller	E	Pvt.	James Taylor	I	Pvt.	
Mills A Higgins	C	Pvt.				

---

[149] Due to the severity of his wound, Gen. Trimble was left behind with the wounded and became a prisoner of war.

[150] Levi Costner's information comes solely from a pension application. He probably enlisted around May or June of 1863 during which time there was no muster records.

Mortally Wounded

John Sr Bare	A	Pvt.	John R Steadman	I	Pvt.	
George J Huntley	I	2Lt.				

Wounded

Henry Atwood	A	Pvt.	James H McCall	G	Pvt.
William P Beam	B	Cpt	Nevin C McLeod	K	2Lt.
Noah G Bess	E	Pvt.	Andrew D Metcalf	E	Pvt.
William B Bess	E	Pvt.	Richard T Morris	H	Pvt.
John Brotherton	G	Pvt.	George W Norment	G	1Lt.
John M Collins	E	Pvt.	George M Overcash	D	Cpl.
Burwell T Cotton	K	Sgt.	William Patrick	A	Pvt.
Leonard Cranford	K	Pvt.	James W Riddick	F	Adj.
Whitson O Davis	B	Pvt.	Elijah W Sanders	K	Sgt.
William C Dennis	K	Pvt.	John M Sanford	G	Pvt.
Virgil H Elliott	F	Sgt.	James F South	A	Pvt.
Leonard Fowler	I	Sgt.	James T Steadman	I	Pvt.
William M Goodson	F	Sgt.	Francis L Twitty	C	Maj.
George T Gordon	Lt. Col.		Levi Wacaster	E	Pvt.
James T Griffin	I	Pvt.	Joseph Weaver	H	Pvt.
Jacob A Hogue	F	1Lt.	William T Wilkins	C	2Lt
Henry Jenkins	I	1Lt.	James Wood	I	Cpt.
Hamilton Koonce	A	Sgt.	Thompson J Wood	I	Pvt.
John Scott Lawing	G	Pvt.	George W Woods	A	2Lt.
William L. Lowrance		Col.	John F Yoder	E	Sgt.
Charles S. Martin	E	Pvt.			

Captured

William M Barnhardt	D	Cpl.	Joseph D Kennedy	I	Pvt.
Alexander A Cathey	G	1Lt.	George W Koone	C	Sgt.
John L Cathey	G	Cpl.	John Lemaster	E	Pvt.
George Cauble	E	Sgt.	John W Lutz	F	Pvt.

Henry E Clay	F	Cpl.	Bartlett Y Martin	A	1Lt.
George W Coggin	K	Sgt.	Orson Mays	I	Sgt.
Alfred W Cook	C	Pvt.	James M McDaniel	B	Pvt.
John H Crawford	I	1Sgt.	Carmi K McNeely	D	Cpt.
Marshall A Douglas	D	Pvt.	Jeremiah J Moore	K	Pvt.
John Eaker Jr	F	Pvt.	Ross J Moore	H	Pvt.
Samuel P Foster	C	Pvt.	James R Morrow	I	Cpl.
Daniel W Fowler	I	Pvt.	John A Newton	F	Pvt.
Jacob Friday	E	Pvt.	George W Parks	G	Pvt.
George F Fulbright	E	Pvt.	Moses P Petty	F	Pvt.
William J Gibbons	F	Pvt.	Andrew Jackson Powell	F	Pvt.
Francis M Green	B	Pvt.	Joseph A Ray	D	Pvt.
Marcus L Heavner	E	Cpl.	Matthew Reynolds	E	Pvt.
Phillip J Henson	I	Pvt.	John Richardson	A	Pvt.
John M Hodgins	D	Pvt.	Elisha C Sanders	K	Pvt.
Marcus A Holly	E	Sgt.	Miles A Stroup	F	Pvt.
Samuel Hoyle	E	Pvt.	Wiley Taylor	A	Pvt.
Freeman Hurley	K	Pvt.	James Tiddy	E	1Lt.
Abram C Irvin	F	Pvt.	John L Todd	G	Pvt.
Robert G James	B	Sgt.	William V White	F	1Sgt.
Eli Jenkins	I	Pvt.	Lawson M Williams	F	Pvt.
John Jenkins	I	Pvt.	Marcus L Withers	E	Pvt.
Henry Keeter	C	Pvt.			

Missing in Action

A J Webb	H	1Sgt.

"Humbug sir!"

The 34th NC was crushed when the battle was over. The field hospitals for Pender and Heth were located along the Chambersburg Road, mostly around the farms of the Lalu and Heintzelman families. Every farmhouse, barn, or outbuilding was crowded with wounded. It is estimated that wounded soldiers at Gettysburg outnumbered citizens twelve to one. Many of the 34th NC's men suffered in the crude hospitals. Lt. Alexander A. Cathey's leg wound was severe and was eventually amputated. The regiment's surgeon, John F. Miller, amputated John Newton's leg due to a canister-shot wound from the first day. The 20-year-old Cleveland County man survived his wound. Captain James Wood was recovering from his wounds received on July 1st. He had a gunshot wound that cracked his skull and an arm wound. Lt. Tiddy had been helped to the rear by Malachi Hovis's Yankee prisoner and Levi Wacaster. Tiddy faced the amputation of the front half of his foot and an awfully long recovery.

Pvt. Charles S. Martin related that he was hit by a piece of a shell that burst over his head struck him behind the left ear and across the neck and right shoulder causing him to be left for dead on the field. He was later found alive and taken to the hospital. He was three months in recovering. The scar from the wound was as wide as two fingers.[151]

The wounded Col. Gordon was taken back to the brigade field hospital where General Scales was being treated. The two spoke, and Scales asked what he thought of the fighting. Gordon replied, "The charge at Balakiva was a damned humbug, a damned humbug, sir!"[152] The 34th NC's experience at Gettysburg was bloody and demoralizing. Like the rest of the Army of Northern Virginia, they would never be the same.

"Woe is me, whose duty was to die!"

The men led by Trimble and Pettigrew that day were overshadowed by Pickett's division from the start. Virginia newspapers lauded Pickett's division and diminished the role of Pettigrew's and Trimble's troops. To their dying days, the veterans were bitter about the slight. They were angrier over the lack of credit for their courage than the defeat itself. They could accept defeat, but not an insult to their honor. For years after the war, articles appeared in North Carolina newspapers defending their part in the fateful attack. One of those slights came from General Longstreet himself. Longstreet is well-known for having opposed the attack. In the highly defensive account

---

[151] Martin's muster card after Gettysburg shows him "Absent sick." This was a often a general term that was used when a man was recovering from wounds. The wound is told of in a post-war account.

[152] Gordon was comparing the charge on Cemetery Ridge to the Charge of the Light Brigade at the 1854 Battle of Balaclava in the Crimean War. The encounter with Scales was found in an article titled North Carolina In the Civil War published in The Goldsboro Headlight on 12/12/1901. (digitalnc.org)

in his memoirs, he refers to Trimble and Pettigrew in a complimentary but ephemeral way, dedicating the bulk of his narrative to Pickett's troops and protecting his own immense ego. In recent years, some have begun calling it the Pickett-Pettigrew-Trimble charge, but full justice has yet to be done for the equally brave men from the Third Corps who fought that day.

General Longstreet did put it well when he wrote, "Weird spirits keep midnight watch about the great boulders, while unknown comrades stalk in ghostly ranks through the black fastnesses of Devil's Den, wailing the lament, 'Someone blundered at Gettysburg! Woe is me, whose duty was to die!'"[153]

---

[153] (Longstreet 1992) Longstreet's memoirs, page 403

Private Mills A. Higgins, The Rutherford Rebels - Company C, was killed in action July 1, 1863, at Gettysburg.[154]

---

[154] Photo courtesy Elliott Family Heritage by Ivarea Flack and Genevieve Elliott Gassner, 1976.

Robert Wells Crowder

Sergeant Robert Wells Crowder, The Floyd Rifles – Company F. Killed in action at Second Manassas.[155]

---

[155] Photo courtesy Van A. Hoyle

Flags of the 34th North Carolina

This flag was captured July 3, 1863 at Gettysburg. It was issued to them in the weeks after Chancellorsville before they started north to Gettysburg. It is not known what happened to their flag at Chancellorsville. Notice the eleven battle honors the 34th had already earned. Note that the Cold Harbor (Gaines's Mill) designation was spelled "Coal Harbor." In the Spring of 1864, the flag was part of an exhibition in New York City. In 1905, this flag was one of several flags returned to North Carolina by the U. S. War Department. In 2010 the NC Division of the Sons of Confederate Veterans funded the total conservation price and presented it to the North Carolina Museum of History where it is currently on display. (Photo and information courtesy of the North Carolina Museum of History).

This was one of several North Carolina flags made by Frances Johnson Devereux Miller. It was received by the QM Department on January 4, 1862. The flag was reportedly captured by the 2nd New Hampshire Infantry, but which battle is not known. The flag was said to have been kept by Cpt. George H. Colby of the 2nd NH. After his death, his widow agreed to return the flag to North Carolina. To date, researchers have not confirmed that the 2nd NH did capture the flag or determined where it was captured. Though tattered, it is now preserved and on display in the museum. (Photo and information courtesy of the North Carolina Museum of History).

This is the flag surrendered by the 34th North Carolina at Appomattox. It is a Confederate first National Flag. When it was surrendered at Appomattox it was on a stave that was field-made from a tree branch. It was also one of the flags returned to the state in 1905 by the War Department. Note several sections have been cut out, possibly by some of the men as souvenirs. The flag was apparently carried at Appomattox by Able Hartzog of Lincoln County who was Ensign and color bearer since October 25, 1864. (Photo and information courtesy of the North Carolina Museum of History).

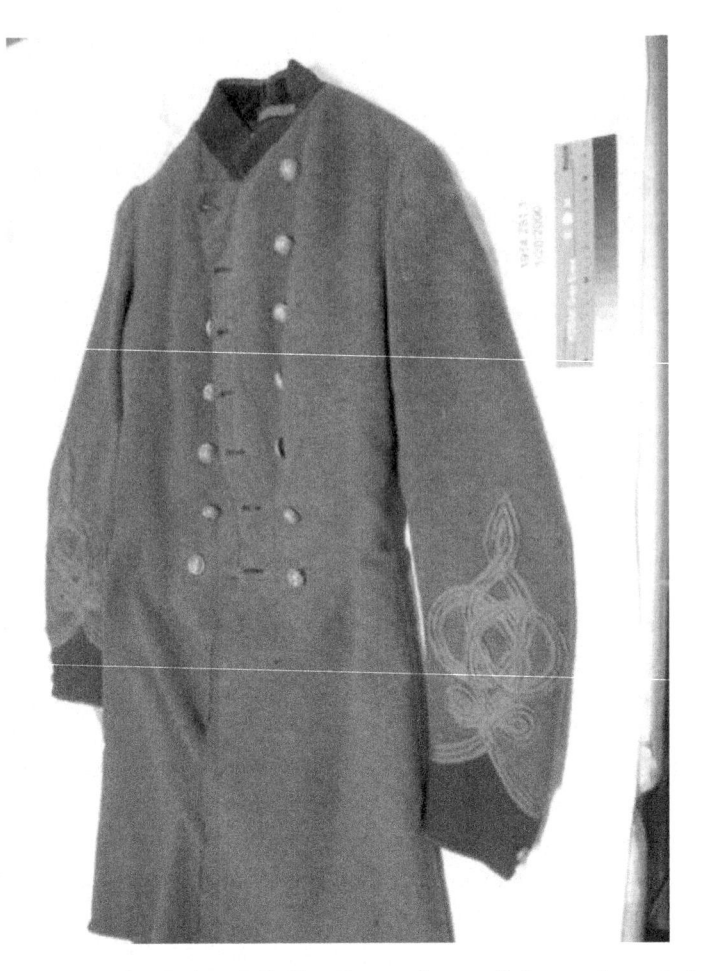

Frock coat worn by Colonel Collett Leventhorpe. It has unique dark blue facings on the collar and cuffs. The coat is currently on display at the North Carolina Museum of History. (Photo courtesy of the North Carolina Museum of History).

Chapter 10.
The Agony of Retreat

Late in the afternoon after the failed attack, the clouds burst in a torrential downpour. The surviving rebels huddled near Seminary Ridge and braced for a counter-attack, but Meade declined to go after Lee's wounded army. This gave General Lee time to plan and organize the retreat. There wasn't a minute to spare. Thousands of wounded men had to be evacuated. Wagon trains had to be assembled and supplies loaded. The logistical challenges of the retreat were far greater than what they faced getting to Gettysburg, and the stakes were higher. They were deep in enemy country with thousands of wounded men and truly little ammunition for the artillery. A poorly executed retreat would spell disaster.

The medical staffs toiled through the night as wagons were rounded up for the wounded. They were ordered to have the wounded ready to go early the next morning. The task was immense. Surgeons like the 34th NC's John F. Miller and his steward, Theo Twitty, worked tirelessly. In addition to treating wounds, they had to decide who was able to travel and who wasn't. Treatment became more like triage in many cases. Those who could walk were made ready. Others were prepared to be loaded onto wagons. Those too severely injured had to be left behind. Lt. Alexander A. Cathey's leg was amputated. Fearing he would not survive the trip, he was left behind. James Tiddy was also left behind following the partial amputation of his foot. Most of the 34th NC's POWs from Gettysburg were wounded men who were left in the field hospitals.

July 4th dawned quietly as neither side made any major moves. Preparations for the retreat continued. Lee decided to split up and use two routes for the retreat. The most direct route to Williamsport where they would cross the Potomac into Virginia, was southwest through Fairfield and Monterey Pass. The Pass, however, was steep, and the road was narrow and featured several sharp turns. It would be exceedingly difficult for the wagon train of the wounded to take this route, so the wounded would take the route west. They would travel back through Cashtown Gap westward, turn south near Greenwood to avoid Chambersburg, then move directly to Williamsport. The infantry columns would take the Monterey Pass route.

Of the estimated 1,300 injured men from Pender's division, roughly 700 were left behind. Volunteers were needed to stay with the wounded until Federal troops came with surgeons. Two men from the 34th NC volunteered, Privates George Parks from Mecklenburg County and George Fulbright from Lincoln County. Parks was slightly wounded himself. Parks and Fulbright helped care for their buddies until Federal doctors arrived. Dr. Miller and Theo Twitty boarded the wagons bound for Virginia.

The Column of Misery

Getting the wounded ready took several hours. Wagons were brought in, and volunteers began loading the wounded. A brigade of cavalry and an artillery unit arrived to serve as an escort. The job was made more difficult when shortly after noon, another heavy rain came into the area. Roads turned to mud, and everything was soaked. The canvas coverings on the wagons provided minimal protection for the wounded. Finally, about 4:00 p.m., wagons carrying the wounded began lumbering down Chambersburg Road. The wounded from A. P. Hill's Third Corps were first in line. By dark, they were heading through Cashtown Pass. It was after three the next morning before all the wagons were in line. Once they were all moving, the train stretched some seventeen miles.

General Imboden was placed in charge of protecting the train. He deployed detachments of cavalry and artillery every quarter of a mile. Pender's division was first, followed by Heth, then Anderson. The wounded of Scales' brigade were near the front. One ambulance near the head of the column conveyed two injured generals, Pender and Scales. Both were suffering leg wounds. Scales' wound appeared to be the worse of the two. They had come up through the ranks together, Scales following Pender up the chain of command. Were it not for their rank, they may have been left behind, but they were considered too valuable to fall into enemy hands. Another ambulance held the wounded Colonel Collett Leventhorpe. With him was his gravely wounded adjutant, Henderson Lucas.

The suffering of these wounded men is indescribable. Some of the wagons had straw for the men to lie on. Others laid on bare boards.

Roads were rough and muddy, and progress was slow. The wind and rain tried to drown out the cries of the suffering men, their pain made worse by every jolt on the road. All night, men wailed in agony. Many begged the teamsters to stop and leave them to die on the side of the road. William P. Beam, from Company B, was in one of those wagons suffering a gunshot wound to his chest. Every bump in the road was sheer torture. Cpt. James Woods carried shell fragments in his head, neck, and right hand. William Wilkins, from Company C, had gunshot wounds to the left thigh and left hand. Many others from the regiment had excruciating wounds that were amplified by the bone-jarring road. The column had to keep moving due to threats of enemy cavalry attacks. If a wagon broke down or got stuck in the mud, they left it, and the wounded crowded onto other wagons. Through the night, the column of misery made slow but steady progress as rain kept coming in sheets. Sporadic thunder and lightning added to the gloom. Men on horseback slept in the saddle. At times, some of the walking wounded came to a farmhouse and begged for food or bandages. Others didn't ask and just took what they could find.

By 4:00 a.m., the head of the train arrived at Greencastle, roughly 31 miles from Gettysburg. There, they were stopped by ax-wielding citizens who attacked the wagon wheels, disabling several wagons. Then, 100 Union cavalry troopers attacked part of the column. Several wounded men were captured before Imboden's men beat them back. After sunrise, the rain stopped, and the sun warmed the shivering men. The teamsters were soaked to the bone. They hadn't eaten or slept and were worn out from the long ride. Locals taunted them as they passed through the Pennsylvania countryside, but the column of casualties kept moving. Wagons broke down and were left in the mud. At times, there was no extra space on other wagons, and wounded men were left by the roadside. If a horse or mule became weak, some teamsters lightened the load by leaving wounded men on the side of the road. Local citizens came behind the train and provided aid to injured men left behind.

On the afternoon of July 5th, the front of the column crossed into Maryland. Some of the men may have felt safer there, but that feeling was short-lived. Part of the train was ambushed by Federal cavalry at Cunningham's Crossroads. The wounded from the 34th NC were fortunate. The attack came just as Pender's division had passed by. Two hundred Union troopers took the Confederates by surprise, capturing 134 wagons, 600 horses and mules, 2 artillery pieces, and 645 prisoners.[156] One of those captured was Colonel Collett Leventhorpe of the 11th North Carolina. His aide, Henderson Lucas, was also captured briefly, but the wagon driver turned off on a side road and escaped. Henderson survived the trip back to Virginia but succumbed to his wounds on July 25th in Martinsville. A post-war article stated, "Lying on the field, unable to move in consequence of his death wounds, he seemed to forget his sufferings and danger, and there are some of us who will never forget the sheering accent of his voice, as he encouraged all who passed him to press on to victory."[157] Leventhorpe's shattered left arm was treated by a Yankee doctor who recommend amputation, but Leventhorpe refused. He would spend the next eight months as a prisoner of war. His friends in England sent him money while he was in prison.

Around 6:00 that evening, the column started arriving at Williamsport, MD with Pender's wagons first in line. The train consisting of over 6,000 wounded men had travelled sixty bitter miles attacked repeatably by Union cavalry. At Williamsport, they planned to cross the Potomac into Virginia. The river, however, was flooded from the storms and could not be forded, forcing Imboden to stop. Four miles downstream at Falling Waters, Federal cavalry had destroyed a vital pontoon bridge. The army was stuck.

The small town was quickly overwhelmed by 5,000 wagons pulling into town. Every church or schoolhouse and many private homes were converted into hospitals. Doctors went to work caring for the wounded. Horses and mules were fed. Every field around town was full of wagons, animals, and troops. Local citizens were called upon to give aid to the wounded. Food was gathered, and beeves were killed. Dead horses were everywhere, inviting the pesky green flies. The threat of another raid by the enemy was a major concern, so cavalry and artillery units deployed.

---

[156] (Eric J. Wittenberg 2008) Page 22
[157] (Ernsberger 2008), Page 259. Written by Cpt. Louis Young and published in the Richmond Enquirer

Private Elijah Daves was dog-tired. The teamster from the 34th North Carolina couldn't remember the last time he had a good night's sleep. He had hauled every kind of freight for the rebel army; ordinance, supplies, equipment. He pulled into Williamsport with damaged human cargo. He had been behind the reins ever since leaving Gettysburg, half asleep at times, struggling to keep his team moving. His body ached from the exertion, but there was no time to rest. The only way across the Potomac was Lemen's Ferry. Three flat raft-like boats went across on cables attached at each end of the river. Two wagons and forty men could cross on each slow seven-minute trip. As soon as they got it running, wounded men were sent over. The first to cross were the wounded who could walk to hospitals in Winchester. Unfortunately, two of the rafts sank in the river, drowning some of the men. The able-bodied men set to work building pontoon boats for a new bridge.

The Battle of Williamsport
Elijah Daves and The Wagoner's Battle

On the morning of July 6th, word came that Buford's Federal cavalry were headed their way. General Imboden scrambled to arm as many men as possible. Any wounded man who could stand and fire a weapon was armed. About 700 injured men picked up muskets. Every available cavalry and artillery unit was deployed around town. Needing more troops, he recruited a few hundred teamsters and quartermaster troops, and organized them quickly into 100-man companies commanded by mostly wounded officers. Private Elijah Daves of the 34th North Carolina was one of the teamsters who took up a weapon. He had survived Gettysburg unhurt and had driven a wagon to Williamsport. By late in the afternoon, he and the rest of Imboden's rag-tag army of wagon drivers and wounded troops could hear artillery firing. With ammunition brought from the other side of the river, Confederate artillery answered. The ragged, desperate men were deployed in an arching semi-circle on the ridges around the town with artillery pieces supporting their line. They took full advantage of the terrain. The defensive position was quite strong considering its hasty construction.

Soon, they were engaged in a sharp battle with Buford's troopers. The motley army of wagon drivers and bandaged men held their ground for several hours against Buford's well-armed cavalrymen. Finally, Confederate cavalry reinforcements arrived and turned the Federals back. In the action, Private Elijah Daves, the 24-year-old teamster from Rutherford County, was killed. He was the only known casualty of the 34th North Carolina at the Battle of Williamsport, also known as the Wagoner's Battle.

The Infantry Retreat

The moment the fighting stopped in Gettysburg, the clock was ticking for Lee's army. If Meade could cut them off from Virginia, the war was over. Lee's army was badly weakened and did not have enough ammunition for another major battle. One third of Lee's Army had been killed, wounded, or captured. The day after the battle ended, General Lee requested an exchange of prisoners. Up to this point, the two sides had exchanged prisoners soon after battles ended, often within hours or a few days after the fighting. This time, the Federals refused. They had decided to end the practice of prisoner exchange to deprive the south of manpower. From then on, those captured would spend many months in prison. Lee's army would also be burdened with Federal prisoners on their way back to Virginia. The 34th NC marched away from Gettysburg leaving behind 53 men who were being marched off to northern prisons or treated in Union hospitals.

Hill's Corps was the first to leave Gettysburg, right behind the supply wagons. Near dark on July 4th in a heavy rain, they formed up and started marching down Fairfield Road. Anderson's division was first, followed by Pender, then Heth. Lowrance's survivors of the 34th NC were somewhere in the middle of the long gray procession trudging through the rain. They plodded along well into the night. Some found food at Fairfield; most went hungry, as did the 4,000 Federal prisoners marching with them. T. D. Lattimore never forgot that night spent slogging through the mud. He wrote, "The retreat from Gettysburg to Hagerstown, MD cannot be described. The soldiers were so completely covered with mud that the color of their clothing could not be distinguished."

The next day, July 5th, Federals found Lee's army gone from Gettysburg, leaving behind thousands of wounded. There, Privates Parks and Fulbright waited with the wounded. Federal troops came, and the injured rebels became prisoners. Federal surgeons came to treat the wounded. Private Moses Petty had a severe leg wound, but the doctors managed to save it. James Tiddy was there, minus the front half of his right foot that was amputated. Alexander A. Cathey and John Newton were both recovering from leg amputations.

"Our men did very bad in MD and Penn."

Progress was difficult after the rain started. Mud was knee deep in places. Company commanders struggled to keep their men together. Colonel Lowrance's regiment was in a terrible condition but kept going. He was still in charge of the brigade since Scales was in the wounded's wagon train. Despite the situation, their spirit was surprisingly high. They marched more like an army simply redeploying for a new mission rather than the badly defeated army they were. They marched much of the night over roads that grew worse as more men slugged through. Men slipped and fell in the mud; boots were sucked off their feet. They were splattered with mud from head to toe and soaked to the core. Teamsters driving the supply wagons in the front struggled. At times, the infantry had to stop while the wagon masters freed up wagons stuck in the mud. Ahead of the supply train was the survivors of Picket's division escorting prisoners.

Rain showers continued off and on for several days. There was little to eat, so they foraged what they could. In accordance with Lee's wishes, most behaved respectfully, but some did not. Some took anything they could find from local citizens including whiskey. Many were found drunk on the march. Lt. Burwell Cotton wrote, "Our men did very bad in MD and Penn. They robbed every house about such battle field not only of eatables but of everything they could lay their hands on. They tore up dresses to bits and broke all the furniture. I think a good many of our officers were drunk all the time. I have suffered much since I have been on the march. I do not think I can hold out much longer. Our army is badly whipped."[158]

Early July 6th, the lead units marched through the foggy Monterey Pass. It was a crucial point in the route, just twelve miles north of Hagerstown. Time was of the essence, so they marched through the day and into the night, approaching Leitersburg, MD by midnight. They paused for a very brief rest and resumed the trek,

---

[158] (Taylor 1994) Quoting from a letter by Cotton dated July 16th, 1863. NOTE: All letters from Cotton are from this source.

nearing Hagerstown by the morning of July 7th. The army was in danger of being trapped at the rain-swollen Potomac, and General Lee issued a plea to his troops calling for fortitude and endurance. The men went to work building a defensive line.

By July 10th, with their backs against the Potomac, the Federal army seemed to have them cornered. Lee's men had built a nine-mile defensive line as strong as the Federal line at Cemetery Ridge. Longstreet's First Corps was on the right, Ewell's Second Corps was to the left. A. P. Hill's Third Corp was in the center near the College of St. James. Instead of being a cornered prey, the defiant rebels dared Meade to attack. Meade, however, delayed while he brought up more troops, showing a healthy respect for the rebels who still had plenty of fight in them. At Falling Waters, a new pontoon bridge was being built to allow the army to escape back into the Old Dominion.

July 12th dawned with heavy fog. While infantry continued to strengthen their line, the pioneers kept working on the pontoon bridge. The river's water level was dropping, but it still could not be forded. Pioneers scoured the countryside looking for lumber for the bridge, stripping barns and houses. They also brought in pitch needed to seal the boats once constructed. It all took time, and time was not on their side. More Federal troops were arriving by the hour, and Yankee cavalry seemed to be everywhere, scouting, and probing lines. Scattered fighting occurred nearby at Hagerstown and Funkstown. Lieutenants John and Joseph Camp were taken prisoner in the Funkstown area. Private Henry Revel was captured near Hagerstown. These men may have been skirmishers or detailed men.

The little ferry at Williamsport was still their only way across. Most of the wounded from the original train were in Virginia by this time. Only the most seriously wounded were still in Williamsport. The ferry had done great service but was inadequate for Lee's infantry. It did bring in desperately needed supplies and ammunition. With the strong fortifications and replenished supplies, they could mount a stiff resistance to an attack. Rains continued to complicate their efforts. On the afternoon of the 12th, a sudden heavy thunderstorm came through, dumping more rain and adding to their problems.

The next day, it seemed that the long-awaited attack was coming as heavy skirmishing occurred all along the line. Still enduring periodic showers, the two sides sparred heavily at times, but no general advance came. The 34th NC held their part of the Light Division line south of Hagerstown and north-east of Williamsport. To the north was Ewell's Corps. To their south, Longstreet's Corps extended the line to the Potomac south of Downsville. This protected the Falling Waters crossing, where the pioneers were putting the finishing touches on the pontoon bridge which finally spanned the river.

Falling Waters, July 14, 1863

The night of July 13th, Lee's infantry began filing across the newly christened pontoon bridge at Falling Waters. Longstreet's corps slipped away from the line in the darkness and started for Falling Waters, replaced by Stuart's cavalry troops. Ewell's troops were closer to Williamsport where they would ford the river, since the water level had dropped there. Once again, heavy rain pelted the area as they made their way to the river. Lee ordered regimental bands to play to give the appearance nothing was happening and to mask the sounds of the movement. The men marched through the rain to Dixie, Bonnie Blue Flag, and other southern favorites. Federal bands answered with their selections, and a battle of the bands ensued. Stuart's cavalry rode along the lines talking and laughing loudly to make things appear normal. Bands on both sides played for hours, as rebel troops fell back away from the lines completely undetected by Federal troops less than 1,000 yards away.

The Light Division stayed in place while the bulk of Longstreet's and Hill's corps started marching. Finally, the Light Division started toward the river with Heth's Division behind as the rear guard. It rained all night, hard at times, but the rain helped conceal the movement. The marching columns and wagons struggled through the rutted-out roads. It took all night for Longstreet's Corps to cross the river. The men of the 34th NC with the rest of the Light Division marched slowly through the night and kept going past sunrise. They were mud-splattered and hadn't eaten or slept. They had answered Lee's call for fortitude.

"The writer and two men were all that escaped of his company."

At least the rain stopped. July 14th brought heaven-sent sunshine to the men of the Light Division. By 10:00 in the morning, Lowrance's brigade was halted two miles from the bridge waiting their turn to cross. The only men still north of the Potomac were from Heth's and Pender's divisions. Having marched all night, the men stacked arms and caught some shut-eye while waiting their turn. Their respite was short. Musket fire coming from behind them brought them back to their feet. Heth's men had been briefly attacked by two companies of Federal cavalry. They quickly opened fire on the Yankees, and the small Federal force was driven back. In a matter of minutes, the attack was over. The short attack, however, was costly. General James J. Pettigrew, the "Scholar General" from North Carolina, was mortally wounded.

Lowrance's brigade, roused by the skirmish, began filing toward the river with the rest of the division. But having gone no more than 300 yards, an order came from General Heth to turn back and support the rear guard. The skirmish had turned out to be only the beginning, and Heth needed help. Additional cavalry troopers led by General John Buford, the Union's Gettysburg hero, arrived, and a more serious engagement developed. Lowrance led his brigade back and took up a position right of center in Heth's line. Heth then ordered them to the extreme left. Lowrance moved his men at the double-quick. There, he found his men exhausted, but they held their part of the line prepared to give battle. Soon, Lowrance saw that the line to the right was giving way. The rebels were out-gunned by Union cavalry. Lowrance sent Lt. John D. Young of the 34th NC, serving as his temporary aide-de-camp, to rally them. After some time, the right held their ground.

Lowrance was then directed to take his men to the right to the high ground overlooking the river. At the top of the hill, he rode forward and surveyed the situation. To his dismay, he saw the entire rebel line in full retreat 300 yards to his rear with the enemy in pursuit directly between Lowrance and the bridge. He later learned that a general retreat had been ordered, but he had not gotten the word. His entire brigade was cut off from the pontoon bridge with no support. Lowrance was alarmed but never panicked. He quickly ordered his men to the rear to find a way across the river. They reached the river about three-quarters of a mile from the bridge and started toward it. Near the bridge, they found that the enemy had passed through the woods and blocked the way to the bridge, cutting them off a second time.

Lowrance somehow found a small avenue of escape, but the window of opportunity was closing. His men had to move fast. Unfortunately, many of them were exhausted and unable to keep up. Confederate artillery from across the river began firing at the Yankee troopers, providing just enough cover for the men to make it to the crossing. Those that could, fled across the bridge. After they crossed, the pontoon bridge was cut loose to float down the Potomac. Around 200 men from Lowrance's brigade were left on the northern banks of the river and taken prisoner, 44 of them from the 34th North Carolina.

It was a staggering loss. One man from the regiment was killed that day, Pvt. Robert A. Taylor, 23, from Lincoln County. His brother Thomas had died of disease the past December. They had volunteered together in September of 1861, both now sacrificed for a cause many were beginning to see as lost.

One of those captured was 27-year-old Captain Carmi K. McNeely of Rowan County. After the war he wrote, "We had had little to eat that day and were hungry. The Federal officer who had us in charge asked one of the prisoners if he had any money. On his saying no, the officer pulled out a twenty-dollar bill and gave him to buy something for all of us. He got some crackers and cheese and handed the remainder of the money back to the officer. When we offered to repay him he said, 'You don't owe me anything. The only thing I ask of you is to do the same for me if I ever become your prisoner.'" The kindness of the unidentified Union officer was never forgotten.

T. D. Lattimore wrote, "The thirty-fourth...was among the last troops to cross the river. Many were captured near the bridge, some crossing after the artillery duel began across the river. The writer and two men were all that escaped of his company." Burwell T. Cotton was able to cross before the bridge was cut loose. He wrote, "We retreated in the night but were overtaken and surprised by yankee cavalry next morning about two miles from the river. We formed and repulsed them but their infantry soon came up. Then a regular stampede occurred. Every man ran to save himself. They got a good many of us prisoners. Four out of our company." He also wrote, "They came very near getting me. I was exhausted having marched all night and mired knee deep. I never saw such a time before. I would have stopped and give up if I had not been afraid the yankees would have killed me."[159]

Col. Lowrance noted in his official report, "...the enemy had penetrated the woods, and struck the river between us and the bridge, and so cut off many of our men who were unwilling to try to pass and captured many more who failed from mere exhaustion; so, in this unfortunate circumstance we lost nearly 200 men."[160] Lowrance left a detailed account of the brigade's actions, carefully documenting his moves in obedience to General Heth's orders. He certainly did not need to feel defensive about the action. Colonel Lowrance was at his best this day. He acted quickly and guided his men out of a death trap. Without his leadership, the entire brigade would have been forced to surrender. Col. Lowrance particularly praised Cpt. John D. Young and Lt. Monroe Gillon for their gallant conduct during the fighting at Gettysburg and Falling Waters in his report.

Falling Waters was the insult added to the injury they suffered at Gettysburg. Col. Lowrance deeply regretted the loss of so many men at Falling Waters. Especially painful was the 44 men captured from his 34th NC.[161] Less than 100 men from the 34th NC crossed back into Virginia at Falling Waters.[162] It would take months to rebuild the once proud regiment. The following soldiers from the 34th NC were captured at the battle of Falling Waters:

Captured at the Battle of Falling Waters

William B Brown	H	Pvt.	Presley Norman	F	Pvt.
James A Cobb	H	Pvt.	Calvin Osborn	A	Pvt.
John Crow	F	Pvt.	James B Overby	H	Pvt.
Abraham Eaker	E	Pvt.	John H Peeler	F	Pvt.

---

[159] (Taylor 1994) Letter from Cotton dated July 16th, 1863 written from Bunker Hill, VA, now West Virginia.
[160] Roughly 500 were captured in all between the two divisions, 200 of them from Lowrance's brigade. Lowrance provided as much, or more, detail on the Falling Waters action than he did of the charge on July 3rd. It is apparent that Falling Waters was a painful event for him.
[161] Official reports show 43 captured but 44 were identified in the records.
[162] The exact number is not known, but 150 went into action on July 3rd and an unknown number of those were lost. With 44 captured at the river-crossing, they likely had well under 100 left.

Daniel Eaker	E	Pvt.	George W Pinson	B	Pvt.
William Fisher	I	Pvt.	James A Proctor	E	Pvt.
John Mc E Freeman	C	Pvt.	John L Putnam	H	Pvt.
John C Gantt	F	Pvt.	P G Putnam, Sr	H	Pvt.
James G Henson	I	Pvt.	Elijah Reynolds	K	Pvt.
Joseph Calaway H	I	Pvt.	Eli Russell	K	Pvt.
John Hodge	I	Pvt.	Jacob Sane, Jr	E	Sgt.
Martin S Hoyle	F	Pvt.	Jeremiah Shittle	C	Pvt.
William A Kilpatrick	D	Sgt.	Robert Smith	H	Pvt.
John W Ledbetter	C	Pvt.	David A Thompson	K	Pvt.
William Crook Lee	F	Pvt.	William H Turner	F	Pvt.
William M Long	H	Pvt.	T A Ware	H	Pvt.
Ahijah Oliver Lynch	C	Pvt.	Emory E Warren	F	Pvt.
Alexander McCall	G	Pvt.	William C Wesson	H	Cpl.
Carmi K McNeely	D	Cpt.	Adam Whisnant	F	Pvt.
D Walter Miller	H	Pvt.	John B Williams	A	Pvt.
William D Morris	K	Pvt.	John Womack	B	Pvt.
William Nelon	C	Pvt.	Perry Wright	F	Pvt.

Back at Williamsport, 300 wounded men were not well enough to travel any farther, so surgeons were forced to leave them behind. Dr. J. M. Gaines of the 18th Virginia Infantry was responsible for the wounded there, and General Lee asked him to remain with the men left behind.[163] One of those was Pvt. Levi Wacaster of Lincoln County.[164] Once the Federals took control of the area, a hospital was established at Hagerstown, and the men were transferred there under Dr. Gaines's supervision.[165] Later, they were transferred to better hospitals like the

---

[163] Dr. Gaines's list of the wounded under his care at Williamsport and Hagerstown is found in the Southern Historical Society Papers Volume XXVII, Richmond, VA, Jan. – Dec. 1899, Page 242-250. (Gaines 1899)

[164] Levi's initial Gettysburg wound did not appear very serious. We suspect that his condition had either worsened, or he may have participated in the Wagoner's Battle and was wounded a second time.

[165] Dr. Gaines kept a list of the wounded under his care at Williamsport and Hagerstown, nearly 300 men in all. Pvt. Levi Wacaster is the only member of the 34th NC on this list. One record for Levi says he was captured at Gettysburg, but Dr. Gaines's list shows that he made it to Williamsport.

one at Chester, PA. With little prospect of exchange, Levi and the others faced a long recovery.

On July 16th, the tattered survivors of A. P. Hill's Corps arrived at Mill Creek west of Bunker Hill and made camp. There, they found rest but still had little to eat. The next day, word came that the highly respected General Pettigrew had died at Bunker Hill. He was known as an intelligent officer and a true North Carolina gentleman. The next day in a hospital in Staunton, Major General William Dorsey Pender died two hours after the amputation of his leg. His fourth wound of the war had proved fatal. Burwell Cotton said of Pender, "I am very sorry we lost Gen. Pender He was a great Gen. and as brave a man as ever lived."[166] William Dorsey Pender was 29 years old.

Brandy Station – August 1, 1863

The 34th NC was soon moving again and marched into Culpepper around July 26th. After a few days of rest, they were marching to Orange Court House fifteen miles south. On the way there on August 1st, the little-known Second Battle of Brandy Station occurred. Here, the regiment once more found itself in trouble. Buford's Federal Cavalry attacked the part of Hill's line occupied by the 34th North Carolina.[167] The regiment was suddenly cut off by fast moving, heavily armed cavalry. Nearly surrounded and facing the possibility of having to surrender, the 34th North Carolina was saved by reinforcements that arrived just in time to drive the Yankee cavalry back. In the struggle, however, another seven men from the regiment were bagged by the speeding cavalry troopers:

Captured at the Battle of Brandy Station August 1, 1863

Levi Cox	A	Sgt.	James H Hudgins	C	Pvt.
Lorenzo A Daves	C	Pvt.	William W Sorrells	C	Pvt.
Jesse Eaker	E	Pvt.	Hiram J White	B	Pvt.
Bedford Hendrick	F	Sgt.			

---

[166] (Taylor 1994) Page 152, letter by Cotton dated August 8, 1863.
[167] Little has been written about this engagement, and details are hard to come by. The 34th may have been manning a skirmish line when they were attacked. Cotton's letter gives the most detail found.

Sgt. Theo Kistler of Company D was the only man listed wounded in the battle. Colonel Lowrence made only brief mention of the action at the end of his Gettysburg report, calling it a "skirmish with the enemy's cavalry." Burwell Cotton gave more detail in a letter to his brother, "I was in a cavalry fight on the 1st inst near culpepper but were defeated as usual. The yankee cavalry run our cavalry and the 34th N.C. & one South C. regt. were surrounded. I thought we would all be taken prisoner. Just at that time our cavalry rallied and were reinforced by one Florida Brigade of infantry & saved us. Our soldiers are getting very tired of fighting. The first thing a greater portion thinks about when there is a fight on hand is running."[168] Cotton's words are striking. Only a few weeks before, after Chancellorsville, they felt like they could conquer the world. Their confidence fell dramatically after Gettysburg.

With the short fight at Brandy Station, the Gettysburg Campaign was over. One demonstration of how hard the 34th NC had fought is the inventory of the regiment's munitions. Ammunition lost and expended since going to Pennsylvania included 3,252 rounds of .58 caliber bullets and 6,821 rounds of .69 caliber, a total of over 10,000 rounds. They also lost 49 .58 caliber rifles and 146 of .69 caliber.[169] Clearly, the 34th NC did their share of the bloody work at Gettysburg.

Thus, ended the great drama of the Gettysburg Campaign. The regiment was shattered at Gettysburg, suffered irreplaceable losses at Falling Waters and Brandy Station, and narrowly escaped complete capture twice. They nearly ceased to exist as a unit, limping into camp with only a few tired survivors. They had lost two-thirds of the men that went to Gettysburg including several officers and senior enlisted men. Many of those lost were veterans that could never be replaced. The regiment and the army would never be the same.

---

[168] (Taylor 1994) Page 151, Letter by Cotton dated August 8, 1863.
[169] The inventory was found in the records of Lt. Henry Jenkins. It is interesting that the regiment seemed to have been equipped with more .69 caliber rifles rather than the .58 caliber.

Captain Marcus Overton Dickerson, The Rutherford Rebels – Company C[170]

[170] Photo courtesy Robin S. Lattimore

Chapter 11.
To Fight Another Day – Recovering From Gettysburg and the Winter of 1863-64

The 34th NC spent the next three months with the rest of the division rebuilding at Orange Courthouse. Units that had been severely damaged were sometimes consolidated with other regiments, but enough core officers and men survived to allow the 34th NC to rebuild. On August 3rd, General Hill placed Cadmus Wilcox in command of the Light Division to replace the fallen Dorsey Pender. Wilcox was a career army officer who was breveted for bravery in the Mexican War. He was forty-seven, a life-long bachelor, and a former West Point classmate of Generals A. P. Hill, George McClellan, and George Pickett. He performed well on July 3rd supporting Pickett's division in the attack on Cemetery Ridge. When General Scales returned from his wounds, the 34th NC was part of Scales' Brigade, Wilcox's Light Division, of A. P. Hill's Third Corps.

In addition to the loss of manpower, the morale of the army was severely damaged. Desertions were up, and volunteering was down. In North Carolina, a peace initiative was gaining momentum led by William Woods Holden. The goal was to convince the Confederate leadership to negotiate an end to the war. Peace meetings were held across the state. Lincoln County and their neighboring Gaston County each hosted at least one peace meeting that summer. Rowan, Rutherford, and Montgomery Counties each had at least two.[171] Counter-meetings were also held by citizens who remained dedicated to southern independence.

The peace movement was denounced by Governor Vance who was strongly supported by North Carolina fighting men. On August 8th, the 34th NC held a patriotic meeting led by Colonel Lowrance.[172] The men were unified in denouncing Holden's peace initiative and reaffirmed their devotion to the war effort. They would accept only an honorable end to the war, meaning victory and southern independence.

---

[171] (Auman 2014) Pages 81-82. Details of the meetings were published in The Weekly Standard.
[172] The meeting was in conjunction with a larger convention held by North Carolina soldiers in Lee's army to denounce Holden's peace initiative.

One outspoken leader in the meeting was Corporal Hamilton Koonce of Ashe County. To encourage the men to stay strong, the men were reminded of the many who had died in the struggle.[173]

General Hill ordered daily drills and frequent inspections, giving the men a sense of normalcy. Food became more plentiful. Beef, bacon, potatoes, and vegetables were brought in. Pies were baked from the ample Blackberries in the area. General Lee reviewed the division in late August and issued a proclamation saying, "God is our only refuge and strength. Let us humble ourselves before him." Faith remained a sustaining influence for the war-weary veterans. A religious revival stirred the men in the late summer months. General Scales wrote to his wife saying that he was feeling better about the brigade's strength.

Some furloughs were granted. General Lee allowed one for every fifty men present. On the muster at the end of August, five men were on leaves granted by Colonel Lowrance, (one more than the regiment's allowance). Of course, there was grumbling over who got the coveted leaves. Lt. Burwell Cotton wrote, "Our Col. is very partial. He sent one from his old company and one who did not go the rounds in Penn. The officers were very much dissatisfied about it of course." This criticism seems unfair, given that of the five men on leave, none were from Lowrance's old company while three were from Cotton's company. A leave was granted to surgeon John F. Miller. He finally married his Goldsboro sweetheart, Sarah Lavinia Borden, on September 21, 1863. He was back on duty by the end of October.

In May, the 34th NC had gone to Chancellorsville with 507 fighting men. They marched into Gettysburg with 337. The muster taken at the end of August, two months after Gettysburg, showed 199 present which included many of the Gettysburg wounded who had returned. The total enrollment was 529. Fifty were absent without leave, and 18 had deserted since Chancellorsville. They reported 158 absent sick or wounded. Ninety-five were prisoners of war.[174] The Laurel Springs Guards, from Ashe County, had only four men present,

---

[173] (Crawford 2001) Page 122.
[174] Most of those being held as prisoners of war were listed "Missing in Action" for several more weeks. They are counted here by their correct status for accuracy's sake.

First Sgt. Hiram Stampler and three loyal privates. Of the 50 AWOL's, 27 were Ashe County men. Most of them never returned. For the rest of the war, this company continued to struggle with desertion. These men were the first to become disaffected by a war started over the institution of slavery that few of them had anything to do with.

Captain Joseph C. Byers

Captain Joseph Byers had been as steadfast as any man. He helped organize the Sandy Run Yellow Jackets and was elected Captain in April of 1862. He led his men all the way to Gettysburg. His story was told in a post-war article written by his friend James C. Elliott, a Cleveland County resident who served in the 56th NC. Byers was eligible for promotion to a field grade position, but his promotion had not come through. Disgruntled, he deserted on September 1, 1863, and started for home. He was arrested near Richmond and brought before the court martial which reduced him to a private.[175] William P. "Posey" Beam replaced him as Captain of the company. Byers never lost favor among the men. He was a tried-and-true veteran who was respected no matter his rank.

Prisoners of War

The Union army was not fully prepared for the number of prisoners it would house following their change in policy concerning exchanges, so a new prisoner of war depot was ordered to be built at Point Lookout, Maryland. Until the prison was ready, the men were held in other facilities. Those with severe wounds were sent to hospitals like the one in Chester, Pennsylvania or David's Island, New York.

Thirty-three men from the 34th NC were sent to Baltimore, probably to the Baltimore City Jail which temporarily held rebel prisoners.[176] They were transferred to the newly opened Point Lookout prison in August, some of the first prisoners sent there. Twenty-four of

---

[175] Forest City Courier December 19, 1929 (digitalnc.org). The article was titled "Officers of Co. B 34th Regiment C.S.A., by James C. Elliott. The article agrees with Byers' record except for the date of his desertion and reduction in rank. According to the record, Byers deserted September 1, 1863. Elliott stated he deserted in March of 1864. The records also show he was reduced to a private in October of 1863, the same month Posey Beam was promoted to captain.

[176] (Speer 1997) Page 324.

the regiment's men were held temporarily at Old Capital Prison in Washington D.C. This building served as the Capitol of the United States from 1815-1819.[177] They were also transferred to Point Lookout in August. At least twenty-one men from the 34th NC arrived at Fort McHenry near Baltimore on July 6. Fort McHenry was a star-shaped coastal fort. Its historical significance was its role in the War of 1812, when the fort's flag inspired Francis Scott Key to write the Star-Spangled Banner. Six days later, they were sent a day's boat ride to Fort Delaware, an imposing five-sided granite structure on Pea Patch Island. They were transferred to Point Lookout in October.

The prison pen at Point Lookout was ten acres surrounded by a board fence with a parapet at the top for guards to patrol. A second smaller pen next to it housed officers. There were no barracks in the prison. They were housed in tents. The prison sat on a patch of land that jutted out into the Chesapeake Bay. Much of the ground was covered with white sand which caused some of the men to be temporarily blinded in the bright sunlight. With only tents, men suffered from intense cold in the winter. The tents had stoves, but firewood was severely rationed. When the prison eventually became overcrowded, some were transferred to Elmira. By the end of the war, 50,000 prisoners passed through Point Lookout. About 4,000 of them died, giving Point Lookout one of the worst reputations of any of the Federal prisons.[178]

Five men from the 34th NC died in prison by the end of August. Private Joseph Ray's leg had been amputated. He died at Hart's Island, NY on July 31. Corporal Henry Clay also died of his wounds. Privates Ross Moore and Elijah Sanders both died of disease at Fort Delaware. Private Andrew Jackson Powell died of disease at David's Island, NY. Alexander A. Cathey survived the amputation of his leg.

Captain Carmi McNeely and Lieutenants Bartlett Martin and Joseph Camp were sent to Johnson's Island on Lake Erie. This prison housed officers and covered sixteen acres. The prison wall surrounded

---

[177] The building stood until 1929. The site is now occupied by the U. S. Supreme Court building.
[178] (Beitzell 1983) This book provides much information on Point Lookout including statistics and correspondence.

twelve two-story barracks for the prisoners. Over 15,000 prisoners eventually passed through, with the population never exceeding 3,200. Only 200 died there, giving Johnson's Island one of the lowest mortality rates of the northern prisons.

Private John Jenkins

Private John Jenkins of Company I found a way to avoid a long prison stay. Jenkins was a conscript assigned to the 34th NC just prior to Gettysburg, where he was captured. While being held at Fort Delaware, Federal authorities took Jenkins to a private room and asked him four questions: "Do you wish to be sent south as a POW for exchange?" Jenkins answered no. "Do you wish to take the oath and be sent north to work on public works, under penalty of death if found in the south before the end of the war?" Jenkins answered no. "Do you wish to take the oath and go to your home within the lines of the U. S. Army under like penalty if found beyond those lines before the end of the war?" He answered no. "Do you wish to take the oath of allegiance and enlist in the Army of the United Sates?"[179] Jenkins answered yes and became a Private in the U. S. 3rd Maryland Cavalry.[180] In March of 1864, the unit was transferred to New Orleans and was preparing to go into battle when Jenkins deserted. He was not heard from again by either army.

Stalemate

The two armies in Virginia were stalemated. Federal troops across the Rapidan River stood guard as pickets from the two sides bantered and bartered for newspapers, coffee, and tobacco. In mid-September, Longstreet's two divisions were sent to Tennessee to reinforce Braxton Bragg's army. Two Federal corps were also reassigned, bringing the Union's numerical advantage in Virginia down considerably. Lee's army was bringing in new recruits. They were

---

[179] (Randolph W. Kirkland 2002) The book references the four questions asked each prisoner who volunteered for the US Army or Navy, per President Lincoln's directions. The passage does not reference Private Jenkins, this is an inference. It was Lincoln's policy was that the questions be asked in private with the soldier signing his name in a ledger with the questions to assure his action was voluntary.

[180] This was the only unit made of former Confederate prisoners that was sent south to fight in the war.

mostly conscripts, but at least they were gaining strength. The 34th NC's progress was slow. They added only 22 new recruits the first four months after Gettysburg. Col. Lowrance remained a steady leader. He wasn't flashy, rarely got his name in the papers, but he was exceptionally reliable and became General Scales' right-hand man. Scales' wounds continued to hinder him. When he needed someone to take his place, he turned to Colonel Lowrance.

"...one tolerable good soldier to be shot."

Rising desertion rates forced the army to impose stricter discipline. General Scales noted that 15 to 20 men from the division were shot for desertion that summer. On September 26th, a 34th North Carolina man faced the firing squad. John Thomas volunteered in September of 1861, in Montgomery County. He had been present on every muster and fought his way to Gettysburg. Lt. Cotton wrote, "Two were shot last Saturday and one of them was a member of our company viz John A. Thomas." Cotton noted, "He deserted sometime in August and was taken up near the state line. I learn the crowd that he started with have got home. Some of them will meet the same fate if they catch them. I think it will be a warning to others. I do not think Thomas would have deserted if it had not been for Bright's Union meeting in Montgomery so the Union…has caused one tolerable good soldier to be shot."

Bristoe Station and Mine Run

Seeing the numerical odds improving, General Lee decided to take the offensive. On October 9, the Light Division was marching. General Scales' health kept him from joining the campaign, so Colonel Lowrance rode at the head of the brigade with Lt. Col. Gordon leading the 34th NC. They marched for two days. The roads were dusty and dry, but it was perfect marching weather. They arrived at Culpepper on October 11th. The Federal army had abandoned the town when they learned of Lee's advance. The Light Division reached Warrenton around dark on the thirteenth where they were supplied by the wagon trains. At Greenwich, they marched past campfires and trappings left behind by Union troops. As the division marched south toward the Rappahannock River, the divisions of Heth and Anderson continued past the river and turned east toward Bristoe Station. General Hill, anxious to strike a decisive blow, launched an uncoordinated attack that did not involve the Light Division. Heth's and Anderson's divisions suffered heavy casualties in the Union victory at Bristoe Station.

The campaign did force the Union army back, and they destroyed a large quantity of supplies. For the next several rainy days, the men of the 34th NC joined the division in tearing up several miles of railroad track from Bristoe to the Rappahannock. When they finished, they set up camp along the south bank of the river as temperatures were dropping. Food was in short supply, and men had few coats and blankets. Shoes, for those that had them, were in tatters. The camp became cold and dreary. General Hill was often seen riding alone wearing a long black cape.

On a cold November 7th, Federal troops caught Ewell's men off guard at Rappahannock Station and took 2,000 of his men prisoner. The Light Division built a line of entrenchments on the south banks of the Rapidan and were placed in a thirteen-mile line to the left of Ewell's corps. On November 24, President Davis visited and reviewed Hill's corps, praising them for their fortitude. Two days later, Federal troops waded across the icy Rapidan. The Light Division marched behind Mine Run to man the earthworks there. The atmosphere was tense for several days, as the men tried to stay warm and alert. Lee grew tired of waiting for Meade to move and ordered an attack. The men moved out after dark November 30th to their assigned position. That night, an icy wind caused intense suffering. At dawn, the men rushed forward finding only abandoned Yankee camps. The men pursued, but Meade got away, ending the Mine Run campaign. The men returned to their winter quarters along the Rapidan.

The 34th NC suffered few casualties in the actions. Pvt. James Williford of Rowan County was wounded during Mine Run, his second injury of the war. This time, he suffered a gunshot wound to the shoulder that kept him out of action for a year. Lt. Col. Gordon suffered his third wound of the year. At Gettysburg, he was shot in the left leg. Around the middle of September, in an incident not recorded, he was shot in the right foot. On October 22, he was hospitalized for another gunshot wound to the left leg. His wounds made future service difficult, and he would be hospitalized several times over the next few months.

Christmas of 1863 was surprisingly upbeat considering the circumstances. The camp was relatively quiet. At the end of the year,

310 men were present in the 34th North Carolina. Seventy-nine of their friends were languishing in Yankee prisons, most at Point Lookout. Morale was still low, and many considered deserting. But the regiment, as did the army, had a core of dedicated veterans who were determined to do their duty. Through victory and defeat, it was these men that kept the fight going.

"...shall he be executed in this condition?"

Pvt. Wiley Bare from Ashe County deserted in January of 1863, and was arrested several months later. On December 12th, Wiley was sentenced to death. When he learned of the sentence, he became, "partially deranged" and "insensitive to everything." His case was appealed to President Davis, but no pardon was granted. General Scales was inclined to intervene and wrote to the authorities, "I learn further that he has been for some time past subject to these spells. If he continues so up to the day of execution, shall he be executed in this condition?" The regiment's surgeon John Miller also wrote on Wiley's behalf, "I certify that I have carefully examined Pvt. Wiley Bare...and find him laboring under what appears to be partial derangement of his intellectual facilities. He has presented these symptoms of great nervous excitement, such as spasms, since he has heard of the decision of his case." He also wrote, "How much of these symptoms may in his case be feigned I am unable to determine. It has been reported to me that he was similarly afflicted before the war, but I have no personal knowledge of the fact."[181]

The year ended with three of the regiment's men under sentence of death. Wiley Bare, Calvin Woodie, and George McSwain were all to be shot by firing squad on Saturday, January 9, 1864.

Calvin Woodie

Ashe County resident Calvin Woodie had been granted a leave early in 1863, but did not return. The Court Martial sentenced him to death. His case was being appealed, but Calvin didn't wait to hear the answer. Around January 4th during the night, he asked to go to the sink (latrine) and ran away. The guard's gun misfired, and the condemned man fled into the darkness. He made his way into enemy lines with frost-bitten feet but was glad to be alive. Colonel Lowrance wrote a

---

[181] Dr. Miller seemed to suspect that Wiley was feigning derangement.

report stating that he had ordered the prisoner tied hand and foot and kept in vigilant guard. Lowrance recommended the officer in charge be punished for neglect of duty.[182] Woodie's escape turned out to be unnecessary. He was pardoned in February.

Saturday, January 9th came. Wiley Bare and George McSwain awaited their fate in the guardhouse. Early that day, Dr. Miller wrote a letter recommending further evaluation of Wiley Bare. Wiley was given a one week stay of execution. George McSwain received no reprieve.

George W. McSwain

George McSwain was 5'8" tall, had red hair, and was 35 when he enlisted in Shelby in October of 1861. He fought through the Seven Days battles and deserted August 1, 1862. He returned in March of 1863, and was convicted of being Absent Without Leave and given 15 days under guard with bread and water. He deserted again a month later and was arrested around the middle of November. This time, the sentence was death.

"God bless my wife and little children. Farewell."

Too often, the assumption is that men deserted out of cowardice. To the contrary, most were more afraid of being called a coward than of being killed in battle. Men like George McSwain deserted because they had families back home who needed them. He had sworn an oath to the Confederate States of America, but he also had a duty at home. By this stage in the war, times were very hard back home. McSwain, like many, received a letter from his wife that told of the hardships she faced. McSwain was a yeoman farmer. He did not have wealth to provide for his family in his absence or slaves to plant crops and help them through the winter. He was no coward. He fought. His crime was caring more about his family than the war. Days before his sentence was carried out, he wrote his farewell letter to his family: "Hannah, Dear wife and dear children:[183]

It is with painful regret that I have to say to you in way of writing my last letter that I ever expect to write in this world to you, as my days are

---

[182] (Perry 2012), Page 55-56. Lowrance's letter was in reply from General Hill who inquired who was responsible for the escape.
[183] http:\obigenealogy.com George Washington McSwain by Orville Boyd Jenkins

but few that I have to spend in this unfriendly world, as I expect to part this life next Saturday by sentence of a general court martial to be tied down to a stake on that day the 9th of this month, and shot to death with muskets. But little thought I had of this when I volunteered in the service of my country to protect my home and family that my life would be taken by my own people simply from absenting myself from my post with the view of protecting my little helpless children and affectionate wife who are as near and dear to me as my own life. Hannah, I was in very good heart and didn't think they would shoot me until yesterday morning. My sentence was read to me that I had to be shot next Saturday. It washed against me like the raging billows against a lonely rock in a sweeping storm, and I carefully examined myself and I feel well assured that when I leave the world that I will be better off than here. But to my little children and affectionate wife may the Lord prepare and fit them to meet me in heaven, for there will be no more parting of husbands and wives and dear children, but be rest forever. Hannah, dear wife, and dear little children, and I never expect to see you anymore in this life. My prayers are that you will meet me in heaven. Do the best you can, and may God in his mercy rest and remain with you forever. Dear wife, don't grieve nor trouble after me, for I feel that I am going to a better world and be at rest. Then I won't be here to be punished any longer. My afflictions have been severe, and I feel that I will be better off when I leave this world. Tell all my friends farewell for me, and farewell dear wife, farewell dear children. Prepare to meet me in heaven. I will close by saying, God bless my wife and little children. Farewell.
[Signed] George W. McSwain"[184]

On Saturday, January 9th, the men of the regiment lined up to witness George McSwain's execution. It was a cold gloomy day, the coldest day of the entire month. Temperatures were in the teens at sunrise and near zero by dark. Charles J. Hamrick and William Jasper Jones were chosen for the firing squad. Hamrick was relieved from the terrible duty because he was related to McSwain. It is said that Jones delayed pulling the trigger, so McSwain was shot before Jones fired.

---

[184] (Jones 1920) Letter from George McSwain to his wife Hannah.

Hamrick and Jones both said that McSwain was one of the best men in the company.

Wiley Bare

For Wiley Bare, his one-week reprieve was crucial. A second evaluation was done by the surgeon of the 38th North Carolina, Dr. P. W. Young, who wrote, "I regard his condition as critical and he cannot in my opinion survive but a few days without a change for the better and under the most favorable circumstance I do not think he will recover for a period less than ten or fifteen days." Fortunately for Wiley, he managed to regain enough command of his faculties to escape from the guardhouse. On February 4th, Wiley made it into enemy lines. He had a sprained wrist and frostbitten feet, but the Federal authorities made no mention of an impaired mental state. Wiley was released on oath and made his way back to Ashe County.[185]

William H. Abshear

The regiment had one more execution to witness. William H. Abshear, from Ashe County, had served through 1862, and had been given a furlough in February of 1863. He did not return and was arrested, found guilty of desertion, and sentenced to death. He was the third and last man from the 34th North Carolina to be shot for desertion. The sentence was carried out on Monday, April 5th.

Whether the executions had the desired effect seems debatable. From October through December, not a single man from regiment deserted. In January-February, after two men from the 34th had been executed, eight men deserted. Seven of them were from Ashe County who all deserted together on February 8th. If anything, the executions may have had the opposite effect there, as the men grew increasingly disheartened over the war. Back home in January of 1863, large numbers of broken-down cavalry horses were turned loose on Ashe County to graze. Worse than the horses, however, were the soldiers taking care of them. They took grain and fodder, chickens, hogs, anything they wanted, at gun point at times. In the winter of 1863-64, General Longstreet's men were camped in Eastern Tennessee, and his foraging parties came through Ashe County taking livestock and wagon

---

[185] It seems odd that two of the three condemned men escaped the guard house in separate incidents. It appears they were not heavily guarded. Wiley went on to raise a large family and lived to old age in Ashe County.

loads of corn and grain desperately needed by the families. When the people resisted, they were bullied and even beaten.[186] Many of the citizens described them as being worse than the Yankee troops that had already been through.

In 1863, the Confederate Congress responded to criticism of the exemptions allowed under the Conscript Law. They added restrictions to the "Twenty-Slave" rule and required a $500 fee for an application. In February of 1864, they dropped the number of slaves to 15 but added more restrictions. They also abolished the practice of hiring substitutes and enacted price controls. The Tax-In-Kind law remained in effect, burdening poor rural families. Collectors frequently abused their power and took beyond ten percent of the family's crops and livestock. Families struggling to survive could ill afford to see food taken from their tables. Many of the poorer families saw the Confederate government as more oppressive than the one they had seceded from. Life for them had been tolerable before the war. Now, they were growing desperate.

Galvanized Yankees

January was very cold at Point Lookout where many of the regiment's men were held. Their tents were not adequate protection from the cold. They never had enough firewood, blankets, or clothing. It was common for men to wake up in the mornings with a man beside them who had died during the night. In January of 1864, men were offered a way out of their bleak existence. The Union army was recruiting Confederate prisoners. This helped relieve overcrowding in the prisons and provided men to garrison western frontier forts, freeing those troops to come back east. Those who volunteered came to be called "Galvanized Yankees." That January, six men from the 34th North Carolina took the oath of allegiance to the United States of America and joined the 1st U.S. Volunteers. All but one had volunteered in 1861. More would join later in the year. Soon, these men would head west. The war would go on without them.

"Murder, Violence and Treason"

Back in Virginia, the men soldiered on through the winter. In February of 1864, the Montgomery County men heard about rising

---

[186] (W. R. Trotter 1988) Pages 142-143.

levels of violence back home. The Bill Owens band had again struck Pleasant Simmons's home. According to a newspaper report, at least four members of the band, including Owens himself, went to Simmons's Montgomery County home late at night and proceeded to clean out the smokehouse.[187] Mr. Simmon's friend Jacob Sanders and his wife were staying with Simmons that night. As Owens's men were robbing the smokehouse, Simmons and Sanders grabbed guns and went out to confront the robbers. In a brief shootout, Sanders was killed, and Simmons was mortally wounded. The wife of Mr. Sanders came out to help her dying husband but was ordered back by Owens's men who called them all a "...damned set of secessionists!" Several Sanders men from Montgomery County were members of the 34th NC and were related to the slain Mr. Sanders.

Bill Owens was finally captured in April. The information on his whereabouts was obtained from his wife who was tortured by his pursuers. Owens was held in the Randolph County jail.[188] His trial was moved to Chatham County in early 1865. The judge there refused to hear the case, for fear of reprisals. On March 22, 1865, a group of armed citizens forcefully removed Owens from his jail cell. Without judge or jury, Bill Owens was shot to death. Throughout the region, similar bands roamed the countryside, and more incidents of violence occurred. In September of 1864, a group led by a man named Northcutt was pursued and caught in Randolph County. Tried by what was described as a "little drumhead court martial," he was promptly executed. Such scenes of violence at home contributed to increased desertion rates, especially among the regiment's Montgomery County soldiers.

"...more than ever determined."

As Spring of 1864, approached, patriotic meetings continued to be held in the army. Colonel Lowrance exhorted his men to stay the course. The regiment resolved on March 12th to be, "...more than ever determined to be free from the power and dominion of the wicked foe,

---

[187] An article titled "Murder, Violence and Treason" published in The Western Democrat / March 8, 1864 (digitalnc.org). The story is also related in Victoria E. Bynum's The Long Shadow of the Civil War.
[188] Owen's capture was reported in The Fayetteville Observer / April 28, 1864 in an article titled "Capture of a Noted Outlaw. (digitalnc.org)

who daily seek our destruction as a nation and people." In the race for Governor, William W. Holden was running against Gov. Vance. Holden was gaining support by challenging the Davis administration. The fighting men in this regiment stood firmly with Governor Vance.[189] The Governor appeared at least twice to the North Carolinians in Hill's Corps over the winter, making light hearted speeches to try and cheer the gloomy troops.

Bureaucracy

Colonel Lowrance's appointment to the Colonelcy of the regiment had still not been confirmed by the War Department, so General Scales wrote a letter on Marth 27th to recommend that the promotion be finalized. Scales noted that Captains Wilson and Hoey had both resigned, leaving nothing to hinder the appointment.[190] Though it had been over a year since Sam Hoey's resignation, the department had not acted, the bureaucracy in Richmond being even less efficient than Washington's. Finally, three weeks after Scales' letter, Secretary of War James Seddon approved Lowrance's appointment, back-dating the effective date to February 10, 1863, the date of Sam Hoey's resignation.[191]

Special Forces

The nature of the war was changing. Conscription was bringing men into the ranks, but most were older men who found it difficult to bear up under the strain of hard campaigning. They also had wives and children at home to worry about. They did not have the same enthusiasm for the war that the original volunteers had. The northern army, on the other hand, had an endless supply of fresh well-equipped young troops ready to fight and increasingly confident of success. The south was forced to use its resources more efficiently. Part of that effort was a more prolific use of trenches and fortifications instead of open-field lines of battle. Another change was the creation of Sharpshooter battalions in the Spring of 1864.

Each brigade formed a battalion of hand-picked men for the Sharpshooters. From each regiment, men were chosen who best

---

[189] (Crawford 2001) Page 138.
[190] Steven Wilson resigned shortly before Col. Riddick was killed. Samuel Hoey resigned February 10, 1863.
[191] Col. Lowrance formally accepted the appointment August 31, 1864.

possessed the qualities of the ideal soldier. They were men who had shown gallantry in battle and had a reputation of devotion. They were physically fit, skilled marksmen, and obedient to orders. The officers chosen to lead them were proven combat leaders. In Scales' brigade, the Sharpshooters were led by the 34th North Carolina's Captain John D. Young. Captain Young had only been with the regiment for a year but had shown himself a strong leader. He had served on Scales' staff and was Col. Lowrance's Aide de Camp in the Gettysburg campaign. His actions at Gettysburg and Falling Waters led to his opportunity to lead the Sharpshooters.

The Sharpshooters were, in Young's words, the "the spike-head of the division." They were the tip of the spear, the "special forces" of the Confederate army. They would be at the forefront of every action and called upon for special, often dangerous assignments. As such, they were given a level of autonomy other units did not enjoy. They camped separately from the rest of the brigade, given the best arms, and were exempted from the onerous picket duty except in the face of the enemy. They were assigned the right of the column, the front of every advance, and the rear in retreat. Wherever the most danger existed, you would find the Sharpshooters. Two of the best narratives concerning the Sharpshooters came from the post-war writings of Captain Young[192] and Major W. S. Dunlap[193] of McGowan's Sharpshooters.

According to Young, each battalion had a commandant, eight commissioned officers, ten non-commissioned officers, one hundred and sixty privates, four scouts, and two buglers. They were divided into four companies and then further divided into groups of four. Young describes these small groups of four as "something like the comrades de bataille of the French army." They messed and quartered together

---

[192] Captain John D. Young wrote an extensive article published in the Philadelphia Weekly Times January 26, 1878 titled "Annals of the War, Chapters of Unwritten History, A Campaign with Sharpshooters: The organization of the Riflemen in the Confederate Service, Their work in the Wilderness and at Petersburg, Personal Reminiscences of some distinguished Confederate Officers."

[193] Major Dunlap wrote Lee's Sharpshooters, The Forefront of Battle, a Story of Southern Valor with Robert F. Ward. Originally published in 1899, Published in 2012 by Forgotten Books, www.forgottenbooks.org.

and were never separated in action except by disability or death. Thus, the men came to know and rely on one another, essential elements of small units designed for outpost fighting and special assignments. They were self-reliant, intelligent, and confident.

General Wilcox instituted a system of drill for the Sharpshooters modeled after one used by the French army. It comprised of a skirmish drill, bayonet exercise, and instruction for estimating distances. Estimating distances was so important that if a man could not pass the test he was dismissed from the Sharpshooters. Likewise, marksmanship was thoroughly drilled. Men were required to hit a target on a board 6x6 feet at 900 yards. Those who failed were sent back to the ranks. The Sharpshooters were armed with the improved Enfield rifles. The scouts were given Whitworth rifles with telescopic sights. The Sharpshooters were the envy of the army, the best of the best.

In late March, a new Union commander arrived in Culpepper. He was Ulysses S. Grant, the successful western commander Lincoln brought east to deal with Lee. He would prove to be the most formidable foe they had encountered.

"this grand old regiment toward the close of the war was not what it had been from the beginning"

As warm weather approached, the army prepared for the coming season of slaughter. Ordinance departments stockpiled ammunition. Medical departments gathered supplies. Recruiting efforts continued. From December to the end of February, the 34th NC brought in only 37 new recruits. In March and April, a major push was undertaken to fill the ranks. Very few willing volunteers were found, so the conscript agents went to work. The regiment gained 86 men in March and April, all conscripts, mostly older men, older than the conscripts from 1863. Some had been discharged in 1862, and were brought back. Milas Stanhope Jamison was 44 years old. He had volunteered in 1861, but was discharged in April of 1862. He returned at the urging of a conscript agent. Troy Miller and Alexander Richards also returned after two years at home. These returning men found a regiment that had changed dramatically since they left. The regiment also got a new assistant surgeon. Dr. Barr, who had treated Stonewall Jackson, was transferred, and Dr. Bodisco Williams replaced him. Dr.

John F. Miller continued to serve as the regiment's chief medical officer.

The recruits mostly came through Camps Vance and Holmes for training. The veterans universally regarded them as poor replacements for the men they had lost. By the end of April 200 of the men on the regiment's rolls were replacement troops, 40% of their total enrollment. T. D. Lattimore expressed it this way, "The regiment received many recruits during this winter, mostly men between forty and forty-five years, who, with rare exceptions, made poor soldiers, and fell far short of filling the places of those who had been killed or disabled. Candor compels the admission that this grand old regiment toward the close of the war was not what it had been from the beginning, and without presuming to speak for others, the same may be said of all regiments which have seen like service."

Private Asa Hazelwood

Private Asa Hazelwood was one of the new conscripts from the Camp Holmes class of 1864. Asa was 32 years old and lived in Stokes County. He was the son of a Patrick County, Virginia blacksmith. A tenant farmer, he leased a small farm in Stokes County. Three of his brothers had volunteered in 1861, in Virginia regiments. One died of measles in 1861, one deserted, the other was still serving. Asa and his wife had six children ranging in age from two to thirteen. He had shown no interest in going off to fight. But the day the conscription agents knocked on his door, Asa was found doing what he always did in the spring, getting ready to plant crops. He obeyed the call, leaving behind a tearful family to trade his plow for a musket. He was assigned to the 34th NC. He didn't have a single relative or friend in the entire regiment, a difficult adjustment for a man who had never been away from his family.

He went to Camp Holmes, received a quick course in soldiering, and boarded a train to Virginia, where the 34th NC had spent the winter. He was assigned to Company I commanded by Captain James Wood. Half of the original company was gone, killed, or disabled by wounds. He found the camp muddy and dismal. Half the men were sick. The tiny log huts that had sheltered them through the winter were crude and cramped. Food was slim, and water was bad. He was met by gaunt veterans who looked at him with an air of derision.

Governor Vance's policy was to place the conscripted soldiers in companies from their native counties whenever possible. Asa did not benefit from that policy. And he was joining the regiment on the eve of a major battle.

Near the end of April, the regiment formed up for their ninth formal muster. They had 403 in camp out a total enrollment of 563. Only 18 were listed AWOL, down from 50 after Gettysburg. Only three had deserted since last muster. Forty-three were absent due to sickness or wounds, and fifty-seven were still POWs. 72% of their total roll was present, the highest since before Chancellorsville. On paper, they seemed ready for battle, but the number of untested recruits worried the veterans. One in four of the men in camp had never seen a battle, and 75 had been in the regiment less than two months. Very soon, however, they would all be veterans.

Pvt. Jacob Riley Dellinger was on leave at the end of April. His cousin Lt. Emanuel Houser wrote to him about the state of the regiment. He wrote, "Col. Gordon is with us at this time and we got two new officers, Laban Reef and Bill Rab...Ely Eaker will get a furlough at last. He will get well now. You said you wanted to know if we was going to move. I cannot say. We may and then we may not, but I don't think we will move this month unless the Yankees compel us to move and then we will move. Longstreet is coming back to our army he is at Charlottesville now. There are good many troops coming from North Carolina and South Carolina and some from all parts of the armies. This Campaign is going to be one of the worst campaigns ever has been in Virginia."[194] Houser's prophetic statement about the coming campaign would prove to be true.

---

[194] Letter from E. M. Houser to Jacob R. Dellinger dated 4/20/1864. Letter courtesy Mike Stroupe.

Sergeant Maxwell H. Hoyle, The Floyd Rifles – Company F[195]

---
[195] Photo courtesy Van A. Hoyle

Privates Franklin Lattimore (left), and his brother James Lattimore (right), The Floyd Rifles – Company F[196]

---

[196] Photo courtesy Robin S. Lattimore

Chapter 12.
A Long Bloody Trail – The Overland Campaign

The trees were starting to bud, and the generals' wives were leaving camp, sure signs a battle was coming. Longstreet's corps had returned from Tennessee, and Hill's Corps of 22,000 men was still at Orange Courthouse, 25 miles southwest of the Wilderness. On the night of May 3-4, the Union army crossed the Rapidan inaugurating one of the war's bloodiest campaigns.

The men were ordered to cook rations. On May 4th, the 34th NC decamped with the rest of the Light Division and marched northward on the Orange Plank Road. Heth's division led the way followed by Wilcox. General Cadmus Wilcox was leading the Light Division into the first major battle of his command. General Scales was back in command of the brigade, and Colonel Lowrance led the 34th North Carolina into their third summer of the war. General Lee could muster 62,000 men of all arms when they were all consolidated. General Grant had twice that number. The Light Division was heading back to the Wilderness where they had fought at Chancellorsville a year before. The veterans remembered that battle all too well. General Hill's men were in remarkably high spirits, laughing and joking, seeming glad to be moving after the long winter. Shortly before dark, the men halted for the night having marched twelve miles. They were about halfway to the Wilderness where Lee wanted to fight. Grant's numbers wouldn't matter as much there where Lee humiliated Hooker the year before.

The Battle of the Wilderness

At dawn on May 5th, the men were back on the road. Around noon, the leading columns were approaching the Wilderness, where Ewell's corps was already in action. They moved quickly along the Plank Road with the ireful sounds of the battle emanating from the dark forest. Their objective, the Brock Road intersection, was four miles ahead. These roads were crucial. In the tangled jungle of the Wilderness, the army that controlled this intersection had the advantage of mobility. On this day, the troops in blue won the foot race to the junction.

Heth's men at the head of the column halted a mile and a half from the intersection at the Widow Tapp's farm, a rare clearing in the area. Not far behind, General Wilcox halted the Light Division to wait for orders. The sounds of Ewell's battle came through the woods from the north. Heth's division moved up and was skirmishing a mile or so from the Brock Road. Shortly before 4:00 in the afternoon, Lee ordered Wilcox to take his division north to try and link with Ewell's men, and unite the divided army. Lee had not intended to divide the army this time. The limited roads and pre-battle disposition of troops had caused the split. With no road, the Light Division began moving northward through the brush. After going only a few hundred yards, a furious battle erupted to the east. Three full divisions of Federal troops, some 30,000 men, came tearing through the woods and attacked Heth's lone division of 6,700 troops. Thousands of muskets and scores of angry artillery pieces fired blindly through the woods. Instead of continuing north, the Light Division was ordered to Heth's immediate support.

Moving as quickly as possible in the terrain, they turned in Heth's direction. General Scales, in action for the first time since Gettysburg, pushed his brigade through the woods. McGowan's brigade had paused at the Tapp farm for a quick prayer service before going into action. Scales' and McGowan's brigades then joined together and made their way through the woods with McGowan's prayed-up men leading the way. When they found their enemy, they raised their best rebel yell and hurled themselves at the Federal troops. Stunned by the sudden reinforcements, the Yankees retreated, leaving behind some 200 men who became prisoners. Scales sent his brigade to fill a gap in Heth's beleaguered line. When the Federal troops returned, they attacked with a vengeance. Wave after wave of Yankees slammed into the thinning Confederate line.

"Rally to the flag! Stand to your colors!"

Four color bearers from the 34th NC fell that day. One was Private Alexander Cathey from Company G. He was a cousin of the lieutenant with the same name that had been captured at Gettysburg. It was said that when the colors fell, Colonel Lowrance asked who would take up the flag, and Private Cathey was among the first to volunteer, holding the banner until he too fell wounded.[197]

---

[197] This information comes from Alexander Cathey's obituary in 1913.

Jim Lattimore was another of the color bearers that day. A post-war account stated, "In the battles of the Wilderness, 1864, they were hard pressed, falling back and becoming demoralized. After their flag had gone down three times, Jim Lattimore picked it up, waving it, calling out, "Rally to the flag, stand to your colors!" and sticking the staff in the ground stood by it, loading and shooting, under cover of the hill, while the men knelt to load and rise to shoot. And soon Jim was shot through the shoulder and was carried out, leaving his flag standing. His brother, Frank Lattimore, relating the story of Jim's bravery, said, "That flag would have been laying there yet before I would have picked it up.""[198]

"He appeared to be as cool as if he was squirrel hunting."

Private Leonard Cranford braved very heavy enemy fire which inspired his buddies to keep fighting. Burwell Cotton wrote, "Len Cranford went about twenty paces in advance of our regt. I expected he would get killed but did not get hurt. Was very much surprised to find him so brave. He appeared to be as cool as if he was squirrel hunting."[199]

As the sun began to set, the reliable General Lane reinforced Scales' brigade. The two brigades advanced in the direction of the Brock Road junction. They were slowed by a patch of swampy ground, when out of nowhere two fresh Yankee brigades broke through to check them. All up and down the line, the bloody melee continued as Yankees seemed to grow on the trees all around them. They came in waves, crashing into the southerners with near reckless abandon. They could hear them coming long before they could see them. Never had the Confederates fought a more determined enemy. Never did the rebels fight so hard to hold their ground.

Nightfall brought the fighting to an end. The rebels were tenuously holding the line after beating back at least six violent attacks. They were woefully outgunned. Only Longstreet's corps could save them, and no one knew where they were. The woods were on fire in several places reminiscent of their first battle there. The lines were

---

[198] (Center 2017) An article published February 2, 1927 in The Forest City Courier titled, "North Carolina Regiments in the War Between the States" by James C. Elliott, Lattimore, R-1, N. C.

[199] (Taylor 1994) Letter from Cotton dated May 20, 1864.

disorganized, many brigades were badly shot up, and the dangerous gap still existed between Hill and Ewell as darkness blanketed the thickets. The stench of smoke and death spread over the area. Many wounded men bled helpless and alone in the war-ravaged woods. The divisions of Wilcox and Heth were arranged like a horseshoe. They stayed motionless all night. Instead of trying to consolidate and strengthen the lines, Hill and Lee wanted the men to rest.

At five the next morning, the woods erupted with thousands of furious Federal troops rushing through the woods. The badly outgunned Confederates fought steady, firing, and slowly falling back. An hour into the fight they gave way under the weight of thirteen Federal brigades. In places, the retreat was orderly. In other places, it was chaotic and desperate. Around seven in the morning, the hard-pressed rebels encountered the fresh brigades of Longstreet's corps, stepping along full of swagger and ready to fight. The survivors of Wilcox's division took heart as Longstreet's men moved up. Col. Lowrance rallied the 34th NC in support of the counter-attack. Soon they were again heading northward to try and link with Ewell's corps. Noise and confusion still reigned as the men in the ranks could do nothing except follow orders. Yankees continued to pound the line, and Confederate units mounted counter-attacks. The 34th NC was close to the area where Stonewall Jackson had been shot a year ago. In a strange twist of fate, General Longstreet was accidentally shot in the same area by his own men. Longstreet would survive his wound.

The day wore on in a grinding fight to survive but ended in stalemate. Longstreet's timely arrival staved off disaster, but they could not drive the enemy back. Smoke from burning pines drifted through the woods as the sun set. The area was a nightmare of wounded men crying out, trapped in the burning woods. Unburied dead were everywhere. The distinctive smell of burnt flesh bothered even the hardest veterans. Many men became lost and wandered into the wrong lines. After two days of hell on earth, the exhausted men strengthened the lines and caught a few precious hours of sleep. Everyone expected the slaughter to continue at dawn.

At first light, the skirmishers began firing. The spattering of muskets continued for some time, but a general assault never came. Both armies were too spent to try again. Grant pulled his bloodied army back out of the forest. The losses in the two-day fight were appalling. Grant's army suffered 16,000 men killed, wounded, or missing. Lee's army lost over 11,000, of which Hill's corps accounted for 7,000. It was an atrocious loss of life for an inconclusive battle that ended near where it began. The 34th North Carolina lost 48 men, most on the first day of the fight. Eight were killed, at least twenty-one were wounded, and nineteen were captured or missing. One of the slain was Seth Bedford whose brother had been killed at Ox Hill. The grief of losing a second son lay heavy on his parents back in Rutherford County. At least two of the wounded men later died. John Sanford of Mecklenburg County was hit by a large piece of buckshot that lodged in his brain. It took his life ten days later.

The following were the known casualties from the Battle of the Wilderness:

Casualties from the Battle of The Wilderness

Killed in Action

John C Clark	G	Pvt.	Archibald N McLeod	K	Pvt.
Seth Bedford	B	Pvt.	Berry Queen	E	Pvt.
Jesse C Dobbins	B	Pvt.	James M Wilson	B	Sgt.
W. M. Loftis	D	Pvt.	William J Gibbons	F	Pvt.

Mortally Wounded

Tilman Sarrat	H	Cpl.	John M Sanford	G	Pvt.

Wounded

Harvey S Adams	H	Pvt.	John P Henson	I	Cpl.
George A Atwell	E	Cpt.	Maxwell H Hoyle	F	Sgt.
Albery Bishop	C	Pvt.	Thomas A Johnson	G	Sgt.
Wesley W Brown	A	Cpl.	John Kiser	E	Pvt.
Alexander Cathey	G	Pvt.	James H Lattimore	F	Pvt.
Felix C Dobbins	B	Sgt.	James F Miller	D	Pvt.
Vincent Dobbins	B	Pvt.	James C Talbert	K	Pvt.
William Foster	C	Pvt.	Thomas H White	E	Pvt.
Robert N Hart	D	Pvt.	George W Woods	A	2Lt.

Captured

Green Van Buren Todd**	G	Sgt.	Jesse Hall	H	Pvt.
William B Smith**	I	Pvt.	Eli Hamrick	B	Pvt.
David M Taylor	E	1Sgt.	Miles M Hartness	D	Pvt.
John F Bess	E	Pvt.	James Keever	E	Pvt.
William C Bowman	C	Pvt.	Charles S Martin	E	Pvt.
William M Burlison	D	Pvt.	E A Miller	H	Pvt.
Ezekiel W Corn	C	Pvt.	Caleb Rhyne	E	Pvt.
Augustus C Davis	A	Pvt.	Charles D Shull	E	Pvt.
John Q Adams Dillworth	G	Pvt.	Robert Chapman*	H	Pvt.

**Listed Missing   *Listed captured at Mine Run

The 34th could not account for two men after the battle. One was Sgt. Green Van Buren Todd. Green was severely wounded in the arm and leg and taken prisoner. The Federal surgeons treated his wounds but unfortunately did not record his exact fate. No date of death was recorded. No record was found that he was ever transferred to a hospital or prison or sent for exchange. Each time such a transfer was made, the Federal officers created a roll. Lists of prisoners were eventually sent to Richmond. With no such record for Green, it is likely that he died shortly after the battle in one of the field hospitals. He was the son of Samuel and Sarah Todd and married Sarah Cathey in 1859. Green Van Buren Todd was 28 years old. The other was Pvt. William B. Smith of Rutherford County. He received a wound to the abdomen. Like Todd, he was treated but his fate was not recorded, and he never made to a Federal hospital or prison. He too likely died of his wound.

A Narrow Escape for Pvt. Martin

When Pvt. Charles S. Martin was captured, he narrowly escaped being bayonetted by a Union soldier. During the fighting, Martin fell with a severe leg wound and became mixed in with a group of Louisiana Zouave troops fighting under a black flag. A Yankee soldier came up and was about to bayonet Martin thinking he was one of the Louisiana troops. A Yankee lieutenant struck the man across the face with the flat side of his sword and said, "You damn fool, can't you see that this man is no Zouave?" The Zouaves had distinctive clothing that Martin did not wear, and he was thus spared and taken prisoner. Martin would spend the rest of the war as a prisoner.[200]

Thomas H. White was a Gaston County resident assigned to the 34th a few days before the Wilderness battle where he received a head wound. On his way home on leave, he was interviewed by a reporter with The Western Democrat and said, "Grant is the worst whipped man who ever started to Richmond with an army." The paper noted that White spoke in "glowing terms of our victories over the enemy."[201] Grant had taken a lot of casualties, but he was far from "whipped." Instead of taking his casualty-ridden army back north to lick their wounds as his predecessors had done, Grant moved southward, trying to get between Lee and Richmond. The fight would go on.

Spotsylvania Courthouse – The Bloody Angle

Rain showers fell across the area on Saturday, May 7th. Grave details worked quickly, while the army prepared to move. Just after dark, Longstreet's corps started marching followed by Hill's men around ten that night. Rain showers continued, turning the roads to mud. As they marched into the darkness, the distant sound of thousands of voices was heard. At first it sounded like the head of the column was under attack, but there was no gunfire, only voices. Slowly the sounds of cheer ran down the ranks in a wave, Hill's men joining in when their time came. Three times, the waves of cheer washed through the ranks.[202] With almost nothing to cheer about as they marched away from another bloody battlefield, the men were defiantly joyous.

On the afternoon of May 9th, Hill's corps reached Spotsylvania where Lee was setting up a defensive line. The line was an inverted V with the flanks anchored against two streams. Hill's division was sent to the right side of the angle and threw up breastworks. The total line was some five miles long. In the center was a large salient that stood daring the enemy to attack. Hill's corps defended the line on the right of the salient for a mile and a half, well entrenched. May 11th featured spotty rain showers. The only fighting was by the Sharpshooter battalions who traded fire with their Federal counterparts. In one exchange, two men of Captain Young's battalion were killed by a

---

[200] (Martin n.d.) Essay courtesy of Patti Martin
[201] The Western Democrat May 17, 1864 (digitalnc.org)
[202] (Dunlop 2012) Page 43.

single shot fired by a Yankee sharpshooter.[203] At sundown, the rain started back up and flooded their trenches.

At 4:30 the next morning, in heavy wet fog, Federal troops charged the northwest section of the salient defended by Ewell's Second Corps. The dampness rendered gunpowder useless for many of the troops, and much of the fighting was hand-to-hand. Soon after the attack on the salient started, Ambrose Burnside attacked Wilcox's part of the line. The line, however, was one the strongest positions they had ever held, and they drove Burnside back with little loss of their own. Much of the work was done by artillery which demoralized Burnside's troops. The extreme right flank was held by General Lane, who was initially driven back. Parts of Scales' and Thomas's brigades reinforced Lane. The strengthened flank drove the Federal troops back and took 300 prisoners. With their area secure, the brigades of McGowan, Perrin, and Harris were sent to the salient to help Ewell.

"The scenes of the dead and wounded piled up are sickening."

For twenty hours, the Bloody Angle earned its name as one of the most violent clashes of the war. In the rain and fog, one assault after another was made by Federal troops fighting like demons. The rebels held the ground as if their lives depended on it. Men were trampled into the mud; some were nearly buried alive. The mud became tinged red. Dead bodies were piled up and used as shields against the assaults. The slaughter continued after dark. A little past midnight, the rebel survivors fell back to a new line a mile to the rear, leaving the gruesome salient to the Federals. Over 10,000 men on both sides were killed, wounded, or captured. The water ran through the trenches blood-red.

For two days, the lines held with only skirmishing amid scattered rain showers. On May 15th, the weather cleared, and the firing stopped. For five more days, the armies stayed in the lines eyeing each other warily. Ancil Dycus tried to describe the scene at the horrible angle by writing, "…I can't put into words what my eyes have seen. It

---

[203] (Dunlop 2012) Page 54. The identities of the two men were not stated. They were apparently not members of the 34th NC.

is too terrible to tell you. The scenes of the dead and wounded piled up are sickening."[204]

The North Anna-May 23, 1864

On the 20th, Grant started pulling his army back and swung again to the southeast. The march to the North Anna River began. Late that afternoon, as Burnside's men pulled away, General Hill ordered the brigades of Scales and Lane to conduct a reconnaissance in force to determine the Federal strength at Spotsylvania Court House. The 34th NC moved out with the rest of the brigade onto Massaponax Church Road near Zion Church. Scales sent his men to Lane's right, both brigades advancing in dense woods with the road between them. They suddenly came upon 250 Vermonters who rose and fired a heavy volley at them. Rebel artillery near the church fired, and Scales and Lane ordered their men to rush forward. The Vermonters were outnumbered and fell back. In addition, a sudden violent wind storm broke loose and felled several trees, and the fighting stopped. When the wind died down, the Federals were reinforced and checked the rebels' advance.[205]

Scales and Lane retired, having accomplished their mission of locating the enemy and determining their strength. In the process, three men of the 34th NC were killed, an unknown number were wounded, and one was captured. Sgt. Charles Wriston of Mecklenburg County was a veteran from 1861. He was killed along with Samuel Jarrett and William Gantt, who had both been with the regiment for a year. John Hipp and George Todd, both also of Mecklenburg County, were wounded. They would survive and return to duty. James T. Blackburn was captured. Blackburn was an 18-year-old conscript who had been with Company A since January. Blackburn was from Wilkes County, where Unionist sympathies were quite strong. On his record, the Federal authorities remarked, "Born in N. Carolina, 18 years old. Conscripted. Never the south was right. Forced into the service. Wishes to go to Pennsylvania and take the oath."[206]

---

[204] (Tisdale 1997) Letter from Dycus page 47. NOTE: All letters of Ancil Dycus are from this source.
[205] (Rhea 2000) The action is described on pages 244-245.
[206] Blackburn was not released on oath. Perhaps the Provost Marshall did not believe he was sincere. He was sent to Point Lookout, then transferred to Elmira where he died on September 13, 1864.

The skirmish at Spotsylvania Court House ended after dark, and Scales and Lane rejoined the division. There was no time to rest. Through the night and to noon the next day, they marched urgently southward. After trekking thirty grueling miles, they stopped at Anderson's Station on the Virginia Central Railroad west of Hanover Junction. Three miles northwest was the Jericho Mills crossing on the North Anna River.

On May 23rd, Union V Corps commander Gouverncur K. Warren discovered the crossing at Jericho Mills undefended. Uncharacteristically, Lee and his generals had neglected to guard the important crossing. Warren exploited the oversight by sending troops wading across to establish a toehold on the south banks, while engineers worked on a pontoon bridge. Lee discovered the movement but believed it to be a ruse. He felt the real threat would be farther down the river. General Hill directed Wilcox to conduct a reconnaissance and find out what the Yankees were up to. In mid-afternoon, Wilcox reported that Federals troops had crossed the river and were moving south. Hill believed they were a small isolated force and ordered Wilcox to attack. The four brigades of the Light Division, including Scales,' were sent to block the Federal troops. They marched two miles along the railroad, turned north, and switched to line of battle. By then, it was six in the evening. Warren's entire corps, four divisions strong, was across the river and ready for a confrontation. Wilcox had no idea what was waiting for them.

Wilcox's division formed with Thomas, McGowan, and Lane in the front. General Scales was again not able to take the field and yielded command to Colonel Lowrance. Lowrance's men formed behind Thomas and planned to swing around and crush the enemy flank. The attack went well at first. The Federals seemed to be caught off guard and fell back. But the success was short-lived. Thomas's brigade came under heavy fire and began falling back, creating a weak spot between Lowrance and McGowan. Meanwhile, Lowrance was already directing his men in the pre-planned flanking movement. Lowrance was in contact with the enemy flank but was aware of Thomas's faltering attack, so he wisely held his men back. To the far right, Lane's men were also meeting heavy resistance. The attack withered and then completely broke apart as the sun was going down.

Lowrance's keen awareness of the battle saved many lives that day. Instead of blindly following orders, he exercised judgment in holding his men back. Wilcox's four brigades had blindly attacked four full divisions of Federal troops; four times their number. Heth's Division arrived too late to get into action. Fortunately, the lateness of the hour and incoming rain kept the Federals from making a stronger counterattack. Wilcox's men were forced to retreat through the shadowy woods. Because of the way the attack had splintered, the withdrawal was piece-meal. In the confusion, many became separated from their commands and fell into enemy hands. One of those was Private Asa Hazelwood. His time with the regiment had been short but eventful. From here, he would fight for survival as a prisoner of war.

Theo Kistler

Only one man from the 34th was killed that day. Theo Kistler's skill and gallant conduct in battle so impressed Colonel Lowrance that he had bestowed an unusual honor on the young Rowan County man. He promoted him to Ensign. This was normally a naval rank, but Confederates sometimes used it as an honorary title. Technically, it was an officer's rank, but he had no command authority. Most Ensigns served as color bearers, as did Kistler. His loss was deeply felt by his fellow Tar Heels. He was 23 years old. The following were casualties of the May 23rd battle at North Anna:

Casualties from the Battle of North Anna - May 23, 1864

Theo H Kistler	D	Engn	Killed in Action		
Sanders Thompson	A	Pvt.	Wounded		

Captured

Alfred S Alcorn	G	Pvt.	Asa Hazelwood	I	Pvt.
Adam R Clark	E	Pvt.	William Hipp	G	Pvt.
Abraham H Davis	B	Pvt.	John A Moore	B	Pvt.
James Davis	B	Pvt.	Lemuel S Self	F	Cpl.
William F Eades	A	Pvt.	James F Shehan	I	Pvt.
John A Gentle	A	Pvt.	Daniel Upchurch	I	Pvt.
James T Griffin	I	Pvt.	Marcus Wood	I	Pvt.
Gilbert W Hamilton	K	Cpl.	John G Yancy	C	Pvt.

Hanover Junction-The Battle of Ox Ford-May 24, 1864

The next day's action could only be described as strange and confused. Wilcox's men planned to rest and work on fortifications. Most of the day's fighting took place to the right of their position. In mid-afternoon, word came of Federal troops heading their way. Additional Federal troops had crossed at Jericho Mills and joined Warren's corps, heading south roughly along the railroad. Hill sent Wilcox's Division forward with Heth and Mahone supporting. Once again, they left strong fortifications to attack an enemy of unknown strength out in the open. General Hill did not appreciate the advantages of fighting behind breastworks. Wilcox's men were in the center and ahead of the other two divisions. Whether due to terrain or timing, Wilcox's advance was embarrassingly uncoordinated. Fortunately, the Federals had not planned an all-out attack in that sector. Thus, casualties were light. Though losing no men killed or wounded, the 34th NC again lost several men taken prisoner in the afternoon advance. The following were taken prisoner in what came to be known as the Battle of Ox Ford:

Captured at the Battle of Ox Ford - May 24, 1864

Perry Allen	H	Pvt.	Andrew D Metcalf	E	Pvt.
Hamilton Bare	A	Cpl.	George W Parks	G	Pvt.
Mathias Brown	A	Pvt.	Alex Richards	E	Pvt.
Geo. Champion	B	Pvt.	Esley Shittle	C	Pvt.
John M Collins	H	Pvt.	Hiram T Stampler	A	Cpl.
J M Dixon	E	Pvt.	Alexander Taylor	A	Pvt.
Alfred Eades	A	Pvt.	Henry B Woods	A	Pvt.
Hamilton Koonce	A	Sgt.			

Two days later, General Grant moved his army away from Hanover Junction, again moving southeast, inching ever closer to Richmond. Lee and his army were frustrated by the nature of the campaign. Though they had inflicted horrendous casualties on Grant, the Army of the Potomac was showing never-before-seen resilience. Lee's army was under constant pressure, and it was starting to wear his men down. Grant could replace his losses, Lee could not.

On May 27th, Lee's embattled army again set out after Grant. Hill's troops stayed in the trenches all day until the rest of the army had left, then fell into line after dark as the army's rear guard. The next two days was a mind-numbing, punishing forced march. Once again, by sheer force of will, Lee's army stayed between Grant and Richmond and established another defensive line. Lee detested being on the defensive, but he proved highly effective in keeping Grant just far enough to the east to block him from Richmond. Every man in the ranks knew, however, that every southward step they took meant they would fight that much closer to Richmond. In the past, they were the ones setting the pace and holding the initiative. Now, all they could do was to react. On May 29th, they were defending familiar territory. Wilcox's division held a position only a few miles north of Mechanicsville, where less than two years prior, the 34th NC received its first baptism of fire. Much had changed since then. They barely resembled the men they once were. After all the miles they had marched, and all the battles fought, they were back to where they started, fighting a tough and determined enemy.

Hill's Third Corps occupied the left of Lee's new line, anchored on the Totopotomony Creek. The Confederate right was at New Cold Harbor, near the scene of the battle of Gaines's Mill. Wilcox's division enjoyed a strong position and were disappointed when the enemy declined to attack. On June 1st, Confederate brigades on the right attacked near Gaines's Mill but failed to disrupt Grant's plans. The Federals launched an attack on the Confederate left which was easily repulsed.

That night, Wilcox's division, along with Mahone's, began moving to the southeast to strengthen the Confederate right. Heth's men became the left flank. It was unusual for the Third Corps to be divided, holding both flanks, but the needs dictated the deployments. June 2nd was steamy hot as the men completed their march. They trekked past Gaines's Mill and Boatswain's Creek remembering the battle they had faced there in 1862. No matter where they had fought since, the contest there was as intense as anything they had experienced. They remembered the long hours pinned down on that bloody slope, pounded mercilessly by thousands of enemy guns. They remembered the final surge that brought victory, and the many friends who died there.

Scattered firing was heard all day June 2nd as the men marched to the right. In the afternoon, scattered rain showers fell as they drove a small Federal force from Turkey Hill, then finished their march and arrived at their new position at the far right of the rebel line with the Gaines's Mill battlefield at their backs. Burwell Cotton remembered the place well and wrote in a June 11, 1864, letter, "I am near the place where I fought on Friday evening in 62. Passed over the battlefield. Everything looked as if it had been only a few days since that powerful battle." They spent the rest of the day improving works and then hunkered down for the night. Rain came down during the night, heavy at times, making small streams in their trenches.

The Battle of Cold Harbor – June 3, 1864

At dawn, there was heavy fog and spotty showers. In the mist, an assault force of 50,000 Yankee troops stood ready to advance. At 4:30 the area exploded with muskets and artillery fire. Wave after wave of Federal troops marched to their death in front of well-fortified Confederates with an endless supply of shot and canister rounds for their artillery. It was reminiscent of Burnside's attack at Fredericksburg and Lee's at Gettysburg. Federal troops gave up the attack just after noon, leaving 7,000 dead and wounded men on the field. The 34th NC was not directly involved but witnessed the battle to their left.

"We are seeing very hard times"

For the next nine long days, the two angry armies sat in the lines sniping at one another and waiting to see who would move first. Helpless wounded men trapped in no-man's land begged for help. On the 7th the armies agreed to a two-hour truce to gather the wounded from the field. By then, they were all dead.

The smell of decaying bodies made men sick. Buzzards circled the area. Drinkable water and food were scarce. The men baked in the sweltering sun with no shelter. Both sides shot at anything that moved, and sleep was impossible. Only one man from the 34th North Carolina sought to escape by going into the enemy lines. Washington Blankenship was a conscript who had recently joined the regiment. On June 2nd, when the regiment left Totopotomoy Creek, Washington slipped out of the ranks, during the night, and found a place to hide out. He surrendered to Federal troops the next day. He told the Federal captors that he wanted to take the oath and go to Missouri where he had two brothers. He died six weeks later at Point Lookout.

Burwell Cotton wrote a letter while in the line, "We are seeing very hard times losing so much sleep makes us feel very bad. One third of the company kept up all the time." He continued, "Have not changed clothes but once since the 1st of May. Do not know how long I will have to remain in this place. We are all very dirty..."[207] Even though the 34th NC had not been directly involved in the battle of Cold Harbor, the violence they witnessed was shocking. Ancil Dycus was usually very willing to describe their situation in his letters home, but here he was at a loss for words. He wrote, "I hardly know what to write you this morning. I want to hear from you the worst I ever did. We are in line of battle here now. We have been here 2 days. We have got good fortification here. We have not had any fighting right here, but in sight on our left there has been as hard fighting as heard yesterday."[208]

On the night of June 12th, Grant once again pulled away from the battlefield. It didn't take long for the men of the 34th to gather their meager possessions and join in pursuit. As they did, Sgt. Wilson Bridges was wounded by a stray shot from a retreating skirmisher.[209] One man, Pvt. Robert Kiser, was taken prisoner in the Turkey Hill area, a deserter who hid out and surrendered to the enemy. The day was hot and humid, but the troops marched urgently.

The Battle of Riddles's Shop – June 13, 1864

As they did after Gaines's Mill, they crossed the Chickahominy and headed south. They passed through the area of Frayser's Farm and remembered the hard fighting there. Near Riddle's Shop, the 34th North Carolina, with other units of Hill's Corps, engaged in a sharp skirmish with Federal troops. T. D. Lattimore described it as a running fight where they drove the enemy for more than a mile. Burwell Cotton says they drove them "several miles." Privates F. M. Holland and J. Wortman had both joined the regiment in April. The two conscripts died together at Riddle's Shop. No official record of the wounded is given, but Burwell Cotton named three from his company, Eli

---

[207] (Taylor 1994) Letter from Cotton dated June 11, 1864.
[208] (Tisdale 1997) Letter from Dycus dated June 4, 1864, pages 49-50.
[209] Bridges survived and returned to duty by October 1864.

Cranford, Wilson Kime, and James Reeves. Scales' Sharpshooters out front, led by Captain John D. Young, did much of the work.

The 34th NC bivouacked that night on the 1862, Frayser's Farm battlefield, weary after a long march and skirmishing with the enemy. Men fell from the ranks completely fatigued. Many were sick. The weeks of constant marching and fighting was taking a toll. They had little to eat, and no clean water. They hadn't changed clothes or bathed in weeks. The men got a day's rest, and on the morning of the 15th were marched southeast. They put in another long day marching, stopping at sundown to establish a new line between White Oak Swamp and Willis Church Road. During the day, five Company K men deserted together. They had only been with the regiment a few weeks, recent conscripts who had no desire to go further. Men were wearing down. Lee's army had been whittled down to barely 30,000 men to oppose 100,000 Federal troops. The 34th NC was barely over half the strength it started with on May 1st.

Lee's army was badly out of position. All that stood between the Federal host and Petersburg was P. G. T. Beauregard's ragged force. On the 16th and 17th of June, Burnside's and Hancock's Federal corps assaulted the lines but were turned back with heavy losses. Beauregard was heavily outnumbered, but the strong fortification system made the difference. At three in the morning June 18th, the 34th NC and the rest of the division was urgently rushed into marching columns and started toward Petersburg. They began in the cool night air at a quick pace, covering several miles. They rested for two hours near Chaffin's Bluff, then shortly before daybreak resumed the trek. Never had a greater emergency existed. If Petersburg fell, Richmond would fall. Beauregard could not withstand another powerful attack. They marched furiously, choking on dust and baking in the sun with precious little water and no food. They had twenty miles to go and sounds of battle were already audible. Straggling was the worse they had ever seen. Officers urged them on, but many just did not have the legs. All day long, the Union army pounded the Confederate lines. The closer the hard-pressed Third Corps got to the city, the louder the sounds of battle. Hill's leading units reached the outskirts of Petersburg by mid-afternoon. It was the longest twenty miles of their lives. Those that made it were covered in dust and desperate to rest their aching legs. The weary infantrymen took their place in the trenches. At 6:30 in the evening, one final Union assault slammed the Confederate line, fortunately not the area occupied by the depleted 34th NC. Once more, the line held and inflicted heavy casualties on the Union forces. It had been three awfully bad days for Union general George Meade, who was furious at their inability to break the thin rebel lines at the cost of 10,000 Union casualties.

    The men looked around and observed the complex system of trenches and fortifications that would be their home for the next nine months. Much of their time would now be spent below ground in trenches and bomb-proofs. They would use picks and shovels more than their trusty muskets as the war entered its final phase.

Lieutenant Romulus M. S. Hopper, The Rough and Readys – Company H, later commanded The Laurel Springs Guards[210]

---

[210] Photo Courtesy of Crystal Jarrett Inman

Private Martin S. Hoyle, The Floyd Rifles – Company F[211]

---

[211] Photo courtesy Van A. Hoyle

Chapter 13.
Hard Times

The last thing General Lee wanted was a siege. Siege was a game of attrition, and that was a losing proposition for the dwindling southern army. The north had always had the advantage of numbers, but Lee had been able to beat them by being bold and unpredictable. Lee's army was at its best when it was out in the open, mobile, and on the offensive. After Gettysburg, things changed. Once Grant and Meade seized the initiative, they never let go. Though Lee's army had inflicted horrendous casualties on Grant, the tenacious Union general kept coming, forcing Lee to back-peddle all the way to Richmond. When Grant deprived Lee of mobility, he took away the air his army needed to breathe. When Lee was driven into the trenches, it was only a matter of time.

The Battle of Jerusalem Plank Road – June 22-23, 1864

On June 21st, Federal troops moved against the vital Weldon Railroad to try and sever the important supply line. The divisions of Wilcox and William Mahone were sent to meet the threat. On June 22nd, they found two Federal divisions divided and vulnerable to attack. Wilcox faced off against one of them but was under orders to avoid a general engagement and did not attack. Mahone launched a surprise attack on the other vulnerable Union division at five in the evening. Wilcox sent only two regiments to take part in Mahone's attack. One of them was the 34th North Carolina Infantry.[212] The 34th NC went forward with Mahone's men in a stinging attack that drove the enemy back until they formed a second defensive line. Only the coming darkness prevented greater success. The southerners were forced to drop back. The area was covered in dense underbrush, and with the darkness, another assault was impossible.

The next day, the Federals moved toward the railroad, but Mahone, 5' 5" tall and weighing barely 100 pounds, once again fought like a giant. His men, again including the 34th North Carolina, were on

---

[212] The identity of the other regiment is not known. Most accounts do not mention the 34th NC's involvement in the attack, however their casualty reports and accounts written by members of the regiment show their extensive involvement in the battle.

the move when they found and attacked the Federal troops. While not the rout of the day before, they again drove the bewildered Yankees back. The Federals were able to tear up a short section of the track, but the Weldon Railroad was back in rebel hands.

"Death seems to pick a shining mark and passes in turn to all."

Of great loss to the 34th NC was the very well-liked Lt. Burwell Thomas Cotton, whose letters were often quoted here. Cotton was killed on the first day of the action when the regiment was falling back. A teacher when the war broke out, he enrolled in Montgomery County's Company K and wrote diligently of his war experiences. He was wounded at Frayser's Farm and promoted to Lieutenant after the Seven Days battles. The day after his death, his friend James C. Reeves wrote to Cotton's sister with the sad news, "It becomes my painful duty to pen you these lines which I know will afford you sorrow irrepressible. Yesterday…your brother, Lieut. B. T. Cotton fell a sacrifice upon the alter of his country. He was pierced through the head by a fragment of shell and instantly killed while falling back from the enemy's fortifications." He went on to explain, "he was left lying where he fell-it being an impossibility to bring his body out. He was killed about four miles south east of Petersburg at about 5 P.M." Later, he noted, "While his dear friends will deeply mourn his instant death, his fellow soldiers and especially his company join them in their sorrows and sadly regret the loss of so gallant an officer and courageous gentleman. We can all join in the hope of his transit into a more happy and peaceful world. Death seems to pick a shining mark and passes in turn to all."[213]

Cotton's cousin William B. Coggin served in the same company. He wrote of Cotton's death, "We went into battle on the 22 of June together & we went within fifty or sixty yards of the enemy's fortifications. Then we had orders to fall back. Then I remember well hering cosin Thomas say men try and fall back in good order & load and fire as you fall back. This was the last words I heard him speak and in a few moments afterwards the Major of our regt told me he saw my Lieut fall dead and thought he was shot thrue the head he sayd he fell on his fase…I was a fue steps of him when he fell but the woods was

---

[213] (Taylor 1994) Letter from James C. Reeves dated June 24, 1864. Page 181.

very thick with bushes so I mist seeing him. He was a man I always thought a grate deal of & hope he is at rest the co all seems to regret his death & me in particular I miss him more than anyone…cosin Thomas was not buried at tall as we know of if he was burried he was burried by the yankees tha have held the battle ground ever since the battle I was very sorry we had to leave him on the field but it was unavoidable."[214]

The mark of the 34th NC's effort is shown in blood. Three men were killed, at least eleven were wounded, and eight were captured.[215]

Casualties from the Battle of Jerusalem Plank Road

Killed in Action

William Bowers*	I	Pvt.	Samuel L Hayes	G	Pvt.
Burwell T Cotton	K	Lt.			

Wounded

John Brotherton	G	Pvt.	Thomas E Mitchell	C	Sgt.
Martin Earls*	H	Pvt.	Carter Shuford	D	Pvt.
George T Gordon	Lt. Col.		Joseph Sparks*	I	Pvt.
Robert M Harrill	C	Sgt.	Woody B Wells	B	Pvt.
William Lyall	A	Cpl.	Sidney Wright*	F	Pvt.
William C McCall	C	Pvt.			

Captured

Robert G Batton	B	Pvt.	John L McFadden*	C	Pvt.
Winborn W Cranford	K	Cpl.	James L McRae	K	Pvt.
Franklin Dowell	C	Pvt.	George W Sizemore	B	Pvt.
Thomas J Elliott	C	Pvt.	Elisha Wallen	I	Pvt.

*Casualty from June 23rd.

For "English" George Gordon, his fourth wound of the war was a gunshot wound to the right leg, a wound that effectively ended his military career. John McFadden joined the regiment in May. He was wounded and captured on the second day of the battle, and his right leg

---

[214] (Taylor 1994) Letter from William B. Coggin dated July 22, 1864. Page 182.
[215] Official reports of casualties are very incomplete, showing one killed and two captured. The figures here come entirely from the information gathered from the service records of the men involved.

was amputated. He died a month later as a prisoner of war. Samuel Hays was 29 and had been with the regiment since 1861. A pre-war carpenter, he was wounded at Chancellorsville, returned to duty, and served the entire war to this point. He was present on every muster and a dependable member of The Mecklenburg Boys. William Bowers had joined Company I in February of 1864. Many conscripts showed little desire to fight, but Bowers had stayed with the regiment throughout the year. He was 26 years old.

With the railroad safe, the 34th NC rejoined the Light Division. The 34th had added another star to its impressive service record.

Trench Rats

For the next several weeks, their main weapons were picks and shovels. The 34th North Carolina manned a section of trenches southwest of Petersburg as both sides extended trench lines as close as 400 yards apart. The landscape slowly grew barren as trees were cut for firewood and earthworks. Any exposure above-ground invited several musket shots, and harassing artillery fire was constant. Men became experts in building bombproofs and abatis works. Trenches were quite elaborate. They used logs to construct walls with cutouts to fire through. Any high ground was used as a fort or artillery position. In the distance, the Federals erected a large observation tower. The two sides engaged in a game of trench-counter-trench. The entire area became a maze of trenches, traverses, and redoubts dotted with small forts. Work even went underground as tunnels were dug. Soldiers doubled as construction workers while dodging enemy fire. They quickly learned to stay underground.

The heat was unbearable. At times, the temperature topped 100 degrees. There was little shelter from the merciless sun. There had been no rain for some time. The dust was terrible, and insects were very troublesome. The rain that fell on July 19th was the first in six weeks. Rumors were everywhere that Grant was mining the area. Men listened to the ground for any signs of underground activity. Disease again spiked. Every day, men were sent to the hospitals in Petersburg or Richmond.

At the end of June, the 34th NC took another muster. In May and June, the 34th NC added 96 new recruits, all conscripts. The regiment had 616 on the rolls, but only 266 were in line, the lowest percentage since Gettysburg. Many of these had joined the regiment in the last few months. They reported 189 absent due to sickness or wounds, 97 prisoners of war, and 28 AWOL. They listed 27 on detached duty, mostly on light duty assignments due to injuries or sickness. They had dropped 43 from the rolls since last muster, 32 of those due to death, and eleven desertions. Death and desertion were the only way out.

"I look upon the man with suspicion."

Thomas Powell of Company D deserted at the end of July after being with the 34th NC only a month. According to the Federal records, Thomas left the regiment near Swift Creek and swam the river around July 28th. Thomas had an incredible story to tell the Provost Marshall. The official report states, "He says that about a month ago, then being employed at Wilmington, North Carolina, he knows that an expedition consisting of three steamers and 1,600 men, with 30,000 stand of arms, left Wilmington for the purpose of liberating the rebel prisoners at Point Lookout. I look upon the man with suspicion on account of some great improbabilities in his story, which I think is known to General Butler…I will mention it to General Grant."[216]

Thomas's story was so incredible that the Federal officer could hardly believe it, but it turned out to be true. General Lee had developed a plan during the winter of 1863, to free the prisoners at Point Lookout to provide his army with desperately needed manpower. The prison at the time held around 15,000 men. The first attempt did not get off the ground, but in July of 1864, Lee ordered Brig. General Bradley T. Johnson to try again. The first part of the plan worked well. Johnson burned railroad bridges and cut the telegraph lines from Baltimore to Washington D. C. From there, he was to proceed overland to Point Lookout and be supported by the naval force Powell mentioned. The plan fell apart, however, when details of the plot were published in the Richmond Times Dispatch.[217]

Why Thomas Powell decided to reveal what he knew is uncertain. He may have been unhappy at being assigned to an infantry

---

[216] O.R. – Series I – Volume XL/3 [S# 82] Union correspondence, orders, and returns relating to operations in southeastern Virginia and North Carolina, from July 5, 1864, to July 31, 1864.
[217] (Norris 2017)

unit when he had had a safer position at Wilmington. It is also unknown whether it was his report that caused the plot to be foiled. Had the plan succeeded, though, Lee's army would have had thousands more troops, enough to change the odds now stacked so heavily against them.

"I can tell you that it is terrible in the hospital"

The danger was constant. On August 5th, Private David Richardson from Montgomery County was killed. He enlisted in 1861, at age 17 and had given the regiment three years of service. He had been present on every muster, never disciplined for unauthorized absence or any other infraction. He was added to the growing list of men whose lives were lost for a cause that was beginning to slip away. Sgt. John Ellis suffered a gunshot wound on June 25th, and Pvt. Zimri Kiser was shot on June 27th. They survived their wounds. Lt. Monroe Gillon, who was praised by Colonel Lowrance for his actions at Gettysburg, was shot in the shoulder on July 5th. He would survive and be back in the line after several weeks in the hospital. Pvt. Jesse Wells was shot and severely wounded on July 6th. He stayed in the hospital until the middle of August, was given a furlough, and never returned. Cpl. George Goode's wound on August 9th ended his military career as well. Most who were wounded never returned.

On July 22nd, Privates James McClurd and Jack Towry were killed in an accident involving an unexploded shell.[218] They were looking over the projectile which had landed in their line. As they worked to remove it, the shell exploded and killed them both. McClurd had only been with the regiment a brief time. Towery had joined in April but had been sick most of his enlistment.

Private Ancil Dycus had been in the hospital for acute diarrhea. On July 18th he wrote, "I can tell you that it is terrible in the hospital when one of the men has to have his leg or arm amputated after an injury. We have no chloroform to deaden the pain." He continues, "We are just below Petersburg in sight of the city and picket. There has been

---

[218] (Girvan 2010) Letter from Joseph J. Hoyle dated July 25, 1864. Joseph Towry's service record shows he enlisted in April of 1864 and was listed Absent-sick for all the 1864 musters. This letter indicates he must have returned to the regiment, his death being unrecorded. McClurd's death is listed as "accidental."

no fighting here more than skirmishes and shooting across the river and some cannons that throw shells at our batteries and ours at theirs."[219] Despite the conditions, only two men from the regiment deserted in June and July, both recent conscripts. The troops were determined to hold on. The fortitude of the 34th NC did not go unnoticed in Richmond. The Confederate congress passed joint resolutions in June to recognize and express appreciation to certain units for distinguished service. The 34th NC was among those regiments recognized.[220]

Prisoners of War

As the besieged troops stuck it out, the regiment's prisoners of war languished in northern prisons. Between May and June, over 10,000 rebel prisoners arrived at Point Lookout from Grant's summer campaign. There were 15,500 men at Point Lookout. Disease was everywhere. Twenty-eight of the regiment's prisoners of war had died by the end of July. Most of them had been captured in the Gettysburg campaign. July 4th, 1864 was hot and sunny at Point Lookout. Federal gunboats in the bay were firing guns to celebrate Independence Day. Private Asa Hazelwood had been suffering a fever for several days since coming down with the measles. As the gunboats roared and guards cheered, Asa, a husband and father of six, quietly died. It would be several months before his regiment or his family back home would be notified. His status had been "Missing in Action" since North Anna. He was one of 204 prisoners that died in July of 1864, at Point Lookout, three from the 34th North Carolina. John McFadden and Washington Blankenship died later in the month.

The Battle of the Crater

On July 30th, at 4:45 a.m., some of the men were asleep in the trenches, and others were standing guard as the sun was about to usher in another scorching day. Temperatures had been in the 90's the last few days. It hit 98 the day before. It had rained truly little all month long. The men choked on dust and swatted at flies. Without warning, the largest explosion of the war erupted north of their position. Explosions were normal, but this one was different. The 34th NC was far enough away not to be harmed by the blast, but they could see it from their position. Ancil Dycus described the explosion this way,

---

[219] (Tisdale 1997) Letter from Dycus dated July 18, 1864, page 53.
[220] The Western Democrat June 28, 1864. (digitalnc.org)

"When they lit the fuse the earth shook beneath our feet. Then a huge mass shot into the air with flames and sounds of loud thunder. I was far enough away that I wasn't hurt, but I could see a rain of rocks, earth, beams, timber, and even mangled bodies of men fall. After the smoke cleared some, we could see a great crater and many of our men fell back."[221]

Suddenly, A. P. Hill's line had a smoldering hole 170 feet long, 70 feet wide, and 30 feet deep. For over a month, Federal troops, many of them coal miners from Pennsylvania, had been tunneling toward the Confederate line. After digging the 511-foot main line, they extended out in T-shaped fashion. The top of the T was a 75-foot gallery under the rebel line. They packed the gallery with 320 kegs holding 8,000 pounds of gunpowder twenty feet below the surface. The explosion killed 278 members of the 18th and 22nd South Carolina regiments, virtually destroying several entire companies. A few minutes after the explosion, Federal artillery began firing, and the infantry advanced. General Hill ordered Mahone's division to counter-attack. The men of the 34th North Carolina and the rest of the Light Division stayed in place and were not involved in the action. In a bitter back and forth action that lasted several hours, Confederates fought and eventually held the line. It was a bizarre and ugly battle, but the daring Union assault failed.

Both sides now settled in for an extended siege. Hill's line stretched east and south of Petersburg. Trenches continued to be dug. Most of the trees in the area were cut for trench supports and firewood, leaving just small patches of trees here and there. Dust clouds rose at the slightest movement. For shelter from the sun, troops placed canvas, blankets, tree limbs, and anything they could find over trenches. Rations were very scarce. What they had was barely fit to eat. Much of it was wretched bacon with old peas or wormy corn meal. Much of the meat was spoiled, and clean water was in noticeably short supply. Diarrhea hospitalized many. The line occupied by the Third Corps was continually threatened. The line eventually extended around the lower half of Petersburg to protect the vital railroads, without which they could not supply the army.

---

[221] (Tisdale 1997) Letter from Dycus dated August 26, 1864, page 54.

Ream's Station – August 25, 1864

On August 17th, the Union V Corps advanced and occupied a mile of the Weldon Railroad near Globe Tavern and moved northward toward Petersburg. On the 18th and 19th, the divisions of Heth and Mahone blunted the advance in severe fighting, but the Federals still held the railroad. On August 20th, the fighting quieted down, and rain came through the area and settled the dust and provided some much-needed water to the men in the trenches. The next day was rainy and stormy. Confederates attacked but were viciously driven back, unable to reclaim the vital rail line. On August 21st, The Federal II Corps, under Winfield Scott Hancock destroyed six miles of track around Ream's Station. "Hancock the Superb" had been severely wounded at Gettysburg but was back in command. On the afternoon of August 24th, the Light Division, minus Thomas's brigade, slipped out of the trenches and began moving toward Ream's Station, taking a circuitous route[222] approaching by Dinwiddie State Road. At dark, they bivouacked three miles west of Ream's Station.

Around 8:00 the next morning, they moved to within a half mile of the station and formed a line of battle with Wilcox's division on the right and Heth's men on the left. Around two in the afternoon, Wilcox's three brigades, led by Scales,' opened the attack with Young's Sharpshooters in front engaging their Federal counterparts. The 13th North Carolina drove in the Yankee skirmish line and fell back for the main assault. The division made two gallant assaults, but they were driven back with considerable loss. Much of the fire came from enfilading musket and artillery from the right. They fell back in good order.

The 34th's Captain Young and his Sharpshooter battalion kept busy. Supported by McGowan's Sharpshooters, they charged a strongly entrenched line of Federal Sharpshooters on the Confederate right. The Federals put up stiff resistance but eventually broke to the rear. They chased the retreating enemy until they came into Hancock's main line and ran into a blizzard of lead. They dropped back to the crest of a ridge about 400 yards back and fired into the Yankee line. For five

---

[222] (Dunlop 2012) The brigade's movements are described on page 190 and following.

hours, they traded fire and held their ground, keeping constant pressure on the enemy lines.

"O! The majesty of that scene!"

Confederate artillery went to work on the Federal lines while reinforcements came up. At 5:40, the final attack went forward. This time, six brigades assaulted the Federal line. The brigades of Lane, Cooke, and MacRae led the assault. Scales' brigade, with Anderson and McGowan were to the left and rear, advancing as reserves. They advanced 200 yards over fallen trees and abatis. The three front brigades yelled and jumped the main Union line, fighting wildly, hand-to-hand. General Heth personally led his men in the attack, at one point carrying the colors himself exposed to deadly fire. Soon, the Yankee regiments broke as Hancock tried in vain to rally his men. T. D. Lattimore wrote, "Scales' North Carolina and Anderson's Georgia Brigades made the first assault on the enemy's works and were repulsed with considerable loss, the right of the line being exposed to frightful enfilading fire of artillery and musketry; but, while feeling the sting of defeat in our attack, with swelling hearts we witnessed the gallant charge of Cook's, MacRae's, and Lane's brigades."

The main Federal line was broken, but the Federals were still entrenched on the railroad on the Confederate right. General Scales ordered an assault on the railroad. His proud brigade swept forward and drove the remaining Yankee defenders away just as darkness was settling in.

The battle of Ream's Station showed that plenty fighting spirit remained in Scales' brigade. Scales' final assault at the railroad is overshadowed by the main assault on the Federal line, but it was no less important. At dark, their hearts swelled with pride as they climbed the railroad and planted their flag. The sky turned black and flashed with lightening as troops searched for the wounded. They had seen defeat and hardship all summer. The victory here gave them one final burst of pride.

Captain Thomas C. Evans of the 13th North Carolina wrote proudly of the brigade's part in the battle. He felt that the brigade was not given due credit for its part. His regiment had been in every phase of the battle and had served alongside the 34th North Carolina. He wrote, "As we stood with arms in hand...the heavens grew blacker than

I have known them, and lurid streaks of lightning so vivid, so fierce, that the eyes would blind, played above our heads, while thunder rattled and rolled, peal after peal, that made the very earth shake. O! the majesty of that scene! "God is in His holy temple!" spake the storm. Hushed be the shouts of victory! Silenced every thought of war and bloodshed! Let all the earth keep silent before him. Poor fool man! His proudest battle yell – his loudest clamor of arms and roar of artillery – is but poor mimicry of that grand voice!"[223]

The 34th North Carolina suffered at least seventeen casualties from the battle. Seven were killed in action.

Casualties from the Battle of Ream's Station

Killed in Action

Thomas Carpenter	E	Pvt.	Daniel Goodnight	D	Pvt.
John T Clodfelter	D	Pvt.	James K McNeely	D	Sgt.
Andrew G Dickson	F	Pvt.	Hiram P Milligan	F	Pvt.
Andrew D Flack	C	Pvt.			

Wounded

Stephen D Baber	C	Pvt.	James Presnel	C	Pvt.
John Black	A	Pvt.	Joshua Richardson	A	Cpl.
Benjamin Carpenter	E	Sgt.	Richard Stephens	G	Pvt.
Joel Corriher	D	Sgt.	Lorenzo T Wilkie	C	Pvt.
Benjamin O Newton	F	Pvt.			

Captured

Henry Sheets	A	Pvt.	

Richard Stephens of Company G had volunteered in 1861, He was shot in the arm at Frayser's Farm and was wounded in the head by artillery fire at Fredericksburg. He went AWOL in September of 1862, and did not return until August 19, 1864. Six days later, he was wounded at Ream's Station. On August 30th, he deserted to the Yankees and was sent to public works in Columbus, Ohio. He later escaped from the work detail and was arrested and confined in Wheeling, WV until the end of the war.

---

[223] (Evans 2017) "Scales' Brigade," *Raleigh Confederate*, September 8, 1864, p. 1 col. 2

Lt. Lorenzo T. Wilkie was shot in the lower left lung. He had been with the regiment since 1861, and was discharged due to the wound. The 27-year-old veteran survived and headed home to Rutherford County. Benjamin Newton had joined in April of 1864. He was wounded in the left leg and right hand, losing two fingers. He was discharged. Joshua Richardson of Ashe County had also been with the regiment since 1861, He had missed only two musters due to sickness. His left arm was amputated on the field by Dr. Miller. After recovering, he was discharged.

Surgeon John F. Miller

Richardson's battlefield amputation may have been the last performed by Dr. John Miller. Miller had been on every battlefield. He had seen more blood and gore than anyone could imagine and had lost two brothers in the war. When he enlisted in 1861, at age 27, he had never seen a gunshot wound back home in Cleveland County. After three years of service, he treated such wounds routinely and amputated arms and legs quickly and easily. Miller's skill had saved numerous lives. He spent many long days and nights treating mangled men in barns, sheds, under tents, or shade trees, sometimes able to patch them back together, sometimes not. Shortly after Ream's Station, Miller was commissioned an Examiner of Hospitals for the Army of Northern Virginia, taking him from the front lines to the hospitals in Petersburg and Richmond. In December, he was appointed Chief Surgeon of the Department of Eastern North Carolina and Southern Virginia. The position took him to eastern North Carolina where he could be near his wife, whom he had not seen since their marriage the year before.

At the end of August, the 34th NC took another muster. In the past two months, another 72 conscripts were brought in. The regiment had 310 men present for duty, up by 44 over the last muster. Most of the volunteers from 1861, were gone. Only 152 of those men were present for duty.

Battery Number 45

The victory at Ream's Station temporarily lifted spirits, but once they returned to the trenches, the tedium of life under siege returned. The 34th was stationed at a point in the line known as Battery Number 45. Cooler temperatures and rain brought some relief, but rations were still short, and the trenches were as dangerous as ever. A new assignment broke the monotony when Scales' brigade was employed as miners. A short distance from the line was a house owned by a Dr. Duval. The house was on a slight elevation, and if the Federals put a battery there, they would have a good range of fire on a large part of the Confederate line. The rebels could not extend their line to include this area, so they decided to dig a mine to the location, and if the Yankees planted a battery there, they would blow it up. It was slow work. Because the Federals had cut the Weldon Railroad tracks, supplies took longer to reach the men. The tools were poor in quality and quickly wore out or broke. They dug the gallery barely ten feet from the surface. When finished, it would extend out 323 yards to Dr. Duval's house. They would then dig the chambers and be ready to pack it with explosives if needed. It would be November before the mine was finished.

Across Lee's army, desertions began to rise. Four men from the 34th NC deserted in August and twelve more in September. Most deserters crossed no-man's land and surrendered to the Yankees rather than try and survive in the Virginia countryside. It happened all over the line. Usually under cover of darkness, often in small groups, hungry Confederates crossed into the Yankee lines and handed in their weapons. Federal authorities devised a way to deal with the many Confederate deserters without taxing the already over-crowded prisons. They sent them to various cities in the north for employment on public works details. They built fortifications, roads, bridges, sewer systems, and various other projects. Rebel deserters were given a hot meal and medical care, even cash if they brought in their musket. Once they "swallowed the oath," the war was over for them.

Hiram Brewer enlisted in 1861, in Montgomery County. He deserted in August of 1862, but returned in May of 1864, and had served through the summer. He left the line on September 7th with his friend Alexander Boyd, who had been with the regiment for four months. Hiram was sent to Philadelphia on public works for the war's duration. Brothers Henry and Hiram Overcash from Rowan County enlisted together in 1861, Hiram died of disease in July of 1862. Henry went AWOL after his brother's death and returned after a fourteen-month absence. He deserted in late September and went to Philadelphia. Enoch Parker had joined the regiment in April. He took the oath and went to Cincinnati. John Peterson had been with the regiment only a month when he deserted. He told the Yankees he wanted to go to Knoxville, TN where he had three sons in the Union army. He was sent instead to Cleveland, Ohio.

There was little the Confederate or state authorities could do to stem rising desertions. Governor Vance issued a proclamation promising pardons for deserters who returned to duty.[224] Perry Steadman deserted shortly before Gettysburg. Asbury White deserted during the Overland Campaign. Both returned and were pardoned.

Where in the World is Colonel Gordon?

On July 18, 1864, Lt. Colonel George T. Gordon was granted a 40-day leave to visit Bermuda. The records do not state whether he made the trip or not, but on August 28, he had not returned and was listed AWOL from the regiment. General Scales wrote to inquire if the leave had been extended. Gordon has lost favor with General Scales who was prepared to take steps to have his commission removed due to prolonged absence. Gordon had been in and out of hospitals much of 1864, due to his health and wounds, but he had recovered and was expected back at his post. He was at the Spotswood Hotel in Richmond on September 24th but had not been heard from since.[225] On September 29th, he was hospitalized for incipient Phthisis, early-stage Tuberculosis. He was given a temporary certificate of disability, and so his absence was satisfactorily explained. On November 25, 1864, Gordon was retired to the Invalid Corps. In the remaining months of the war, the irascible Englishman served on the staffs of Generals Whiting and Braxton Bragg, performing administrative duties as Assistant Inspector General.

Post-war writings say that he was George Tomline Gordon who was born in England in 1823 and moved to Canada after a scandalous affair and resulting legal trouble. He was married with children. He was called many things: gambler, charming con-man, and adulterer. It is

---

[224] This was at least his third such proclamation, which brought at least a few men back to the ranks.
[225] Spotswood was one of the largest and most luxurious hotels in Richmond. It was also said to be a place where much gambling went on. Many prominent individuals stayed there during and after the war. It was destroyed by a fire in 1870.

believed that he was never actually in the British Army, only the Canadian Militia during the Pig War incident. He was convicted of embezzlement and left Vancouver after escaping from debtor's prison and then came to Virginia and volunteered his services to the Confederacy. The men of the 34th NC knew him as a real fighter, and his record of war wounds stand as proof. If legend is correct, he died in New Orleans in 1868 at the hospital named Hotel Dieu (French for House of God) at age 44. Judging from his medical records, he may have died from Tuberculosis.

The Siege Drags On

By September 29th, Federal troops had taken Fort Harrison north of the James River. Scales' brigade was lent to Hoke's division to retake it. The attack, however, was poorly executed. Scales' men were never engaged and returned to Battery 45. Early the next morning Federal troops took Fort Archer south of Battery No. 45 and advanced northward toward Jones's Farm and occupied Peebles's Farm. Brigades from Heth and Wilcox caught the Yankees off guard and drove them back by dark, capturing some supplies in the process. Yankees still held Peebles's Farm. On October 1st, a dark and rainy day, Heth and Wilcox's divisions tried once more to drive them away, but the attack stalled against stiff resistance. The Yankees were then able to extend their line in the area, edging closer to the Boydton Plank Road and the vital Southside Railroad.

The regiment suffered few casualties in these actions. Alfred Foster and James Henderson, both long-time members of Company C, were wounded but both eventually returned to duty. John Black, from Company A, left the regiment in December of 1862, with an illegal discharge. John was ordered back to the regiment and returned a year later, under protest. He was shot in the lower left leg at Ream's Station but returned to duty. He was shot in the left arm in one of the recent actions. The war was over for John. His arm required amputation.

The regiment returned to Battery No. 45 and resumed digging the tunnel they had started earlier in the month. Hill's part of the line was the flank and the strongest part of the line. Other areas were so thin that men stood fifteen feet apart in places. Lee ordered every man on extra duty or detached service that could be spared to be sent to the trenches. Some of the men from the 34th had been working at hospitals or ordinance details and returned to the line. Even some who had been under arrest were released on condition they would return to duty.

In October, desertions across the army were rising. The picket lines between the fortifications were close enough that opposing troops could converse. Yankee troops taunted Confederates into deserting with hot coffee, food, and a warm place to sleep. They also enticed them with offers to go on the public works projects. They sometimes held unofficial truces to work out the details. Jeremiah Patterson, a conscript who had joined just after the Wilderness, took their offer in October, and was sent to Henry County, Indiana for the duration of the war. James and Aaron Capps were conscripts from Company E who had only been with the regiment since the 21st of August. They deserted on October 7th, making their way home through the countryside rather than crossing over to the Yankees. Not a single man from the regiment deserted in November and only two in December.

Calvin J. Murchison

On the night of October 6th, a tragic accidental shooting occurred. Calvin J. Murchison was 20 when he enlisted in 1861, in Montgomery County. He had been wounded at Chancellorsville which prevented him from going to Gettysburg, but he returned and had been everywhere else with the regiment. He had been standing vidette duty all day and was relieved around dark. He was walking back to the line when a member of the 13th North Carolina mistook him for a prowling Yankee and shot him in the bowels. He died around four o'clock the next morning. He had survived so much violence during the war, only to be shot accidentally while coming off guard duty.

"According to the talk, that "olde Abe" was born right here in Rutherford County."

On October 19th, Ancil Dycus's wife wrote him a letter that caused some stir among the Rutherford County men. She wrote, "I want to tell you what the local talk is around here – besides the war. According to the talk, that "olde Abe" was born right here in Rutherford County. Mrs. Martin told some folks that she knew for sure he was born here in the county because she knew Nancy Hanks, his mother, personally. She said when Nancy Hanks left here with a wagon train headed west, she was holding Abraham in her lap."[226] Indeed there was considerable talk about this subject and has been ever since. The local legend is that Nancy Hanks gave birth to Lincoln as the illegitimate son of Abe Enloe. She then moved to Kentucky and married Tom Lincoln. Many people note that Tom Lincoln was average height, while Abraham Enloe was tall, like the 6' 4" President Lincoln. The Enloe's were said to be "tall, raw-boned, with high cheeks and immense ears." A friend of President Lincoln said that Lincoln once told him, "My right name is Enloe, but I have always gone by the name of my step-father." One Kentucky man was said to have frequently walked to school with Lincoln in 1811, casting doubt on Lincoln's birth year being 1809. Several Elizabethton, KY residents claimed to have seen him as a toddler, two years before he was supposed to have been born in 1809.[227]

    The letter gave the men something to talk about in the trenches, but the reality of life on the war's front line remained. Life on the home front had gotten worse as well, as deserter and outlaw bands roamed freely and citizens in parts of the Quaker Belt were in a state of near revolt. In September, Collett Leventhorpe was given command of the Home Guards and promoted to Brig. General with the mission of rounding up deserters and Unionists. He established a HQ in Asheboro, and his companies fanned out through the region. Some used brutal tactics including what was described as a Bull Pen to incarcerate forty-two Randolph County women whose husbands, fathers, or sons refused to fight and die, as one paper put it, "in the slave-holder's rebellion." The troops were also implicated in the brutal tactics used to arrest William Owens, as well as the execution of Northcutt. Commanding his troops from a distance, Leventhorpe likely did not personally order these tactics, but the stigma followed him the rest of his life. In 1872 he

---

[226] (Tisdale 1997) Letter from Mary Dycus dated October 19th, 1864, page 57
[227] Information from the article "Abraham Lincoln – A Rutherford County Native?" by Tom Melton in The Heritage of Rutherford County, published by the Genealogical Society of old Tryon County. The Bostic Lincoln Center in Bostic, NC is dedicated to this part of history. So far, the history books haven't been rewritten but evidence exists to support the belief that President Lincoln was born in Rutherford County. See http://rutherfordcoc.org/media/history/The_Abraham_Lincoln_of_Rutherford_County.pdf

ran for State Auditor, but his opponents labeled him "Bull Pen Man." Leventhorpe vigorously denied responsibility for those actions, but he was defeated.[228]

The Last Winter

At the end of October, the regiment took its final muster of the war. From there, the regiment either stopped taking musters, or the records have been lost. They recorded 64 new recruits, but dropped 43, mostly due to death or desertion. They had 390 men present for duty out of 669 on the rolls. Nearly half of them had been with the regiment a year or less. Winter quarters officially began on November 12th, but the men hardly noticed. Near the end of the month, the mine shaft and gallery they had started in September was finished. It was never used, however. Deserters from the brigade told the Yankees of its existence, and they never placed a battery in the area. They hardly needed it anyway. By then, they had extended the line farther south and had control over much of the area.

Weather was getting colder. Mornings became frosty. Clothing was entirely lacking. Shoes were nearly worn out if they had them at all. Yankees carried out raids on portions of the line, and artillery and rifle fire continued to harass the besieged rebels. President Lincoln had just been reelected. He declared the last Thursday of November Thanksgiving Day. Yankee troops were treated to a fare of turkey and all the trimmings. The smell that drifted across no-man's land was torture to the famished Confederates who had nothing but cornbread and rancid bacon. Hungry as they were, the rebels ceased fire out of respect for the holiday. The Confederacy was on life support by this time. They could not muster enough for one good hot meal.

The situation was also growing increasingly dire back home. Holden's Peace Movement that began in 1863, with rallies across the state waned after he was defeated by Governor Vance in a landslide election, but problems with bands of deserters and conscription dodgers continued. Newspapers reported many incidents of violence and robbery.

---

[228] After the war, Leventhorpe moved to New York and collected antiques for a while and travelled to England several times. He finally settled back in Wilkes County, NC. He died there on December 1, 1889 at age 74.

Organizations like the Heroes of America gained strength. In early November, Linville Price, a deserter from Company A, was arrested for being a member of the Heroes of America. Linville was a relative of the Price men who were hung in Ashe County in 1863. He and another member of the HOA were on a train from Wytheville, VA and were arrested between Dublin and Lynchburg after passing the secret signs and passwords to an undercover agent.[229] Price and his companion were confined at Castle Thunder in Richmond.[230] The Rowan County men learned that the organization was active in their area. The Western Democrat published a letter from a repentant member of the organization from the county who denounced the organization claiming he had been deceived into joining.[231] A second article in the papers, by another member of the organization who claimed to have been deceived into joining, named several Rowan men who were members.[232] Hearing that the organization was operating in Rowan County on such a scale was troubling to the men in the regiment.

"During the winter, the regiment made a forced march, through rain, sleet, and snow"

In the first week of December, the Yankees again tried to sever the Weldon railroad. The weather was atrocious, but Lee had no choice but to respond. Hill's Third Corps left the trenches on the eighth of December. The 34th NC prepared to march as they had done so many times before. They cooked three days rations and stowed them in their haversacks, checked weapons, and filled canteens. They slung their bed rolls over their shoulders and wrapped themselves in blankets. The forty-mile march was memorable. The men battled high wind and cold

---

[229] Official Records of the Union and Confederate Armies, Washington 1902, memo signed by Jno. B Williams and Thos. McGill dated November 9, 1864 forwarded to the Secretary of War.

[230] Linville Price's record with the 34th NC shows that he signed a receipt for a clothing issue in December of 1864, indicating he was released and returned to the regiment. It is his last record with the regiment. Some records indicate he may have served briefly in a Virginia regiment.

[231] The Western Democrat / July 19, 1864 (digitalnc.org), article titled "The Secret Society in Rowan County

[232] The Western Democrat / August 2, 1864 (digitalnc.org) None of those named were members of the 34th NC.

rain as they started out, and the weather got worse from there. They braved rain, sleet, snow, ice, and wind. Several of the men were impressed when they saw General Scales dismount his horse to put two sick men from the brigade on. The General walked the last ten miles to Bellfield beside the horse, despite the ill soldiers offering to give his horse back. He remounted only after his leg could take him no farther. Scales' leg had given him problems ever since Gettysburg, so marching ten miles in these conditions was difficult. The men long remembered the selfless act.[233]

At the railroad, they found sixteen miles of track destroyed with piles of smoldering cross ties and bent rails littering the area. The Yankees had done their work and were gone. General Hill tried to mount a pursuit, but the weather and weariness of the troops kept them from finding the raiders. A year ago, they could have given the Yankees a run for their money, but the tired legs of the Third Corps just couldn't make a go of it. A sleet storm added to their misery. The night was spent sitting or lying around campfires wrapped in blankets and gum cloths trying to keep warm. By morning, they were dazed and tired as they started back. General Hill wrote after returning to camp that it was the hardest trip he had ever made. They had marched forty miles in one day and one night in some of the worst weather they had ever marched in.

T. D. Lattimore made that march. He wrote, "During the winter the regiment made a forced march, through rain, sleet, and snow to Bellfield Station on the Petersburg & Weldon railroad. The objective of the march was to look after a raiding party of Federal cavalry. On our arrival, we found that they had retired. This also was a winter of intense suffering among the soldiers. Almost destitute of provisions and clothing, many of them deserted and crossed the line to the enemy."
"they have had all they can take of these hard times."

The regiment returned to Battery No. 45. Misery increased in the weeks ahead. Ancil Dycus wrote to his wife about life in the trenches, "It has been a hard time this winter, as we are almost destitute of provisions and clothing. Many of our men have deserted and crossed the lines to the enemy. They feel they have had all they can take of

---

[233] Article titled "A War Incident" in The Danbury Reporter / October 9, 1884. (digitalnc.org).

these hard times. I pray that I won't get to the place where I might do that. Here in the trenches and bombproofs, life gets hard, but sometimes we talk and can even joke and laugh. Some of the men play cards or checkers, but mostly we talk of home and our loved ones. We have dug and dug more trenches, sometimes in the mud and sometimes through frozen ground."[234]

    The winter weather did indeed make life much harder. Every necessity was in short supply. They drew one issue of clothing in November and two in December, but it wasn't enough. The socks were made of cotton and wore out quickly. General Hill was frequently seen riding along the lines. He was very courteous and attentive to the needs of the men. Many soldiers walked barefoot in the snow and slogged through ankle-deep water and mud in the trenches. They sat shivering in bombproofs and cut-outs. Even their meager soldier's pay was far behind schedule. All was borne with minimal complaint.

Seine-hauling

    On the last day of 1864, a daring group of men decided to take matters into their own hands to provide clothing and supplies. Captain John D. Young of the 34th North Carolina still led the sharpshooter battalion from Scales' brigade. His group, with their counter-parts in McGowan's brigade, decided to go seine-hauling. Seine-hauling had been done before in the Petersburg lines with some success. A seine was a fish net held by two fishermen to catch fish. The Sharpshooters would be the seine and the Yankees would be the catch. Basically, the two battalions would advance on the enemy pickets in single-file lines with sixteen hand-picked men out front to protect the advance. The formation roughly resembled an arrow with the advance men forming the point and the two battalions the shaft of the arrow. They were to hit hard and fast and penetrate the enemy picket lines in the early morning hours of December 31st. Once through the line, they would fan out east and west, turn back toward their lines and bag as many Yankee prisoners as they could with their fine winter coats, boots, and camp equipment. At 4:00 in the morning, the raiders slipped stealthily forward. The night was darker than usual, giving them an advantage.

---

[234] (Tisdale 1997) Letter from Dycus date unknown, page 62.

A hundred yards from the enemy rifle pits, an unseen ditch posed a problem. One by one, the men hopped in and quietly climbed back out the other side, until one of McGowan's men slipped and his gun went off. Alerted, the Federal troops fired a volley into the darkness. The raiders raced ahead and punched through the Yankee line. Once through, Captain Young led his men to the right as planned, and McGowan's men turned left. Yankees became disoriented. They had been attacked from the front, but suddenly rebels were behind them. Feeling surrounded, they dropped their weapons and surrendered. Had it not been for the misfired gun, they could have been more successful, but they brought in 37 Yankee prisoners and a good supply of clothing, food, and equipment. The only rebel wounded was the man who slipped and accidentally fired his gun. The raiders were back in their lines by sunrise with their prisoners and captured goods, receiving slaps on the back from grateful comrades. For the Yankees, it turns out they had been forewarned of the raid the day before by a rebel deserter. The Yankees hadn't taken the report seriously or they would have been better prepared.

The small victory gave them something to cheer, which was rare in 1864. In a brutal year of warfare, another one hundred men from the regiment had died. Thirty-seven died of battle-related wounds the rest from disease.[235] Twenty-four had died in the northern prisons at Point Lookout and Elmira, two from wounds, the rest from disease. Times were especially bad at Point Lookout, where 500 prisoners died over the winter.

Lt. Alexander A. Cathey and the Immortal 600

Lt. Cathey's ordeal as a prisoner of war began at Gettysburg where he was wounded and left behind to be taken prisoner. On July 17, 1863, recovering from the amputation of his leg, he arrived at Decamp General Hospital at David's Island, NY. There, he was hospitalized for over two months. On October 1st, he entered the prison population at Fort Wood on Bedloe's Island. This fort was completed in 1811 and had a star-shaped stone wall with eleven points. The walls are prominently seen today surrounding the base of the Statue of Liberty on what is now called Liberty Island.

---

[235] Thirteen died in 1864 of causes not stated in the records.

By the end of October, Lt. Cathey was sick again and was sent back to Decamp General. After recovering, he was back at Fort Wood at the convalescent hospital. His condition improved further, and in January, word came he was being exchanged. At the end of the month, he was deemed fit to travel, so on the first day of February, he boarded a ship filled with prisoners headed for City Point, Virginia to be exchanged. Something happened to derail the exchange, however, and he and the other disappointed prisoners were detained at Fortress Monroe. They were then put on a boat to Fort McHenry, arriving there February 10th. On June 15, 1864, he was transferred to Fort Delaware.

Getting acquainted with the Fort Delaware prisoners, he learned that the camp commander, General Albin Schoepf, was viewed as a tolerable officer. His subordinates, however, had brutal reputations and were despised by the prisoners. Lt. Cathey was housed with the officers in wooden barracks outside the prison walls and fared better than the enlisted men inside the fort. But rations were quite short. Earlier that year, Secretary of War Edwin Stanton had ordered prison rations cut in retaliation for what was viewed as unfair treatment of northern troops held in southern prisons. In August, he ordered package deliveries to prisoners stopped and limited trade with prison sutlers.

By then, however, things were looking up for Lt. Cathey. It was announced that 600 prisoners would be exchanged soon, and he hoped to be among them. On the day, the list came out, the names were read alphabetically, and when they got to C, Lt. Cathey's name was called. Some were skeptical at whether they would be exchanged, including Lt. Cathey who had been through this before. But he was hopeful that the exchange would happen this time. On August 20th, the 600 hopeful prisoners, including the one-legged Lt. Cathey, boarded the steamer *Crescent City* bound for South Carolina.

The prisoners were sent to the hold below deck. There were four rows of bunks, each containing three tiers. There were ports fore and aft, and small air holes every ten feet. With 600 men crammed inside, there was little air circulation. The bunks and machinery took most of the space. Only two three-foot-wide rows between bunks allowed the men to move around. Prisoners had to stand or lay on the bunks. The sinks were on the upper deck. Only two prisoners were allowed there at a time. The water was foul and made many of them sick. When the boilers ran, the temperature soared. The men sweltered in the cramped dark hold. They mostly stayed in their bunks and suffered. This was Lt. Cathey's home for nineteen long days.

On August 24th, the boat dropped anchor at Port Royal Harbor, South Carolina. They sat motionless for several days, and the heat in the ship's hold was stifling. A few times, they received fresh water, then the water supply stopped. For forty desperate hours, they had none. Finally, the ships condensers were fired up and produced boiling water for the prisoners. For the rest of their stay on the boat, that was their only water supply. It was a miracle that none of them died during the nineteen-day ordeal. Many attributed their survival to the hope of being exchanged soon.[236] Their skin had been tanned when they boarded but had turned bleach white after being in the hold with no sunlight.

The unhealthy conditions were hard on Alex Cathey. He had been hospitalized much of his time as a prisoner. The conditions on the boat made him sick again, along with several others. On August 28th, Lt. Cathey was one of forty prisoners taken from the *Crescent City* and sent to a hospital at nearby Beaufort. The next day, the *Crescent City* left for Charleston. Cathey recovered at the U.S. General Hospital for Prisoners of War at Beaufort, SC.

Cathey was fortunate the day he was carried off the hell-hole of the *Crescent* and taken to Beaufort. He would not have survived the rest of the journey. At Charleston, the boat stayed at anchor for several more days before the prisoners were let off. There was no exchange in store for these men. They were confined at Morris Island, where the cross-fire between Union and Confederate forts unnerved the prisoners. Confederate gunners were aware of their presence and were careful not to hit them, but shells did occasionally fall too close for comfort. In October, they were moved to Fort Pulaski on the Savannah River. The winter was unusually cold, and the prisoners were housed in casemates with little protection from the cold. At Beaufort on December 13th, Lt. Cathey was part of a group of prisoners taken from the hospital and sent to Charleston for exchange. After enduring seventeen months in captivity, Lt. Cathey was back in Richmond where he was hospitalized.

---

[236] (Stokes 2013) Quoting Captain George W. Nelson

For the rest of the prisoners that left Fort Delaware with Lt. Cathey, the worst part of their ordeal started in January. For six weeks, their rations were ten ounces of insect-infected cornmeal and a small supply of pickles. These were retaliatory measures for the suffering of Union troops at Andersonville and other southern prisons. Had Lt. Cathey been among them in his weakened state, he would have perished. Forty-six of them did. The men were called the Immortal 600 and were admired throughout the south for their fortitude. The survivors were sent back to Fort Delaware.

Lt. Cathey's health improved over the next few weeks. In March, he was retired to the Invalid Corps.

Lieutenant David Beam Harrill, The Sandy Run Yellow Jackets - Company B[237]

---

[237] Photo courtesy Rick Calert, and G. Thompson

Chapter 14.
The Bitter End

In early February, President Lincoln met with Confederate representatives to discuss peace. Lincoln was negotiating from a position of strength and would consider nothing short of the unconditional surrender of the Confederate armies, which was rejected. When the results of the meeting were made known in the trenches, many of the regiments mustered their troops and asked if submission to President Lincoln's terms was acceptable. According to Major Dunlop of McGowan's Sharpshooters, "The poll was taken, and every mother's son of them voted to fight it out to the bitter end."

And so, began the bitter end.

Disease and desertion had thinned Lee's ranks. Morale plummeted as stomachs growled and men shivered in the frozen trenches. Lee's army was outnumbered at least three-to-one. Pvt. Jacob R. Dellinger wrote on February 14, "They say that we will hafto {have to} fite it out and I don't think it will take us long to do it if the men keeps going to the Yankees like they have bin for the last munt {month}. They will soon all bee gone. The men is desertin, goin home and goin to the Yankees. They was 25 men left our Brigade and started home the other night." He also noted, "Brother Washington (Frederick Washington Dellinger) is with me and Henry, he has bin here about 10 days. He is very well satisfied heare. We are all three well at this time. I don't think that any of us will get home this winter. Lieut E. Houser is well and expects to come home shortly on a furlough. Cousin W. C. Childeress sends you all his best wishes. He is well."[238]

"...two double handfuls of corn meal that is supposed to last three days"

Ancil Dycus wrote home in January after returning from a leave, "They say rations are shorter than they were when I left. I had enough rations to do me when I was here before, but I don't know how it will be now. I drew two days rations today and got two double handfuls of corn meal that is supposed to last three days and a small bit of bacon." He closed the letter by saying, "...if I never see you in this

---

[238] Letter from Jacob Dellinger dated 2/14/1865. Letter courtesy of Mike Stroupe.

world, I hope to meet you all in Heaven to part no more. Write soon and often. I remain your affectionate husband until death. Ancil."

In February, he received a reply that read, "As I take my pen in hand to write you a few lines, I find myself wanting to see you so bad…We have managed, in spite of the shortages, for which I am thankful to the Lord. Some of the people in this area are suffering from want of food. We try to share what we can. Some of the people say they are down to eating sour kraut, even for breakfast. I pray you are getting enough to eat, but I hear the shortages for the troops are great. When I go to bed at night and lay there thinking about you being so far away from home and in danger, the tears roll down my face. It is very hard not to let Louisa and Dory see me cry. Today I made Louisa a little dress out of one of my old dresses. Dory can wear the few clothes Louisa has out-grown. I was getting low on wood, but your father came and brought some help yesterday and they cut wood and I was glad to see my wood pile build up. I am very tired tonight and I will close by saying I remain your affectionate wife and send up my petition for God to keep you safe. Write as often as you can. Mary"[239]

Special Orders

General Grant issued Special Orders Number 3 in January. Any rebel who surrendered to Federal troops would not be confined if they were willing to take an oath not to take up arms against the United States. They would also be paid for weapons, horses, and equipment they brought in and could go to one of several northern cities for employment on public works projects. It was a good deal for freezing, half-starved rebels, and many took it.

In accordance with General Orders No. 64 from the War Department dated February 18, 1864, the Provost Marshall examined deserters. If judged to be truly deserting the rebel cause for good, Lincoln's Amnesty Proclamation of December 8, 1863, was read to them. By agreeing to it, they were pleading guilty to treason but were granted a full pardon. They then took an oath pledging to obey the laws of the United States, including those passed during the rebellion and proclamations issued by the President regarding slavery. They were

---

[239] (Tisdale 1997) These letters found on pages 67-68.

then asked if they desired employment from the United States. If so, they became laborers instead of soldiers.

From June through October 1864, 39 men from the 34th NC deserted, mostly new conscripts. None deserted in November and only two in December. Then, eight deserted in January followed by eighteen in February and thirty-six in March. Men started deserting from companies that had experienced little or no desertion up to this point. Company D had only two deserters for the whole war before the siege began; they had thirteen by the end of March of 1865. Company E had none until September-October 1864, when they had three. They had ten more from January-March. Companies F and G had not had a single deserter prior to arriving at Petersburg. Company F had seven after January, and G had six during the siege. The regiment had a total of 101 deserters in the final nine months of the war. Of these, 33 had been with the regiment since 1861, Even some core members of the regiment were giving up. Pride and devotion had carried them a long way, but the only thing that mattered in the end was survival.

Joseph Hogan from Montgomery County enlisted in 1861, at age 38. He was given the Badge of Distinction for his actions at Chancellorsville. Hogan deserted in the middle of March 1865, and spent the remainder of the war on a work detail in New York City. Joseph Byers was another unfaltering soldier. A post-war newspaper article stated, "I saw Byers carrying a musket at Petersburg in the summer of 1864, and he carried it until March 1865, dropped it and went home. He was popular with his men and was with his company almost continuously."[240] Byers was one of the few who made his way home instead of surrendering to the Yankees. This was a far more dangerous way to desert, but he made it home without being arrested.[241]

The fact that so many of the deserters from the war's final months were long-time veterans shows the toll the war had taken. Certainly, there was no lack of fortitude among them. Most bore the scars of wounds, badges of courage they wore with pride. But looking at their thinning lines and then staring across the bleak no-man's land

---

[240] Forest City Courier December 19, 1929 (digitalnc.org). The article was titled "Officers of Co. B 34th Regiment C.S.A.
[241] Byers' popularity continued after the war. He was the first post-war Sheriff elected in Cleveland County. He was prosperous and lived to age 85.

separating them from their foes, they knew that they had no chance of stopping the attack that was coming, and no one wanted to be the last man to die in a war they were going to lose.

Desertion and AWOL
34th North Carolina Infantry

Company	AWOLs All Musters	Desertions 1862-1864	Desertions Jan-Mar 1865	Total Desertions
A	146	30	2	32
B	41	7	2	9
C	31	4	9	13
D	4	7	7	14
E	7	3	10	13
F	11	0	7	7
G	18	4	2	6
H	39	8	7	15
I	46	6	5	11
K	44	22	9	31
Unknown			2	2
Totals	387	91	62	153

Colonel Lowrance Leaves the War Behind

On February 2nd, Colonel William Lee Joshua Lowrance was granted a leave of absence by General Lee. Lowrance had been with the regiment since 1861, and led it since late 1862, suffering multiple battle wounds in the process. Unlike his two predecessors, he had no military experience prior to the war, but he quickly became a seasoned professional, even leading the brigade on several occasions. He was thoughtful and intelligent, attentive to his duties, and showed great care for his men. Only lack of opportunity prevented his promotion to Brigadier General.

Col. Lowrance had been joined on Christmas day in 1864, by his younger brother, Samuel Newton Lowrance, who had transferred to the 34th NC from the 56th NC. Samuel had also seen much of the war and showed the signs of a soldier who was weakening. On January 2nd, the 24-year-old brother of Colonel Lowrance died. It is believed that when Col. Lowrance took his leave in February, he took his brother home. Samuel was laid to rest in the cemetery by the Prospect Presbyterian Church in Iredell County, only a mile from their boyhood home. Col. Lowrance then travelled south. On March 5th, he was hospitalized in Mobile, Alabama for chronic rheumatism and then was transferred to Oxford, Mississippi. On March 16th, 1865, he married Sarah Cordelia Stewart. He did not return to the war.

Lowrance yielded command of the 34th NC to George Norment who was promoted to Lt. Colonel. Norment was a 27-year-old farmer when he enlisted in 1861, as a Lieutenant in Company G. He was wounded at Gaines's Mill and Gettysburg and was promoted to Captain after the Battle of Ox Hill. He appears to have been a favorite of Colonel Lowrance. Norment was promoted to Major in September of 1864. When Lowrance went on leave, Norment was promoted to Lt. Colonel in the place of George Gordon who had been retired to the Invalid Corps. To facilitate Norment's promotions, Captains Wood and Hoyle both waived their right to consideration.

General Scales also went home on leave and did not return before the war's end. Scales had been wounded severely at both Chancellorsville and Gettysburg. The demands of his position never allowed time to heal, and he continued to have health problems. Command of the brigade fell to Colonel Joseph H. Hyman. General A. P. Hill remained with the Third Corps, but his health had been a constant struggle for over a year. He looked frail and sickly but was frequently seen riding his favorite horse, Champ, around the lines.

"The boys are bad out of heart."

Ancil Dycus wrote a despairing letter in the middle of February in which he said, "I got up the other morning to make a fire and started to fall. I hit my foot against something in the dark and tore off a piece of skin about as big as a silver half dollar from the ball of my foot. It is very sore, and I can't walk except on my heel. The boys are bad out of heart. A great many talk of running away and some talk of going home. I don't know how they will make it. Times are hard here and getting worse. A great many soldiers are barefoot and half naked. The weather is cold…We have no tents to shelter our heads and the mortars fall every evening and we have to dodge them. Mary, teach our little girls to read the scripture when they are older for they will find treasure there…Whether I live long or die soon, I have a hope to meet all of you and live eternally in heaven. Teach Louise and Dory to put their trust in the Lord Jesus Christ. We will pray and hope for the best although the worst may come. Ancil."

His wife replied saying, "We have heard how General Sherman has been taking his army of men through South Carolina…All the talk has been of burning homes, houses knocked to pieces by balls and of the famine and murder…Columbia was set ablaze. To think of how the poor women and children must have been so terrified. Columbia is in ruins and the talk is that Sherman has struck out toward Goldsboro, North Carolina."[242]

Eight Dollars Cash for a Musket

Desertions increased as spring approached. Most of the regiment's deserters were sent to public works details. Philadelphia was the most popular destination. Others went to Washington, D.C., Baltimore, Pittsburgh, and Indianapolis. Some were sent to Indiana, and Illinois. They often deserted in small groups, sometimes pre-arranging their moves with Yankee pickets to avoid being accidently shot. Once safely in Yankee hands, they were given their first decent meal in months and $8.00 cash if they brought their musket in.

Six men deserted together February 21st including John Dobbins, A. J. Dobbins, James Presnel, and John Presnel.[243] Five men from Company F defected on February 26th and were sent to Oil City, PA.[244] William Crook Lee had enlisted in 1861. His cousin William Capers Lee joined in 1863. Along with the Lee's, John Hardin, Sidney Wright, and Simpson Warlick spent the rest of the war at Oil City. John Hardin had been in the war since 1861. He had enlisted with his brother William and cousin Benjamin, who were both killed at Gaines's Mill.

---

[242] (Tisdale 1997) These letters found on pages 69-70.
[243] According to the records, the Dobbins' were transported to Utica, NY, and the Presnels went to Baltimore.
[244] The town was so-named because oil had been discovered there. By war's end, the population had boomed. With the increased need for public works, they took in some rebel deserters and put them to work.

Six men from the 34th deserted on March 7th. Eight left the next day, two the day after that. Five left March 18th, and two more on the 19th. Of the eight men who deserted on Marth 8th, four were members of the Rollins family from Rutherford County; Dock, Lawson, Drury, and John. They deserted with James Scoggins, William Scoggins, Robert Price, and Alex Keever. Price and Keever went to Philadelphia. The Scoggins' and Rollins' all went to Chattanooga, TN. Five days earlier, Alex Keever had written his wife saying, "I think now it is a verry good plan for a man *not* to desert atall for I think the war will end this spring anyway and them that stays with their company will do the best."[245] Keever apparently changed his mind.

Everyone knew that once the weather broke, Grant would unleash his troops on the fragile rebel lines. The Confederacy was crumbling. Columbia and Charleston were in Union hands. Wilmington had fallen, and Sherman was marching toward Virginia. Lee's army already faced impossible odds. With Sherman on the way, they were completely hopeless. Desertion bred desertion, as men lost hope.

Fort Stedman – March 25, 1865

As April approached, those remaining in the trenches watched with anxiety for any sign of movement. The first move came from General Lee. On the night of March 24-25, two Light Division brigades, Lane and Thomas, slipped quietly out of the trenches. Leading the way was Captain John D. Young and his Sharpshooters. The rest of Scales' brigade, with the 34th North Carolina, remained in place. The men marching away were part of a strike force assembled to attack Fort Stedman on the eastern part of the line. The 34th North Carolina stretched out to cover the thinning line.

According to Major Dunlop, Captain Young's Sharpshooters preceded the assault columns and helped the engineers clear the way of obstructions.[246] Behind them were three groups of 100 sharpshooters each, ready to storm the fort relying on speed and surprise. They carried unloaded muskets, so no one would accidentally fire and alert the enemy as happened during the December 31st raid. Nearing the Yankee skirmish line, the men exchanged banter with the Yankee

---

[245] (Perry 2012) Quoting Perkins, Alexander Keever papers, March 5, 1865.
[246] (Dunlop 2012) Page 246. Some accounts say that engineers were employed in the removal of obstructions.

troops. The Federals believed they were deserters and were not alarmed, since such exchanges had become commonplace.

At around 4:00 on the morning of March 25th, the assault began. The three 100-man teams stormed the fort and took it by complete surprise. Then, the main columns rushed in. The attackers quickly succeeded in capturing the fort and several hundred prisoners. Unfortunately, the attack was not followed through properly. As the sun rose, advance troops were wandering in the rear with no orders and had stopped to consume some captured Federal rations. Pickett's division had been delayed and had not arrived in time to reinforce the strike force. The delays gave Federal troops time to organize a counter-attack. By 7:45, Union troops were in a semicircle a mile and a half long around the area. The final counterattack drove the rebels away. Lee's last offensive action of the war had accomplished nothing but the loss of 4,000 men killed, wounded, or captured.

Back in the trenches, the men of the 34th North Carolina watched and waited. The line was severely weakened by the troops sent to Fort Steadman, so they feared the Federals would attack. At around 1:00 in the afternoon, the skirmish line in front of the trenches was assaulted by a small Federal force.[247] The 34th NC was thrown forward to support the picket line which held, but two hours later, a second larger assault drove them back. One Federal brigade attempted to assault the main line but was blocked by the Rohoic Creek. Two Georgia regiments staged a counterattack and drove them back, but the Yankees came back at 5:00 in the evening and again pushed the rebel pickets back. Had the Federals staged a stronger attack, they could have broken the weak rebel line and opened the door to Richmond.

The 34th NC suffered significant losses in the sharp back-and-forth fighting that afternoon. Between the regiment's Sharpshooters engaged at Fort Stedman and the afternoon fighting on the skirmish line, at least nine men were wounded and a stunning fifty-five were captured. The following were casualties from March 25, 1865:

---

[247] T. D. Lattimore noted that the skirmish line was a mile from the main line, indicating the distance between the two main lines in this area.

Casualties from the Battles at Petersburg - March 25, 1865[248]

Wounded

Samuel Dellinger	H	Pvt.	Thomas M Ruppe	F	Pvt.
Jabez Hamrick	B	Pvt.	George W Walker	K	Pvt.
William Martin	I	Pvt.	Jonathan L Whiteside	B	Pvt.
John J Plonk	F	Pvt.	George Hovis	D	Pvt.

Captured

Elias A Alexander	I	Pvt.	Stephen A Hensley	C	Pvt.
William D Bailey	A	Pvt.	Andrew B Hoover	G	Pvt.
John Bannard	C	Pvt.	Lansford M Hopper	I	Pvt.
Hamilton Bare	A	Cpl.	Timons J Hughes	H	Cpl.
John S Barnett	D	Pvt.	Noah Koone	C	Pvt.
Jacob W Barnhardt	D	Pvt.	Timmons G Lee	F	Pvt.
James M Barnwell	A	Pvt.	Hiram Littleton	K	Pvt.
James T Brooks	I	Pvt.	William Martin	I	Pvt.
Frederick Carpenter	E	Pvt.	William C McCord	G	1Sgt.
Levi Cox	A	Sgt.	William McCrary	A	Pvt.
Willis Cranford	K	Pvt.	Alexander D McNeilly	F	Pvt.
Emanuel Crotts	F	Pvt.	William D McNeilly	F	Pvt.
Matthew Crowder	B	Pvt.	Miles W Medlen	H	Pvt.
William C Dennis	K	Pvt.	John H Paschal	A	Pvt.
Felix C Dobbins	B	Sgt.	Thomas F Philbeck	B	Pvt.
G W Elliott	K	Pvt.	Perry G Jr. Putnam	H	Pvt.
Virgil H Elliott	F	Sgt.	David M Ray	I	Pvt.
Elias Green	B	Pvt.	Elisha Robbins	I	Sgt.
Martin A Green	B	Pvt.	Thomas M Ruppe	F	Pvt.
Eli Hall	K	Pvt.	Leonard F Russell	K	Pvt.
Eli O Hamrick	B	Pvt.	William Snotherly	K	Sgt.
Elphus Hamrick	F	Pvt.	Caleb L Sparks	B	Cpl.
Jabez Hamrick	B	Pvt.	Perry Steadman	I	Pvt.
David Harrill	B	Pvt.	Jacob Frank Stirewalt	D	Pvt.
James Harrison	I	Pvt.	Mark T Talbert	K	Pvt.

---

[248] Some of these casualties could have been from the Sharpshooter Battalion at Fort Stedman but they cannot be identified as such. Most are assumed to have been from the actions on the skirmish line.

Thomas W Hearn	K	Pvt.	George C Todd		G	Cpl.
William F Hearn	K	Pvt.	Joseph G Willis		F	Pvt.
James F Henderson	C	Sgt.				

Jonathan Whiteside lost a leg due to his wound. George Hovis was shot in the face. Sam Dellinger received his third wound of the war but was back with the regiment a few days later.[249]

"...it had better be stopped on some terms as soon as it can be."

The day after the battle, Ancil Dycus wrote home saying, "Times are hard here now and worse coming. I expect our rations will get shorter before long....I hear the Yanks have taken the railroad 20 miles from Greensboro...I will close by saying that if I never more am permitted to see you in this world, I hope and trust I will meet you in heaven to part no more and where there will be no roar of cannons and musket to be heard, but joy and peace forever. Ancil."

He also penned a short letter to his father with a sharper tone, "I'd like to know what you think of this war and tell you what I really think of it. All I really know right now is that it had better be stopped on some terms as soon as it can be. If the higher men don't stop it, the soldiers will. They will not stay here and be run over as they have been. There were seventeen who ran away from the 13th regiment last week. I hear that they have called all the men out from age 17 to 50 into the war. If the number already out can't whip the Yankees, then we'd better quit. If they take all the men, who will stay at home and raise crops?" Ancil had been in the war from the beginning, and his frustration was evident.

With the losses on March 25th, the Third Corps had barely 11,000 men to defend some twenty-two miles of trench lines. They were stretched thin, several yards between men in places. There was nothing they could do but wait. It was Grant's move to make at the time

---

[249] Beginning with this battle, accurate casualty records were not kept. Many of those killed or wounded went unrecorded. Those who were captured turned up on Union POW registers. Thus, most of the recorded casualties are men who fell into Union hands. Roughly 75 men from the regiment have records that end in November -January with no record of what happened to them. We can only assume they were killed, wounded, or deserted in the final weeks of the war.

and place of his choosing. The matter seemed already settled. How it would play out was all that remained to be seen.

McIlwain Hill

On the night of March 26th Captain John D. Young was given orders. An important part of the skirmish line called McIlwain Hill was lost on March 25th, and it was up to the four battalions of Light Division Sharpshooters to take it back. They were ordered to take the hill and hold it until reinforcements came up, but it was easier said than done. They were attacking an enemy five times their number on a fortified position on high ground. Entire brigades had failed to carry the hill the previous day. The danger was apparent. As a reward, every man who survived would be given a 30-day leave.

At 1:30 the next morning, Captain Young formed his battalion, including the Sharpshooters from the 34th NC, and read the order to them. Soon, the four battalions, 400 men altogether, met in front of McIlwaine Hill. The officers decided to attack in two lines of two battalions each. The two lead battalions were Dunlop's of McGowan's brigade and Major Wooten of Lane's brigade. Young's battalion was in the second line in support of Dunlop's men. The two lead battalions would carry the hill by storm and then sweep left and right, while the two supporting battalions would seize and hold the crest against counterattack.

At 5:00, they started quietly forward. One hundred yards from the enemy pickets, they encountered a deep ditch lined on both sides with briars and thorns. Each man crawled down and out the other side with as little noise as possible. According to Major Dunlop, they got within thirty paces of the vidette before they were fired upon.[250] With a yell, they stormed the hill, taking the enemy by complete surprise. The crest of the hill blazed with the flashes of muskets. The stunned defenders fled in disarray. As planned, the lead battalions turned right and left and swept the enemy "tooth and toe nail—from center to circumference."[251] The two supporting battalions, including Young's, seized the crest and fired at the retreating enemy. When the sun rose, the hill belonged to the Sharpshooters.

---

[250] It seems incredible that they got that close without being detected. Apparently, the sentries were not prepared for an attack.
[251] (Dunlop 2012) Page 254.

The reinforcements they had been promised never came. Three times during the day, the enemy tried to retake the hill, and three times the Sharpshooters held, driving the enemy back with heavy loss. Major Dunlop declared that, "The storming of McIlwaine Hill was unquestionably one of the most daring and successful engagements of its dimensions ever witnessed upon any field during the great struggle, and our generals did not hesitate to so declare." Dunlop stated that the four battalions lost no more than ten or fifteen men. Pvt. Lawson Williams of the 34th North Carolina received a gunshot wound to the face that day, during the assault. He had volunteered in February of 1863, at age 18. He was captured at Gettysburg and was exchanged only eight days before this battle. He spent the war's final days in the hospital before going home to Cleveland County.[252]

The Final Days

On March 29th, Union cavalry under General Philip Sheridan arrived at Dinwiddie Courthouse. A corps of Federal infantry was moved to within a mile of Boydton Plank Road. Another corps of infantry was also moving. Lee ordered Pickett's division to the area of Sutherland Station on the Southside Railroad, ten miles west of Petersburg. This was a strategically important location. If it could be secured, the Confederates could extend their line to Five Forks. It was also important to the Confederate retreat should their lines break. A short fight with Federals at Lewis's Farm revealed the location of Warren's V Corps. That night, McGowan's South Carolinian's were pulled from the trenches and marched toward White Oak. It rained all night, heavy at times. The line was further weakened when McRae's brigade was pulled away.

It rained for eighteen hours, into most of the next day. Early on the rainy morning of March 30th, the 34th North Carolina moved along with the rest of the brigade a short distance to the White Oak Road area, taking up a position near the intersection with Boydton Plank Road. To the north, Hatcher's Run meandered past Burgess's Mill. Beyond that was the vital Southside Railroad. Skirmishing occurred

---

[252] It is not known for sure if Williams was a Sharpshooter, therefore it is possible that he was wounded with the regiment on the trench line. Given that the regiment was not actively engaged this day, it seems more likely he was wounded at McIlwaine Hill.

during the day. Eventually, Federal troops moved toward the area occupied by Scales' troops. In doing so, they captured a large section of the skirmish line. Four men from the regiment were captured that day, three from Company K and one from Company I, in this movement.

As was customary, the captured men were questioned. Private William Guest of Company I was from Transylvania County. He had been with the regiment since May of 1864. His capture on March 30th is referenced in Federal correspondence of that day:

HEADQUARTERS FIFTH ARMY CORPS,
March 30, 1865-8.15 p. m.
Brevet Major-General WEBB,
Chief of Staff:
General Griffin has taken no prisoners to-day except from Scales' brigade. One of them, Private Guest, Thirty-fourth North Carolina, states his brigade is composed of Thirty-fourth, Twenty-second, and Sixteenth North Carolina. Scales was not present in their charge to-day; the brigade was led by Major Norman [Norment]. There are four brigades in Wilcox's division, commanded by General Scales, Colonels Howe [Hyman], Gallaway, and Stowe. They left the works in front of our signal tower at 3 o'clock this morning. Thinks all the brigades of his division were present to-day, but is not sure. General Wilcox is absent on leave.
Respectfully,
G. K. WARREN,
Major-General.

Evaluating Pvt. Guest's information along with all the other intelligence from the field, General Meade sent a message to General Wright, whose corps had been stationed opposite Wilcox's division, saying that Scales had left his front. Early the next morning, General Lee ordered three Confederate brigades to attack a vulnerable part of the Federal line in the Battle of White Oak Road. Showing great fighting spirit, three Confederate brigades took the Federals off guard and drove back two Federal divisions before being pushed back by reinforcements. The battle delayed Grant's plans but left the Confederate position at White Oak disorganized. The battle did not involve Scales' brigade, though two men from the 34th NC were listed as captured that day, skirmishers.

The next day, April 1, 1865, rebel troops concentrated at Five Forks, an important intersection. General George Pickett had assembled five brigades to defend the area with hastily constructed works. Scales' brigade was not part of this group and was not involved in the action. Throughout the day, the battle raged, as Confederates fought hard but in vain, eventually giving up three separate battle lines.

At 10:00 that evening, 150 Yankee artillery pieces opened fire on the Confederate lines. The three-hour cannonade was unnerving. It also masked the sounds of Federal troops moving into position to attack the next morning. The long-awaited day of reckoning was at hand.

Sunday, April 2, 1865

At 4:40 a.m., Federal infantry advanced across no-man's land. Some 14,000 troops of the VI Corps (Wright's) lined up against 2,800 rebels holding a one-mile stretch of Hill's line. The strong fortifications and artillery were to their advantage, but it wasn't enough against the weight of the Federal numbers coming at them. The brigades of Lane and Thomas bore the brunt of the assault with McGowan's Sharpshooters manning their picket line. Scales' brigade was farther to the right. The Federal VI Corps attacked in force. Within thirty minutes, the line was breached near Boydton-Plank Road. The Federals quickly exploited the breach, turning in the direction of Scales' brigade. The rest of the division was posted south of Hatcher's Run with MacRae, then Scales, Cooke, and McGowan to the right. When word came that the line was broken, Scales' brigade fell back, and Federal troops captured their works around 7:30 a.m. with little resistance. The men from the regiment fell back in as good order as possible under the circumstances. Some were captured near the works. Some were captured at Hatcher's Run before getting away from the Federals who advanced from the left within their lines.

Lane and Thomas were forced back to the Dimmock Line near Battery 45 where the regiment had spent the winter. General Longstreet was struggling to defend the area with what troops were available. News began circulating that General A. P. Hill had been seriously wounded. In fact, he had been killed that morning. Hill had been their commander for most of the war, and the men were loyal to him. Lt. General Ambrose Powell Hill was 39 years old. The situation was controlled chaos. As Scales' brigade headed for the Southside Railroad,

Generals Wilcox and Lane gathered men to the area of Forts Gregg and Whitworth near the Dimmock Line. Their troops held the positions, buying Longstreet and Lee valuable time. Every minute counted, and Lane's men doggedly held Fort Gregg two desperate and bloody hours before being forced to abandon it. It was General Cadmus Wilcox's finest hour of the war. The stand he made there gave Lee's retreating army valuable time. The area west of Petersburg was vital to Lee's retreat. With Five Forks lost and the Confederate line disintegrating, the Southside Railroad became crucial. Unless this area could be held for a few more precious hours, the Yankees could trap much of Lee's army before they could get away from the city. Command of the Third Corps fell to General Heth, who selected Sutherland Station on the Southside Railroad as the place for their last stand.

The Southside Railroad and Sutherland Station

T. D. Lattimore wrote, "On 1 April 1865, the regiment with the brigade occupied a position on the right, south of Hatcher's Run. We learned soon after daylight that the Confederate lines between us and Petersburg had been broken. After this saddening news, the regiment repulsed a force of Federal cavalry and then retreated to Southerland's Station…" Scales' brigade crossed Hatcher's Run and was ordered by General Heth to move to Sutherland Station. Marching north, they reached the Southside Railroad and turned east toward Sutherland Station. They were followed by Nelson Miles's division and elements of Federal Cavalry under General Philip Sheridan who was in the area. Twenty-seven men from the regiment were taken prisoner on the Southside Railroad on the way to Sutherland Station.[253]

By late-morning, the brigades of Scales, Cooke, MacRae, and McGowan were arriving at Sutherland Station, around 1,200 men.[254] General Heth placed Brig. General John Cooke in charge of the station, where supply trains were parked. Feverishly, the men threw up works

---

[253] Details are sketchy. It is unclear whether the brush with enemy cavalry referred to by T. D. Lattimore occurred here or closer to their original trench line. In a review of General Sheridan's official report, it seems more likely to have been closer to the railroad since Sheridan joined Miles north of Hatcher's run.

[254] One estimate of total Confederate strength at Sutherland Station was around 4,000.

of logs, earth, rocks, anything they could find. They dug with bayonets, tin cups, and bare hands, and formed a battle line one-half mile long. Cooke was the right flank with Scales to his left, followed by MacRae and McGowan on the left. The Sharpshooter battalions were in place. By 11:00 a.m., they were ready to receive the Federal attack. Against these ragged rebels were massed 8,000 Federal troops under the command of General Nelson Miles. The longer the rebels held, the more time Lee had to get his army safely away from Richmond. If they retreated too soon, the Yankees could cut off the route of retreat for much of Lee's army.

Soon, one brigade of Yankee troops attacked Cooke and Scales on the Confederate right. The rebels beat back the assault. At 1:00 p.m., a second assault occurred at the other end of the line, and it too was repulsed. The Federals took their time, not launching the third assault until 4:00. This time, they attacked McGowan on the flank. After an hour of desperate fighting, the Confederate line weakened and finally gave way. At least twelve men from the 34th NC were taken prisoner at Sutherland Station. In all, sixty-five men from the 34th NC were taken prisoner in the actions of April 2nd. An untold number were killed and wounded. Sharpshooter commander John Dunlop said of Sutherland Station, "I never saw finer fighting anywhere than was done by the...brigades at Sutherland Station."

Captured April 2, 1865

Place not specified

Alex Axion	G	Pvt.	T D Munn	K	Pvt.
John S Barnwell	A	Pvt.	David C Peeler	F	Pvt.
Noah G Bess	E	Pvt.	William A Philbeck	B	Pvt.
Thomas Clary	A	Pvt.	James O Sanford	G	Pvt.
Samuel Dellinger	H	Pvt.	George Shepherd	A	Pvt.
John Eaker Sr.	F	Pvt.	Phillip Siceloff*	B	Pvt.
Alfred Foster	C	Pvt.	William W Sorrells	C	Pvt.
G W Hall	K	Pvt.	Joseph Sparks	I	Pvt.
Joseph Hatley	A	Pvt.	Oliver P Taylor	C	Pvt.
Bedford Hendrick*	F	Sgt.	Woody B Wells*	B	Pvt.
Henry L Humphries*	I	Pvt.	Thomas H White	E	Pvt.
Franklin Lattimore	F	Pvt.	Joseph Williams*	D	Pvt.

John N London	F	Pvt.	William H Williams	F	Pvt.
D Walter Miller	H	Pvt.	Joseph S Willis	F	Pvt.

*Probably Hatcher's Run

Captured on the Southside Railroad

William S Blackburn	E	Pvt.	Jacob Sane, Jr	E	Sgt.
John Brown	H	Pvt.	Jonas Senter	E	Pvt.
Thomas Bryant	E	Pvt.	A B Shuford	B	Pvt.
James Y Cavin	E	Pvt.	Isaac Smith	K	Pvt.
Joseph Cooper	I	Pvt.	William Sutton	I	Pvt.
Joel Corriher	D	Sgt.	William L Vaughn	F	Pvt.
Henry Dellinger	E	Pvt.	H M Warren	H	Pvt.
Elias J Henson	I	Pvt.	John Warren	E	Pvt.
James Hill	C	Pvt.	Francis Wright	F	Pvt.
Daniel Cephas Holly	E	Pvt.	Richard Wright	E	Pvt.
Orrin D Johnson	D	Pvt.	William H Wright	F	Pvt.
Hiram Kiser	E	Pvt.	Daniel Yarborough	K	Pvt.
Emanuel Mooney	E	Pvt.	David Zimmerman	B	Pvt.
William Roberts	B	Pvt.			

Sutherland Station

Stephen F Blanton	B	Pvt.	Walter R Roberts	B	Pvt.
Richard Davis	D	Pvt.	J L Rudd	B	Pvt.
Harberd Fortenbery	F	Pvt.	Thomas S Rudd	B	Pvt.
Daniel W Fowler	I	Pvt.	Noah Stalker	B	Pvt.
John T Harrill	B	Pvt.	M Tallman	K	Pvt.
G F Hurley	K	Pvt.	Bartlett Towery	F	Pvt.
Samuel H Jordan	G	Pvt.	James M Wallace	K	Pvt.
Wilson Kime	K	Sgt.	Thompson J Wood	I	Pvt.

The stand at Sutherland's station bought Lee just enough time to extract his army and start west on his pre-planned route of retreat. By evening, the regiment, with the rest of the brigade, pulled back toward the Appomattox River. There, they found a boat scarcely big enough for a few men. With no time for a slow river crossing, they turned west, marching south of the river, with Lee's main body marching north of the river. Their destination was Amelia Courthouse, thirty-six miles north-west of Petersburg. They marched all night April 2-3rd and much of the next day to get to Amelia. The next morning, April 3rd, Union soldiers marched into Richmond unopposed. Trailing units were still skirmishing around Sutherland Station and the Southside Railroad. Six more men from the regiment were taken prisoner that day, either from the fighting or picked up as stragglers.

Billy Philbeck

Records of men who were killed or wounded are virtually non-existent, but one wounded man was Company B veteran Billy Philbeck a member of Cpt. Young's Sharpshooters. His records do not reveal the final days of his service, only a newspaper article published years after the war show what happened to him the day the Petersburg lines broke. Philbeck was described as lank and sinewy and hard as nails. He was part of Scales' sharpshooter battalion because of his skill with a gun. It was said he could "get a squirrel if he could see its ear above a high limb." He had gone to war with the Sandy Run Yellow Jackets in 1861. He was one of only a handful of men to be present on every muster, serving throughout the war in every battle, every campaign.

That morning, he was on the skirmish line in an open field taking his last stand behind a persimmon tree "popping away at the advancing enemy when a bullet struck him on the cheek an inch under the eye knocking him senseless." Yankee troops took him to a hospital in Petersburg and told him they would send him home when he was able. Not trusting the Yankees, he slipped away two weeks later and started for home with the ball still lodged in his head. A year after the war, the roof of his mouth became infected and the ball was finally removed by a doctor.[255] He kept it for many years. When he was in his 80's, someone asked if he still had it and he said he had lost it.[256]

---

[255] The Forest city Courier, May 31, 1928. An article titled A Surviving Hero of the Lost Cause.

[256] Philbeck was one of the last surviving members of his company, living to age 88. Several hundred people attended his funeral.

Private Linville Price, The Laurel Springs Guards - Company A. Linville was a member of the Heroes of America, also known as the Red Strings.[257]

---

[257] Photo courtesy Chad Riggs

Lieutenant Colonel Charles J. Hammarskold led the regiment at the Battle of Frayser's Farm. (Photo courtesy of the Lincoln County Historical Association.)

Chapter 15.
Appomattox - Duty Faithfully Performed

Once away from the city, the men marched with a strong and determined gait. After nine long months in the trenches of Petersburg, underfed and ill-equipped to face the cold Virginia winter, they were glad to be moving. It was April, and they were marching through the Virginia countryside free of the yoke of protecting Richmond. A fair fight out in the open was better than withering away in the trenches.

At least forty-three men from the 34th NC were in Richmond hospitals when Yankee troops occupied the city. Most weren't well enough to travel, but those who could were transported to northern prison hospitals. The rest stayed in Richmond under the care of Yankee doctors. Jonathan Whiteside, a veteran from 1861, had recently lost a leg. After a few more days of recovery, he was sent to Point Lookout aboard the Steamer *Mary Powell*. Aboard the same ship was George Walker who had been wounded March 25th. William Norton and S. T. Sarvice were put aboard the Hospital Transport *Thomas Powell* bound for Point Lookout. Sarvice was recovering from Typhoid. At least seven from the 34th NC did not survive to go home. William Conner's leg had been amputated recently. He died on April 8th.

Amelia Courthouse

Because Grant had to secure Richmond before going after Lee, the rebels had a one-day lead. But the progress to Amelia was hampered by washed-out bridges and skirmishes with Federal cavalry. They had left Petersburg with one day's rations, and that was gone. But they expected to be resupplied at Amelia, so they marched undaunted by their hunger and weary legs. Five more men from the regiment fell into Yankee hands on April 4th, men who were unable to make the long march.

Completing their thirty-six-mile trek, they arrived at Amelia Courthouse late in the day, April 3rd. They expected boxcars full of food. Instead, the cars were full of munitions and no rations. Foraging parties were dispatched the next day to collect anything they could from the local citizens. Another problem was that Lee's army was still not consolidated. They had left Richmond in five separate columns. Some units were not yet at Amelia. The delay caused by the need to forage and waiting for trailing units cost Lee much of his lead over Grant.

The next morning, April 5th, was cold and rainy, and bellies were growling. The forage wagons came back with little food. The countryside had been stripped bare during the siege, and people had little to give. A million rations were stored at Danville, but that was a hundred miles away. Lee planned to have supplies rushed toward them by rail. If the men could march eighteen miles to Burkeville, they could be supplied the next day. Their situation was critical. He could not keep pushing his army without food. Early that morning, Lee learned that Union cavalry had destroyed rebel supply wagons seven miles away. He roused his army and quickly marched westward. He wanted to give his men every chance for victory, so he pushed them on. Around one in the afternoon word came that Federal troops had gotten to Jetersville ahead of them and had thrown up a strong defensive line. Lee was cut off from his supplies as well as his escape route into North Carolina via Burkeville. It was a critical point in the march. Lee considered an assault on the Federal line, but the Yankee position was too strong. He decided instead to move his men farther west.

They had gone three days with little sleep and little or no food. They had marched more than forty miles across uneven and sometimes challenging terrain, passing through stretches of thick mud they called Virginia quicksand. The pace required to stay ahead of Grant was brutal. Feet were bleeding, muscles ached, and senses became numb. Lack of sleep and nourishment made the men weak. Many could not continue and dropped to the ground, watching helplessly as the column marched on. At every rest stop, men wandered into the woods in search of anything edible they could find. Some stripped the bark from trees to get some nourishment. Horses and mules also became victims of exhaustion, forcing caissons and wagons to be abandoned. The roads were often too narrow to accommodate thousands of troops, wagons, and animals, and precious time was spent repairing bridges. They marched through April 5th. When darkness fell they kept going. They marched again all night of April 5-6th with little sleep. They received word that 80,000 rations were waiting for them at Farmville, nineteen miles away. If they could hold out one more day, they could be resupplied and have a chance to escape to North Carolina.

Sailor's Creek

The morning of April 6th was rainy as the shabby column inched along. They were tired and hungry beyond description but not ready to give up. There was still plenty of pluck in these hungry rebels. An army can't march forever on determination alone, but these men were giving it their best shot. Where there was no food, there was plenty of resolve. No matter how many miles lay ahead, they kept placing one bloody foot in front of the other. They still had their muskets and 40 rounds per man, and they were ready to fight it out if they had to.

Every man could see that the odds were heavily against them. Yankee cavalry was attacking the line daily. Union infantry could cover 30 miles a day, while the rebels could barely make half that time. With the Confederacy spiraling toward defeat, there was only one thing that kept their tired legs going. It wasn't the "cause," and it wasn't even patriotism. All of that was long gone. What kept them going when they knew they were going to lose, was pride. That's all they had left. That stubborn southern pride compelled them to keep going when every instinct told them to quit. They would rather die than give up their flag. After all the deprivations, the victories, and heartbreaking losses; they would not quit, not now, not ever. So long as they had breath in them, they were determined to keep going.

Lee was desperate to get to Farmville. Grant was determined to cut him off. What was left of the old Light Division marched near the front of Lee's column in a combined 1st and 3rd Corps under General Longstreet. Due to cavalry attacks, tired legs, and two very narrow bridges over Sailor's Creek, two dangerous gaps developed in Lee's column. Aggressive Union commanders pounced on the opportunity at Sailor's Creek. The 34th North Carolina took up a line of battle along the Southside Railroad near Rice's Station but were not engaged.[258] Instead, it was Ewell's and Anderson's corps who faced the day's carnage. The rebels fought like wounded animals, unleashing their full fury. The vicious hand-to-hand fighting stunned even the hardest veterans. They wanted a fair fight on open ground. They got it there. For all their rage, however, the Federal army fought back just as hard.

---

[258] (Calkins 2008, 2011) This line of battle mentioned on page 115.

Finding themselves cut off, much of Ewell's corps was forced to surrender. The crushing defeat cost Lee over 8,000 casualties, including Lt. General Richard S. Ewell who was taken prisoner. His corps was virtually destroyed. Over one-fifth of Lee's remaining army was gone.

High Bridge and Farmville

For what was left of Lee's army, every minute counted. They were approaching Farmville and their much-needed rations, but with Grant's men on their heels, the weary rebels again marched most of the night of April 6-7. They had to cross High Bridge to get to Farmville and their supplies. Once across the bridge, they were ordered to burn it to buy time to rest and get ahead of Grant. Confederate cavalry protected the rear, defending against slashing attacks by Federal cavalry backed by fast-marching infantry. The rebels had been trying to burn every bridge behind them, but Union troops stayed close enough to put out the fires and preserve the bridges. High Bridge was critical. Unless it could be burned behind them, Lee's army would have to keep marching.

High Bridge was an impressive structure, spanning 2,400 feet across the Appomattox River with a maximum height of 160 feet.[259] Its twenty piers contained four million bricks to support the wooden structure. Completed in 1852, it had been a vital part of the Southside Railroad during the war. Importantly to Lee's army, it also had an adjacent wagon bridge. Before reaching the bridge, General Longstreet relieved the cavalry of the job of rear guard and passed the critical responsibility to Scales' brigade. The 34th North Carolina and what was left of the brigade had to defend against Federal Cavalry while the rest of the army raced toward Farmville. For several miles, the regiment was in constant line of battle against marauding cavalry troopers. Most of the army was arriving at Farmville by around 9:00 a.m. on April 7th. There, they found the desperately needed rations and quickly distributed the food to the starving troops while the 34th North Carolina and the rest of Scales' brigade kept the Federal army at bay. At the bridge, a traffic jam had caused a delay, but finally, the rest of the army crossed High Bridge and headed for Farmville. Scales'

---

[259] High Bridge still stands today. The damaged portions have been rebuilt over the years. Anyone visiting Appomattox should make High Bridge part of their trip.

brigade, still in contact with the enemy, was the last to cross, doing so under artillery fire.

T. D. Lattimore described the scene this way, "The regiment, with the brigade, protected the rear of the army at Farmville, marching several miles in line of battle, beating back the enemy's cavalry, and was the last to cross the river. As we went out from the river a heavy artillery fire was poured down upon the regiment." Due to a lack of records, casualties are unknown.

Lee's army was fully across. The 34th NC marched into Farmville eager for some food and rest, but it was not to be. The bridge was set afire, but not in time. Though severely damaged, Federal engineers had gotten to it and put the fire out, cutting away one section to stop the spread of the fire. Grant's relentless army marched on. When Lee learned the Federal troops had crossed, he put his men back in motion. Scales' brigade was among the last to arrive. They got the least rest and had to eat on the run. By early afternoon, Farmville was filled with blue-coated troops while the gray-backs marched away.

Appomattox

The Union army was closing in. At Cumberland Church, just five miles away, the column again came under attack as Lee struggled to put distance between his and Grant's army. That night, as the men paused for a brief rest, General Lee received a note from Grant asking him to avoid further bloodshed and surrender his army. His chief lieutenant, Longstreet, stated simply, "Not yet." For the third night in a row, the men marched on. They had been on their feet for most of forty straight hours. The exhausted troops shuffled on, minds and bodies numb. Sensing that the end was near, men began dropping from the ranks. April 8th was calm as they neared Appomattox. When they bivouacked that night, campfires from Federal troops glowed all around them. The routes west and south were blocked. Federal troops were at their rear. The checkmate was complete.

April 9th, 1865 was Palm Sunday. A heavy fog hung over the area as the sound of battle woke everyone at 5:00 a.m. The 34th North Carolina stood with the rest of the frazzled army prepared once more to do their duty. A few miles ahead, Grant's army had once again gotten ahead of Lee. General Gordon's men were trying one last time to punch through the Federal line. After a valiant effort, Gordon was forced to fall back through the Appomattox River Valley to the higher ground beyond. There, General E. P. Alexander was forming a second battle line made up of Wilcox's division along with Field's and Mahone's. The gaunt rebels waited, clutching their muskets. The steely veterans would not flinch if a fight came. Those that remained were the hardest and most determined men. Their skin was weathered, their eyes were sunken but alert. Their feet bled, and their muscles ached as they stood in tattered clothes beneath bullet-pierced flags. How many miles had they marched, how much blood had shed, only to come down to these final few hours.

The 34th NC stood within musket range of Federal troops, the combatants staring each other down and waiting for orders. From those first bright days in Raleigh when the young farm boys first put on uniforms and started "playing war," they had marched so many miles, more than they could count. They experienced the stunning victories at the Seven Days, Chancellorsville, and Fredericksburg, followed by the heart-breaking loss at Gettysburg. They fought through the appalling violence at the Wilderness and Spotsylvania. The grinding last winter in the trenches to the final effusion of blood, all was borne with courage and fortitude.

The death knell for the Confederacy was not signaled by one last raging battle, but distant gunfire that gradually faded away. Around 11:00, firing stopped, replaced with silence. The stillness was sweet and dreadful, familiar but strange. It was a sound they had longed for and dreaded, desired but feared.

It was the sound of peace.

General Order No. 9

Men bearing white flags passed between the armies, and General Wilcox joined the procession of generals moving forward. The 34th NC was ordered back toward an open field. There, an apple tree stood where General Lee had waited for the return of the flag of truce he had sent to General Grant. Barely a word was spoken by the men. They knew.

The troops rested and nibbled on anything they had to eat. Sometime after 3:00 in the afternoon, General Lee, atop Traveler, arrived back at camp. Men cheered his arrival as they always did, but the general was somber as he delivered the news of the surrender.

Many expressed emotions ranging from despair to anger. Some shouted defiantly that they would fight on till the last breath. General Lee told his men, "Boys, I have done the best I could for you. My heart is too full to say more." He added, "Go home now, and if you made as good citizens as you have soldiers, you will do well, and I shall always be proud of you."

And it was over, finally over. Union troops celebrated loudly at first but were ordered to stop out of respect for their defeated foes. The Confederates sat in camp with heavy hearts and heads hung low. They had nothing to eat, so Lee asked General Grant for rations. That evening, rations of meat and hardtack were delivered by Union troops, and Lee's half-starved rebels ate their first post-war meal.

The next morning, April 10th, was chilly and rainy. More rations came, and the men had breakfast and chatted. Men on both sides were ordered not to enter one another's camps, but groups from both armies did so anyway. They talked and traded items, looking for souvenirs. Paroling the army would take time. Printing presses had to be brought in to print each soldier's parole slip. The men were considered prisoners of war and had to be formally paroled before going home. Each man would receive a parole to allow passage through Union-controlled territory, without which they could be arrested and sent to a POW camp.

During the day, General Lee issued his final orders to his army. The men were gathered, and the order was read by their commanders:

General Order No. 9
Headquarters, Army of Northern Virginia
April 10, 1865

After four years of arduous service, marked by unsurpassed courage and fortitude, the Army of Northern Virginia has been compelled to yield to overwhelming numbers and resources.

I need not tell the brave survivors of so many hard-fought battles, who have remained steadfast to the last, that I have consented to this result with no distrust of them.

But feeling that valor and devotion could accomplish nothing that would compensate for the loss that must have attended the continuance of the contest, I determined to avoid the useless sacrifice of those whose past services have endeared them to their countrymen.

By the terms of the agreement officers and men can return to their homes and remain until exchanged. You will take with you the satisfaction that proceeds from the consciousness of duty faithfully performed, and I earnestly pray that a Merciful God will extend to you His blessing and protection.

With an increasing admiration of your constancy and devotion to your country, and a grateful remembrance of your kind and generous considerations for myself, I bid you all an affectionate farewell.

R. E. Lee
General

The formal surrender ceremony would be on April 12th. The 34th North Carolina Infantry Regiment was surrendering 166 men, only 74 of whom were at High Point on October 25, 1861. Almost half of the original volunteers and one-third of the regiment's total roll were dead. They died of wounds and disease. They died on marches, in battle, and as prisoners of war. They died in North Carolina, Virginia, Maryland, and Pennsylvania. A few even died in the frozen Dakota territory, wearing Yankee blue uniforms. Some died on scorched battlefields, others in POW camps. Many died in hospitals. Some died peacefully at home with their loved ones. The regiment's long march through the war could be traced by the graves left behind. Records were found of 1,536 men who served in the hard-fighting 34th North Carolina Infantry.[260] Of those, 523 died before their service ended. The 34th NC served for 1,262 days. The regiment suffered one death for every two and a half days of its existence. It is estimated that only one-third of all Confederate deaths in the war were from battle-related wounds. The 44% of battle-related deaths in the 34th NC is a testament to their courage.

---

[260] Most of the men had records easily found, but some enlisted during times where there were no muster records and were found in pension applications, transfers from other regiments, and North Carolina Troops. There were likely some who served during times of no muster records such as May-December 1862, or the last few months of the war which have not yet been found.

Number of Deaths by Company

34th North Carolina Infantry

Company	Battle	Disease	Executed	Unknown Cause	Total
A	16	24	1	3	44
B	20	35	0	10	65
C	25	28	0	9	62
D	22	17	0	0	39
E	25	22	0	4	51
F	41	21	0	2	64
G	23	15	0	1	39
H	16	29	1	1	47
I	8	26	0	5	39
K	30	37	1	3	71
Field Staff	3				2
Totals	228	254	3	38	523

  The war's brutality had known no bounds. Death was not considerate of families back home or social status, wealth, or occupation. Death cared not if a man was married or how many children he had. It struck all with equal and devastating effect. More tears were shed for fallen men in the Civil War than all other American wars. Some families in the regiment were hit harder than others. No family was more devastated than the Callicott family from Montgomery County. Five Callicott men enlisted in Company K's Montgomery Boys. All five died before the war was half over.

  Waiting for the final formalities to take place, the men visited with friends and relatives from other units camped in the area and made plans for how they would get home and who they would travel with. Ancil Dycus was glad to see his younger brother, Joseph, who was with the 2nd NC Junior Reserves. They embraced and talked. Ancil looked much older than his 23 years. It was hard to believe how much they had all changed. The Dycus brothers would go home with other friends from Rutherford and Cleveland Counties.

  John L. McDowell stood proudly with Company I. He was once the Lt. Colonel of the regiment, but he went AWOL in 1863. With the governor's intervention, he had been permitted to reenlist as a private and was later promoted to the company's supply sergeant. McDowell had gone all the way and was as proud as any man at Appomattox.

The Lattimore and Hoyle families anchor the Floyd Rifles

The Lattimore and Hoyle families anchored Company F throughout the war. They were there through the good times and the bad. More Company F men died in battle than any other company in the 34th NC. Lt. Thomas D. Lattimore was at Appomattox with Jim and Jesse. Thomas had come through the war without serious injury to lead the company at the end. Jim rallied the 34th NC at the Wilderness by grabbing the colors and was shot in the shoulder. Frank Lattimore was captured when the lines broke at Petersburg and was at Point Lookout. Jesse Lattimore was said to be the hero of several daring exploits. On one occasion, a bombshell fell within their works with the fuse still hissing. Jesse seized it and threw it away only a second before it exploded. In another battle, he carried a wounded friend from a corn field under withering fire. The Yankees were so impressed with the feat that they applauded loudly. Jesse was a big strong man who would often carry a gun for a weaker friend on a march.[261]

The Hoyle men were core members of the regiment from the start. The family contributed five men to Company F and two more in Company E. At Gaines's Mill, Henry was killed, and Benjamin lost a leg. David replaced Captain Waters after Gaines's Mill and led the company until the final months of the war. Samuel was wounded and captured at Gettysburg, and Martin was captured at Falling Waters. Jonas served faithfully up to the final two months of the war, and Maxwell went home late in the war due to a severe wound to his side. Maxwell and Benjamin were both called to preach during the war and became respected ministers. Martin was released from Point Lookout in March of 1865 and was sent home. It is said that he arrived home to

---

[261] Jesse Lattimore's feats were found in an article by M. L. White in the Forest City Courier titled Corn Cracker Lauds Deeds of Confederate Heroes dated June 6, 1929. White does not identify the battles. The one in which Jesse carried a wounded man from the field may have been Shepherdstown in which the men fought across a corn field. Ox Hill was also fought in a cornfield, but the nature of that battle does not seem to fit with this story.

find his wife pregnant from a rape at the hands of one of the Unionist/deserter bands roaming the area. Martin raised the child as his own with the rest of his large family.

The Final Muster

Preparations continued. The officers were to provide each man a signed parole slip to prove he was a properly paroled prisoner of war. With this, he would be given free passage on government railroads if he had to pass through Union-controlled territory to get home. On the 10th, cavalry troops surrendered their flags, arms, and equipment. The artillery units followed the next day.

Steady rain set in on the 11th. They built campfires, smoked pipes, and hung their camp kettles over the fires as they had done hundreds of times before. The rain was refreshing. Soon the earth would begin to heal. Scorched earth, trees shredded by bullets, even soft mounds of shallow graves would all begin to disappear and erase every trace of war. Thoughts soon turned to home. Some of these men hadn't been home in over three years. Some had children they had never seen. With the war ending in time for spring planting, the men began thinking about repairing their farms and starting crops as soon as they got back. It gave them a sense of normalcy to think of plowing fields and mending fences. They watched the artillery units slowly drive toward the surrender like a funeral procession. Lee's army was no more.

The infantry rose early on April 12th, 1865. By 6:00 a.m., Gordon's corps was marching toward Appomattox Courthouse. Marching along the Richmond-Lynchburg Road, they approached the two waiting columns of Federal infantry. Presiding over the ceremony was General Joshua Lawrence Chamberlain, the hero of Little Round Top. As Gordon's men approached, the Union troops snapped to attention and respectfully saluted the defeated Confederate troops who returned the salute in an act of mutual respect. Only days before, these same soldiers had fought viciously at Sailor's Creek. Here, they showed one another all the respect due soldiers who had done their duty. Their differences remained, but the issue had been settled on the field of battle with honor.

Longstreet's Corps came next. Longstreet's men had fought beside Hill's Third corps many times. It took most of the day for the

Third Corps to watch the rest of Lee's army file by. When their time came, they followed suit. They marched between the two columns of Federal infantry, paused, turned to face the center, and on command fixed bayonets for the last time. They stacked their muskets, removed their cartridge boxes, and piled them beside the muskets, and solemnly and painfully draped their flag over the stacked muskets. Giving up their flag was like losing a piece of their soul. Men had died fighting for possession of that flag. The ceremony ended when the last of Hill's Corps surrendered around 4:00 p.m.

In their final muster, the 34th North Carolina Infantry surrendered the following 166 men at Appomattox:[262]

The 34th North Carolina Infantry - Surrendered at Appomattox
Field and Staff

Lt. Col.	George W Norment*	Surgeon	Bodisco Williams
Sgt Maj.	Henry H Rickert*	Steward	Theophilus B Twitty
Sgt Maj	Charles B Todd*	Sgt.	Willis W Hargroves
Ensign	Abel C Hartzog*		

Company A - The Laurel Springs Guards

2nd Lt.	Romulus M Hopper	Pvt.	Joseph Hamby
Sgt.	James C Miller*	Pvt.	John Koonce
Cpl.	Soloman Pless	Pvt.	John Roope*
Pvt.	Jacob Bare, Sr*	Pvt.	Elbert J Wiles*
Pvt.	George W Dean		

Company B - The Sandy Run Yellow Jackets

Cpt.	William P Beam*	1st Lt.	David B Harrill*
1st Sgt.	Doctor N Hamrick*	Sgt.	Wilson W Bridges*
Pvt.	Samuel T Allen	Pvt.	Ancil N Dycus*
Pvt.	John H Beam	Pvt.	Joseph C Gatis

---

[262] The National Park Service list says the regiment surrendered 168 men. Ancil Dycus, Elber Wiles, and Peter Heavner are each listed twice under different spelling variations. Robert Sommerall is not on the NPS list, but a parole card is found in his record. With these corrections, the number gathered from regimental records stands at 166 and is believed to be the correct number.

Pvt.	Elijah Blanton	Pvt.	David F Hage
Pvt.	James Blanton	Pvt.	Amos Hamrick
Pvt.	David A Bowen*	Pvt.	James A Harrill
Pvt.	Samuel Bridges	Pvt.	John H Harrill
Pvt.	William Brooks*	Pvt.	Nathaniel S Harrill
Pvt.	David Craver	Pvt.	William A Jones
Pvt.	Joel J Daily*	Pvt.	Joseph J McDaniel
Pvt.	Robert A Durham	Pvt.	William A Sparks

Company C - The Rutherford Rebels

Cpt.	John D Young	2nd Lt.	William T Wilkins
Sgt.	Noah H Whiteside*	Sgt.	Joseph W Wilson*
Cpl.	Humphrey P Lynch*	Pvt.	Martin O Forester
Pvt.	William Anderson	Pvt.	Henry London*
Pvt.	Stanhope Bagwell*	Pvt.	Cebun S Lynch
Pvt.	William H Elliott*		

Company D - The Oakland Guards

1st Lt.	Monroe M Gillon*	Lt.	Tilman H Davis*
Sgt.	Phillip A Sloop*	Cpl.	Milas Stanhope Jamison*
Pvt.	Joseph A Douglas*	Pvt.	John H McLaughlin*
Pvt.	David Z Gray	Pvt.	George N Peacock
Pvt.	James K Guy	Pvt.	George W Thompson
Pvt.	James C Lowrance*	Pvt.	John C Woodside*
Pvt.	Ezekiel W McCall		

Company E - The Shady Grove Rangers

1st Lt.	Simon B Bradley	Sgt.	Benjamin F Carpenter
Sgt.	Marcus A Holly*	Cpl.	Devany Putnam*
Pvt.	George J Conner*	Pvt.	John Kiser
Pvt.	Jacob R Dellinger*	Pvt.	Zimri Kiser
Pvt.	George F Fulbright*	Pvt.	Henry H Long
Pvt.	Peter Heavner	Pvt.	Jesse Reep*
Pvt.	Pinkney M Huss	Pvt.	David V Ried

Company F - The Floyd Rifles

2 Lt.	Thomas Lattimore*	2nd Lt.	Nathan McGinnis*
1st Sgt.	William V White*	Cpl.	Robert A Fortenbery*
Cpl.	Albert I Borders	Cpl.	Drury D Price*

Pvt.	David H Beam	Pvt.	Andrew J London*
Pvt.	Henry J Borders*	Pvt.	Isaac Mooney*
Pvt.	John C Canipe*	Pvt.	Andrew Peeler*
Pvt.	William Crotts*	Pvt.	Doctor D Peeler
Pvt.	James M Davis	Pvt.	Samuel S Putnam
Pvt.	Jacob S Earls*	Pvt.	Miles A Stroup
Pvt.	John C Gantt*	Pvt.	Joshua Vandyke
Pvt.	John C Haynes	Pvt.	Adam Whisnant*
Pvt.	James H Lattimore*	Pvt.	Newton Wright*
Pvt.	Jesse R Lattimore*	Pvt.	Noah Wright

Company G - The Mecklenburg Boys

Cpt.	James C Todd*	Sgt.	Thomas A Johnston*
Cpl.	Scott B Hutchison*	Pvt.	Ezekiel King
Pvt.	Columbus Abernathy	Pvt.	John Scott Lawing*
Pvt.	Alexander S Beaty	Pvt.	Thaddeus C McGahey
Pvt.	William Brotherton	Pvt.	Thomas T McGee
Pvt.	Alexander Cathey*	Pvt.	George W Rosich
Pvt.	Franklin C Downs	Pvt.	William F Smith
Pvt.	Andrew M Fox	Pvt.	Robert Sumerville
Pvt.	John M Hipp	Pvt.	David S Todd
Pvt.	Moses S Hovis	Pvt.	John W S Todd
Pvt.	Isaac M Johnson	Pvt.	Lawson N Todd
Pvt.	John T Johnston		

Company H - The Rough and Readys

Cpt.	John A Roberts*	2nd Lt.	William McK Mittag*
2nd Sgt.	John T Howell*	1st Sgt.	James D Wesson*
Sgt.	Champion Allen*	Pvt.	Richard T Morris
Pvt.	David Allen*	Pvt.	James F Scism*
Pvt.	William Cosand	Pvt.	Robert Smith*
Pvt.	James P Francis*	Pvt.	Robert H Ware
Pvt.	William Howell	Pvt.	William Ware
Pvt.	David R Huffsteter	Pvt.	John W Williams
Pvt.	John H Kendrick		

Company I - The Rutherford Band

Cpt.	James Wood*	1st Lt.	Henry Jenkins*

2nd Lt.	Thomas P Phillips*	Sgt.	Thomas L Carson*
Sgt.	John L McDowell*	Pvt.	James B Hawkins
Pvt.	William J Blanton*	Pvt.	Joseph Calaway Henson
Pvt.	Robert B Crisp	Pvt.	Lewis Humphries
Pvt.	Miles W Flinn*	Pvt.	John Hutson
Pvt.	Burrel B Harris	Pvt.	Decator S Smith

Company K - The Montgomery Boys

Cpt.	William B Lowrance	1st Lt.	George C Mills
Pvt.	Eli Cranford	Pvt.	Peter P Milsaps
Pvt.	Leonard Cranford*	Pvt.	George W Ried
Pvt.	Dewit Clinton Hall	Pvt.	John Walker

*Denotes volunteers from 1861.

Never had a defeated army walk away with more pride then the Army of Northern Virginia. The Confederacy was a nation that never was, an elusive dream, doomed before it ever began. These men fought because they had to, caught up in a war that should never have happened. It was their duty, borne out of a sense of loyalty to their native south. They left Appomattox with the memories of all the men who had died. Now, each time they saw flames from a fire, they would remember the scenes at the Wilderness. When it snowed, they would recall the march to Fredericksburg and the trail of bloody footprints in the snow. The cries of the wounded and the hush of the forever-muted dead would never leave them.

Lt. Thomas D. Lattimore expressed their emotions this way, "The Confederate soldier which had cast their fortunes with the destiny of the South, had suffered untold and indescribable hardships and privations, but when their grand chieftain rode in among them and announced the terms of surrender, the agony of soul and the depth of suffering exceeded anything ever before endured in the cruel war. In the vast array of ragged braves, whose courage and zeal had carried them to the very mouths of the bronze war-dogs of the enemy, not a dry eye could be seen anywhere. It seemed that they preferred to make one last charge and become engulfed in death, the last long sleep, to the painful duty of giving up their tattered flag which had waved over them in so many victories; but all was over, and the remnant of two hundred officers and men marched out and stacked their trusty muskets, laid down their bullet-pierced flag, never again to be unfurled in the rage of battle."

Dr. James I. "Bud" Robertson, one of the great Civil War historians of our time, once said, "Johnny Reb never apologized for what he did, Billy Yank never asked him to." That was the spirit at Appomattox, a solemn respect among soldiers. Quoting T. D. Lattimore once more, "Thus ended the great drama in which the Thirty-fourth played no mean part." Lattimore's history was dated April 9, 1901, the 36th anniversary of Lee's surrender at Appomattox.

Private Jacob Riley Dellinger, The Shady Grove Rangers – Company E[263]

---

[263] Photo courtesy Mike Stroupe

Private Michael Dellinger, The Rough and Readys – Company H[264]

---

[264] Photo courtesy Mike Stroupe

Chapter 16.
The End of the Beginning – The War's Closing Chapter

The war was over in Virginia, but there was much to be done before it was all finished. Lee's army was only the first of several still in the field. Each one had to surrender separately. Prisoners remained confined, and the folks at home had to deal with Stoneman's Raid.

Stoneman's Raid – The War Hits Home

On the day the 34th NC laid down its flag at Appomattox, Union General George Stoneman rode into Rowan County with 5,000 troopers, converging on Salisbury. Local citizens had long feared such a raid. They had heard reports of Stoneman's men in North Carolina. Finally, the raid became a reality. The rebels had little resistance to offer. Some accounts say there were 3,000 rebels, while other accounts say there were only about 500. Some were Home Guard troops and Senior Reserve Guards. Others were convalescent troops and even some local citizens. The rag-tag rebels fought for two hours before giving way in a rout with an unknown number of casualties. Scattered fighting ensued through the streets, frightening the citizens who were seeing the first real fighting of the war. The defenders fled into the nearby hills.

Stoneman's primary objective was to liberate the prisoners at the infamous Salisbury prison, but the prisoners were long-gone. All but those too sick to travel had been sent to Richmond and Wilmington in February. All that was left for them to do was to burn the prison, which they promptly did. The fire and exploding shells were seen and heard for miles. Many thought they were burning the whole town. They then began the occupation, which involved searching every home and building, sometimes taking valuables, horses, food, and supplies.

Lincolnton

On April 17th, cavalry commanded by Brig. General William J. Palmer crossed the Catawba River and took control of Lincolnton late in the day. Only one shot was fired in defense of the town. A 16-year-old boy fired at Palmer as he rode at the head of the column. The boy was arrested, but his mother intervened, and Palmer released him. Palmer's occupied Lincolnton 15th Pennsylvania and 12th Ohio regiments. Overall, they found Lincolnton to be a pleasant place despite the citizens' fierce Confederate loyalty. The people were courteous to the troopers, who treated them well. The day after the raiders came to Lincolnton, a Federal trooper named Corporal George French and two others went looking for a stray mount and were ambushed a mile from town. In a brief skirmish, Corporal French was killed, a sad and unnecessary death at the end of the war. The young Federal trooper was buried in Lincolnton's Episcopal Cemetery.

Other raiders encountered Anna Jackson, the widow of Stonewall Jackson, living in Lincoln County. The soldiers couldn't resist the target and took several horses and other animals from the farm. Stonewall Jackson had been a friend of General Stoneman, so Anna wrote and asked for the animals back. The animals were returned with a note of apology and three soldiers to guard Cottage Home.

Rutherfordton

Palmer occupied Lincolnton for five days, scouting down the Catawba River and keeping the area secure. On April 23rd, they struck camp and headed toward Rutherfordton, arriving there the next day. It was the third straight day Union troops had come to town. Tennesseans had been there for two days and were not as kind toward the residents as Palmer's men had been in Lincolnton. Some were eastern Tennessee Unionists who dealt unkindly to their neighbors to the south. Considerable damage was done in the town, and at least three structures were destroyed by fire. Palmer's men, however, were better behaved.

As the troopers made their way through Rutherford County, they came to the home of a farmer named Richard Smith. Smith was polite and gave them no trouble. They searched his home and took a few things. In the front yard was a fresh grave with a headboard, marked Daniel. When they inquired about the grave, Smith said that a faithful old servant had died a few days before. As the troopers started to leave, one of them became suspicious and said he would like to see Daniel before they left. He dug up the grave, opened the box, and discovered that Daniel was several nice hams Smith had hidden. The soldier said, "Daniel looks natural; seems like I've seen him before. Well boys, I guess we will take Daniel with us." Mr. Smith watched in chagrin as the prized hams rode away.[265]

---

[265] (Elliott n.d.) Story related by James C. Elliott.

One of the worst scenes during this time was not at the hands of Union soldiers, but rebels. Joseph Biggerstaff was a 56-year-old farmer and merchant in Rutherford County. On April 28, 1865, he was visited by six mounted rebels claiming to be Wheeler's men on their way home. They demanded money and searched his home, finding $600. Four of the men counted the money on the kitchen table while the other two watched outside. Biggerstaff attacked them with an axe. He killed two of them and had the third one down when the fourth man drew a pistol and shot him dead. A neighbor named Waters saw the commotion, and one of the robbers shot and killed him as well. The robbers left the four dead men, took the money, and fled.[266]

Athens, Georgia

Soon, Stoneman's troopers left the area. Johnston and Sherman signed a preliminary surrender on April 18th and the final agreement on the 26th. With the war ending, General Palmer was sent south to join in the pursuit of Jefferson Davis. On May 8, 1865, Palmer occupied Athens, Georgia. Athens was a major supply and railroad hub for the Confederacy. They captured the remaining Confederate troops there, including the last members of the 34th North Carolina still in active military service. Seven men from the 34th NC were there. They were men whose health made them unfit for field duty and were given a light duty assignment.

Captured May 8, 1865, at Athens, GA

J. B. Bess	B	Pvt.	W P Longston	I	Pvt.
A. H. Burr	A	Pvt.	J Mitchell	I	Pvt.
John Camp	C	1Lt.	J. P. Moor	C	Pvt.
Noah Carpenter	E	Pvt.			

Lt. John Camp had gone to war in 1861, with his friends from Rutherford County. He was captured at Funkstown on July 12, 1863 and sent to Point Lookout. Following his exchange, he returned to duty and served until the final winter of the war. His friend Noah Carpenter enlisted in Lincolnton in 1861 and served throughout the war. The others had all been conscripted in the final four months of the war. Also

---

[266] (Elliott n.d.) Related in an article titled "Confederate Troopers Commit Outrages, Plunder, and Murder, written by James C. Elliott.

paroled in Athens was an old Rutherford County friend, James M. Taylor. James enlisted with Company C of the 34th NC at the start of the war but transferred to the 62nd NC in July of 1862, with a promotion to Lieutenant. General Palmer paroled each man, allowing them to go home.

The 34th NC at Ford's Theatre

On April 14, 1865, Good Friday, President Abraham Lincoln was shot at Ford's Theatre. Our nation's greatest president had lived to see the successful conclusion of the war only to be senselessly killed two days later. Two members of the 34th NC were said to be witnesses to the tragic event. Fredrick Washington "Wash" Dellinger and Jonas Hoyle crossed the lines together at Petersburg on March 18, 1865 and surrendered to the Yankees. Both men had been in the war since near the beginning. Wash enlisted in the 11th North Carolina early in 1862. He was wounded at Gettysburg, captured, and confined at David's Island, NY. It is said that one of the best meals he had there was when he caught a black snake and ate it.[267] He was exchanged in 1864, returning to his company in October. He transferred to the Company E of the 34th NC in February of 1865, to be with his brothers Jacob and Henry. His friend Jonas Hoyle had been with the 34th NC since 1861.

Like others that crossed the lines in the final weeks of the war, they were given a work detail instead of being sent to prison. A newspaper article published years after the war relates that Wash and Jonas were housed just south of the Potomac and employed at a nearby cemetery. On April 14th, the Federal officer in charge gave them his tickets to the theatre. One account indicates that they helped set up the theatre before the play. The article states that they had not yet taken their seats when John Wilkes Booth "took three steps and shot Mr. Lincoln."[268] Because Wash and Jonas were rebels, they feared they

---

[267] Per information on his Find A Grave memorial page, as told by one of Wash's granddaughters.

[268] (Carpenter 2016) Carpenter quotes an undated Gastonia Gazette article and another from the same paper dated May 5, 1968. The story is believable. Both of their service records place them in the area at time of the assassination. They deserted only days before the fall of Richmond. The records state they were to be transferred, Wash to Illinois and Jonas to Philadelphia. However, their assignments may have been cancelled due to the war's end, or they may have not gone until after April 14th.

would be arrested, so they "slipped quietly out the iron door and went back across the river to their compound."

The Catawba River

Ancil Dycus and his brother Joseph headed home with a group of men from Rutherford and Cleveland Counties. Their friends James Blanton and Drury Price from the 34th NC were in the group of twenty or thirty rebels making their way home. They had the rags on their backs, and a few days' rations. Many of them were sick, and progress was slow. The stronger ones helped their weaker friends along. Finding a working railroad was not easy. They hopped a few wagons, anything they could find, but much of the way was on foot.

They followed the rail lines south to Greensboro. There, they learned that the lines north and south of town had been demolished. Roads everywhere were muddy and difficult to travel, but on they went. They reached Salisbury by the 16th of April. Every step brought them closer to home. Ancil's wife and daughters Louise and Dora were waiting. How much his girls must have grown, and there was so much work to be done. As the group made their way through Salisbury, they filed by the prison which was in smoldering ruins, the handy work of Stoneman's troopers.

When they arrived at the Catawba River, they were home, but there was a problem. The bridge they planned to use was washed out by the heavy rains. The current was too strong to ford and there was no other bridge for miles. They would have to wait until the water settled down, which could be several days or a week or two. After waiting a few days, they met a local lad of about 12 years and talked him into taking them across on a small barge pulled by a mule.

Ancil and his brother Joe climbed aboard. James Blanton and Drury Price also climbed on. Three other men went aboard. The mule pulled the raft into the water with the seven men on board. The rest of the group watched, shouting encouragement, and hoping they could get across themselves on the next trip. The mule-drawn raft struggled. The water was too rough for the small raft with seven men aboard. Halfway across, the raft turned over, and the men found themselves fighting the powerful current. Of the seven, only Ancil made it across. Once safely on the bank, he saw that his brother was still floundering in the current. Without hesitating, he dove back in to rescue him. He never made it back out. All seven men drowned in the raging Catawba River, only a few miles from home. Three of them, Ancil Dycus, James Blanton, and Drury Price, were members of the 34th North Carolina. Drury Price was a fifer and had survived the entire war, including being wounded once. James Blanton enlisted in late 1863, and had served faithfully the last half of the war.

Once more, hearts shattered, and bitter tears fell. Families faced the shock of losing their loved ones on the way home from the war. It was more than they could bear. The letters of Ancil Dycus provided us with valuable insight into the lives of the men of the 34th NC. Today, seven markers stand on the banks of the Catawba to memorialize the men who perished there April 25, 1865. They are known as the Flat Rock Seven.

Swallowing the Oath

On May 9th, 1865, President Johnson declared the hostilities over. Over 200 men from the 34th North Carolina, more than those surrendered at Appomattox, remained prisoners of war. Most were at Point Lookout and Hart's Island, New York. Most of the men had been captured since March 25, 1865. A few had been prisoners since the Wilderness and Hanover Junction. Only four of the regiment's POWs from the Gettysburg campaign remained confined. Privates Joseph Kennedy and John Lutz remained at Fort Delaware since Gettysburg. They were released June 8th. Lt. Joseph A. Camp and Capt. Carmi K. McNeely remained at Johnson's Island in Ohio until June 11th. These men had been in confinement longer than any of the regiment's prisoners, two full years and two terrible winters. After Lee's surrender, another thirteen men from the regiment died as prisoners of war. Private James Sharpe from Company A was the last man from the regiment to die in service on June 20, 1865. He was captured when Petersburg fell and was sent to Hart's Island where he died of Typhoid.

Elmira

Only seven men from the regiment remained at Elmira when Lee surrendered. All but one had been captured between May and June of 1864, spending time at Point Lookout before transferring to Elmira. After taking the oath, they were given a train ticket back to North Carolina. Pvt. Chares S. Martin was there. Martin had been wounded at Chancellorsville and Gettysburg, and was wounded and captured at The

Wilderness. His father had died of disease in July of 1863, as a member of the 42nd NC. Martin remembered that as prisoners they were always filthy, and body lice were "thick and furious." Being a prisoner was rough, but he said that he fared better there than as a soldier in the field. The worst part of Elmira to him was the humiliation they were subjected to. The guards had erected a platform from which people from the town could come out and, for a fee, view the prisoners, referred to as the, "barbarians, or apes, from the south." On warm Sunday afternoons, families from town would come out and gawk at the prisoners for hours. The humiliation was hard for them to take.

Private Sam Dellinger was the last of the regiment to leave Elmira. He had been severely wounded in the left leg and left arm when Petersburg fell, his third wound of the war. He took his oath at the Elmira hospital on July 19th and was sent home to Shelby, NC. It had been a long war for Sam. He was there for it all. He was his company's selection for the badge of distinction at Chancellorsville. Except those times when he was wounded, he was with the regiment every step of the way. At 26 years of age, he was a battle-hardened veteran with scars to show for his service. He was among the first to join and one of the last to go home.

Hart's Island

At Hart's Island in New York Harbor, 60 men from the regiment waited to go home. All of them had been captured April 1-3. Typhoid was an acute problem there. Despite their short stay, privates James Sharpe, John Brown, and William Vaughn died of Typhoid before their release. T. D. Munn died of an unspecified disease, probably Typhoid. They were among the 235 who died at Hart's Island in the prison's four months in operation. They were buried near the prison but reinterred at Cypress Hill Cemetery in Brooklyn in 1941.

The 34th NC's Drum Major, Fred Bourquin was one of the last to leave Hart's Island on June 21st. He had been with the regiment since just before the Seven Days battles. He was one of very few from the regiment who was not a native Tar Heel. He was a Virginian, a resident of Fredericksburg. Sgt. Robert James was among those afflicted with Typhoid, and his release had to be delayed another month as he recovered at nearby David's Island Hospital. He was finally well enough to go home on July 21st. He had been shot in the ankle and captured at Gettysburg, then paroled from Point Lookout in March of 1864. He served on light duty for a while, eventually returning to the regiment during the siege of Petersburg. He was captured again when the city fell and was sent to Hart's Island. The two-time POW survived and headed home to Rutherford County.

Point Lookout

At Point Lookout, 109 men from the regiment waited to be released. Five died before that day came. Most were captured between March 25th and April 2nd. The prison housed over 20,000 men when Lee surrendered. They were released in groups starting in May by a combination of alphabetical order and inverse order in which the states seceded. Thus, the South Carolina men would leave last. Men were selected going A to Z in two rounds. The first round was slow, not getting to the W's until the last half of June. On June 22nd, Harvey Adams was released, starting the second round, which went faster. The last prisoner from the 34th NC took the oath on June 30th, when Private James Williford got his ticket home. Private James Harrison had taken his oath earlier, but he was sick and had to spend time in Hammond General Hospital before leaving on July 13th, becoming the last of the regiment's Point Lookout prisoners to head home.

Because of the way they were released, the men had some idea when they would leave. This gave some a way to get out earlier. Privates Calvin McCallum and Thompson Wood underwent unofficial name changes to get out sooner. Some prisoners throughout the camp did this. They arranged with buddies to trade names. They were recorded on a "Roll of prisoners who arrived under an assumed name or assumed one to be released."

The Way Home

A notice was posted at Point Lookout on June 11th, "All men whose homes are in Virginia and North Carolina who wish to return via Richmond, whose names begin with D and E, will be discharged upon taking the oath of allegiance to the United States on to-morrow—12th June." This included Felix Dobbins of Rutherford County and Virgil Elliott of Cleveland County of the 34th NC, and their friend James C. Elliott of the 56th NC from Cleveland County. The trio stood in a line of 300 men waiting their turn, as 32 at a time entered the building where the oath was administered. A large American flag hung above them, as their names, occupation, place of residence, etc. were recorded. After taking the oath, they were each given six hardtacks and a half pound of cod fish and put aboard a transport ship.

Felix, James, and Virgil stayed together. It was raining when they arrived at Richmond after dark the next day. At the Provost Marshall's office, they were told where they could find shelter and were ordered to report back the next morning. They sheltered for the night, having eaten extraordinarily little since leaving Point Lookout. A store keeper gave them two loaves of bread and some dried herring.

The next morning, they were furnished a train ride to a commissary to draw rations. Two men at a time stood in line. When James's turn came, he said, "Meat for two men, please." He was given his request and waived on. He divided his extra meat with his friends. They crossed the James River on a pontoon bridge and then took quarter in a freight car. A heavy rain came through that night which delayed them another day. They drew more rations of crackers and salt pork. They left Richmond on the 16th, but the train could not cross the Appomattox River because high water had damaged the trestle. They walked to another station. They stayed at Burkeville until dark and hopped on a boxcar. The door of the boxcar was full, but they fought their way in, only to find that the men at the door were the only ones in the car. The men at the door were "hospital rats" who did not want to mix with lousy, dirty prisoners. After Felix, Virgil, and James got in, they let no one else aboard. Many prisoners rode on top in the all-night ride through a rain storm. They passed through Greensboro to Charlotte. From there they walked the last sixty miles, arriving home on June 20th, weary but glad to be home.[269]

Scott B. Hutchison

Scott Hutchison made his way home from Appomattox to Charlotte with a group of war-weary veterans. Scott received an "illegal discharge" back in 1862, but was one of the handful of men who returned to duty rather than go home. He went all the way with the regiment, missing only one muster in 1864, due to sickness. He came home with the memories of the war and clothes on his back. Near home, the other members of the group wanted to take an extra night to

---

[269] (Elliott n.d.) A collection of post–war recollections by James C. Elliott.

get some rest, but Scott was anxious to get home and went on alone. When he got home, he wouldn't even go into the house until he had changed clothes and burned the lice-infested rags he came home with.[270] The war had changed him, like it had all the men who fought. Many were unrecognizable to even their own families. From the day they left home to now, everything about them was different. They would never be the same.

Rev. Maxwell Humphrey Hoyle

Maxwell H. Hoyle was sick and weakened from wounds when he came home late in the war. He was shot in his right side in May of 1864 and had not fully recovered when the war ended. He was in the hospital in Richmond when his sister came and took him home. Max had been with the regiment from the beginning and was in many hard battles. But unlike many of his friends, he never doubted that he was survive the war, because he had been called to preach and knew God would spare him. One day, he went out to work in the fields and fell on his face praying. His brother David, with whom he served in the 34th NC, came and asked him what was wrong. Max said that he had been called to preach and was unprepared. David told him to go to the house and get his books. He would do his work for him.

Max studied hard and got his license to preach in 1867. He married Mary Francis Lee in 1870, and they raised a large family. Max read and studied, especially bible history, all his life. He spent forty years in the ministry, a highly respected minister with an impeccable reputation. He died in 1908 at 66 years of age.

---

[270] Hutchison is said to have known by name one of the Confederate agents involved in a failed plot to set fire to several locations in New York City in late 1864.

Sgt. Simon D. Davis, The Sandy Run Yellow Jackets – Company B

Simon's left leg was amputated above the knee from a wound received the night of May 2, 1863 at Chancellorsville.[271]

---

[271] Photo courtesy Judith Parker-Proctor

Corporal George Washington Lookadoo, The Sandy Run Yellow Jackets – Company B. Lookadoo was mortally wounded at Ox Hill.[272]

---

[272] Photo Courtesey FindaGrave member.

Chapter 17.
Tar Heels in Yankeedom – The Galvanized Yankees

When Lee surrendered at Appomattox, twelve men from the 34th NC were wearing the blue uniform of the United States Army. As the 34th NC faced Grant in the war's final showdown, these men went west.

Name	Company		Residence	34th NC Company
White, Hiram J	A	1 USV	Rutherford Co.	B
Revel, Henry B	A	1 USV	Cleveland Co.	H
Eaker, Abraham	B	1 USV	Lincoln Co.	E
Peeler, John H	B	1 USV	Cleveland Co.	F
Brown, William B	B	1 USV	Cleveland Co.	H
Long, William M	C	1 USV	Cleveland Co.	H
Corn, Ezekiel W	H	1 USV	Henderson Co.	C
Dillworth, John QA	H	1 USV	Forsyth Co.	G
Hartness, Miles M	K	1 USV	Catawba Co.	D
Kiser, Robert G	K	1 USV	Cleveland Co.	H
Allen, Perry	C	4 USV	Cleveland Co.	H
McRae, James L	C	4 USV	Montgomery Co	K

1st USV – Fort Rice

Six members of the 34th North Carolina joined the 1st United States Volunteers in January of 1864, at Point Lookout.[273] Four more joined in May and June. Most of the 1st USV recruits were from North Carolina. After mustering in at Norfolk, VA, they did provost duty briefly in Portsmouth, and Elizabeth City, NC before being sent west. The 1st USV was host to a small Cleveland County contingent; Henry Revel, William B. Brown, William M. Long, Robert B. Kiser, and Perry Allen were all former members of the 34th NC.

On August 15, 1864, the 1st USV sailed to New York City. The sights there were the likes of nothing these farm boys had ever seen. From there, they took a train to Chicago where the regiment was

---

[273] The principle source for information on the 1st and 4th USV comes from <u>The Galvanized Yankees</u> by Dee Brown. Select portions pertaining to the companies the men from the 34th NC were assigned are summarized here.

split up. Four companies went to Milwaukee including Company A with Hiram White and Henry Revel, both 1861, volunteers from the 34th NC. The rest of the regiment, including eight former members of the 34th NC, was sent to St. Louis, Missouri, arriving there August 22nd. Five days later, they boarded a steamboat for the 1,000-mile trip up the Missouri to Fort Rice. On September 27, a sandbar prevented the boat from going any farther. They had to march the remaining 272 miles. William Brown, Abe Eaker, William Long, and John Peeler all made the march to Gettysburg as members of the 34th NC, covering 157 miles in twelve days. The march to Fredericksburg in December of 1862, covered 175 miles in 13 days. They marched the 272 miles to Fort Rice in 20 days, reaching the fort on October 17th.

The men settled into their new surroundings and received assignments. John Peeler and Abe Eaker in B Company worked as herders. William Long worked as a cook for C Company. By the time they were settled in, winter came. The Virginia winter had been hard, the winter at Point Lookout was harder, but neither was anything like the Dakota weather. The temperatures were brutal, and they were isolated in a sea of white. They had plenty of meat but lacked vegetables. It was impossible to have supplies brought in. Many were sick, and medicine ran low.

In November, K Company Private Miles Hartness became sick. It started with stomach cramps and diarrhea. He was nauseated, his muscles ached, he ran a fever, and lost weight. There was little the post doctor could do. Miles was 19 when he joined the 34th NC in April of 1864, from Catawba, NC. He was captured at the Battle of the Wilderness, his only engagement of the Civil War. He joined the 1st USV in June. Miles was unable to survive the winter at Fort Rice. He died on November 21, 1864, of Dysentery.

Ezekiel Noah Corn was 36 years old from Henderson County, NC. He was conscripted in May of 1864, and was captured at the Wilderness. He joined the 1st USV three weeks later. His family was as southern as they came. All his brothers enlisted in the Confederate army. His wife, Leathanna, was back home taking care of their children aided by his parents Noah and Elizabeth. In January, he complained of being tired and achy. By February, he was short of breath. His bones ached, his gums were hurting, and his teeth were loosening. The doctor diagnosed the problem easily. He had seen a lot of Scurvy that winter due to the lack of vegetables. Ezekiel's condition worsened through February. He became jaundiced, his skin became rough and he developed edema and dehydration. He suffered convulsions at the end. It was a terrible way to die. Ezekiel succumbed to the disease on March 4, 1865. Just a year earlier, he had been at home with his wife and kids. He was laid to rest in the frozen Dakota landscape by Fort Rice.

John Quincy Adams Dillworth also felt the effects of the disease. Like Ezekiel, John had entered the war shortly before the Wilderness, where he was captured. John was from Forsyth County, North Carolina. On March 21st, the man with the presidential name died. Three former members of the 34th NC were among the 11% of the garrison to die during the winter, most from scurvy.[274] When spring finally came, the fort was re-supplied, and the winter-weary men gained strength. In April, word came of Lee's surrender at Appomattox. They quietly hoped the war's end might bring an early discharge. In May, two companies, B and K, were transferred out. They were sent to Forts Union and Berthold in Montana. The transfer took all the remaining men from the 34th NC out of Fort Rice except William Long, whose C Company remained. Two companies of the 4th USV were sent to Ft. Rice.[275]

A fight with Sitting Bull

Trouble with the Indians had been brewing for several weeks. At dawn on July 28th, Sioux warriors in full war paint, led by Chief Sitting Bull, captured the garrison's entire herd, and then gathered to attack the fort itself. The remaining companies of the 1st USV with the two companies of the 4th USV and a detachment of cavalry prepared to defend themselves. The soldiers came out armed and ready to give battle. They weren't merely staying in the safety of the fort. They formed a line of battle and faced the threat out in the open. They were

---

[274] The soldiers buried at Fort Rice were reinterred in March of 1905. Ezekiel Corn, John Dillworth, and Miles (Milus) Hartness are now buried in marked graves in the Custer National Cemetery in Big Horn County, Montana, also known as Little Big Horn National Cemetery.

[275] Companies A and D of the 4th USV were sent to Fort Rice. Company C went to Fort Berthold. In this company were two former members of the 34th NC, Perry Allen and James McRae.

greatly out-numbered but counted on superior firepower to win the day. Fort Rice was virtually surrounded by mounted Sioux warriors. The artillery was ready including the fort's two howitzers, and the cavalry was in support.

The Sioux raced forward so fast their horses seemed to stretch straight out. Some of the warriors stood on the backs of their horses and fired arrows and swung tomahawks in stunning feats of skill and bravery. The battle raged for three hours. The composed troops at Fort Rice never gave an inch. Just after noon, the Sioux withdrew from the area. Only one soldier was killed by an arrow and gunshot wounds early in the attack. Another later died of wounds. Three suffered severe arrow wounds but survived. Several suffered minor wounds. William Long of the 34th NC was not injured.

The rest of the summer was quiet. They cut and stacked 300 tons of hay along the river, a chore that must have reminded them of home. They hunted buffalo and antelope. Meat was plentiful. They grew every kind of vegetable in the fort's gardens. On August 26th, word came that they were to be transferred to Fort Leavenworth, Kansas to be mustered out of the service. On August 31st, Companies B and K rejoined them, and together they travelled to Fort Leavenworth and were mustered out on November 27, 1865.

Forts Union and Berthold

Companies B and K missed the Battle of Fort Rice in July of 1865, having been sent to forts Union and Berthold. B Company with Abe Eaker, William Brown, and John Peeler went to Fort Union-2 in Montana[276]. Abe Eaker joined the 34th NC in 1861, in Lincoln County along with several other Eaker men.[277] William B. Brown volunteered in 1861. John Peeler joined the 34th NC in February of 1863. All three had been captured at Falling Waters. Fort Union-2 was located near Frazer, Montana and was established in 1829 by the American Fur Company. The company's time there was peaceful.

In K Company going to Fort Berthold was Robert G. Kiser. Robert was born in Gaston County and enlisted in 1861, in

---

[276] This fort is sometimes confused with Fort Union-1 in North Dakota, which was established three years sooner.

[277] Daniel and Jesse Eaker also joined the U. S. Army. They were placed in an "Unassigned Regiment." Further records for them were not found.

Montgomery County. As the 34th NC pulled away from the trenches at Cold Harbor on June 13, 1864, Kiser slipped out and surrendered to Union troops. Two weeks later, he joined the 1st USV and wound up at Fort Berthold.

Also sent to Fort Berthold was C Company of the 4th USV, with a pair of friends from the old outfit, Perry Allen and Jim McRae. Perry Allen was the youngest of six Allen men who volunteered at Shelby in October of 1861. He was 19 then. Other than one short AWOL, his record with the 34th NC was excellent. He was captured at the North Anna and joined the 4th USV. Counting his two years in the U.S. Army, Perry was in uniform the longest of any from 34th North Carolina, five full years. Perry busied himself in the fort as a cook and worked in the post hospital.

Jim McRae was 32 when the conscription agents called on him in March of 1863, forcing him to leave behind a teaching job. He was captured June 22, 1864, at the battle of Jerusalem Plank Road and joined the 4th USV after a month and a half at Point Lookout. Picking up a similar duty he had performed for the 34th NC, he worked in the commissary with the 4th USV. He was also company clerk and a hospital steward. The company had one of the best surgeons around, 22-year-old Washington Matthews.[278] Perry Allen and Jim McRae assisted Dr. Matthews in the post hospital. Fort Berthold was another old fur-trading post formerly owned by the American Fur Company. It was described as a gloomy place on a high bluff near the river. There were few problems with Indians at Berthold during their time there. Their main battles were with bed bugs and boredom.

In early June of 1866, word came that both the 1st and 4th USV regiments would be mustered out. Companies B and K of the 1st USV were sent to Fort Rice on August 31st to join the rest of the command to go to Fort Leavenworth. The 4th USV proceeded to Fort Leavenworth, mustering out as they arrived. C Company, with Jim McRae and Perry Allen, was the last company mustered out on July 2, 1866, fourteen months after Appomattox.

---

[278] Dr. Matthews had a highly successful career and became very well known, especially for his studies of the Navajo.

The Last Battalion

Hiram White joined the Sandy Run Yellow Jackets in September of 1861, with his brother Albert. Hiram was 18, Albert only 16. Albert died of disease the following June. Hiram soldiered on, fighting his way through 1862. He fought at Chancellorsville and Gettysburg. Henry Revel was the same age as Hiram and enlisted at Shelby in 1861. Henry and Hiram had served together since the beginning. Henry was captured at Hagerstown on July 12th, 1863, Hiram at Brandy Station August 1st. On January 22, 1864, the pair joined the 1st USV. On enlistment they had to pass a physical examination. Henry's exam was fine, but the doctor had some pause when Hiram told him he had been kicked in the head by a horse when he was a boy. The injury did not appear to have caused permanent damage, however, and both men were accepted. Their A Company was detached from the regiment and spent a monotonous year at Fort Abercrombie in the Dakota Territory along the Red River. Henry had a short stay at Fort Ridgley caring for the captain's ailing wife. Henry and Hiram occupied themselves with various chores in the frigid Dakota weather.

Around July of 1865, Hiram and Henry were told they would be mustered out and were sent to Fort Snelling in Minnesota to await transport to Fort Leavenworth. They waited for orders, but the paperwork moved too slowly. Henry could wait no longer and deserted at Fort Snelling, saying goodbye to Hiram and starting for home.[279] Hiram White and the rest of the company went to Fort Leavenworth in early October. There, instead of being discharged, they were reassigned. A Company and three other companies of the 1st USV were to guard the stations of a new stage line across Kansas to Denver. The battalion was to march the 225 miles west to establish a new outpost in Kansas. On November 1, 1865, the last battalion of the 1st USV started west with 250 men and 108 wagons loaded with supplies. With them marched Hiram White, the last member of the 34th NC in the 1st USV.

The weather and roads were good. Hiram found marching in the plains much easier than the rolling hills of Virginia. On November

---

[279] Henry was mustered out at Fort Leavenworth October 1, 1865, presumably for desertion. In 1928, the U.S. Army dropped the charges of desertion against Henry Revel.

20th, they reached Big Creek and established Fort Fletcher as battalion headquarters.[280] Hiram White and A Company helped get things in order and left two days later. His company was assigned to an outpost 100 miles farther to the west at Monument Station, while I Company was sent to Pond's Creek Station, 50 miles west of Monument Station.

The first few days on the way to Monument Station were fine, and Hiram marched along without complaint. They passed by a large herd of buffalo and killed a few for meat. On Sunday, November 26, an Indian raiding party attacked swiftly, taking many of their mules and horses and disappearing into the prairie. That evening, they observed ominous smoke on the horizon. Nerves were on edge. Cheyenne were taking revenge for the Sand Creek Massacre in November of 1864, in which over 100 Cheyenne and Arapaho were killed.

The next morning, teamsters were ordered to roll back the canvas covers on the wagons and be ready to corral their wagons at the first sign of an attack. Throughout the day, Hiram marched by several disturbing sights. Near Downer's Station, three dead men were found, each shot by numerous arrows, one burned to death. Several such sickening scenes were encountered. They kept close watch that night with wagons corralled. They were still 40 miles from Monument Station but decided to push hard and make it in one day. They started early and covered the 40 miles in one grueling forced march without incident. They arrived at Monument Station and found a detachment of the 13th Missouri Cavalry waiting. After marching 325 miles in 28 days, they were tired but glad to be in the relative safety of their new position.

After a night of rest, Hiram spent the next day unloading wagons and getting things in order. They were on the west bank of Smoky Hill by a long stretch of grass-covered prairie. Beyond the prairie was the beautiful formations known as The Monuments which gave the area its name. They did not have a fort to protect them, only adobe structures. Early the next morning, an Indian raiding party swooped in and attacked the mule herd, this time beaten back by the troopers. The Indians lingered in the area until their numbers swelled to 500, then began to surround the adobes, making slashing attacks. Later

---

[280] The fort was later renamed Fort Hays.

in the afternoon, the dry prairie grass caught fire as the Indians tried to drive the soldiers away. The soldiers stood their ground. Like Hiram, most of them were veterans of the fighting in Virginia. Flames and smoke from the burning grass only reminded Hiram of Chancellorsville.

For the next few weeks, Hiram White, and the rest of the company, built dugouts and other defenses and guarded the coaches as they passed between stations. In December, traffic slowed. When the snows started from the Rockies, the coaches stopped coming. The men hunkered down for the winter.

The Blizzard March

By January of 1866, it was clear that they did not have enough food for the winter, and the weather was getting bad. From Pond's Creek, I Company marched 50 miles back to Monuments. Together, the two companies started the 100-mile trip to Fort Fletcher. A day into the march, the blizzard struck. Taking shelter in and under wagons, they endured hours of heavy snow and pounding wind. They had just enough firewood with them to keep from freezing. When the storm stopped, they resumed their trek through the deep snow. They still had most of the 100 miles to go to reach Fort Fletcher, their only hope for food and supplies. At night, they spread rubber blankets on the snow with wool blankets over them to sleep on, and then covered themselves with several blankets, not even exposing their faces to the cold. Often the wind would blow drifting snow that completely covered them. The snow insulated them from the wind and helped keep them warmer.[281] In the mornings, their camp resembled a graveyard with snow-covered mounds until the men shook themselves awake. It took a total of 16 long days from Ponds Creek to Fort Fletcher. By the time Hiram and his company reached the fort, they had almost no rations left. The garrison there had little food as well. And there was little hope of being resupplied anytime soon in the terrible weather. Hiram was sick and very weak by the time he reached the fort as were many others. The situation was dire.

Then on February 1st, a supply train miraculously made its way to the fort with a full month's provisions. Hiram White was weak but

---

[281] (Brown 1963) The Blizzard March is described on pages 198-200.

holding up. On March 1st, Hiram's company was ordered back to Monument Station for the resumption of the stage line. Hiram was ill and did not go with his company. By the time he recovered, the ice-covered landscape had thawed, and more supply trains arrived. Men ventured out to hunt. Hiram rejoined his company at Monument Station as the stages began rolling in.

Finally, the long-awaited order came that the battalion would be mustered out. The companies undertook their long march back to Leavenworth. On May 10, 1866, Hiram White mustered out after two full years of service in the United States Army, four years and eight months after joining the 34th North Carolina in Rutherford County. Captain Adams of the 1st USV wrote, "We have a country redeemed from anarchy, redeemed from disunion, which we can call our own. We have served that country honorably, let us preserve that good name. We are the first fruits of a re-united people. Let us prove that it is a golden link, and of no baser metal."[282]

---

[282] (Brown 1963) Captain Adams's quote is from the final edition of The *Frontier Scout*, quoted by Dee Brown on pages 110-111.

Private James A. Harrill, The Sandy Run Yellow Jackets - Company B[283]

---

[283] Photo courtesy Carolyn, Ancestry.com

Chapter 18.
Reverend Lowrance Speaks

In Limestone County, Texas, July 22-24, 1891, a large group of Confederate veterans and their families gathered. There was plenty of food, music, and old friends. They cherished these friendships forged long ago in the trials of war. Among the guest speakers was Reverend William Lee Joshua Lowrance whose 55th birthday was a few days away. He began with these words:

"Confederate veteran, ladies, gentlemen, sons and daughters of the Confederate dead. I greet you this morning as the noblest among the living - and the representatives of the mightiest dead. Twenty-seven springs have brightened into summers, and twenty-six autumns have darkened into winters since the sound of war hushed into silence in this beautiful land, and peace began her blissful reign. And long may this heaven born queen sit in triumph on her white throne.

"We are not here to celebrate the victories of that bloody strife; let those rest in their glory.

"We are not here to stir again the passions of hate and thirst for war; may these sleep forever. We are not here to show cause, just cause or why such a war waged. We are not here to show the world how the battles were won and why the cause was lost.

"We are not here to reproach or hate those we fought, (and just here let me say that should there be one in our midst who wore the blue or marched on the other side of the line, in the name of these brave hearts and noble spirits, I bid you welcome).

"Nor are we here to apologize to governments, princes, kings, the world, or to humanity, for ought that we said or did.

"But we are here to shake hands once more, with the noblest band of heroes that ever drew sword or marched to the sound of a drum—and who waged the grandest contest for civil liberty, in the history of man. We are here to keep bright in memory the cherished names and the chivalrous deeds of the heroic dead. We are here in obedience to the majestic call of duty, to see that these grand and noble deeds find their proper place in history, and that these brilliant and almost sacred names pass down to the heritage of their sons and daughters properly enshrined, and that they be engraven in marble and brass preserved for the guidance and adoration of the ages unborn. Who should blush to perform such graceful deeds as these? Let that son or daughter born in this land of the brave, hide their face for very shame, who should refuse to hang a wreath or do a deed to the memory of the Confederate dead."

Col. William L. J. Lowrance left the war behind in February of 1865, and married Sarah Cordelia Stuart. Shortly after the wedding, the war in Virginia was over. Lowrance made a living at farming and as a merchant in Oxford, Mississippi for a while, then tried his hand at politics. He spent four years in the Mississippi State Legislature. But politics, especially in the dark days of reconstruction, was not his true calling. In 1880, he and his family moved to Texas, and he went into the ministry. He was ordained in 1883 and worked as a City Evangelist. He helped established several churches and earned a Doctor of Divinity degree from Austin College in 1885. He was the founder and for many years pastor of the Oak Cliff Presbyterian Church in Dallas, Texas.

But the war never left his memory, the sacrifices borne by the men he served with and their families at home. Lowrance received great applause when he spoke of the southern army's Grand Chieftain, calling him, "that model southern gentleman and soldier, a very prince among generals – the unparalleled commander, the mightiest leader of armies; the spotless, unrivaled, and immortal, R. E. Lee!" He got another round of applause at the mention of, "…that comet-like, magnetic, military genius, who alone has touched the pinnacle of military glory, and became the mightiest captain and most brilliant general in ancient or modern warfare, Stonewall Jackson! At the very mention of his name the beautiful valley of Virginia bursts into panoramic visions before our minds, and that loveliest plane, made classic by his genius and heroic devotion, light up with the glory of victories won by this Confederate knight."

But Lowrance spoke only briefly about the generals. The focus of his speech was the common soldier. He described the Confederate soldier as a, "plain, simple minded, unostentatious man…not illiterate as he has often been represented; but well informed and oftentimes refined and intelligent." Lowrance described scenes known so well by the veterans.

"I see him arranging to leave his cottage home. His true, loving, and thoughtful wife has carefully folded his blanket on his well filled knapsack and haversack, he looks around for the last time on his well tilled fields; he observes there is plenty of feed in the crib and grain in the bin; and as he passes the stable he bids adieu to his faithful horses, wipes a falling tear and commits them to the care of a loving wife and fond children...He takes his children one by one in his arms...bids them adieu – turns to his wife. Words cease to come.

"I see him in camp life; he reads the sad tender letters from wife and loved ones at home...He folds the letters, opens his little Bible, reads a passage, breathes a silent prayer, folds all away, and is ready for duty again.

"I see him again...this time he falls in battle, is carried with the wounded to the hospital, and from there goes to his home and loved ones for the first time...How changed! The little fields are grown up with grass and weeds. The horses...look lean and hungry. There is but little provender in the barn, and but little grain in the bin...The day to return comes so quickly...to say goodbye is like tearing on his heart strings, for he has had the glimpse of a desolate home and the struggles of a faithful wife. But that solemn call to duty must be obeyed and to the front he goes. "See him again; this time unarmed, wasted, worn, tired and tattered, with empty haversack...in that long, sad, last march, back to wife, loved ones...Once more he takes to his bosom the object of his love, and tells his story in one sentence: 'All is lost but my devotion and my honor, these I bring home to my wife and children.'"

Rev. Lowrance spoke for thirty minutes, his words sometimes partisan, often nostalgic; but his words were mostly personal reflections of a time when war interrupted youth and destroyed homes and lives. William L. J. Lowrance was a Confederate all his long life. He was a man of his times and unapologetically so. He saw no need to apologize for or justify what they had done. Like every man who fought, on either side, he did what he believed was right at the time and fought for a cause that he believed was right and just. William Lee Joshua Lowrance died in Forestville, Texas on March 24, 1916 at age 80.[284]

---

[284] Information courtesy Will Lowrance.

Captain David Ramsour Hoyle, The Floyd Rifles - Company F[285]

---

[285] Photo courtesy Van A. Hoyle

Roster of the Thirty-Fourth North Carolina Infantry Regiment
October 25, 1861 - April 9, 1865

ABERNATHY, Columbus, Pvt, G. Enlisted in Dallas NC on March 5, 1863. Accounted for every muster of enlistment. Wounded at Chancellorsville. Present at Appomattox.

ABERNATHY, Hiram W, Cpt, A. Enlisted in Lincolnton on September 11, 1861, at age 36. Carpenter. Failed re-election in Company E April 18, 1862. Promoted to Captain of Company A in March 1863. Wounded twice at Chancellorsville. Gunshot wound to the right arm in May 1864. Retired to the Invalid Corps in September 1864.

ABERNATHY, John N, 2Lt, G. Enlisted as a private in Charlotte on September 30, 1861, at age 19. Promoted to 2Lt. Killed in action at Gettysburg. Son of Miles Abernathy.

ABERNATHY, Thomas W, 2Lt, E. Enlisted as a private in Lincolnton on August 31, 1861, at age 22. Born in Gaston County. Blacksmith. Son of William B Abernathy. Wounded at Gaines's Mill. Promoted 2Lt. June 27, 1862. Died of disease in a private home in Virginia Nov. 6, 1862.

ABSHER, John L, Pvt, A. Enlisted in Ashe Co. on August 10, 1861, at age 42. Born in Spruce Springs, NC. Discharged due to age December 8, 1862.

ABSHER, William H, Pvt, A. Enlisted in Ashe Co on August 10, 1861, at age 26. Born Spruce Springs, NC. Listed as AWOL since February 16, 1863. Was executed for desertion April 18, 1864.

ADAMS, Harvey S, Pvt, H. Enlisted in Shelby on October 1, 1861, at age 24. Confined in Richmond for desertion. Returned to duty July 31, 1863. Gunshot wound left arm May 1864. Was captured at Amelia Courthouse April 4, 1865. Confined at Pt Lookout until June 22, 1865.

ADAMS, Martin, Pvt, H. Enlisted in Shelby on October 1, 1861, at age 37. Died of disease in Winchester, VA October 25, 1862. Wife Rody.

ADKINS, James, Pvt, K. Enlisted in Montgomery on September 9, 1861, at age 16. Did not reenlist and was discharged November 1, 1862, per Conscription law.

AIKIN, Samuel, Pvt, F. Enlisted in Cleveland on July 17, 1861, at age 19. Born in Burke, NC, son of R H Aikin. Was killed at Gaines's Mill.

ALCORN, Alfred S, Pvt, G. Enlisted in Charlotte on September 30, 1861, at age 37. Captured at North Anna May 23, 1864 and confined at Point Lookout. Exchanged February 13, 1865.

ALEXANDER, Elias A, Pvt, I. Enlisted at Camp Vance on May 15, 1864. Captured at Petersburg March 25, 1865. Confined at Point Lookout until June 22, 1865.

ALEXANDER John D, Pvt, G. Enlisted in Charlotte on September 30, 1861, at age 23. Musician. Killed at Gaines's Mill. Son of Harriet Alexander.

ALLEN, Champion, Sgt, H. Enlisted as a private in Shelby on October 1, 1861, at age 27. Promoted to Sgt. Musician. Present on every muster. Present at Appomattox. Married to Elizabeth Camp.

ALLEN, Clark, 1Sg, H. Enlisted in Shelby on October 1, 1861, at age 42. Died Sept 9, 1863, of wounds received at Second Manassas. Married to Agnes Allen.

ALLEN, Daniel C, Pvt, C. Enlisted at Camp Vance on March 30, 1864, at age 43. Wounded May 12, 1864. Returned to duty. Present to January 1865.

ALLEN, David, Cpl, H. Enlisted in Shelby on October 1, 1861, at age 33. Wounded in May 1864. Returned to duty. Present at Appomattox.

ALLEN, James, Sgt, H. Enlisted in Shelby on October 1, 1861, at age 25. Wounded at Chancellorsville. Disability discharge April 4, 1864.

ALLEN, James M, Cpl, B. Enlisted in Rutherford on September 2, 1861, at age 25. Wounded in June of 1862, finger amputated. Returned to duty. Hospitalized in January 1865, 60-day furlough.

ALLEN, Laban, Pvt, H. Enlisted in Shelby on January 1863, at age 32. Transferred from 15th NC. Deserted from the hospital in August 1863. Returned to duty. Was captured and paroled at Burkesville Junction April 1865.

ALLEN, Perry, Pvt, H. Enlisted in Shelby on October 1, 1861, at age 19. Captured at North Anna and sent to Point Lookout. Joined US Army October 15, 1864. Served in the 4th US Volunteers. Stationed in Ft. Fletcher Kansas. Worked as a cook and on hospital duty. Mustered out at Fort Leavenworth July 2, 1866.

ALLEN, Samuel T, Pvt, B. Enlisted at Camp Vance on September 26, 1863, at age 37. Came to the regiment in May or June of 1864. Present at Appomattox.

ALLEN, William, Pvt, H. Enlisted in Shelby on October 1, 1861, at age 26. Wounded at Chancellorsville, Transferred to light duty at Gordonsville, VA Feb. 1864

ALLEY, Green, Pvt, D. Enlisted after January of 1865. Paroled at Salisbury, NC May 18, 1865.

ALLIS, A. S., Pvt, C. Enlisted at Camp Vance on April 25, 1864. Listed as AWOL since June 7, 1864. Dropped from rolls Sept. 1, 1864.

ALLISON, Albert, Pvt, D. Enlisted at Camp Vance on March 22, 1864. Absent-Sick since May 6, 1864. Did not return to duty.

ANDERS, Meredith T, Pvt, A. Enlisted in Ashe Co on August 10, 1861, at age 29. Enlisted with his brother Thomas J. Anders. Died of disease at Hamilton, NC April 4, 1862. Son of John and Cynthia Anders.

ANDERS, Thomas J, Pvt, A. Enlisted in Ashe Co on August 10, 1861, at age 19. Enlisted with his brother Meredith T. Anders. Killed in action at Gaines's Mill. Son of John and Cynthia Anders.

ANDERSON, Charles J, Pvt, G. Enlisted in Charlotte on November 21, 1861, at age 30. Born in Henry County, NC. Killed in action at Gaines's Mill.

ANDERSON, William, Pvt, C. Enrolled around December 1864. Served as a courier. Present at Appomattox.

ANTHONY, John, Pvt, H. Enlisted in Shelby on October 1, 1861, at age 41. Discharged May 13, 1862, due to age and chronic pneumonia.

ARMSTRONG, W Jackson, Pvt, E. Enlisted in Lincolnton on September 11, 1861, at age 22. Wounded by buckshot in left thigh and captured near Kelly's Ford (Chancellorsville) May 1863. Confined at Old Capital prison and released June 1863. Hospitalized in Petersburg after release. On sick roll for the rest of the war.

ARNETT, J T, Pvt, D. Enlisted after December of 1864. Captured in Jackson Hospital in Richmond April 3, 1865. Date of release unknown.

ASBURY, John R, Pvt, G. Enlisted in Lincolnton on March 12, 1863, at age 39. Wounded at Chancellorsville and returned to duty November 1, 1863. Placed on light duty from October 8, 1864.

ASHBURN, Martin, Pvt, K. Enlisted in Raleigh on May 26, 1864, at age 43. Listed as AWOL each muster of enlistment.

ATKINSON, Thomas J, Pvt, D. Enlisted in Rowan on September 6, 1861, at age 21. Promoted to Sgt. April 18, 1862. Reduced to Pvt due to AWOL. Listed wounded September 28, 1863. Returned to duty. Died after October 1864, of unknown cause. Married to Sallie Atkinson.

ATWELL, Burrett M, Pvt, D. Enlisted in Rowan on September 9, 1861, at age 18. Son of W B Atwell. Died July 28, 1862, at home of wounds received at the Seven Days Battles.

ATWELL, George A, Cpt, D and E. Enlisted in Rowan on September 9, 1861, at age 18 as a private in Company D. Accounted for every muster. Promoted to Ordnance Sgt March 1, 1863, then 2Lt in command of Company E. Promoted to Captain August 25, 1864. Paroled at Salisbury May 23, 1865.

ATWELL, George L, Pvt, D. Enlisted in Rowan on September 9, 1861, at age 17. Died of disease at Camp Gregg, Fredericksburg April 25, 1863. Son of James A Atwell.

ATWOOD, Henry, Pvt, A. Enlisted in Ashe Co on August 10, 1861, at age 27. Wounded at Chancellorsville. Returned to duty. Present in December 1864.

AUSTIN, Edwin, 1Sgt, A. Enlisted in Ashe Co on August 10, 1861, at age 32. Died of disease in Richmond July 1862.

AVERY, Vincent, Pvt, E. Enlisted in Lincolnton on August 31, 1861, at age 35. Musician. Wounded in the Seven Days battles. Died following the march to Fredericksburg December 4, 1862.

AXION, Alex, Pvt, G. Enlisted on November 14, 1864. Resident of Mecklenburg County. Captured April 2, 1865, at Petersburg. Confined at Harts Island NY Harbor until June 17, 1865.

BABER, Stephen D, Pvt, C. Enlisted at Camp Vance on May 9, 1864. Wounded August 26, 1864. Transferred to Cherryville, NC Sept 10, 1864. No record after that.

BABER, William, Pvt, C. Enlisted in Rutherford on September 2, 1861, at age 19. Son of William A Baber. Died in Richmond hospital July 1862, of unknown cause.

BAGWELL, Stanhope H, Pvt, C. Enlisted in Rutherford on September 2, 1861, at age 24. Gunshot wound to the right shoulder in Seven Days battles. Wounded again at Chancellorsville, gunshot wound to the right leg. Recovered and was present at Appomattox.

BAILEY, William D, Pvt, A. Enlisted at Camp Holmes on October 3, 1864. Resident of Granville NC. Captured at Petersburg March 25, 1865. Confined at Point Lookout until June 21, 1865.

BAILIFF, Frederick, Pvt, G. Enlisted in Ashe Co on July 16, 1864. Present in December 1864, no record after that.

BAIN, James J, Pvt, G. Enlisted in Charlotte on September 30, 1861, at age 20. Died May 16, 1863, of wounds received at Chancellorsville. Gunshot wound to the shoulder.

BAKER, Daniel, Pvt, G. Enlisted at Camp Holmes on April 29, 1864. Hospitalized for a gunshot wound to the arm August 29, 1864. Granted a 30-day furlough. No further record.

BAKER, George, Pvt, A. Enlisted in Ashe Co on August 10, 1861, at age 19. Deserted August 8, 1862.

BAKER, Henry, Pvt, D. Enlisted November 5, 1864. Resident of Rowan County. Paroled at Salisbury May 16, 1865.

BAKER, Peter, Pvt, K. Enlisted at Camp Holmes on May 26, 1862. Resident of Wilson County. Came to the regiment around August 1864. Paroled at Goldsboro May 15, 1865.

BALTON, James C, Pvt, G. Enlisted in High Point on October 31, 1861, at age 20. Born in Johnston, NC. Discharged Nov 5, 1861,

BANNARD, John, Pvt, C. Enlisted at Camp Vance on May 13, 1864. Captured at Petersburg March 25, 1865. Confined at Point Lookout until June 23, 1865.

BARE, Cleveland, Pvt, A. Enlisted at Camp Holmes on October 1, 1863, at age 18. Absent on sick leave since February 10, 1864. No record of return.

BARE, Eli, Pvt, A. Enlisted at Camp Holmes on November 12, 1863, at age 40. Died of disease at Orange Court House, VA Jan. 13, 1864.

BARE, Hamilton, Cpl, A. Enlisted in Orange, VA on November 17, 1863, at age 24. Present every muster of enlistment. Captured at Hanover Junction May 24, 1864. Confined at Point Lookout. Exchanged March 15, 1865. Captured again at Petersburg March 25, 1865. Released June 23, 1865, from Point Lookout.

BARE, Henry, Pvt, A. Enlisted at Camp Holmes on December 25, 1863, at age 19. Absent with leave since May 23, 1864.

BARE, Jacob Jr, Pvt, A. Enlisted in Ashe Co on August 10, 1861, at age 19. Furloughed due to sickness May 1862, listed AWOL August 27, 1863. Returned. Hospitalized in June 1864. No return to the regiment recorded.

BARE, Jacob Sr, Pvt, A. Enlisted in Ashe Co on August 10, 1861. Wounded at Ox Hill. Listed AWOL in August 1863. Returned and was wounded May or June 1864. Present at Appomattox.

BARE, John Jr, Pvt, A. Enlisted in Ashe Co on August 10, 1861, at age 32. Captured at Chancellorsville. Paroled at Old Capital Prison June 10, 1863. Captured in a Richmond Hospital April 3, 1865. Transferred to Newport News and was released June 30, 1865.

BARE, John Sr, Pvt, A. Enlisted in Ashe Co on August 10, 1861, at age 27. Died of wounds July 13, 1863.

BARE., Wiley, Pvt, A. Enlisted in Ashe Co on August 10, 1861, at age 27. Deserted August 8, 1862, arrested around November 4, 1863. Sentenced to death but escaped the guardhouse and surrendered to Union troops. His wrist was sprained, and his feet were frostbitten. Released on oath.

BAREFIELD, William, Pvt, I. Enlisted in Rutherford on October 6, 1861, at age 19. Received a gunshot wound at Second Manassas. Discharged March 1864, due to disability.

BARLOW, Patrick, Pvt, H. Enlisted at Camp Holmes on June 1, 1864. Resident of Wilmington NC. Deserted at Petersburg January 30, 1865. Took the oath and was sent to Pittsburgh.

BARNETT, John S, Pvt, D. Enlisted after December 1864. Resident of Henderson Co, NC. Captured at Petersburg March 25, 1865. Confined at Point Lookout until June 23, 1865.

BARNHARDT, Jacob W, Pvt, D. Enlisted in Richmond on July 9, 1862, at age 21. Accounted for every muster. Captured at Petersburg March 25, 1865. Confined at Point Lookout until June 23, 1865.

BARNHARDT, William M, Cpl, D. Enlisted in Rowan on September 9, 1861, at age 29. Born in Cabarrus NC. Captured at Gettysburg. Died September 2, 1863, at Fort Delaware.

BARNWELL, James M, Pvt, A. Enlisted after December 1864. Captured at Petersburg March 25, 1865. Confined at Point Lookout where he died of Rubella June 8, 1865.

BARNWELL, John S, Pvt, A. Enlisted at Camp Holmes on October 3, 1864, at age 40. Resident of Caswell, NC. Captured at Petersburg April 2, 1865. Confined at Harts Island, NY Harbor until June 6, 1865.

BARR, Richard R, Surgeon. Joined the regiment at Camp Gregg on June 1, 1862. Moved to NC from Louisiana before the war. Married Martha Ann Atwell in Rowan County on Oct. 24, 1861. Treated Stonewall Jackson at Chancellorsville. Later transferred to another command.

BARRETT, Henry W, Pvt, H. Enlisted in Shelby on October 1, 1861, at age 22. Born Fairfield, SC. Accounted for every muster. Deserted at Petersburg March 18, 1865. Released on oath at City Point Va.

BARRETT, James S, Pvt, F. Enlisted in Cleveland on September 17, 1861, at age 26. Born Fairfield, SC. Died September 27, 1862, of wounds received at Sharpsburg. Married to Cynthia Barrett.

BASINGER, James, 2Lt, D. Enlisted as a Sgt.in Rowan on September 9, 1861, at age 30. Merchant. Promoted to 2Lt July 20, 1862. Died November 21, 1862, of wounds received at Sharpsburg. Married to Elizabeth Basinger.

BATTON, Robert G, Pvt, B. Enlisted at Camp Holmes on May 6, 1864. Captured June 22, 1864, at Petersburg and sent to Point Lookout. Exchanged September 30, 1864. Hospitalized in Richmond October 7, 1864. No record of a return to duty. Paroled May 3, 1865.

BAXTER, Henry E, Pvt, E. Enlisted in Lincolnton on August 31, 1861, at age 38. Teamster. Discharged "by mistake" December 8, 1862. Ordered to return to duty but did not return.

BAXTER, Thomas H, Pvt, E. Enlisted in Lincolnton on September 11, 1861, at age 18. Transferred to 49th NC Infantry October 6, 1862, in exchange for Pvt. Samuel J. Hoyle.

BEAM, David, Pvt, B. Enlisted in Rutherford on September 2, 1861, at age 19. Died in Goldsboro March 11, 1862. Son of Rebecca Beam.

BEAM, David H, Pvt, F. Enlisted at Camp Holmes on April 20, 1864. Gunshot wound to the left shoulder May 1864. Returned after October 1864. Present at Appomattox.

BEAM, John H, Pvt, B. Enlisted at Camp Vance on October 19, 1863, at age 18. Present at Appomattox.

BEAM, Johnson E, Pvt, F. Enlisted in Cleveland on September 17, 1861, at age 19. Son of Andrew Beam. Was killed at Gaines's Mill.

BEAM, Martin L, Pvt, B. Enlisted in Rutherford on September 2, 1861, at age 14. Discharged November 8, 1862, per conscription law, under 18 and did not reenlist.

BEAM, Peter V, Cpl, F. Enlisted in Cleveland on September 17, 1861, at age 26. Died of disease May 26, 1862, at Ashland VA. Married to Margaret Beam.

BEAM, William P, Cpt, B. Enlisted in Rutherford on September 2, 1861, at age 28. Gunshot wound to the chest at Gettysburg, returned after 40-day furlough. Promoted to Captain October 24, 1863, with waiver from Harrill, Present at Appomattox.

BEAMAN, Andrew J, Pvt, K. Enlisted in Troy NC on March 5, 1863, at age 39. Deserted May 3, 1863. Paroled at Troy NC May 5, 1865.

BEAMAN, John A, Pvt, K. Enlisted in Troy NC on March 5, 1863, at age 37. Deserted May 3, 1863. Took the oath in Washington DC, paroled from Old Capitol prison.

BEAN, John, Pvt, K. Enlisted in Troy NC on March 5, 1863, at age 36. Hospitalized multiple times for sickness. Paroled at Salisbury June 5, 1865.

BEATY, Alexander S, Pvt, G. Enlisted at Camp Holmes on April 22, 1864. Resident of Montgomery NC. Present at Appomattox.

BEATY, Archibald W, Pvt, G. Enlisted in Charlotte on September 30, 1861, at age 26. Present or detached duty every muster. Served as a Nurse in Richmond and the Mining Bureau in 1863, wounded in 1864.

BEATY, John, Pvt, G. Enlisted in Charlotte on September 30, 1861, at age 25. Wounded at Chancellorsville. Retired to the Invalid Corp November 23, 1864.

BEATY, Samuel, Pvt, G. Enlisted in Charlotte on September 30, 1861, at age 21. Died of disease August 10, 1862. Son of James M Beatty.

BEDFORD, John H, Pvt, B. Enlisted in Rutherford on September 2, 1861, at age 20. Died of disease in Goldsboro April 18, 1862.

BEDFORD, Joseph B, Pvt, B. Enlisted in Rutherford on September 2, 1861, at age 20. Born in Pickens Alabama. Son of Wiley and Elizabeth Bridges. Killed at Ox Hill.

BEDFORD, Seth, Sgt, B. Enlisted in Rutherford on September 2, 1861, at age 18. Wounded at Chancellorsville. Listed as deserted but returned and was killed in action May 5, 1864, at the Wilderness.

BEDWELL, John A, Pvt, K. Enlisted after December 1864. Surrendered at Troy, NC May 22, 1865.

BELL, Monroe W, Pvt, G. Enlisted at Camp Vance on August 21, 1864, at age 20. Captured April 1, 1865, at Hatchers Run. Confined at Point Lookout until June 6, 1865.

BENNETT, Thomas, Pvt, G. Enlisted in Charlotte on September 30, 1861, at age 29. Born in Franklin VA, 6'4" tall. Listed as AWOL from

January 1, 1863, to August 1864, but produced paperwork of being on detail in Franklin VA, Retired to the Invalid Corps September 7, 1864.

BENNICK, Augustus R, Chaplain. Enlisted at Camp Gregg on January 14, 1863, at age 29. Graduated from Catawba Lutheran College in 1856. Commissioned the regiment's chaplain in January 1863. Resigned his commission December 28, 1863.

BERRYHILL, John H, Pvt, G. Enlisted in Charlotte on September 30, 1861, at age 22. Discharged December 16, 1863, due to gunshot wound received in the Seven Days' Battles.

BESS, J. B., Pvt, B. Enlisted after December 1864. Paroled May 8, 1865, in Athens GA.

BESS, John F, Pvt, E. Enlisted in Lincolnton on September 11, 1861, at age 18. Gunshot wounds to the head and foot at The Seven Days' battles. Returned to duty and was captured at Chancellorsville. Exchanged after a short confinement at Washington DC. Captured at the Wilderness. Confined at Point Lookout and then Elmira. Exchanged February 20, 1865, at the James River.

BESS, Noah G, Pvt, E. Enlisted at Camp Gregg on March 8, 1863, at age 18. Accounted for every muster of enlistment. Wounded at Gettysburg. Returned to duty. Was captured April 2, 1865, at Petersburg. Released from Point Lookout June 23, 1865.

BESS, William B, Pvt, E. Enlisted in Lincolnton on January 1862, at age 21. Accounted for every muster. Wounded at Gettysburg. Returned to duty. Was captured April 2, 1865, at Petersburg. Released from Point Lookout June 23, 1865.

BISHOP, Albery, Pvt, C. Enlisted at Camp Vance on March 30, 1864. Wounded May 5, 1864, at the Wilderness. Present until October 1864, with no record after that.

BLACK, Elsey E, Pvt, H. Enlisted at Camp Holmes on September 11, 1864, at age 19. Resident of Gaston County. Deserted at Petersburg March 18, 1865. Took oath at City Point, transferred to Pittsburgh for public works.

BLACK, John, Pvt, A. Enlisted in Ashe Co on August 10, 1861, at age 35. Discharged illegally in December of 1862 and ordered back. Returned to duty in late 1863. Wounded at Ream's Station. Wounded again October 2, 1864. Arm amputated.

BLACKBURN, James T, Pvt, A. Enlisted at Camp Holmes on January 23, 1864, at age 18. Captured at Spotsylvania May 21, 1864. Transferred from Point Lookout to Elmira. Died of disease at Elmira September 13, 1864.

BLACKBURN, William S, Pvt, E. Enlisted in Lincolnton on Sept. 11, 1861, at age 26. Accounted for every muster. Promoted to Sgt but reduced for protracted sickness. Captured April 2, 1865, at the Southside Railroad. Confined at Hart's Island NY until June 18, 1865.

BLAKE, Isham F, Pvt, K. Enlisted in Troy NC on September 9, 1861, at age 33. Deserted May 20, 1863.

BLANKENSHIP, Andrew, Pvt, C. Enlisted at Camp Vance on May 13, 1864, at age 34. Died in a Richmond hospital August 26, 1864.

BLANKENSHIP, Reuben O, Pvt, C. Enlisted in High Point on December 1, 1861, at age 22. Died of disease at Raleigh, NC January or February 1862.

BLANKENSHIP, Washington W, Pvt, B. Enlisted at Camp Vance on June 8, 1864, at age 34. Captured at Totopotomoy Creek June 4, 1864, and confined at Point Lookout, where he died July 23, 1864. Had desired to take the oath and go to Missouri where he had two brothers.

BLANTON, Elijah, Pvt, B. Enlisted at Camp Vance on September 26, 1863, at age 39. Present at Appomattox.

BLANTON, George W, 2Lt, H. Enlisted in Shelby on October 1, 1861, at age 30. Blacksmith. Enlisted as a private. Promoted to 2Lt in February of 1863. Captured at Winchester December 1862, exchanged March 28, 1863. Wounded May 12, 1864. Granted a leave in December 1864, no records after that.

BLANTON, James, Pvt, B. Enlisted at Camp Vance on October 19, 1863. Shoemaker. Came to the regiment around May of 1864. Present at Appomattox. Drowned on the way home at the Catawba River on April 25, 1865.

BLANTON, James M, Pvt, F. Enlisted in Cleveland on September 17, 1861, at age 21. Accounted for every muster. Wounded at Gaines's Mill. Surrendered by General Joseph Johnston to WT Sherman April 26, 1865.

BLANTON, Stephen F, Pvt, B. Enlisted at Camp Vance on October 19, 1863. Captured at Sutherland Station. Confined at Harts Island, NY until June 18, 1865.

BLANTON, Taylor, Pvt, B. Enlisted in Rutherford on September 2, 1861, at age 15. Discharged due to age November 8, 1862, under 18 and did not reenlist.

BLANTON, William J, Pvt, I. Enlisted in Rutherford on October 6, 1861, at age 19. Present for every muster but one (Jan 62-sick). Present at Appomattox.

BOGGS, Noah C, Pvt, E. Enlisted in Lincolnton on August 31, 1861, at age 29. Extra duty man. Hospital steward, Forage master, and clerk most of the war. Present every muster but one (leave in Jan-Feb 1864). Present to December 1864.

BOLIN, James, Pvt, A. Enlisted at Camp Holmes on October 1, 1863, at age 39. Died of disease Orange Courthouse February 4, 1864.

BORDERS, Albert I, Cpl, F. Enlisted in Massoponax on May 17, 1862, at age 23. Present for every muster during enlistment. Promoted to Corporal August 1, 1862. Present at Appomattox.
BORDERS, Henderson, Pvt, F. Enlisted in Cleveland on May 17, 1862, at age 30. Discharged August 14, 1862, due to hiring a substitute.
BORDERS, Henry J, Pvt, F. Enlisted in Cleveland on October 7, 1861, at age 21. Discharged in October 1862, due to hiring a substitute. Reenlisted in September 1864 and was present at Appomattox.
BORVIG, John F, Pvt, K. Enlisted after December 1864. Paroled at Troy, May 23, 1865.
BOSTIUN, Levi A, Pvt, D. Enlisted at Camp Holmes on September 28, 1864, at age 36. On a detail January 30, 1865. Paroled at Lynchburg VA April 13, 1865.
BOTTS, John W, Pvt, F. Enlisted in Cleveland on September 17, 1861, at age 26. Died July 12, 1862, of an accidental wound. Son of Judah D Botts.
BOURQUIN, Frederick W, Drum Maj. Enlisted in Guinea Station on May 16, 1862, at age 28. Resident of Fredericksburg, VA. Present every muster. Captured at Petersburg April 3, 1865. Confined at Harts Island until June 21, 1865.
BOWEN, David A, Pvt, B. Enlisted in Rutherford on September 2, 1861, at age 26. Present on every muster but one (sick leave). Present at Appomattox.
BOWERS, William, Pvt, I. Enlisted in Lancaster SC on February 16, 1864, at age 26. Killed in action June 23, 1864, near Petersburg.
BOWMAN, John R, 2Lt, C. Enlisted in Rutherford on September 2, 1861, at age 28. Provost Sgt. Promoted to 2Lt August 18, 1862, and resigned October 25, 1862. Gospel minister, resigned his commission stating, "I now find it is not agreeable for a Minister of the Gospel to hold a Military Office and in accordance with my feelings and profession I find that I am utterly incapable of enforcing Military Discipline."
BOWMAN, William C, Pvt, C. Enlisted in Culpepper VA on July 27, 1863. Resident of Morganton, NC. Captured at the Wilderness May 6, 1864. Confined at Point Lookout, then Elmira until June 19, 1865.
BOYD, Alexander W, Pvt, K. Enlisted at Camp Holmes on May 21, 1864. Deserted at Petersburg September 7, 1864. Took oath and was transferred to Norfolk, resident of New Hanover NC.
BRADLEY, Simon B, 1Lt, E. Enlisted on October 21, 1864. Present at Appomattox. A paroled prisoner remaining in Richmond May 19, 1865.
BRADLEY, William A, Pvt, C. Enlisted in Rutherford on September 2, 1861, at age 24. Killed in action July 1, 1862, near Malvern Hill.

BRAY, Allison, Pvt, H. Enlisted at Camp Vance on April 6, 1864. Died of disease in a Richmond hospital October 3, 1864.

BREWER, Hiram, Pvt, K. Enlisted in Montgomery on September 9, 1861, at age 20. Deserted August 14, 1862. Returned, deserted from Petersburg September 7, 1864. Took the oath and was transferred to Philadelphia on public works.

BREWER, Robert, Pvt, K. Enlisted in Troy NC on September 9, 1861, at age 20. Reenlisted, collected $50 bounty March/April 1862, Deserted September 12, 1862.

BREWER, William A, Pvt, K. Enlisted in Troy NC on September 9, 1861, at age 18. Reenlisted, collected $50 bounty March/April 1862, Deserted September 12, 1862.

BRIDGES, Aaron, Pvt, I. Enlisted in Rutherford on December 29, 1861, at age 38. Died of disease, July 27, 1863.

BRIDGES, Abram, Pvt, H. Enlisted in Shelby on October 1, 1861, at age 29. Died at Raleigh Jan. 6, 1862, of disease, widow Mary Bridges.

BRIDGES, David, Pvt, B. Enlisted in Rutherford on September 2, 1861, at age 20. Died June 14, 1864. Son of Ezekiel and Permilia Bridges. Cause and place of death not stated.

BRIDGES, David K, Pvt, H. Enlisted in Shelby on October 1, 1861, at age 32. Listed AWOL August 28, 1863, to February 28, 1864. Returned to duty. Hospitalized March 31, 1865 and was granted a 60-day furlough. No further record.

BRIDGES, Greenberry, Sgt, B. Enlisted in Rutherford on September 2, 1861, at age 30. Promoted to Sgt May 1, 1862. Killed in action at Frayser's Farm.

BRIDGES, James, Pvt, K. Enlisted in Salisbury NC on May 9, 1864. Resident of Montgomery NC. Captured April 5, 1865, at Amelia Courthouse. Confined at Point Lookout until June 23, 1865.

BRIDGES, John H, Pvt, B. Enlisted in Rutherford on September 2, 1861, at age 18. Sick several times. Dropped from roll by order April 10, 1864.

BRIDGES, Lawson H, Pvt, H. Enlisted in Shelby on October 1, 1861, at age 27. Listed AWOL April 1863. Returned in August. Present all other musters. Paroled at Burkesville Junction April 1865.

BRIDGES, Lorenzo D, Pvt, B. Enlisted in Rutherford on September 2, 1861, at age 16. Killed in action at Frayser's Farm, son of Ezekiel Bridges.

BRIDGES, Samuel, Pvt, B. Enlisted at Camp Vance on October 19, 1863, at age 18. Present at Appomattox.

BRIDGES, Wiley, Pvt, B. Enlisted in Rutherford on September 2, 1861, at age 18. Died January 22, 1863, at Guinea Station, VA. Cause not stated.

BRIDGES, William, Pvt, B. Enlisted in Rutherford on September 2, 1861, at age 15. Wounded at Frayser's Farm. Discharged December 1862, per conscription law. Reenlisted after December 1864. Was captured at Petersburg June 16, 1864. Confined at Point Lookout and Elmira until July 3, 1865.

BRIDGES, Wilson W, Sgt, B. Enlisted as a private in High Point on October 19, 1861, at age 25. Promoted to Ordnance Sergeant. Wounded at Ox Hill. Wounded again June 13, 1864. Present at Appomattox.

BRILES, Oliver P, Pvt, B. Enlisted at Camp Holmes on July 17, 1864, at age 37. Wounded at Rcam's Station. Died Oct. 12, 1864.

BROADWAY, P F, Pvt, H. Enlisted at Camp Holmes on June 20, 1864. Hospitalized in Richmond January 4, 1865. Furloughed for 60 days. No records after that.

BROOKS, Benjamin, Pvt, B. Enlisted in Rutherford on September 2, 1861, at age 20. Son of Ransom Brooks. Died of disease March 15, 1862, at Goldsboro.

BROOKS, James T, Pvt, I. Enlisted in Person NC on March 10, 1863, at age 39. Absent sick much of enlistment. Captured at Petersburg March 25, 1865. Confined at Point Lookout until June 23, 1865.

BROOKS, Samuel, Pvt, B. Enlisted in Rutherford on September 2, 1861, at age 18. Severe head wound at Frayser's Farm. Returned to duty, on detached service from February 1864.

BROOKS, William, Pvt, B. Enlisted in Rutherford on September 2, 1861, at age 22. Gunshot wound hand and back at Fredericksburg. Hospitalized for debilitas July 27, 1863. Hip wound May 1864, Present at Appomattox.

BROTHERTON, John, Pvt, G. Enlisted in Lincolnton on March 12, 1863, at age 38. Wounded at Gettysburg, returned in November. Wounded June 22, 1864. Present in November 1864. No further record.

BROTHERTON, William, Pvt, G. Enlisted in Lincolnton on March 12, 1863, at age 39. Accounted for every muster of enlistment. Present at Appomattox.

BROWN, Gray J, Pvt, A. Enlisted at Camp Holmes on August 13, 1862. Present in November 1864. No records after that.

BROWN, Henry H, Pvt, H. Enlisted in Dallas NC on March 1, 1863. Died of Typhoid fever in Richmond June 23, 1863.

BROWN, Henry T, Pvt, D. Enlisted in Rowan on September 9, 1861. Hospital nurse in Richmond 1863, Transferred to Augusta Ga in Ordnance department March 1864. Paroled at Salisbury June 27, 1865.

BROWN, John, Pvt, H. Enlisted at Camp Holmes on September 1, 1864. Captured at Southside Railroad April 2, 1865. Confined at Hart's Island. Died in prison of Typhoid June 3, 1865.

BROWN, Mathias, Pvt, A. Enlisted in Ashe Co on August 10, 1861, at age 21. Badge of Distinction at Chancellorsville. Captured at North Anna. Confined at Point Lookout. Exchanged October 11, 1864. In hospital in a Richmond October 15. No record after that.
BROWN, Wesley W, Cpl, A. Enlisted in Ashe Co on August 10, 1861, at age 32. Wounded around August 10, 1862. Promoted to Corporal May 1, 1864. Received a gunshot wound in the left hand May 5, 1864. Listed Absent Wounded on remaining musters.
BROWN, William B, Pvt, H. Enlisted in Shelby on October 1, 1861, at age 21. Captured at Falling Waters. Confined at Point Lookout. Released on joining 1st US Volunteers January 25, 1864. Discharged November 27, 1865, at Fort Leavenworth.
BRYANT, James A, Pvt, F. Enlisted in Cleveland on January 1862, at age 25. Born in South Carolina. Son of Lewis and Jennette Bryant. Killed in action at Gaines's Mill. Married to Sarah G Weathers. They had two children.
BRYANT, Thomas, Pvt, E. Enlisted at Camp Vance on August 21, 1862. Joined the regiment around July of 1864. Resident of Yancey County. Captured at Southside Railroad. Confined at Hart's Island until June 18, 1865.
BUMGARDNER, Amos, Pvt, F. Enlisted in High Point on October 23, 1861, at age 21. Died at Goldsboro February 11, 1862, of disease. Son of John Bumgardner.
BURGESS, William P, Pvt, I. Enlisted in Rutherford on October 6, 1861, at age 23. Gunshot wound in the hand at Frayser's Farm. Deserted July 21, 1862, from camp near Richmond. Returned, deserted again around May or June 1863. Arrested near Orange Courthouse. Jailed until December 1, 1864. No record after that.
BURLISON, William M, Pvt, D. Enlisted at Camp Vance on April 10, 1864. Listed as captured at the Wilderness. No records after that. Possibly died of wounds.
BURNET, Alfred, Pvt, I. Enlisted at Camp Vance on May 25, 1864. Died in a Petersburg hospital July 17, 1864. Unknown cause.
BURR, A. H., Pvt, A. Joined regiment after December of 1864. Paroled May 8, 1865, in Athens GA.
BURROUGHS, John, Pvt, K. Enlisted in Montgomery on September 9, 1861, at age 20. Deserted August 14, 1863, near Orange Courthouse. In a hospital in Greensboro NC April 1, 1865.
BYERS, Joseph, 1Lt, B. Enlisted in Rutherford on September 2, 1861, at age 29. Elected Captain April 18, 1862. Deserted September 1, 1863. Reduced to private by court martial October 24, 1863. On duty for through all of 1864. Deserted in March of 1865. Was present every muster but one (leave).

CALLICOTT, Charles, Cpl, K. Enlisted in Troy NC on September 9, 1861, at age 29. Died May 13, 1863, of wounds received at Chancellorsville.

CALLICOTT, Claiborn, Pvt, K. Enlisted in Troy NC on September 9, 1861, at age 19. Died in Richmond April 15, 1863, of wounds received at Chancellorsville.

CALLICOTT, Henry, Pvt, K. Enlisted in Troy NC on September 9, 1861, at age 22. Died of disease February 27, 1862, at Williamston.

CALLICOTT, John, Sgt, K. Enlisted in Troy NC on September 9, 1861, at age 29. Died of pneumonia December 28, 1861, at Raleigh.

CALLICOTT, Martin T, Pvt, K. Enlisted in Troy NC on September 9, 1861, at age 20. Died July 5, 1862, in Richmond of wounds received at Gaines's Mill. Son of Martha Callicott.

CAMP, Abner, Pvt, H. Enlisted in Shelby on October 1, 1861, at age 28. Head wound at Gaines's Mill. Deserted from the hospital August 18, 1863. Returned January 14, 1864. AWOL July-September of 1864 but was in the hospital in Richmond. Medically discharged July 1864.

CAMP, John H, Pvt, C. Enlisted in Rutherford on September 2, 1861, at age 23. Captured at Falling Waters. Confined at Point Lookout. Exchanged August 16, 1863. Sent to Cherryville, NC February 1865. Captured and exchanged May 8, 1865, Athens, GA. Present or accounted for every muster.

CAMP, Joseph A, 1Lt, H. Enlisted in Shelby on October 1, 1861, at age 21. Wounded at Gettysburg. Captured at Funkstown, Md July 12, 1863. Held at Ft McHenry and Johnson Island until June 11, 1865.

CAMP, Joshua G, 1Lt, I. Enlisted in Goldsboro on April 18, 1862. Elected from civilian life April 18, 1862. A physician by profession, resigned his commission on July 24, 1862, due to chronic bronchitis.

CAMP, Nathan, Pvt, H. Enlisted in Shelby on August 1, 1863, at age 18. Accounted for his entire enlistment. Present November 1864.

CAMP, Soloman, Pvt, C. Enlisted in Rutherford on September 1, 1861, at age 21. Died in Richmond June 15, 1862, son of John Camp.

CAMP, Tyrell, Sgt, H. Enlisted in Shelby on October 1, 1861, at age 26. Wounded at Chancellorsville. Right arm amputated. Discharged January 30, 1864.

CAMP William P, Pvt, H. Enlisted in Shelby on October 1, 1861, at age 24. Wounded in the Seven Days. Returned to duty. Died May 9, 1863, of wounds received at Chancellorsville. Son of Margaret Camp.

CAMP, William T, Pvt, H. Enlisted in Shelby on October 1, 1861, at age 18. Wounded at Second Manassas with a gunshot wound near the eye. Dropped from the rolls May 7, 1863. Married to Corilla Camp.

CAMPBELL, George L, Sgt, G. Enlisted as a private in Charlotte on September 30, 1861, at age 40. Promoted to Sgt. April 22, 1862. Died of disease September 22, 1862, at Martinsburg, Va. Widow Martha J Campbell.

CAMPBELL, Lewis, Pvt, D. Enlisted at Camp Holmes on June 15, 1864. Disability discharge January 24, 1865, convalescent from Typhoid fever.

CANIPE, John C, Pvt, F. Enlisted in Cleveland on September 17, 1861, at age 18. Wounded at Gaines's Mill. Light duty as a bridge guard in Raleigh. Returned to the regiment in October 1864. Present at Appomattox.

CAPPS, Aaron, Pvt, E. Enlisted at Camp Vance on August 21, 1864. Deserted October 7, 1864.

CAPPS, James, Pvt, E. Enlisted at Camp Vance on August 21, 1864. Deserted October 7, 1864.

CARGAL, Sansbury, Pvt, I. Enlisted in Rutherford on October 6, 1861, at age 29. Killed in action at Gaines's Mill.

CARPENTER, Absalom, Pvt, E. Per NC Pension Application served in Company E. Died of disease in a Richmond Hospital on an unknown date. Was married to Fannie Carpenter.

CARPENTER, Benjamin F, Sgt, E. Enlisted in Lincolnton on May 11, 1862, at age 18. Gaston County resident. Wounded at Ream's Station and Petersburg March 25, 1865. Present every muster of his enlistment and was present at Appomattox.

CARPENTER, Frederick, Pvt, E. Enlisted in Dallas NC on March 15, 1863, at age 36. Gaston County resident. Confined for desertion in November 1863. Returned to duty. Captured at Petersburg March 25, 1865. Confined at Point Lookout until June 24, 1865.

CARPENTER, James L, Pvt, C. Enlisted in High Point on November 15, 1861, at age 21. Died in Richmond Nov 17, 1862, of Small Pox.

CARPENTER, Joseph, Pvt, G. Enlisted in Lincolnton on March 12, 1863, at age 38. Killed in action at Gettysburg.

CARPENTER, Michael, Pvt, F. Enlisted in Cleveland on September 17, 1861, at age 42. Discharged December 8, 1862, due to age, per conscription law. Was wounded at least once.

CARPENTER, Noah, Pvt, E. Enlisted in Lincolnton on September 11, 1861, at age 17. Present every muster but one (sick). Wounded at Chancellorsville. Returned to duty. Captured and paroled May 8, 1865, at Athens GA.

CARPENTER, Perry D, 2Lt, E. Enlisted as a private in Lincolnton on September 11, 1861, at age 25. Born in Lincoln County and resided in Gaston County. Plasterer by trade. Promoted to 2Lt in 1862. Wounded at Gaines's Mill. Promoted to 1Lt May 1863. Killed in action at Chancellorsville. Son of Andrew Carpenter.

CARPENTER, Soloman, Pvt, F. Enlisted in Cleveland on September 17, 1861, at age 35. Killed at Mechanicsville. Widow Jane Carpenter.
CARPENTER, Thomas, Pvt, E. Enlisted in Petersburg on August 1, 1864. Killed at Ream's Station August 25, 1864.
CARRIER, Joseph B, Sgt, C. Enlisted in Rutherford on September 2, 1861, at age 23. Regimental quartermaster. Died in Goldsboro in 1862, exact date unknown. Son of H D Carrier.
CARROLL, Edward J, Pvt, F. Enlisted in Cleveland on September 17, 1861, at age 20. Discharged at High Point for disability.
CARSON, Thomas L, Sgt, C, and I. Enlisted in Rutherford on September 2, 1861, at age 24. Transferred to Company I October of 1863. Sgt in both C and I companies. Accounted for on every muster. Present at Appomattox.
CARTER, Jesse J, Pvt, F. Enlisted in Cleveland on September 17, 1861, at age 18. Killed in action at Gettysburg.
CASS, William F, Pvt, A. Enlisted at Camp Vance on April 11, 1864, at age 21. Captured at Petersburg March 25, 1865. Confined at Point Lookout until June 24, 1865.
CASTELOW, P, Pvt, G. Enlisted at Camp Vance on June 29, 1864. Sick through October 1864. No further records.
CATHEY, Alexander, Pvt, G. Enlisted in Charlotte on September 30, 1861, at age 27. Wounded May 5, 1864, at the Wilderness while bearing the colors. Wounded again in May or June of 1864. Returned to duty. Was Present at Appomattox.
CATHEY, Alexander A, 1Lt, G. Enlisted in Charlotte on September 30, 1861, at age 26. Enlisted as a Sgt and was promoted to Lt April 18, 1862. Wounded and captured at Gettysburg. Leg amputated. Confined at Bedloe's Island NY and Charleston SC. Part of the "Immortal 600." Retired to the Invalid Corps in March of 1865.
CATHEY, John L, Cpl, G. Enlisted in Charlotte on January 1862, at age 19. Shot in the foot November 1862. Shot in left shoulder at Gettysburg and captured. Released from the US Army hospital in Chester, PA Sept 23, 1863. Retired to invalid corps July 25, 1864.
CATHEY, William A, Pvt, G. Enlisted in Charlotte on September 30, 1861, at age 40. Granted a medical discharge due to chronic rheumatism July 20, 1862.
CATHEY, William H, Pvt, G. Enlisted in Charlotte on January 1862, at age 23. Died of disease at Hamilton, NC March 25, 1862. Widow Elizabeth Cathey.
CAUBLE, George, Sgt, E. Enlisted in Lincolnton on September 11, 1861, at age 23. Wounded at Second Manassas. Captured at Gettysburg. Confined at Fort Delaware and Point Lookout Exchanged

February 18, 1865 and was present at Camp Lee Feb. 23, 1865. Did not return to the regiment.

CAUDILL, Hugh, Cpl, A. Enlisted in Ashe Co on August 10, 1861, at age 35. Severely wounded in 1862. Granted medical discharge March 18, 1863.

CAVIN, James Y, Pvt, E. Enlisted in Lincolnton on September 11, 1861, at age 23. Stone mason. Nurse in Richmond 62-63' and returned to the regiment around December of 1863. Captured April 2, 1865, at the Southside Railroad. Confined at Hart's Island until June 18, 1865.

CAVINESS, Riley J, Pvt, K. Enlisted in Troy NC on September 6, 1861, at age 30. Died around July 1863, in a Petersburg hospital. Exact date and cause not stated.

CHAMPION, George, Pvt, B. Enlisted in Raleigh on April 10, 1864, at age 24. Captured at Hanover Junction May 24, 1864. Confined at Point Lookout. Exchanged September 18, 1864. No further records.

CHANCY, Eli, Pvt, I. Enlisted in Montgomery on March 10, 1863, at age 27. Deserted May 8, 1863.

CHANDLER, Eli, 2Lt, A. Enlisted in Ashe Co on August 10, 1861, at age 38. Shoemaker, resigned his commission on May 6, 1862.

CHAPMAN, Robert, Pvt, H. Enlisted at Camp Holmes on April 20, 1864. Captured at the Wilderness. Confined at Point Lookout and Elmira. Died September 29, 1864, at Elmira.

CHILDERS, Wiley B, Pvt, E. Enlisted in Lincolnton on September 11, 1861, at age 49. Enlisted with his sons, Wiley C and William J Childers. Discharged April 17, 1862, due to disability.

CHILDERS, Wiley C, Cpl, E. Enlisted in Lincolnton on August 31, 1861, at age 20. Carpenter. Present on every muster. Deserted March 7, 1865, at Petersburg took the oath transferred to Philadelphia.

CHILDERS, William J, Cpl, E. Enlisted in Lincolnton on August 31, 1861, at age 27. Son of W B Childers. Died August 5, 1862, of disease in a Richmond Hospital.

CLARK, Adam R, Pvt, E. Enlisted in Gaston, NC on March 5, 1863, at age 46. Gaston County resident. Substitute soldier. "Shamefully abandoned colors" at Chancellorsville and wore a ball and chain for a month. Present or accounted for the remainder of the war. Captured May 23, 1864, at North Anna. Died February 16, 1865, at Pt Lookout.

CLARK, Almarine, Pvt, G. Enlisted in Charlotte on September 30, 1861, at age 33. Wounded in 1862. Nurse in Richmond March 1863-Oct 1864. Present to November 1864. No record after that.

CLARK, George M, Major. Enlisted in Troy NC on September 6, 1861, at age 22. Student at the University of NC Chapel Hill before the war, mother was born in Scotland. Enlisted as a 2Lt in Company K.

Failed reelection April 18, 1862 but returned as Captain by January 1863. Promoted to Major May 6, 1863. Killed in action at Gettysburg.
CLARK, John C, Pvt, G. Enlisted in Charlotte on Sept 30, 1861, at age 28. Present every muster. Wounded in 1862, date unknown. Returned to duty. Killed in action at the Wilderness May 5, 1864.
CLARKE, John W, Captain. Enlisted on May 1, 1862. Asst. Quartermaster transferred to Brigade quartermaster to replace Joseph Carrier September 1864.
CLARY, John, Pvt, A. Enlisted at Brandy Station on October 23, 1863, at age 26. Deserted February 8, 1864.
CLARY, Thomas, Pvt, A. Enlisted in Ashe Co on August 10, 1861, at age 22. Accounted for every muster but one (AWOL). Wounded twice, dates unknown. Captured April 2, 1865, at Petersburg. Confined at Harts Island, NY until June 17, 1865.
CLARY, William, Pvt, A. Enlisted in Ashe Co on August 10, 1861, at age 28. Born in Iredell, NC. Wounded once. Listed AWOL February-November 1863. Returned. Deserted February 8, 1864.
CLAY, Henry E, Cpl, F. Enlisted in Cleveland on September 17, 1861, at age 19. Died August 17, 1863, of wounds received at Gettysburg.
CLAY, William S, Pvt, F. Enlisted in Cleveland on September 17, 1861, at age 23. Born in Lincoln Co. Killed in action at Gaines's Mill.
CLAYTON, Jacob L, Pvt, I. Enlisted in Granville NC on January 19, 1863, at age 22. Wounded at Chancellorsville. Disability discharge granted December 18, 1863.
CLIFTEN, J S, Pvt, K. Enlisted at Camp Holmes on April 15, 1864. Deserted June 15, 1864.
CLODFELTER, John Travis, Pvt, D. Enlisted in Rowan on September 9, 1861, at age 19. Accounted for every muster. Killed in action August 25, 1864, at Ream's Station.
COBB, James A, Pvt, H. Enlisted in Cleveland on February 28, 1863, at age 35. Captured at Falling Waters. Confined at Elmira. Exchanged October 29, 1864. Died some time before Feb 1865.
COBB, Rufus, Pvt, H. Enlisted in Shelby on October 1, 1861, at age 18. Discharged November 1, 1862, per the conscription law.
COCHRAN, Atlas J, Pvt, K. Enlisted at Camp Holmes on October 31, 1863. Died at Gordonsville of a stroke January 1864.
COCKRAN, David R, Cpt, K. Enlisted in Montgomery on September 9, 1861, at age 49. Resigned his commission on October 9, 1861,
CODY, Henderson, Pvt, E. Enlisted in Lincolnton on September 11, 1861, at age 18. Died of wounds June 28, 1862.
CODY, Turner, Pvt, E. Enlisted in Lincolnton on September 11, 1861, at age 44. Born in Davidson Co. Present every muster. Discharged September 1864, due to age.

COFFMAN, J R, Pvt. Captured at Fredericksburg May 6, 1863. Paroled May 10th at City Point, VA. No further records.

COGGIN, George W, Sgt, K. Enlisted in Troy NC on September 9, 1861, at age 26. Promoted to Sgt. April 1, 1863. Was thought to have been killed at the third day of Gettysburg but was captured July 5th with the wounded. Confined at Ft Delaware where he died of disease September 29, 1863.

COGGIN, William A, Pvt, K. Enlisted at Camp Mangum on December 21, 1861, at age 23. Died of disease July 19, 1862.

COGGIN, William B, Sgt, K. Enlisted in Troy NC on September 9, 1861, at age 26. Accounted for every muster. Wounded at Orange CH November 30, 1862. Promoted to First Sgt. July 2, 1863. Paroled at Lynchburg, VA April 15, 1865.

COLBERT, Lewis, Pvt, I. Enlisted in Rutherford on December 26, 1861, at age 25. Died of disease at Goldsboro February 11, 1862.

COLLINS, John M, Pvt, E. Enlisted in Lincolnton on September 11, 1861, at age 26. Transferred to the 12th NC in exchange for Devany Putnam April 26, 1863. Was later wounded at Gettysburg.

COLLINS, John M, Pvt, H. Enlisted in Shelby on October 1, 1861, at age 25. 6'2" tall. Captured at Hanover Junction May 24, 1864. Confined at Point Lookout until October 30, 1864.

COLLINS, Robert D, Pvt, G. Enlisted Nov 14, 1864. Captured at Farmville April 6, 1865. Confined at Point Lookout until June 24, 1865.

COLLINS, William W, Pvt, C. Enlisted at Camp Vance on May 18, 1864. On duty until after November 1864.

COLLUMS, Calvin, Pvt, K. Enlisted on November 17, 1864. Captured at Hatchers Run. Confined at Point Lookout until June 10, 1865.

COMPTON, Henderson H, Pvt, C. Enlisted at Camp Holmes on May 24, 1864. Detailed as a butcher. Deserted at Petersburg February 21, 1865. Took the oath and went to Baltimore on public works.

CONNER, George J, Pvt, E. Enlisted in Lincolnton on September 11, 1861, at age 25. Present every muster but one, (Recruiting Service in January 1863). Wounded in the Seven Days' battles. Present at Appomattox.

CONNER, William G, Pvt, C. Enlisted in Rutherford on September 2, 1861, at age 22. Teamster, Ambulance Driver. Wounded at Gaines's Mill. Hospitalized for a gunshot wound March 26, 1865. Captured in the hospital April 3, 1865. Left leg amputated at Fairgrounds hospital. Died of his wounds April 8, 1865. Buried near the hospital.

COOK, Alfred W, Pvt, C. Enlisted in Rutherford on September 2, 1861, at age 17. Wounded and captured at Gettysburg, POW at Point Lookout, took oath and joined US Army.

COOK, John, Pvt, C. Enlisted in Rutherford on September 2, 1861, at age 27. Gunshot wound to the jaw at Chancellorsville, recovered at home. Returned and was detailed as a carpenter. Present in Dec 1864.
COONE, Nobey, Pvt, C. Enlisted after Dec 1864. Captured April 3, 1865, in Amelia Co, VA, released from Point Lookout June 4, 1865
COOPER, James, Pvt, E. Enlisted in Lincolnton on September 11, 1861, at age 23. Born in Wilkes, NC. Medical discharge granted. Died of consumption July 15, 1862.
COOPER, Joseph, Pvt, I. Enlisted at Camp Vance on May 13, 1864. Absent sick last three musters. Captured at Sutherland Station April 2, 1865. Confined at Harts Island, NY until June 17, 1865.
COOPER, Nicholas P, Pvt, C. Enlisted in Rutherford on September 2, 1861, at age 22. Musician. Deserted December 12, 1862.
COOPER, Thomas, Pvt, B. Enlisted at Camp Holmes on April 12, 1864. Medical furlough in August 1864. No further records.
COPPLE, Alphius, Pvt, D. Enlisted in Davidson NC on August 27, 1864. Deserted September 5, 1864.
COPPLE, Joshua, Pvt, D. Enlisted in Davidson NC on August 27, 1864. Deserted September 5, 1864.
COPPLE, Soloman, Pvt, D. Enlisted in Davidson NC on August 27, 1864. Deserted September 5, 1864.
CORN, Ezekiel W, Pvt, C. Enlisted at Camp Vance on May 5, 1864. Captured at the Wilderness and confined at Point Lookout. Released after joining the US Army 1st US Volunteers June 1, 1864. Served in the Dakota territory. Died at Ft. Rice, Dakota of scurvy March 4, 1865. Record states he was "of good character".
CORN, Matthew W, Pvt, C. Enlisted at Camp Vance on May 18, 1864. Transferred to the 16th NC September 6, 1864. Present at Appomattox with that regiment.
CORN, Nathan, Pvt, D. Enlisted on December 19, 1864. Captured at Hatchers Run, release from Point Lookout June 26, 1865.
CORN, William, Pvt, I. Enlisted at " Vance on May 25, 1864. Furloughed in July 1864. No further records.
CORRIHER, Joel, Sgt, D. Enlisted in Rowan on September 9, 1861, at age 25. Wounded May 25, 1864. Returned to duty. Captured April 2, 1865, at Sutherland Station, released from Harts Island, NY June 19, 1865. Accounted for every muster.
COSAND, William, Pvt, H. Enlisted at Camp Vance on May 30, 1864. Wounded May or June 1864. Present at Appomattox.
COSTNER, Levi, Pvt, E. Enlisted on April 30, 1863. Killed in action at Gettysburg. Information from NC Confederate Pension application filed by Elizabeth Costner.

COTTON, Burwell T, Lt, K. Enlisted in Troy NC on September 9, 1861, at age 24. Present on every muster. Enlisted as a Sgt. Wounded at Frayser's Farm. Promoted to Lt July 30, 1862. Wounded at Gettysburg (bruised by grape shot), Killed in action June 22, 1864.

COVIN, James F, Pvt, E. Relieved March 20, 1863.

COWAN, Robert T, Lt, D. Enlisted in Rowan on September 9, 1861, at age 22. Enlisted as a Sgt. Promoted to Lt April 18, 1862. Killed in action at Frayser's Farm. Widow Margaret Cowen.

COX, David, Sgt, A. Enlisted in Ashe Co on October 10, 1861, at age 25. Promoted to Sgt April 8, 1863. Killed in action at Chancellorsville.

COX, Hiram, Sgt, A. Enlisted in Ashe Co on August 10, 1861, at age 22. Enlisted as a Lt but failed reelection. Reenlisted as a private and was promoted to Sgt April 8, 1863. Killed in action at Chancellorsville.

COX, John, Pvt, A. Enlisted in Ashe Co on August 10, 1861, at age 23. Died of disease at Goldsboro April 4, 1862.

COX, Levi, Sgt, A. Enlisted in Ashe Co on August 10, 1861, at age 35. Captured at Brandy Station August 1, 1863, paroled August 1, 1864. Captured again at Petersburg March 25, 1865. Confined at Point Lookout until June 24, 1865.

COX, William C, Pvt, G. Enlisted in Mecklenburg on September 30, 1861, at age 26. Arm amputated from wound received at a date not specified. Medical discharge granted December 1863.

CRANFORD, Ambrose, Pvt, K. Enlisted in Troy NC on September 9, 1861, at age 34. Died in May of 1863, cause unknown.

CRANFORD, Eli, Pvt, K. Enlisted in Raleigh on December 5, 1863. Wounded in 1864, date unknown. Present at Appomattox.

CRANFORD, Joel S, Pvt, K. Enlisted in Troy NC on September 9, 1861, at age 22. Accounted for every muster. Wounded in 1864, date unknown. Retired to Invalid Corp October 21, 1864.

CRANFORD, Leonard, Pvt, K. Enlisted in Troy NC on September 9, 1861, at age 36. Teamster. Wounded at Gettysburg. Present every muster but one (leave). Present at Appomattox.

CRANFORD, Willis, Pvt, K. Enlisted in Raleigh on July 31, 1864. Resident of Davidson Co. NC. Millwright. Captured at Petersburg March 25, 1865. Confined at Point Lookout until May 13, 1865.

CRANFORD, Winborn W, Cpl, K. Enlisted in Troy NC on Sept 9, 1861, age 25. Millwright. Accounted for every muster. Captured June 22, 1864, at Petersburg. Confined at Pt Lookout until March 11, 1865.

CRAVER, David, Pvt, B. Enlisted at Camp Vance on September 26, 1864. Present at Appomattox.

CRAVER, William F, Pvt, B. Enlisted at Camp Holmes on May 10, 1864. Present in November 1864. Paroled at Greensboro May 8, 1865.

CRAWFORD, John H, 1Sgt, I. Enlisted in Rutherford on October 6, 1861, at age 17. Postmaster. Enlisted as a private. Wounded at Shepherdstown. Captured at Gettysburg, released from Point Lookout January 17, 1865.

CRAWFORD, Sylvester, Pvt, C. Enlisted in Rutherford on September 2, 1861. Discharge granted December 1862.

CRESWELL, Anderson H, 1Lt, G. Enlisted in Charlotte on September 30, 1861, at age 26. Born in Marshall, TN, Coach maker. Failed reelection at Goldsboro and discharged April 18, 1862.

CRISP, Robert B, Pvt, I. Enlisted at Camp Vance on May 7, 1864. Present each muster of enlistment. Present at Appomattox.

CROMPSON, William, Pvt. Enlisted after December 1864. Deserted at Petersburg February 24, 1865. Took the oath and was sent to Baltimore for public works.

CROTTS, Elijah, Pvt, F. Enlisted in Cleveland on September 17, 1861, at age 21. Wounded at Ox Hill. Died November 5, 1862, of disease at Winchester, VA.

CROTTS, Emanuel, Pvt, F. Enlisted at Camp Holmes on April 20, 1864. Present each muster of enlistment. Captured at Petersburg March 25, 1865, released from Point Lookout June 24, 1865.

CROTTS, Henderson, Pvt, D. Enlisted in Davidson NC on August 27, 1864. Deserted September 5, 1864.

CROTTS, William, Pvt, F. Enlisted in Cleveland on September 17, 1861, at age 27. Captured June 27, 1862, at Gaines's Mill. Exchanged August 5, 1862. AWOL for three musters in 1863 and returned to duty. Present at Appomattox.

CROW, Calvin M, Cpl, C. Enlisted in Cleveland on September 2, 1861, at age 17. Teamster. Accounted for on every muster. Wounded once. Deserted January 26, 1865, at Petersburg. Took oath and was sent to Philadelphia on public works.

CROW, John, Pvt, F. Enlisted in Cleveland on September 17, 1861, at age 28. Captured at Falling Waters. Confined at Point Lookout. Exchanged March 16, 1864. In hospital in Danville April 9, 1865.

CROWDER, Matthew, Pvt, B. Enlisted at Camp Holmes on August 27, 1864. Captured at Petersburg March 25, 1865. Confined at Point Lookout until June 24, 1865.

CROWDER, Robert W, Sgt, F. Enlisted in Cleveland on September 17, 1861, at age 29. Son of Bartlett and Mary Crowder. Married Eunice Jane Evans in 1860. They had two children. Promoted to Sgt August 1, 1862. Killed in action at Second Manassas August 30, 1862.

CROWDER, William F, Pvt, F. Enlisted in Cleveland on September 17, 1861, at age 23. Gunshot wound in leg at Chancellorsville. Little active duty after that. In the hospital in Richmond November of 1864.

CRYTZ, William, Pvt, E. Enlisted in Lincolnton on September 11, 1861, at age 27. Carpenter by trade. Transferred to the 12th NC June 8, 1863, in exchange for Private Andrew Fulenwider.

DAILY, Joel J, Pvt, B. Enlisted in Rutherford on September 2, 1861, at age 33. 6'5" tall. Discharged by mistake in December 1862. Ordered to return to duty but did not return. Reenlisted June 1864. Present at Appomattox.

DANCY, Alpheus, Leroy, Pvt, D. Enlisted in Spotsylvania on May 15, 1862, at age 18. Died of disease in Danville September 24, 1862, son of Mary Dancy, who was with him when he died and took his body and effects home with her.

DAVENPORT, John W, 1Sgt, G. Enlisted in Charlotte on September 30, 1861, at age 40. Called "Big John." Enlisted as a private. Promoted to First Sgt. April 22, 1862. Died of wounds June 21, 1862.

DAVES, Elijah D, Pvt, C. Enlisted in Rutherford on Sept 2, 1861, at age 24. Teamster, Killed in action at Williamsport, MD July 6, 1863.

DAVES, Lorenzo A, Pvt, C. Enlisted in Rutherford on September 2, 1861, at age 18. Captured at Brandy Station. Died at Point Lookout February 2, 1864.

DAVIS, Abraham H, Pvt, B. Enlisted in Rutherford on September 2, 1861, at age 26. Gunshot wound in the arm at Gaines's Mill. Returned to duty. Captured at North Anna. Exchanged from Point Lookout March 14, 1865

DAVIS, Augustus C, Pvt, A. Enlisted at Camp Vance on Sept 1, 1863. Captured at the Wilderness. Died at Point Lookout June 20, 1864.

DAVIS, James, Pvt, B. Enlisted in Charlotte on April 20, 1864. Captured at North Anna. Exchanged from Point Lookout January 17, 1865. No record of a return to duty.

DAVIS, James M, Pvt, F. Enlisted at Camp Holmes on April 10, 1864. Detailed at Charlotte October 1864. Returned to the regiment and was present at Appomattox.

DAVIS, John H, Pvt, B. Enlisted in Rutherford on September 2, 1861, at age 18. Gunshot wound left hand at Fredericksburg. Deserted December 1, 1863. Dropped from the rolls.

DAVIS, Josiah, Pvt, C. Enlisted at Camp Vance on March 30, 1864. Sick since August 30, 1864. No further records.

DAVIS, Josiah, Pvt, K. Enlisted at Camp Holmes on May 24, 1864. Deserted June 15, 1864. Came in for parole at Goldsboro May 8, 1865.

DAVIS, Micah C, Cpt, E. Enlisted in Lincolnton on September 11, 1861, at age 23. Enlisted as a private. Promoted to captain in December 1862. Minister in Methodist Episcopal Church (SC Conf) since 1859. Resigned October 22, 1863, due to a request from the conference that he return. Chaplain Augustus Bennick wrote to recommend the acceptance of his resignation.

DAVIS, N F, Pvt, B. Enlisted in Raleigh on April 20, 1864. Died of disease at Wayside hospital in Richmond August 17, 1864.

DAVIS, Richard, Pvt, D. Enlisted after Dec 1864. Captured at Sutherland Station. Released from Harts Island June 18, 1865.

DAVIS, Simon D, Sgt, B. Enlisted in Rutherford on September 2, 1861, at age 29. Left leg amputated above the knee from wound received at Chancellorsville. Discharged in October 1864.

DAVIS, Tilman H, Lt, D. Enlisted as a corporal in Rowan on September 9, 1861, at age 33. Born in Cabarrus, NC. Accounted for every muster. Promoted to Lt. March 20, 1863. Recommended for valor and skill by Col. Lowrance. Present at Appomattox.

DAVIS, Whitson O, Pvt, B. Enlisted in Rutherford on September 2, 1861, at age 23. Wounded at Gettysburg, listed as AWOL from December 1863, dropped from the rolls as a deserter.

DAVIS, William F, Pvt, B. Enlisted at Camp Holmes on September 20, 1864. Transferred to the 1st NC Cavalry January 24, 1865.

DAVIS, William P, Pvt, D. Enlisted in Rowan on September 9, 1861, at age 20. Died of disease at High Point November 14, 1861.

DEAN, George W, Pvt, A. Enlisted at Camp Holmes on October 3, 1864. Present at Appomattox.

DEATON, Elias M, Pvt, K. Enlisted in Troy NC on March 5, 1863, at age 35. Died of disease at Guinea Station, VA April 14, 1863.

DECK, Joseph L, Pvt, I. Enlisted in Rutherford on October 6, 1861, at age 26. Discharged November 25, 1861, due to disability.

DELLINGER, Fred W "Wash", Pvt, E. Transferred from the 11th NC February 1, 1865. Deserted at Petersburg March 18, 1865. Took the oath and was sent to Jackson Co, Illinois on public works.

DELLINGER, Henry K, Pvt, E. Enlisted in Gaston, NC on March 30, 1864. Resident of Gaston County. Captured April 2, 1865, at Southside Railroad. Released from Hart's Island June 14, 1865.

DELLINGER, Jacob, Pvt, H. Enlisted in Shelby on October 1, 1861, at age 35. Discharged by mistake December 8, 1862 and ordered back to duty but did not return.

DELLINGER, Jacob R, Pvt, E. Enlisted at Camp Mangum on December 7, 1861, at age 20. Born in Gaston Co, NC. Accounted for on each muster. Present at Appomattox.

DELLINGER, Michael, Pvt, H. Enlisted in Shelby on October 1, 1861, at age 39. Discharged September 17, 1862. Reenlisted August 1, 1863, wounded May or June 1864. Was present in November 1864. No further records.

DELLINGER, Samuel, Pvt, H. Enlisted in Shelby on Oct 1, 1861, at age 22. Badge of Distinction at Chancellorsville. Wounded at Chancellorsville. Wounded May 1864. Received a severe gunshot wound to the right thigh and captured at Petersburg March 25, 1865. Treated aboard the USA Hospital Steamer Connecticut and Lincoln USA General Hospital in Washington DC. Released from Elmira July 19, 1865.

DENNIS, James M, Pvt, K. Enlisted in Troy NC on September 9, 1861, at age 20. Son of James and Mary Dennis. Enlisted with his brother, John. Died November 27, 1861, of disease.

DENNIS, John M, Pvt, K. Enlisted in Troy NC on September 9, 1861, at age 24. Son of James and Mary Dennis. Married to Laura Ann Dennis. Enlisted with his brother, James, who died in 1861. John was killed in action at Second Manassas.

DENNIS, William C, Pvt, K. Enlisted in Troy NC on September 9, 1861, at age 22. Accounted for every muster. Wounded at Gaines's Mill. Captured at Petersburg March 25, 1865. Confined at Point Lookout until May 13, 1865.

DEPRIEST, James R, Pvt, B. Enlisted in Rutherford on September 2, 1861, at age 16. Discharged due to age, per Conscription law after October 1862.

DICKERSON, Marcus O, Cpt, C. Enlisted in Rutherford on September 2, 1861, at age 48. Resigned June 24, 1862, due to his age and duties as Rutherford Co. Clerk of the Court.

DICKERSON, Robert P, Lt, C. Enlisted in Rutherford on September 9, 1861. Son of Capt. M O Dickerson. Transferred from the 16th NC to replace JB Carrier. Promoted to Lieutenant July 1862. Died of wounds received at Shepherdstown, date of death not stated.

DICKSON, Andrew G, Pvt, F. Killed in action at Ream's Station.

DILWORTH, John Quincy Adams, Pvt, G. Enlisted at Camp Holmes on April 29, 1864. Captured at the Wilderness, released from Point Lookout after joining US Army. Served in the 1st US Volunteers in the Dakota territory. Died of scurvy at Fort Rice March 21, 1865. Record states he was "of good character".

DIXON, J M, Pvt, E. Enlisted at Camp Holmes on April 2, 1864. Captured May 24, 1864, at Hanover Junction. Died at Point Lookout August 15, 1864.

DOBBINS, A J, Pvt, C. Enlisted after December of 1864. Deserted February 21, 1865, at Petersburg. Took the oath and was sent to Utica, NY on public works.

DOBBINS, D Calloway, Pvt, C. Enlisted in Rutherford on September 2, 1861, at age 20. Killed in action at Second Manassas.

DOBBINS, Daniel, Pvt, B. Enlisted in Rutherford on September 2, 1861, at age 21. Died at Guinea Station, VA March 1, 1863. Cause of death not stated.

DOBBINS, Felix C, Sgt, B. Enlisted in Rutherford on September 2, 1861, at age 25. Accounted for every muster. Wounded at the Wilderness. Returned to duty. Was captured at Petersburg March 25, 1865. Released from Point Lookout June 12, 1865.

DOBBINS, James L, Pvt, B. Enlisted in Rutherford on September 2, 1861, at age 22. Died August 17, 1862, of wounds received at Frayser's Farm. Son of Lewis Dobbins and brother of Jesse C. Dobbins.

DOBBINS, Jesse C, Pvt, B. Enlisted in Rutherford on September 2, 1861, at age 20. Wounded August 1862, (Gunshot wound shoulder). Returned to duty. Killed in action May 5, 1864, at the Wilderness. Brother of James Dobbins and son of Lewis Dobbins.

DOBBINS, John A, Pvt, C. Enlisted in Rutherford on September 2, 1861, at age 19. Accounted for on every muster. Received a gunshot wound in the hand at Chancellorsville. Deserted from Petersburg February 21, 1865. Took oath and went to public works in Utica NY.

DOBBINS, Vincent, Pvt, B. Enlisted in Raleigh on April 15, 1864. Gunshot wound to the left leg at the Wilderness. Was present to November 1864.

DOGGETT, Peter, Cpl, C. Enlisted in Rutherford on September 2, 1861, at age 43. Discharged November 2, 1862, due to age, per Conscription law.

DOTY, Osborne M, Pvt, B. Enlisted in Rutherford on September 2, 1861, at age 18. Died at Richmond August 11, 1862. Son of Jesse Doty.

DOUGLAS, Joseph A, Pvt, D. Enlisted in Rowan on September 9, 1861, at age 20. Accounted for on each muster with one short AWOL. Present at Appomattox.

DOUGLAS, Marshall A, Pvt, D. Enlisted in Massaponax on May 15, 1862. Wounded and captured at Gettysburg. Exchanged from Point Lookout March 17, 1864. Retired to the Invalid Corps December 30, 1864. Served as a prison guard at Salisbury.

DOUGLAS, Samuel A, Pvt, G. Enlisted in Charlotte on September 30, 1861, at age 36. Discharged at Goldsboro March 29, 1862, for disability.

DOUGLAS, Samuel H, Lt, D. Enlisted in Rowan on September 9, 1861, at age 27. Enlisted as a Sgt. Promoted to Lt April 18, 1862. Died of disease at Richmond July 20, 1862.

DOWELL, Franklin, Pvt, C. Enlisted at Camp Vance on March 15, 1864, at age 18. Gunshot wound to the chest at Williams Farm, VA June 22, 1864, and was taken prisoner. Died in a hospital in

Washington DC June 30, 1864. Was listed as KIA but was captured and died as POW. Was buried at Arlington but was reinterred in 1883.

DOWNS, Franklin C, Pvt, G. Enlisted in Charlotte on May 14, 1864. Present at Appomattox.

DUNN, Thomas J, Pvt, G. Enlisted in Charlotte on September 30, 1861, at age 31. Gunshot wound near Richmond June 26, 1863. Discharged for disability November 14, 1863.

DURHAM, Robert A, Pvt, B. Enlisted after November 1864. Present at Appomattox.

DYCUS, Ancil N, Pvt, B. Enlisted in Rutherford on September 2, 1861, at age 21. Discharged for disability June 6, 1862. Reenlisted February 26, 1863. Present at Appomattox. Drowned on the way home at the Catawba River on April 25, 1865, along with his brother, Joe.

DYER, John W, Pvt, I. Enlisted in Rutherford on October 6, 1861, at age 31. 6'3" tall. Died of disease December 10, 1861.

EADES, Alfred, Pvt, A. Enlisted at Camp Vance on April 7, 1864. Captured May 23, 1864, at the North Anna. Exchanged from Point Lookout September 18, 1864. Hospitalized after release, sent to Statesville, NC. Did not return.

EADES, William F, Pvt, A. Enlisted at Camp Vance on April 1, 1864. Captured May 23, 1864, at the North Anna. Paroled from Point Lookout March 15, 1865.

EAKER, Abraham, Pvt, E. Enlisted in Lincolnton on September 11, 1861, at age 30. Captured at Falling Waters. Confined at Point Lookout. Joined the US Army January 25, 1864. Served in the 1st US Volunteers as a Herder. Mustered out at Ft. Leavenworth Nov 27, 1865.

EAKER, Daniel, Pvt, E. Enlisted in Lincolnton on September 11, 1861, at age 22. Discharged July 1862, due to disability. Reenlisted March of 1863. Captured at Falling Waters. Confined at Point Lookout. Joined the US Army January 25, 1864. Placed in an "unassigned regiment". No further records.

EAKER, Jesse, Pvt, E. Enlisted in Lincolnton on September 11, 1861, at age 19. Wounded in the Seven Days battles and Second Manassas. Captured at Chancellorsville and exchanged after a short confinement. Captured August 1, 1863, at Brandy Station. Confined at Point Lookout. Joined the US Army January 25 1864, and was placed in an "unassigned regiment." No further records.

EAKER, John H, Cpl, E. Enlisted in Lincolnton on September 11, 1861, at age 25. A carpenter. Married to Marth Eaker. Was killed in action at Gaines's Mill.

EAKER, John Jr, Pvt, F. Enlisted in Cleveland on October 10, 1861, at age 20. Captured at Gettysburg, died at Point Lookout Dec 1, 1863.

EAKER, John Sr, Pvt, F. Enlisted in Cleveland on October 10, 1861, at age 23. Gunshot wound in right thigh at Chancellorsville and Gunshot wound in the right hand in June of 1864. Captured April 2, 1865, at Petersburg, released from Harts Island June 17, 1865.

EAKER, Joseph, Pvt, E. Enlisted in Lincolnton on September 11, 1861, at age 28. On duty in October 1864, with no records after that.

EARLEY, Thomas S, Pvt, C. Enlisted at Camp Vance on May 9, 1864. Present in November 1864, with no records after that.

EARLEY, William H, Pvt, C. Enl in Rutherford on September 2, 1861, at age 20. Discharged January 8, 1862. Reenlisted around January of 1863. Accounted for each muster since. Captured in the hospital in Richmond April 3, 1865. Released from Newport News June 30, 1865.

EARLS, Jacob S, Pvt, F. Enlisted in Cleveland on October 2, 1861, at age 19. Accounted for every muster. Teamster, Gunshot wound in the elbow at Gaines's Mill, Present at Appomattox.

EARLS, Martin, Pvt, H. Enlisted in Shelby on October 1, 1861, at age 18. One AWOL, Mar-Apr 1863. Returned to duty. Wounded twice in 1864, Captured April 3, 1865, at Petersburg, released at Harts Island June 14, 1865.

EARLS, Preston, Pvt, H. Enlisted in Shelby on October 1, 1861, at age 20. Died of disease at Raleigh January 4, 1862.

EARLS, William, Pvt, H. Enlisted in Shelby on October 1, 1861, at age 20. One AWOL in Mar-April 1863. Returned to duty. Present all other musters. Gunshot wound September 20, 1862, at Shepherdstown. Captured April 3, 1865, at Petersburg. Confined at Harts Island until June 18, 1865.

EARLY, Drury B, Pvt, C. Enlisted in Rutherford on September 2, 1861, at age 26. Right leg amputated from wound received during the Seven Days Battles. Died August 7, 1862.

EARLY, James, Pvt, C. Enlisted in Rutherford on Sept 2, 1861, at age 32. Captured at Chancellorsville, exchanged May 10, 1863, and returned to duty. Present to Nov 1864. Accounted for every muster.

EARLY, John P, Pvt, C. Enlisted in Rutherford on September 2, 1861, at age 24. Died of disease at Hamilton March 19, 1862, widow Ruth Early.

EARLY, William A, Pvt, C. Enlisted in Rutherford on September 2, 1861, at age 19. Died of disease at Hamilton March 26, 1862, mother Elizabeth Early.

EATON, Henry D, Lt, E. Enlisted in Lincolnton on September 11, 1861, at age 35. 6' 3" tall. Enlisted as a private. Color bearer. Distinguished for actions at Gaines's Mill. Promoted to Lt. Killed in action at Ox Hill September 1, 1862, widow Catherine Eaton.

EATON, John H, Pvt, I. Enlisted in Davie Co NC on October 6, 1864. Captured in the hospital in Richmond April 3, 1865. Released from Newport News June 30, 1865.

EDMISTON, Ahimaaz H, Pvt, D. Enlisted in Rowan on September 9, 1861, at age 23. Nurse and hospital guard in Richmond since Chancellorsville. Captured April 3, 1865, released April 18, 1865. Accounted for every muster.

EDMOND, W Pinkney, Pvt, E. Enlisted in Lincolnton on September 11, 1861, at age 22. Accounted for on every muster. Born in Pickens, SC, Hospital guard, Gunshot wound in shoulder in Seven Days Battles. Returned to duty. Deserted at Petersburg March 7, 1865. Took oath and went to Philadelphia on public works.

EDWARDS, Henry, Pvt, B. Enlisted at Camp Holmes on May 8, 1864. Deserted June 18, 1864.

EDWARDS, John, Cpt, B. Enlisted in Rutherford on September 2, 1861, at age 62. Baptist minister. Organized Co B, died at home in Rutherford April 11, 1862.

EDWARDS, John N, Sgt, B. Enlisted in Rutherford on September 2, 1861, at age 22. Died March 1, 1862, at Tarboro, NC, son of Captain John Edwards.

EDWARDS, Joseph M, Pvt, B. Enlisted in Rutherford on September 2, 1861, at age 36. Died March 2, 1862, at Goldsboro, widow Priscilla Edwards.

EDWARDS, William, Pvt, C. Enlisted at Camp Vance on May 9, 1864. Listed AWOL after October 2, 1864. Was granted sick leave and never returned.

EDWARDS, William D, 1Lt, B. Enlisted in Rutherford on September 2, 1861, at age 29. Commanded Company B. Died of disease at Guinea Station, VA February 27, 1863. Was the son of Amos Edwards.

EDWARDS, Zachariah A, Pvt, B. Enlisted at Camp Vance on October 19, 1863. Resident of Rutherford. Captured April 3, 1865, at Petersburg, released from Harts Island June 19, 1865.

ELAM, George A, 1Sgt, F. Enlisted in Cleveland as a private on September 17, 1861, at age 26. A miller before the war. Elected 1Sgt. April 18, 1862. Killed in action at Gaines's Mill, widow Mary Elam.

ELKINS, John, Pvt, I. Enlisted at Camp Vance on May 7, 1864. Present in November 1864. No records after that.

ELLER, Green, Pvt, D. Enlisted in Rowan on September 6, 1861, at age 29. A miller before the war, Present or accounted for every muster. Present in November 1864. No record after that.

ELLER, Obediah, Sgt, D. Enlisted in Rowan on September 9, 1861, at age 21. Badge of Distinction at Chancellorsville. Color Sgt, Provost

Guard. Present on every muster. Captured April 3, 1865, in the hospital in Richmond, released from Newport News June 16, 1865.

ELLIOTT, Thomas J, Pvt, K. Enlisted in Montgomery on September 9, 1861, at age 25. Accounted for every muster. Captured June 22, 1864, at Petersburg. Confined at Point Lookout. Exchanged October 11, 1864, and hospitalized. Did not return to duty.

ELLIOTT, Elza C, Pvt, F. Enlisted in Charlotte on April 3, 1863. Present in March and April 1863. No further record.

ELLIOTT, Ezekiel A, Pvt, K. Enlisted in Montgomery on September 9, 1861, at age 26. Discharged in November 1861.

ELLIOTT, G W, Pvt, K. Resident of Montgomery County. Enlisted after December 1864. Captured at Petersburg March 25, 1865. Released on oath from Point Lookout May 13, 1865.

ELLIOTT, Hugh W, Pvt, G. Enlisted in Charlotte on September 30, 1861, at age 34. Discharged by mistake in December of 1862 and ordered back to duty. Returned and served as a teamster from June 1863. Severely wounded once, date unknown. Died of disease in hospital at Orange, VA February 17, 1864.

ELLIOTT, James, Pvt, K. Enlisted in Raleigh on August 21, 1862. Present up to November 1864.

ELLIOTT, James G, Cpl, K. Enlisted in Troy NC on September 9, 1861, at age 26. Died July 1863, in the hospital of a gunshot wound received at Hagerstown.

ELLIOTT, Jonathan, Pvt, C. Enlisted in Rutherford on September 2, 1861, at age 39. Died of disease in the hospital in Farmville, VA October 1, 1862.

ELLIOTT, Robert, Pvt, A. Enlisted at Camp Holmes on October 3, 1864. Transferred to the 1st NC Cavalry March 2, 1865.

ELLIOTT, Thomas, Pvt, C. Enlisted in Rutherford on Sept 2, 1861, at age 29. Died of disease at Camp Mason, Goldsboro April 12, 1862.

ELLIOTT, Titus M, Pvt, K. Enlisted in Troy NC on October 9, 1861, at age 23. Killed in action July 1, 1863, at Gettysburg.

ELLIOTT, Virgil H, Sgt, F. Enlisted in Cleveland on September 17, 1861, at age 30. Gunshot wound in the right leg at Gettysburg, returned to duty late in the war. Was captured at March 25, 1865 and confined at Point Lookout until June 12, 1865.

ELLIOTT, William F, Pvt, D. Enlisted in Rowan on September 9, 1861, at age 19. Drummer. Died of Typhoid October 24, 1862, at Winchester. Son of Samuel Elliott.

ELLIOTT, William H, Pvt, C. Enlisted in Rutherford on September 2, 1861, at age 25. Accounted for on every muster. Gunshot wound in the leg at Chancellorsville, recovered at home. Returned as a wagon master in the Ordnance Department. Present at Appomattox.

ELLIS, Benjamin F, Pvt, F. Enlisted in Cleveland on October 10, 1861, at age 24. Accounted for on every muster. Ambulance driver from August 1863. Captured April 3, 1865, at Petersburg. Confined at Point Lookout until June 26, 1865.

ELLIS, Bolivar C, Pvt, F. Enlisted in Cleveland on May 17, 1862, at age 33. Died of unknown cause at Richmond October 6, 1862. Widow Mary Bolivar.

ELLIS, John W, Sgt, D. Enlisted in Rowan on September 9, 1861, at age 20. Accounted for on every muster. Wounded at Chancellorsville. Promoted to Sgt May 3, 1863. Wounded again in June of 1864. Present in December 1864. Paroled at Salisbury May 1865.

ENGLAND, Robert A, Pvt, C. Enlisted in Rutherford on September 2, 1861, at age 25. Died in the hospital in Richmond, October 18, 1862, of wounds received at Ox Hill.

ERWIN, James S, Chaplain. Served beginning Nov. 11, 1861, officially appointed Feb. 13, 1862 at the recommendation of Col. Leventhorpe. Resigned due to health reasons Oct. 1, 1862. (See NC Troops Vol. 9, page 253).

ETTERS, Pinkney P, Pvt, G. Enlisted in Charlotte on September 30, 1861, at age 29. Born in York, SC. Died August 20, 1862, on the march to Manassas.

EWING, John D, Pvt, G. Enlisted in Charlotte on September 30, 1861, at age 23. Deserted March 28, 1863. Present December 1864. Deserted February 2, 1865, at Petersburg. Took the oath and was sent to Pittsburgh on public works.

FALLS, George L, Pvt, F. Enlisted in Cleveland on October 2, 1861, at age 16. Drummer. Discharged October 9, 1862, due to age.

FELMENT, Otho W, Pvt, F. Enlisted in Cleveland on September 19, 1861, at age 31. Killed in action at Gaines's Mill.

FERRIS, George N, Pvt, G. Enlisted in Charlotte on September 30, 1861, at age 27. Died of disease in a hospital in Raleigh Feb 4, 1862.

FINGER, Monroe P, Cpl, E. Enlisted in Lincolnton on September 11, 1861, at age 26. A tanner. Died June 25, 1863, of a gunshot wound to the knee received at Chancellorsville. Son of Daniel Finger.

FISHER, Soloman C, Pvt, A. Enlisted at Camp Vance on April 1, 1863, at age 23. Captured at the North Anna River May 23, 1864. Confined at Point Lookout and then Elmira. Desired to take the oath. Volunteered for the US Army 161 NY Engineers but died at Elmira October 17, 1864, before transferring.

FISHER, William, Pvt, I. Enlisted in Lincolnton on March 12, 1863, at age 39. Captured at Falling Waters and confined at Point Lookout. Treated at Hammond General Hospital for Typhoid from October 29, 1863, until January 15, 1864. Exchanged March 3, 1864. Returned to duty by August 1864. Captured near Appomattox April 4, 1865. Released from Point Lookout June 26, 1865.

FISMIRE, J M, Pvt, K. Enlisted at Camp Holmes on May 28, 1864. Deserted 6/8/64.

FISMIRE, J S, Pvt, K. Enlisted at Camp Holmes on May 28, 1864. Deserted 6/8/64.

FLACK, Andrew D, 2Sgt, C. Enlisted in Rutherford on September 2, 1861, at age 18. Accounted for every muster. Promoted to Sgt June 3, 1863. Killed in action at Ream's Station August 25, 1864.

FLINN, Daniel P, Pvt, C. Enlisted at Camp Vance on May 12, 1864. Absent after September 1864, in the hospital. No further records.

FLINN, Miles W, Pvt, I. Enlisted in Rutherford on October 6, 1861, at age 37. Wounded at 2nd Manassas. Listed AWOL July 23-August 4, 1863 but was pardoned. Promoted to Sgt November 16, 1863 but reduced to private. AWOL September 1864. Present at Appomattox.

FORBUSH, Franklin, Pvt, C. Enlisted at Camp Vance on May 4, 1864. Admitted to the hospital in Danville April 3, 1865.

FORESTER, Martin O, Pvt, C. Enlisted at Camp Vance on May 18, 1864. Furloughed 60 days in December of 1864. Returned and was present at Appomattox.

FORTENBERY, Harberd S, Pvt, F. Joined regiment after December 1864. Captured April 3, 1865, Sutherland Station, released at Point Lookout June 26, 1865.

FORTENBERY, Robert A, Cpl, F. Enlisted in Cleveland on September 12, 1861, at age 34. Blacksmith. Discharged by mistake December 8, 1862. Rejoined November 1864. Present at Appomattox.

FOSTER, Alfred, Pvt, C. Enlisted in Rutherford on September 2, 1861, at age 21. Accounted for every muster. Detailed a short time as a hospital guard at Lynchburg, VA. Wounded September 30, 1864. Returned to duty November 20, 1864. Captured at Petersburg April 2, 1865. Confined at Harts Island NY until June 6, 1865.

FOSTER, George, Pvt, D. Enlisted in Rowan on September 9, 1861, at age 16. Discharged Nov 18, 1862, due to age per conscription law.

FOSTER, Henry F, Pvt, C. Enlisted in Rutherford on September 2, 1861, at age 23. Present or accounted for every muster. Division Pioneer in Wilcox's Pioneer Corp. On duty to December 1864.

FOSTER, James L, Pvt, C. Enlisted in Statesville on July 17, 1862. Resident of Cherryville, NC. Admitted to Jackson Hospital in Richmond April 1, 1865. Captured April 3, 1865, in the hospital, Released from City Point June 30, 1865.

FOSTER, Samuel P, Pvt, C. Enlisted in Rutherford on September 2, 1861, at age 28. Disability discharge April 18, 1862. Re-enlisted October 10, 1862, at Bunker Hill, VA. Captured at Gettysburg, exchanged from Point Lookout February 18, 1865. At Camp Lee in Richmond following release. No further records.

FOSTER, William, Pvt, C. Enlisted in Rutherford on August 18, 1862. Wounded at Chancellorsville. Recovered at home. Returned to duty by December 1863. Present in December 1864. No further records.

FOWLER, Daniel W, Cpl, I. Enlisted in Rutherford on October 6, 1861, at age 25. Born in Union SC. Captured at Gettysburg and confined at Fort Delaware. Exchanged July 20, 1863. Returned to duty. Captured again at Sutherland Station. Confined at Harts Island until June 18, 1865. Record states he was "a good soldier."

FOWLER, Leonard, Sgt, I. Enlisted in Rutherford on October 6, 1861, at age 30. Born Union SC. Wounded at Second Manassas and Gettysburg. Right leg amputated February 1865, from a wound received between Nov 1864, and February 1865. Was discharged.

FOX, Andrew M, Pvt, G. Enlisted at Camp Holmes on July 6, 1864. Present at Appomattox.

FRANCIS, James P, Pvt, H. Enlisted in Shelby on October 1, 1861, at age 23. Deserted September 1, 1862, to September 25, 1864. Returned and Present at Appomattox.

FRANKLIN, Robert B, Pvt, B. Enlisted in Rutherford on Sept 2, 1861, at age 53. Discharged at Goldsboro April 16, 1862, due to disability.

FRAZIER, Isaac, Pvt, G. Enlisted in Charlotte on September 30, 1861, at age 26. Transferred to the 13th NC in January 1863.

FREELAND, James L, Pvt, D. Enlisted in Rowan on September 9, 1861, at age 19. Gunshot wound to the chest at Fredericksburg. Returned by April 1863. Absent, sick from May 1, 1863, to after November 1864. Captured in the hospital in Richmond April 3, 1865. Paroled April 17, 1865.

FREEMAN, John M, Pvt, C. Enlisted in Rutherford on September 2, 1861, at age 24. Died in camp near Richmond July 8, 1862.

FREEMAN, John Mc E, Pvt, C. Enlisted in Rutherford on September 2, 1861, at age 23. Captured at Falling Waters. Confined at Old Capital and Point Lookout. Paroled November 15, 1864. No record after that.

FREEMAN, Noah, Pvt, K. Enlisted in Troy NC on January 1862, at age 25. Died May 17, 1863, in a hospital in Richmond of wounds received at Chancellorsville and pneumonia.

FREEZE, Elijah P, Pvt, D. Enlisted in Rowan on Sept 6, 1861, at age 28. Born in Cabarrus NC. Was killed at Gaines's Mill June 27, 1862.

FREEZE, Miles N, Pvt, D. Enlisted in Rowan on September 9, 1861, at age 25. Accounted for on every muster. From Rowan Mills, NC. Wounded July or August 1864 returned by October 1864. Present in November 1864. No further records.

FRIDAY, Jacob, Pvt, E. Enlisted in Dallas NC on August 31, 1861, at age 37. Captured at Gettysburg and confined at Point Lookout. Exchanged February 18, 1865 and listed with a detachment of exchanged prisoners at Camp Lee in Richmond February 23, 1865. No record after that.

FRONEBERGER, Jacob E, Pvt, F. Enlisted in Massaponax May 17, 1862, at age 24. Died of disease January 6, 1863, in a Danville hospital. Effects included a gold ring.

FRY, William R, Pvt, I. Enlisted at Camp Holmes on June 20, 1864. Present each muster. Paroled at Salisbury, NC June 10, 1865.

FULBRIGHT, George F, Pvt, E. Enlisted in Lincolnton on September 11, 1861, at age 22. Gunshot wound in the arm at Ox Hill. Detailed as a nurse in enemy lines at Gettysburg and was captured with the wounded left behind. Exchanged from Point Lookout May 3, 1864. Returned to duty and was present by August 1864. Present at Appomattox.

FULENVILLER, Andrew, Pvt, E. Age 35. Transferred from the 12th NC June 20, 1863, for William Crytz. Killed in action at Gettysburg.

GANTT, Abel H, Cpl, F. Enlisted in Cleveland on September 17, 1861, at age 24. Millwright. Died June 29, 1862, of wounds received at Gaines's Mill. Son of True Gantt and brother of Marcus A Gantt.

GANTT, John C, Pvt, F. Enlisted in Cleveland on September 17, 1861, at age 17. Captured at Falling Waters and sent to Point Lookout. Exchanged March 3, 1864. Returned to duty by June 1864. Present at Appomattox.

GANTT, Marcus A, Pvt, F. Enlisted in Cleveland on October 25, 1861, at age 22. Died May 6, 1863, of pneumonia caused by wounds received at Chancellorsville. Effects, 1 pocketbook with $11, 1 good pocket knife, Son of True Gantt, and brother of Abel Gantt.

GANTT, Melvin P, Pvt, F. Enlisted at Camp Holmes on April 20, 1864, at age 18. Brother of Abel and Marcus Gantt. On duty to November 1864.

GANTT, William J, Pvt, F. Enlisted in Cleveland on February 28, 1863. Killed in action May 21, 1864, at Spotsylvania.

GARDNER, B M, Pvt, K. Enlisted at Camp Holmes on May 28, 1864. Deserted June 8, 1864.

GARREN, Anderson, Pvt, G. Enlisted at Camp Holmes on August 25, 1864. Deserted at Petersburg September 4, 1864. Took oath and asked for employment.

GARVY, Andrew J, Pvt, D. Enlisted in Tarboro on June 10, 1864. Discharged due to disability September 18, 1864.

GATIS, Joseph C, Pvt, B. Enlisted at Camp Holmes on July 17, 1864. Present at Appomattox.

GENTLE, John A, Pvt, A. Enlisted at Camp Vance on September 1, 1863. Captured May 23, 1864, at North Anna and sent to Point Lookout. Exchanged March 14, 1865.

GETTYS, Alfred W, Pvt, B. Enlisted in Rutherford on Sept 2, 1861, at age 20. Died at Goldsboro April 23, 1862, of disease. Son of A. Gettys.

GETTYS, Lawson G, Pvt, B. Enlisted at Camp Fisher on October 25, 1861, at age 19. Died of a fever at Liberty, VA September 11, 1862. Son of A. Gettys.

GIBBONS, Cornelius C, Pvt, F. Enlisted in Charlotte on February 21, 1863, at age 18. Left arm amputated for wound received at Chancellorsville. Discharged March 5, 1864.

GIBBONS, William J, Pvt, F. Enlisted in Cleveland on September 17, 1861, at age 22. Captured at Gettysburg, exchanged August 23, 1863. Returned to duty and was killed at the Wilderness May 6, 1864.

GIBBS, Henry, Pvt, D. Enlisted in Polk Co on August 27, 1864. Deserted from Petersburg February 16, 1865. Took the oath and transferred to White Co, Ill on public works.

GIBBS, Josephus, Pvt, D. Enlisted at Camp Vance on March 30, 1864. Wounded May or June 1864. Returned to duty. Hospitalized February 26, 1865, for pneumonia. Captured in the hospital in Richmond April 3, 1865. Died at Newport News May 29, 1865. Buried at P. West's farm.

GILBERT, Daniel R, Pvt, E. Enlisted in Lincolnton on September 11, 1861, at age 27. Teamster. Present every muster. Wounded in the Seven Days actions. Present up to December 1864.

GILL, Thomas S, Pvt, F. Enlisted in Cleveland on May 17, 1862, at age 32. Died of disease at his home Aug 1, 1862. Suzanna Gill widow.

GILLON, Monroe M, 1Lt, D. Enlisted in Rowan on September 9, 1861, at age 20. Resident of Concord, NC. Promoted to 1st Sgt June 1, 1862, and Lt. July 1, 1862. Praised by Colonel Lowrance for his conduct at Gettysburg. Gunshot wound to the shoulder in July 1864. Present at Appomattox.

GINGERY, Daniel, Pvt, G. Enlisted at Camp Holmes on July 15, 1864. Record states he deserted to the enemy August 4, 1864, but no POW records found.

GLOVER, James, Pvt, D. Enlisted in Rowan on September 9, 1861, at age 17. Captured July 12, 1863, at Hagerstown, MD and sent to Point Lookout. Volunteered for the US Navy January 26, 1864, but enlistment was rejected.

GOINGS, John C, Pvt, F. Enlisted at Camp Holmes on April 20, 1864. Died July 5, 1864, of disease. Son of G M Goings.

GOLD, Parham A, Cpl, H. Enlisted in Shelby on October 1, 1861, at age 31. Killed in action at Gaines's Mill. Nancy Gold widow.

GOODE, Edward S, Pvt, C. Enlisted in Rutherford on September 2, 1861, at age 21. Accounted for on every muster. Detailed as hospital guard due to disability since April 12, 1864. Present in December 1864. No records after that.

GOODE, George, Pvt, I. Enlisted in Rutherford on October 6, 1861, at age 20. Died at Goldsboro of disease March 27, 1862.

GOODE, George W, Cpl, C. Enlisted in Rutherford on September 2, 1861, at age 20. Wounded in May/June 1863, and Aug 8, 1864. Furloughed August 27, 1864, to Cherryville, NC. No further records.

GOODE, John W, Pvt, I. Enlisted in Rutherford on October 6, 1861, at age 43. Discharged for disability May 1, 1862.

GOODE, William R, Pvt, I. Enlisted in Rutherford on October 6, 1861, at age 26. Died at Halifax, NC March 31, 1862.

GOODNIGHT, Daniel L, Pvt, D. Enlisted in Concord, NC on September 21, 1863, at age 18. Was killed in action at Ream's Station.

GOODSON, William M, Sgt, F. Enlisted in Cleveland on Sept 17, 1861, at age 25. Substitute for Jacob Beaman. Captured August 15, 1862 and exchanged Sept 21, 1862. Promoted to Sgt. May 4, 1863. Wounded during the Gettysburg campaign. Captured April 3, 1865, near Appomattox and was confined at Pt Lookout until June 3, 1865.

GORDON, George T, Lt. Colonel. Commissioned as a Major at Camp Gregg on December 24, 1862, at age 39. Formerly of the British Army. Served on A. P. Hill's staff. Hill Recommend his commission. Was wounded 4 times, Promoted to Lt Col May 6, 1863. Retired to Invalid Corp November 25, 1864.

GRAGG, David H, Pvt, G. Enlisted at Camp Vance on July 1864. Died in the hospital in Richmond November 9, 1864.

GRAHAM, John, 1Lt, D. Enlisted in Rowan on September 9, 1861, at age 37. Failed reelection and was discharged April 18, 1862.

GRANT, Samuel B, Pvt, C. Enlisted in Rutherford on September 2, 1861, at age 19. Went home on sick leave and joined another regiment, dropped from rolls August 11, 1863.

GRAY, David Z, Pvt, D. Enl after Dec 1864. Present at Appomattox.

GRAY, James L, Sgt, C. Enlisted in Rutherford on September 2, 1861, at age 50. Hospital Steward died at home in March of 1862.

GREEN, Elias, Pvt, B. Enlisted at Camp Holmes on July 6, 1864. Captured at Petersburg March 25, 1865. Confined at Point Lookout until June 27, 1865.

GREEN, Francis M, Pvt, B. Enlisted in Rutherford on September 2, 1861, at age 24. Wounded at Gaines's Mill. Captured at Gettysburg. Died at Fort Delaware September 21, 1863.

GREEN, Martin A, Pvt, B. Enlisted at Camp Holmes on May 21, 1864. Captured at Petersburg March 25, 1865. Confined at Point Lookout until June 27, 1865.

GREEN, Pleasant G, Pvt, K. Enlisted in Troy NC on September 9, 1861, at age 35. Killed in action at Gaines's Mill, widow Sarah Green.

GREEN, Reubin H, Pvt, I. Enlisted in Cleveland on April 1, 1864. Present to November 1864.

GREEN, Uel, Pvt, B. Enlisted in Cleveland on February 26, 1863, at age 29. Absent June 5, 1863, to November 1, 1864. Present in December 1864. No further records.

GREEN, William R, Pvt, B. Enlisted in Rutherford on September 2, 1861, at age 28. Wounded at Chancellorsville (Gunshot wound finger). Present up to November 1864.

GREENHILL, Lawson, Pvt, G. Enlisted in Lincolnton on March 12, 1863, at age 37. Died May 5, 1863, of wounds received at Chancellorsville, widow Nancy Greenhill.

GRICE, William J, Pvt, E. Enlisted in Lincolnton on September 11, 1861, at age 20. Died of disease December 29, 1861.

GRIFFIN, James T, Pvt, I. Enlisted in Rutherford on October 6, 1861, at age 41. Wounded at Gettysburg. Captured at North Anna May 23, 1864. Died at Point Lookout February 5, 1865.

GRIGG, Levi R, Cpt., F. Enlisted as a private at Camp Holmes on April 20, 1864. Married to Mary Jane Crowder. Apparently promoted to Captain after December of 1864. No further record.

GRUBBS, M, Cpl, D. Enlisted after December 1864. Captured April 3, 1865, in the hospital in Richmond.

GUEST, William, Pvt, I. Enlisted at Camp Vance on May 25, 1864. Captured at Boydton Plank Road March 30, 1865. Confined at Point Lookout until June 27, 1865.

GUY, James K, Pvt, D. Enlisted at Camp Holmes on September 25, 1864. Present at Appomattox.

GYERE, N, Pvt, K. Enlisted at Camp Holmes on June 25, 1864. Deserted July 11, 1864.

HAGE, David F, Pvt, B. Enlisted at Camp Holmes on May 22, 1864. Deserted June 18, 1864. Returned in July and was present at Appomattox.

HALES, William T, Pvt, B. Enlisted at Camp Holmes on September 28, 1864. Absent with leave Sept/Oct 1864. No record after that.

HALL, Dewit Clinton, Pvt, K. Enlisted in Troy NC on March 5, 1863, at age 36. Conscript. Present on each muster of enlistment. Present at Appomattox.

HALL, Eli, Pvt, K. Enlisted in Raleigh on Aug 21, 1862. Captured at Petersburg March 25, 1865. Held at Point Lookout until May 13, 1865.

HALL, G W, Pvt, K. Enlisted around November 23, 1864. Captured at Petersburg April 2, 1865. Released from Point Lookout June 24, 1865.
HALL, Jesse, Pvt, H. Enlisted at Camp Holmes on April 20, 1864. Captured at the Wilderness May 6, 1864. Died at Elmira Aug 11, 1864.
HALL, N N, Pvt, E. Joined the regiment around December 1864. Deserted at Petersburg March 4, 1865.
HALL, William, Pvt, D. Enlisted around November 1864. Deserted January 09, 1865, at Petersburg took oath and transferred to Indianapolis on public works.
HALL, William H, Pvt, K. Enlisted in Troy NC on January 28, 1863, at age 37. Died August 3, 1863, at his home of gunshot wound to the side received at Chancellorsville, Mary Hall widow.
HALTOM, Elisha, Pvt, K. Enlisted in Troy NC on September 9, 1861, at age 16. Son of James Haltom. Uncles William and Joseph served in the same company. Elisha was killed in action at Ox Hill Sept 1, 1862.
HALTOM, Joseph, Pvt, K. Enlisted in Troy NC on September 9, 1861, at age 29. Son of Sarah Haltom. Died of disease October 1862.
HALTOM, Thomas C, 1Lt, K. Enlisted in Troy NC on September 9, 1861, at age 41. Farmer and hotel owner. Former constable in Montgomery County. Elected Lieutenant April 18, 1862. Wounded at Frayser's Farm. Led the company at Gettysburg. Resigned July 15, 1864, due to injuries and the needs of his large family. Later served as a captain in the 6th NC Senior Reserves.
HALTOM, William B, Pvt, K. Enlisted in Troy NC on Sept 9, 1861, at age 24. Fifer. Deserted Feb 1862. Later enlisted in the 44th NC.
HAMBY, Joseph, Pvt, A. Joined the regiment in December 1864. Present at Appomattox.
HAMILTON, Gilbert W, Cpl, K. Enlisted in Troy NC on September 9, 1861, at age 22. Present every muster until he was captured at North Anna, exchanged from Point Lookout March 11, 1865.
HAMILTON, Harris C, Pvt, K. Enlisted in Troy NC on September 9, 1861, at age 22. Killed in action at Gaines's Mill.
HAMILTON, M R, Pvt, K. Enlisted at Camp Holmes on August 25, 1864. Present to November 1864.
HAMMARSKOLD, Charles J, Lt. Colonel. Born in Sweden. Enlisted as a lieutenant in Lincolnton on September 11, 1861, Elected Lt. Colonel April 18, 1862. Led the regiment at Frayser's Farm. Resigned his commission July 17, 1862, due to failing eyesight.
HAMRICK, Albert, Pvt, F. Enlisted in Cleveland on May 17, 1862, at age 26. Died of Disease in Richmond July 10, 1862.
HAMRICK, Amos, Pvt, B. Enlisted in Guinea Station on May 7, 1862, at age 25. Wounded at an unknown date. On detached service for

most of his enlistment. Present with the regiment in October 1864. Present at Appomattox.

HAMRICK, Doctor N, 1Sgt, B. Enlisted in Rutherford on September 2, 1861, at age 35. Musician. Present on every muster. In Chimborazo Hospital for dibilitis during the Gettysburg campaign. Present at Appomattox.

HAMRICK, Eli, Pvt, B. Enlisted in Guinea Stat on May 7, 1862, at age 24. Captured at the Wilderness May 6, 1864. Died at Elmira prison November 16, 1864.

HAMRICK, Eli O, Pvt, B. Enlisted in Cleveland on February 26, 1863, at age 18. Wounded at Chancellorsville. Captured at Petersburg March 25, 1865. Released from Point Lookout June 28, 1865.

HAMRICK, Elphus, Pvt, F. Enlisted in Cleveland on Sept 17, 1861, at age 25. Present every muster but one (on leave). Captured at Petersburg March 25, 1865. Released from Point Lookout June 27, 1865.

HAMRICK, Greenberry, Pvt, B. Enlisted in Rutherford on Sept 2, 1861, at age 28. Died at Raleigh Jan 18, 1862. Mary Hamrick widow.

HAMRICK, Jabez, Pvt, B. Enlisted after Dec 1864, at age 19. Wounded and captured at Petersburg March 25, 1865. Received a gunshot wound to the ankle. Treated at Lincoln General Hospital in Washington DC. Released June 19, 1865

HAMRICK, Jason, Pvt, B. Enlisted in Rutherford on May 7, 1862, at age 33. Died of Typhoid fever in Richmond September 2, 1862. Widow Sarah Hamrick.

HAMRICK, John, Pvt, C. Enlisted in Rutherford on September 2, 1861, at age 23. Died of Typhoid fever in Raleigh January 15, 1862. Son of Chelsey Hamrick.

HAMRICK, Lewis M, 1Sgt, B. Enlisted as a private in Rutherford on September 2, 1861, at age 22. Promoted to 1Sgt. Died of disease at Guineas Station, VA January 31, 1863.

HANNAH, Levi C, Pvt, K. Enlisted at Camp Holmes on December 3, 1863. Gunshot wound in the back May 1864. Granted a 60-day leave. No records after that.

HANSEL, John P, Pvt, I. Enlisted in Gaston, NC on March 19, 1863, at age 37. Present to December 1864.

HARDESTER, James, Pvt, K. Enlisted in Troy NC on March 5, 1863, at age 38. Killed in action at Chancellorsville.

HARDIN, Benjamin K, Pvt, F. Enlisted in Cleveland on September 17, 1861, at age 22. Killed in action at Gaines's Mill, son of Martha Hardin.

HARDIN, John H, Pvt, F. Enlisted in Cleveland on September 17, 1861, at age 21. Born Chester, SC. Accounted for on every muster. Deserted from Petersburg February 26, 1865. Took oath and went to Oil City, PA on public works.

HARDIN, William L, Pvt, F. Enlisted in Cleveland on September 17, 1861, at age 19. Born Chester, SC, Killed at Gaines's Mill, son of Elizabeth Hardin.

HARGROVES, Willis W, Sgt. Enlisted in Portsmouth on April 20, 1862. Present on every muster of enlistment. Present at Appomattox.

HARMON, John W, Pvt, H. Enlisted at Camp Holmes on April 10, 1864. Captured and paroled at Burkesville Junction April 1865.

HARRELSON, William O, Cpt, E. Enlisted as a private in Lincolnton on September 11, 1861, at age 31. Elected April 18, 1862. Wounded and captured at Gaines's Mill and paroled after a brief confinement. Resigned his commission December 13, 1862, due to disability.

HARRILL, David, Pvt, B. Enlisted in Rutherford on September 2, 1861, at age 19. Accounted for every muster. Captured at Petersburg March 25, 1865, released from Point Lookout June 28, 1865.

HARRILL, David B, 1Lt, B. Enlisted in Rutherford on September 2, 1861, at age 25. Present every muster. Captured at Fredericksburg May 3, 1863. Exchanged May 10th. Present at Appomattox.

HARRILL, Drury, Pvt, B. Enlisted in Rutherford on May 17, 1862, at age 16 as a Substitute. Killed at Mechanicsville. Son of James A Harrill.

HARRILL, George, Pvt, B. Enlisted in Rutherford on September 2, 1861, at age 20. Died at Goldsboro January 18, 1862. Son of Amos Harrill.

HARRILL, James A, Pvt, B. Enlisted at Camp Holmes on May 27, 1864. Enlisted after December 1864. Present at Appomattox.

HARRILL, John, Pvt, B. Enlisted in Rutherford on September 2, 1861, at age 23. Discharged July 13, 1862, due to disability.

HARRILL, John H, Pvt, B. Enlisted on September 1, 1864, at age 48. Brother of David B. Harrill. Had served in the Cherokee war. Present at Appomattox.

HARRILL, John T, Pvt, B. Enlisted at Camp Holmes on June 29, 1864. Captured at Sutherland Station. Released from Harts Island NY June 18, 1865.

HARRILL, Nathaniel S, Pvt, B. Enlisted in Raleigh on April 20, 1864. Present at Appomattox.

HARRILL, Robert M, Sgt, C. Enlisted in Rutherford on September 2, 1861, at age 25. Miller. Present every muster until wounded June 22, 1864. Furloughed to Cherryville Sept 17, 1864. No records after that.

HARRILL, William H, 1Lt, B. Enlisted as 1Sgt in Rutherford on September 2, 1861, at age 30. Elected 1Lt April 18, 1862. Resigned due to disability September 1, 1862.

HARRIS, Burrel B, Pvt, I. Enlisted in Cleveland on April 1, 1864. Present at Appomattox.

HARRIS, Charles G, Cpl, K. Enlisted in Troy NC on September 9, 1861, at age 22. Died of Typhoid August 22, 1862, son of E T Harris.
HARRIS, George, Pvt, A. Enlisted after December 1864. In the hospital March 27, 1865. Paroled by 20 NY Cavalry April 27, 1865.
HARRIS, Nimrod, Pvt, I. Enlisted in Rutherford on October 6, 1861, at age 20. Born Spartanburg SC. Present every muster of his enlistment but one (sick). Died of disease March 25, 1864.
HARRIS, Romulus G, Pvt, H. Enlisted in Shelby on October 1, 1861, at age 18. Died of small pox March 29, 1863, in Petersburg, VA. Son of Robert W Harris.
HARRIS, Samuel, Pvt, K. Enlisted in Troy NC on September 9, 1861, at age 46. Discharged July 1862, due to disability.
HARRIS, William, Pvt, I. Enlisted in Rutherford on October 6, 1861, at age 36. Discharged by Mistake-ordered back to duty December 8, 1862 but did not return.
HARRISON, James, Pvt, I. Enlisted at Camp Vance on May 15, 1864. Resident of Rutherford County. Captured at Petersburg March 25, 1865. Confined at Point Lookout. Took the oath June 27, 1865, hospitalized and released from Hammond Hospital July 13, 1865.
HART, Robert N, Pvt, D. Enlisted in Rowan on September 9, 1861, at age 20. Accounted for every muster. Wounded May or June 1864. Returned to duty. Deserted at Petersburg February 16, 1865. Took the oath and transferred to White Co, Ill on public works.
HARTNESS, Milus M, Pvt, D. Enlisted April 12, 1864, at age 18. Captured at the Wilderness and confined at Point Lookout. Joined US Army June 1, 1864. Served in 1st US Volunteers in Dakota Territory. Promoted to Sergeant but reduced to private. Died November 21, 1864, of dysentery at Fort Rice Dakota.
HARTZOG, Abel C, Ensg, E. Enlisted in Lincolnton on September 11, 1861, at age 19. Present on every muster. Captured at Chancellorsville and paroled after a short confinement in Washington DC. Promoted to Ensign October 24, 1864. Color bearer. Present for the surrender at Appomattox.
HARTZOG, Cephus, Pvt, E. Enlisted in Lincolnton on September 11, 1861, at age 21. Killed in action at Gaines's Mill.
HARVEL, Mark, Pvt, K. Enlisted in Troy NC on September 9, 1861, at age 49. Discharged April 16, 1862, due to disability.
HARVIL, William, Pvt, D. Enlisted in Rowan on September 9, 1861, at age 38. Died in 1862, of wounds received at the Seven Days Battles. Date unknown.
HASSELL, John W, Pvt, K. Enlisted at Camp Holmes on June 25, 1864. Deserted July 11, 1864.

HATLEY, Joseph, Pvt, A. Enlisted at Camp Holmes on August 27, 1864. Resident of Stanley Co, NC. Captured at Petersburg April 2, 1865. Released from Point Lookout June 27, 1865.

HAWKINS, G M, Pvt, I. Enlisted in Cleveland on February 26, 1863, at age 40. Deserted at Lynchburg June 12, 1863.

HAWKINS, James B, Pvt, I. Enlisted in Cleveland on February 26, 1863, at age 23. Received a gunshot wound to the elbow at Chancellorsville. Returned to duty in February 1864. Present at Appomattox.

HAYES, Samuel L, Pvt, G. Enlisted in Charlotte on November 1, 1861, at age 26. Present every muster of enlistment. Born in Union SC, Resident of Mountain Island, Gaston NC. Wounded at Chancellorsville. Returned to duty and was killed June 22, 1864.

HAYES, Samuel L, Pvt, G. Enlisted in Mecklenburg on May 4, 1862, at age 60. Substitute. Granted a 60-day furlough in December 1862, no record after that.

HAYES, Soloman, Pvt, G. Enlisted in Guinea Station on May 4, 1862, at age 59. Born in Union SC. Absent sick every muster. Discharged for disability April 12, 1864.

HAYNES, John C, Pvt, F. Joined the regiment after December 1864. Present at Appomattox.

HAYS, Thomas, Pvt, I. Enlisted in Rutherford on October 6, 1861, at age 26. Accounted for on every muster. Hospitalized 1 April 5, 1865, with a fever.

HAZELWOOD, Asa, Pvt, I. Enlisted in Stokes on April 5, 1864, at age 32. Conscript. Born in Patrick County, VA, resident of Stokes County, NC. Captured at North Anna, died at Point Lookout July 4, 1864, of measles. Son of Edward Hazelwood. Widow Rachael Hazelwood. Had six children.

HEARN, Noah, Pvt, K. Enlisted after December 1864. Captured at Ream's Station and released from Point Lookout June 13, 1865.

HEARN, Thomas W, Pvt, K. Enlisted after December 1864. Captured at Petersburg March 25, 1865. Released at Pt Lookout May 13, 1865.

HEARN, William F, Pvt, K. Enlisted at Camp Orange on April 2, 1864. Captured at Petersburg March 25, 1865. Released from Point Lookout June 27, 1865.

HEAVNER, Franklin A, Sgt, E. Enlisted in Lincolnton on September 11, 1861, at age 30. Died of disease March 11, 1862, at Hamilton.

HEAVNER, Marcus L, Cpl, E. Enlisted in Lincolnton on September 11, 1861, at age 23. Wounded at Gaines's Mill. Captured at Gettysburg. Exchanged from Point Lookout February 18, 1865, on roll of exchanged prisoners at Camp Lee in Richmond.

HEAVNER, Peter, Pvt, E. Enlisted in Gaston, NC on March 5, 1863, at age 35. Gaston County resident. Teamster. Present every muster but one (sick). Wounded at Chancellorsville. Returned to duty and was Present at Appomattox.

HEAVNER, Solomon, Pvt, H. Enlisted at Camp Holmes on April 20, 1864. Absent sick since April 1864, no further records.

HEDGEPETH, George, Pvt, E. Enlisted in Lincolnton on September 11, 1861, at age 33. Wounded at Gaines's Mill. Discharged by Mistake-ordered back to duty December 8, 1862 but did not return.

HELMS, Alexander, Pvt, E. Enlisted in Lincolnton on September 11, 1861, at age 22. Arm amputated due to a gunshot wound received in the Seven Days battles. Disability Discharge granted August 21, 1862.

HENDERSON, George, Pvt, K. Enlisted after December 1864. Deserted from Petersburg March 20, 1865. Took the oath and transferred to Pittsburgh on public works.

HENDERSON, James, Cpl, I. Enlisted in Rutherford on October 6, 1861, at age 21. Present on every muster. Present to November 1864, with no record after that.

HENDERSON, James F, Sgt, C. Enlisted in Rutherford on September 2, 1861, at age 22. Wounded at Fredericksburg (contusion of the right hip from a shell). Wounded again in in September 1864. Captured at Petersburg March 25, 1865. Released from Pt Lookout June 27, 1865.

HENDERSON, Joel G, Pvt, K. Enlisted in Troy NC on March 12, 1864. Transferred from the 28th NC. Deserted at Petersburg March 19, 1865. Transported to Pittsburgh.

HENDRICK, Bedford, Sgt, F. Enlisted in Cleveland on September 17, 1861, at age 26. Captured at Brandy Station August 1, 1863. Exchanged from Point Lookout March 17, 1864. Captured again at Hatchers Run April 2, 1865, released from Point Lookout June 6, 1865.

HENDRICK, James A, Pvt, F. Enlisted at Camp Holmes on August 12, 1864. Captured at the Southside Railroad April 1, 1865. Released from Harts Island June 19, 1865.

HENDRICK, John W, Pvt, F. Enlisted in Cleveland on September 11, 1861, at age 17. Died Nov 21, 1862, of wounds received at Ox Hill.

HENSDALE, Charles C, Pvt, I. Enlisted in Rutherford on October 6, 1861, at age 22. Born New Jersey. Wounded at Chancellorsville. Reduced to Pvt. for extended absence after wounded furlough. Returned by February 1864 and present the remaining musters. Captured near Appomattox April 3, 1865 and was released from Point Lookout June 14, 1865.

HENSLEY, Stephen A, Pvt, C. Enlisted in Rutherford on September 2, 1861, at age 22. Accounted for on every muster. Reduced in rank for straggling August 1864. Captured at Petersburg March 25, 1865. Released from Point Lookout June 3, 1865.

HENSON, Elias J, Pvt, I. Enlisted at Camp Vance on May 15, 1864. Captured at the Southside Railroad April 2, 1865. Released from Harts Island June 17, 1865.

HENSON, James G, Pvt, I. Enlisted in Rutherford on July 9, 1863. Captured at Falling Waters. Exchanged March 1864. Present in December 1864.

HENSON, John P, Cpl, I. Enlisted in Rutherford on October 6, 1861, at age 18. Accounted for every muster. Wounded May 1864, (Gunshot wound right thigh). Present to November 1864.

HENSON, Joseph Calaway, Pvt, I. Enlisted in Rutherford on July 9, 1863. Captured at Falling Waters and exchanged March 17, 1864. Returned to duty and was Present at Appomattox. Accounted for on every muster.

HENSON, Phillip J, Pvt, I. Enlisted in Rutherford on October 6, 1861, at age 17. Wounded and captured at Gettysburg. Confined at David's Island, NY. Exchanged September 16, 1863. Returned to duty and was present till December 1864.

HESTER, James M, Pvt, I. Enlisted in Rutherford on October 6, 1861, at age 36. Discharged by mistake in December 1862. Did not return.

HESTER, Jason, Cpl, I. Enlisted in Rutherford on October 6, 1861, at age 30. Born Polk, NC. Died of disease March 20, 1863, in Richmond.

HESTER, John, Pvt, I. Enlisted in Rutherford on October 6, 1861, at age 35. Born Polk, NC. Discharged July 15, 1862, due to disability.

HIATT, C W, Pvt, Enlisted in Aug 1864. Resident of Forsyth County. Deserted to the enemy Aug 16, 1864. Released from Louisville, KY. Agreed to remain north of Ohio river for the duration of the war.

HICKS, C Greenburg, Pvt, C. Enlisted at Camp Holmes on September 25, 1864. Deserted at Petersburg, March 5, 1865. Took the oath and was sent to Chattanooga, TN.

HICKS, Calvin, Pvt, K. Enlisted in Troy NC on September 9, 1861, at age 37. Died of disease at Goldsboro March 1862.

HICKS, Littleberry, Pvt, K. Enlisted in Troy NC on September 9, 1861, at age 37. 6'4" tall, Died July 12, 1862, of wounds received at Gaines's Mill. Widow Londy Hicks.

HICKS, Riley B, Pvt, K. Enlisted in Troy NC on September 9, 1861, at age 23. Died of disease May 10, 1862. Nancy A Hicks widow.

HIGGINS, Mills A, Pvt, C. Enlisted in Rutherford on September 2, 1861, at age 26. Born in McDowell, NC. Detailed to take a body home April 13, 1862. Killed in action at Gettysburg July 1, 1863. Son of John Higgins. Married Mary Elliott in 1854. They had four children.

HILL, David N, Pvt, C. Enlisted in Rutherford on Sept 2, 1861, at age 23. Died of disease April 20, 1862.
HILL, James, Pvt, C. Enlisted at Camp Vance on May 13, 1864. Captured at the Southside Railroad April 2, 1865. Confined at Harts Island until June 17, 1865.
HILL, James H, Sgt, E. Enlisted in Lincolnton on September 11, 1861, at age 20. Plasterer. Died of wounds received at Gaines's Mill, exact date unknown.
HILL, John F, Cpt, E. Enlisted in Lincolnton on September 11, 1861, at age 44. Resigned July 18, 1862, due to disability.
HILL, John F, Pvt, K. Enlisted at Camp Holmes on May 23, 1863. Died of disease May 4, 1864.
HILL, Reubin R, Pvt, C. Enlisted at Camp Vance on May 13, 1864. Captured in Jackson Hosp Richmond April 3, 1865, died June 3, 1865.
HILL, William, Pvt, K. Enlisted at Camp Holmes on July 6, 1864. Hospitalized December 1864. 60-day furlough. No further records.
HINSHAW, Minus, Pvt, K. Enlisted at Camp Holmes on May 21, 1864. Deserted June 15, 1864.
HIPP, Andrew, Pvt, G. Enlisted in Charlotte on September 30, 1861, at age 43. Died of disease November 22, 1862.
HIPP, John, Pvt, G. Enlisted in Charlotte on September 30, 1861. Died at Raleigh January 24, 1862, of Meningitis.
HIPP, John M, Pvt, G. Enlisted in Charlotte on March 1, 1863, at age 37. Accounted for every muster of enlistment. Wounded May 21, 1864. Returned and was present at Appomattox.
HIPP, Pinkney, Pvt, G. Enlisted in Charlotte on September 30, 1861, at age 33. Died of disease November 25, 1862.
HIPP, William, Pvt, G. Enlisted in Charlotte on September 30, 1861, at age 22. Accounted for every muster except one AWOL. Captured at North Anna, exchanged from Point Lookout March 14, 1865.
HODGE, John, Pvt, I. Enlisted in Rutherford on July 9, 1863. Captured at Falling Waters, confined at Point Lookout. Exchanged August 1864, present in December 1864. No record after that.
HODGINS, John M, Pvt, D. Enlisted in Rowan on September 9, 1861, at age 32. Born in Iredell Co. Mechanic. Wounded and captured at Gettysburg, left leg amputated. Paroled and retired to invalid corps August 18, 1864.
HOEY, Samuel A, Cpt, H. Enlisted in Shelby on October 1, 1861, at age 21. Druggist. Born in Union, SC. Resigned his commission February 10, 1863.
HOGAN, Archibald B, Pvt, K. Enlisted in Troy NC on September 9, 1861, at age 23. Died May 15, 1863, of wounds received at Chancellorsville.

HOGAN, Calvin, Pvt, K. Enlisted in Troy NC on September 9, 1861, at age 26. Sent to hospital August 1862, from Orange Courthouse. "Supposed to be dead".

HOGAN, John W, Sgt, K. Enlisted in Troy NC on September 9, 1861, at age 31. Fell out September 1, 1862. Died of disease September 28, 1862. His death was not known by the regiment until April 1863. Widow Ann Hogan.

HOGAN, Joseph, Pvt, K. Enlisted in Troy NC on September 9, 1861, at age 38. Badge of Distinction at Chancellorsville. Deserted August 14,1863, to November 25, 1863, and placed in guard house. Four months wages stopped by court martial. Present through 1864. Deserted at Petersburg March 13, 1865, took oath and went to NY City.

HOGUE, Jacob A, 1Lt, F. Enlisted as a Sgt in Cleveland on Sept 17, 1861, at age 36. Married Jane E. Borders in 1853. Elected Lieutenant April 18, 1862. Wounded at Gettysburg. Captured April 3, 1865, at Amelia Courthouse. Released at Johnson's Island, OH June 18, 1865.

HOLAWAY, John, Pvt, A. Enlisted in Ashe Co on October 10, 1861, at age 34. Killed in action at Frayser's Farm.

HOLAWAY, Martin, Pvt, A. Enlisted in Ashe Co on August 10, 1861, at age 24. Died February 20, 1862, of disease at Raleigh.

HOLIFIELD, Jacob, Pvt, B. Enlisted in Rutherford on September 2, 1861, at age 16. AWOL part of 1862. Returned to duty. Present on each muster until deserting September 17, 1863.

HOLLAND, F M, Pvt, B. Enlisted in Raleigh on April 10, 1864. Killed in action June 13, 1864.

HOLLY, Daniel Cephas, Pvt, E. Enlisted at Camp Gregg on March 8, 1863, at age 18. Lincoln County resident. Accounted for each muster of enlistment. Captured at Southside Railroad. Released from Hart's Island June 6, 1865.

HOLLY, Marcus A, Sgt, E. Enlisted in Lincolnton on September 11, 1861, at age 22. Miller. Accounted for each muster. Captured at Gettysburg, exchanged February 18, 1865. Returned to duty and was present at Appomattox.

HONEYCUT, Dillard, Pvt, I. Enlisted in Rutherford on May 29, 1863, at age 24. Transferred in from the 16th NC. Listed absent/sick most musters. Present in December 1864. No record after that.

HONEYCUT, Marion, Pvt, I. Enlisted in Rutherford on Oct 6, 1861, at age 20. Born in Wake, NC. Killed at Chancellorsville.

HOOVER, Andrew B, Pvt, G. Enlisted in Charlotte on September 30, 1861, at age 20. Teamster. Present on every muster. Captured at Petersburg March 25, 1865. Held at Point Lookout until June 13, 1865.

HOOVER, David W, Pvt, G. Enlisted in Charlotte on September 30, 1861, at age 21. Wounded in the left leg June of 1862. Died April 15, 1863, of disease, son of Alfred Hoover.

HOOVER, Michael M, Pvt, E. Enlisted in Lincolnton on September 11, 1861, at age 21. Died at Goldsboro April 4, 1862, of disease.

HOOVER, Timothy A, Pvt, E. Enlisted in Lincolnton on September 11, 1861, at age 19. Died at Richmond August 4, 1862, of disease.

HOPPER, John A M, Pvt, I. Enlisted in Rutherford on October 6, 1861, at age 37. Discharged May 24, 1862, due to disability. Returned late in the war. Was present in November 1864.

HOPPER, Lansford M, Pvt, I. Enlisted in Cleveland on November 26, 1864. Cleveland County resident. Captured at Petersburg March 25, 1865. Confined at Point Lookout until June 28, 1865.

HOPPER, Romulas M, 2Lt, H. Enlisted in Charleston SC on January 1863, at age 21. Transferred from the 15th NC Oct 1862. Accounted for every muster of enlistment. Slight wound at Malvern Hill. Promoted to 2Lt commanding Company A October 1864. Present at Appomattox.

HOPPER, William V, Pvt, H. Enlisted in Shelby on October 1, 1861, at age 24. Wounded at Gaines's Mill. Died of Typhoid January 1863, Lucy Hopper widow.

HOUCK, William A, Lt. Colonel. Enlisted in Rowan on Sept 9, 1861, at age 35. Enlisted as a captain. Failed reelection April 18, 1862.

HOUSE, Emanuel, 2Lt, E. Enlisted in Lincolnton on September 11, 1861, at age 20. Enlisted as a private. Promoted to Sergeant in May 1862, and 2Lt May 3, 1863. Received a leg wound in May 1864. Present every muster but one (leave). Granted a leave of indulgence February 1865, no record after that.

HOVIS, Daniel, Pvt, E. Enlisted in Lincolnton on May 1, 1862, at age 28. Killed in action at Chancellorsville.

HOVIS, George, Pvt, D. Enlisted at Camp Holmes on October 3, 1864. Wounded and admitted to the hospital in Richmond March 28, 1865, (Gunshot wound to the face). No record after that.

HOVIS, Malachi, Cpl, E. Enlisted in Lincolnton on September 11, 1861, at age 18. Present on every muster. Present in December 1864. No record after that.

HOVIS, Moses S, Pvt, G. Enlisted in Lincolnton on March 12, 1863, at age 28. Wounded at Chancellorsville. Temporary guard duty at Salisbury. Returned by April 1864, and present rest of the year. Present at Appomattox.

HOWELL, John, Pvt, H. Enlisted in Shelby on October 1, 1861, at age 18. Killed in action at Mechanicsville. Son of Thomas Howell.

HOWELL, John T, 2Sgt, H. Enlisted in Shelby on October 1, 1861, at age 19. Present every muster except two (leaves granted). Promoted to 2Sgt January 1, 1864. Present at Appomattox.

HOWELL, William, Pvt, H. Enlisted at Camp Holmes on March 11, 1864, at age 20. Accounted for each muster. Present at Appomattox.

HOYLE, Benjamin M, Pvt, F. Enlisted in Cleveland on September 17, 1861, at age 26. Son of David and Betsy Hoyle. Left leg amputated for wounds received at Gaines's Mill. Applied for an artificial limb. Disability discharged granted February 1865. Received assistance from the Association for the Relief of Maimed Soldiers. Benjamin was called to preach during the religious revivals in the southern army. Went into the ministry after the war.

HOYLE, David R, Cpt, F. Enlisted in Cleveland on September 17, 1861, at age 31. Millwright. Brother of Maxwell Hoyle. Wounded at Ellerson's Mill. Present every muster. Promoted to Captain June 28, 1862. Resigned Sept 28, 1864. Married Mary D. Elliott in May 1865.

HOYLE, Henry, Pvt, F. Enlisted in Cleveland on September 17, 1861, at age 23. Died June 28, 1862, of wounds received at Gaines's Mill.

HOYLE, Jonas C, Pvt, E. Enlisted in Lincolnton on September 11, 1861, at age 28. Son of Burrell and Mary Hoyle. Present or detached duty every muster. Gunshot wound to the side in December 1862. Detached as a teamster in the Medical Purveyor's Department from 1863, on. Deserted from Petersburg March 18, 1865, took the oath and went to Philadelphia on public works.

HOYLE, Martin S, Pvt, F. Enlisted in Cleveland on February 22, 1863, at age 37. Son of Martin S. Hoyle and Mary Carpenter. Captured at Falling Waters. Confined at Point Lookout until February 24, 1865.

HOYLE, Maxwell H, Sgt, F. Enlisted in Cleveland on September 17, 1861, at age 20. Accounted for every muster. Wounded in May 1864. Present in November 1864. Went home due to wounds. Became a minister after the war.

HOYLE, Samuel, Pvt, E. Enlisted in Lincolnton on August 31, 1861, at age 21. Son of Burrell and Mary Hoyle. Transferred from the 49th NC in exchange for Thomas H Baxter. Wounded and captured at Gettysburg. Treated at Chester, PA Hospital. Exchanged September 17, 1863, and retired to the Invalid Corps.

HUDGINS, James H, Pvt, C. Enlisted in Rutherford on September 2, 1861, at age 18. Captured at Brandy Station, died February 14, 1864, at Point Lookout.

HUDSON, Wesley, Pvt, K. Enlisted in Troy NC on September 9, 1861, at age 26. Died September 3, 1862, of Typhoid in a hospital in Culpeper VA.

HUDSON, Wilborn, Pvt, K. Enlisted in Troy NC on September 9, 1861, at age 26. Killed in action at Fredericksburg December 13, 1862.

HUFFSTETER, David R, Pvt, H. Enlisted at Camp Holmes on April 10, 1864. Present at Appomattox.

HUGHES, James R, Pvt, K. Enlisted in Troy NC on September 9, 1861, at age 33. Resident of Davidson County. Was present every muster but one (leave). Wounded at Ox Hill. Deserted at Petersburg February 11, 1865. Took the oath and was sent to Philadelphia.

HUGHES, Timons J, Cpl, H. Enlisted in Shelby on October 1, 1861, at age 20. Present every muster but one (leave). Captured at Petersburg March 25, 1865. Released from Point Lookout June 6, 1865. In hospital at Farmville until June 20, 1865.

HUGHES, Toliver, Pvt, I. Enlisted in Rutherford on November 10, 1861, at age 31. Died at home in Rutherford County April 17, 1862.

HULL, Marcus M, Pvt, E. Enlisted in Lincolnton on September 11, 1861, at age 18. Wounded at Chancellorsville. Present every muster but one (wounded). Deserted from Petersburg March 7, 1865, took the oath and went to Philadelphia on public works.

HULL, William, Pvt, D. Enlisted at Camp Holmes on October 23, 1864. For Oct/Nov 1864, was "Present in arrest." No other records.

HULLENDER, D D, Pvt, H. Enlisted in Shelby on Oct 1, 1861, at age 21. Furloughed Aug 2, 1862 for sickness, deserted and joined CS Navy.

HULLET, Peter, Pvt, E. Enlisted in Lincolnton on Sept 11, 1861, at age 53. From Gaston County. Disability discharge April 16, 1862.

HUMPHRIES, B B, Pvt, I. Enlisted in Cleveland on April 10, 1864. Died in the hospital in Richmond July 9, 1864.

HUMPHRIES, Henry L, Pvt, I. Enlisted in Cleveland on April 10, 1864. Resident of Cleveland County. Captured at Hatchers Run April 2, 1865. Confined at Point Lookout until June 13, 1865.

HUMPHRIES, Lewis, Pvt, I. Enlisted in Cleveland on April 10, 1864. Present at Appomattox.,

HUNTER, Jonathan, Pvt, C. Enlisted in Rutherford on September 2, 1861, at age 44. Dropped from the rolls August 11, 1863, for AWOL.

HUNTLEY, George J, 2Lt, I. Enlisted as a Sgt in Rutherford on November 10, 1861, at age 21. Recognized for bravery at Chancellorsville and promoted to 2Lt. Died July 2, 1863, of wounds received the first day at Gettysburg.

HUNTSINGER, John L, Pvt, B. Enlisted in Rutherford on September 2, 1861, at age 22. Died July 15, 1862, of wounds received at Frayser's Farm. Son of Catherine Huntsinger.

HURLEY, Alfred H, 2Lt, K. Enlisted as a private in Troy NC on September 9, 1861, at age 23. Elected April 18, 1862. Died July 4, 1862, of wounds received at the Seven Days battles.

HURLEY, Armstead, Pvt, K. Enlisted in Troy NC on March 5, 1863, at age 37. Deserted May 16, 1863. In arrest May 20, 1863. No record after that. Paroled at Troy May 22, 1865.

HURLEY, Caswell D, Pvt, K. Enlisted in Troy NC on September 9, 1861, at age 19. Died March 8, 1862, of disease at Williamston, NC.

HURLEY, Freeman, Pvt, K. Enlisted in Troy NC on September 9, 1861, at age 20. Wounded in both thighs at Gaines's Mill. Captured at Gettysburg and died at Ft. Delaware October 3, 1863.

HURLEY, G F, Pvt, K. Enlisted after December 1864. Resident of Montgomery County. Captured at Sutherland Station April 2, 1865, released at Harts Island, June 6, 1865.

HURLEY, Nathan, Pvt, K. Enlisted in Troy NC on September 9, 1861, at age 22. Killed in action June 30, 1862, at Frayser's Farm.

HURLEY, Oran L, Pvt, K. Enlisted in Troy NC on September 9, 1861, at age 22. Killed in action June 26, 1862, at Mechanicsville.

HURLEY, Pleasant C, Pvt, K. Enlisted in Troy NC on September 9, 1861, at age 18. On duty each muster. Ordnance Teamster. Deserted from Petersburg March 9, 1865. Took the oath and was sent to Washington DC.

HURLEY, Willis, Pvt, K. Enlisted in Troy NC on September 9, 1861, at age 47. Court martialed for stealing coffee in February 1862 and sentenced to hard labor at the Richmond fortifications. Was granted a disability discharge in October 1862.

HUSS, Joseph H, Sgt, E. Enlisted in Lincolnton on September 11, 1861, at age 19. Killed at Gettysburg. Son of David Huss.

HUSS, Pinkney M, Pvt, E. Enlisted at Camp Gregg on March 18, 1863, at age 18. Accounted for every muster of enlistment but one (AWOL). Present at Appomattox.

HUTCHISON, Scott B, Cpl, G. Enlisted in Charlotte on Sept 30, 1861, at age 34. Discharged by mistake in December 1862. Returned to duty. Present on every muster but one (sick). Present at Appomattox.

HUTSON, John, Pvt, I. Enlisted at Camp Vance on September 2, 1864. Present at Appomattox.

IRVIN, Abram C, Pvt, F. Enlisted in Cleveland on September 17, 1861, at age 18. Wounded at Gaines's Mill. Captured at Gettysburg and confined at Point Lookout. Exchanged February 1865 was at Camp Lee in Richmond February 18, 1865.

JACKSON, Silas, Pvt, G. Enlisted on July 15, 1864, at age 36. Deserted to the enemy August 4, 1864.

JACKSON, William W, Pvt, I. Enlisted at Camp Holmes on June 22, 1864. Present to November 1864.

JAMES, Robert G, Sgt, B. Enlisted in Rutherford on September 2, 1861, at age 24. Born Carmel GA. Wounded and captured at

Gettysburg, confined at Point Lookout. Exchanged March 6, 1864 and hospitalized in Richmond. Returned to duty and was captured at Petersburg April 3, 1865. Treated at David's Island, NY for Typhoid, and released from Harts Island July 31, 1865.

JAMISON, Milas Stanhope, Cpl, D. Enlisted in Rowan on September 9, 1861, at age 39. Discharged December 7, 1862, due to age. Reenlisted March 4, 1864 and was present at Appomattox.

JARRETT, Samuel, Pvt, G. Enlisted in Lincolnton on March 12, 1863, at age 38. Killed in Action May 21, 1864.

JARRIL, Doctor J, Pvt, C. Enlisted in Rutherford on September 2, 1861, at age 23. Discharged January 8,1862.

JENKINS, Eli, Pvt, I. Enlisted in Gaston, NC on March 5, 1863, at age 37. Captured at Gettysburg, exchanged September 16, 1863, from David's Island, NY. Returned to duty and was captured in the hospital at Petersburg April 3, 1865. Released April 21, 1865.

JENKINS, Henry, 1Lt, I. Enlisted as a private in Rutherford on October 6, 1861, at age 31. Promoted to 1Lt. Present every muster. Wounded at Gettysburg. Was present at Appomattox.

JENKINS, John, Pvt, I. Enlisted in Rutherford on June 28, 1863. Captured at Gettysburg and confined at Ft Delaware. Joined the US 3rd Maryland Cavalry, deserted at New Orleans March 25, 1864.

JENNINGS, Elijah F, Pvt, A. Enlisted in Ashe Co on August 10, 1861, at age 30. Deserted after April 1862.

JOHNSON, Daniel, Pvt, A. Enlisted in Ashe Co on August 1, 1861, at age 19. Killed in action at Chancellorsville.

JOHNSON, Elisha, Pvt, A. Enlisted in Ashe Co on August 10, 1861, at age 38. Discharged in April 1862, for disability.

JOHNSON, Isaac M, Pvt, G. Enlisted around November 17, 1864. Present at Appomattox.

JOHNSON, John A, Pvt, A. Enlisted in Ashe Co on August 10, 1861, at age 19. Wounded in 1862. Returned October 1863. Deserted February 8, 1864.

JOHNSON, Orrin D, Pvt, D. Enlisted at Camp Holmes on August 26, 1864. Captured at the Southside Railroad. Confined at Island until June 19, 1865.

JOHNSON, Rowland, Pvt, C. Enlisted in Rutherford on September 2, 1861, at age 17. Musician. Discharged due to conscription law September 13, 1862.

JOHNSTON, David H, Pvt, G. Enlisted in Charlotte on Sept 30, 1861, at age 26. Died of wounds July 8, 1862. Son of Thomas T Johnson.

JOHNSTON, Frank E, Pvt, G. Enlisted in Charlotte on September 30, 1861, at age 17. Died Sept 6, 1862, of wounds received at Ox Hill.

JOHNSTON, John T, Pvt, G. Enlisted at Camp Holmes on December 31, 1863. Present each muster of enlistment. Present at Appomattox.
JOHNSTON, Thomas A, Sgt, G. Enlisted in Charlotte on September 30, 1861, at age 27. Promoted to Sgt. September 7, 1862. Was present every muster until he was wounded at the Wilderness May 5, 1864. Returned to duty and was present at Appomattox.
JOLLY, James, Pvt, I. Enlisted in Cleveland on April 10, 1864. Wounded in late May 1864, granted a 30-day furlough. Did not return.
JONAS, John, Pvt, E. Enlisted in Lincolnton on September 11, 1861, at age 43. Discharged December 8, 1862, due to age, per conscription law. Later served in the 4th NC Senior Reserves.
JONES, John A, Pvt, A. Enlisted at Camp Holmes on September 6, 1864. Hospitalized and furloughed in December 1864. Did not return.
JONES, Starling, Pvt, B. Enlisted in Rutherford on September 2, 1861, at age 39. Discharged July 13, 1862, due to disability.
JONES, William A, Pvt, B. Enlisted in Cleveland on February 26, 1863, at age 36. Conscript. Present each muster of enlistment. Wounded at Chancellorsville. Was present at Appomattox.
JONES, William L, Pvt, I. Enlisted in Rutherford on October 6, 1861, at age 38. Wounded Frayser's Farm. Discharged Dec 8, 1862 for age.
JORDAN, Samuel H, Pvt, G. Enlisted at Camp Holmes on August 10, 1862. Captured at Sutherland Station April 2, 1865. Confined at Point Lookout until June 28, 1865.
JUSTICE, B F, Pvt, H. Enlisted at Camp Holmes on April 20, 1864. Wounded May/June 1864. Paroled Burkesville Junction April 14, 1865.
KANADY, Edward D, Pvt, I. Enlisted in Rutherford on May 5, 1864. Missing in Action from May 5, 1864.
KANE, Z, Pvt, Enlisted around May 3, 1863. Captured at Fredericksburg May 4, 1863. Exchanged May 10th at City Point, VA. No further records.
KANEDY, Joseph D, Pvt, I. Enlisted in Rutherford on October 6, 1861, at age 18. Wounded during the Seven Days battles. Absent sick most musters. Wounded and captured at Gettysburg. Confined at Ft Delaware until June 8, 1865.
KEETER, George F, Pvt, C. Enlisted in Rutherford on September 2, 1861, at age 21. Died December 12, 1862, near Guinea Station, VA.
KEETER, George R, Pvt, C. Enlisted in Rutherford on September 2, 1861, at age 24. Killed in action at Gaines's Mill.
KEETER, Henry, Pvt, C. Enlisted in Rutherford on September 2, 1861, at age 17. Wounded and captured at Gettysburg. Exchanged from Pt Lookout April 27, 1864. Retired to the Invalid corps Jan 7, 1865.

KEETER, William M, Cpl, C. Enlisted in Rutherford on September 2, 1861, at age 36. Discharged by Mistake and ordered back to duty in December 1862. Did not return.

KEEVER, Alexander, Pvt, E. Enlisted in Cleveland on September 25, 1863, at age 41. Present every muster of enlistment. Deserted at Petersburg March 8, 1865. Took the oath and went to Philadelphia.

KEEVER, George P, Pvt, E. Enlisted in Lincolnton on September 11, 1861, at age 26. Wagon maker. Died at Goldsboro March 19, 1862.

KEEVER, James, Pvt, E. Enlisted in Lincolnton on September 11, 1861, at age 25. Accounted for each muster. Captured at the Wilderness. Held at Point Lookout and then Elmira until June 30, 1865.

KELLY, James, Pvt, D. Enlisted in Bertie Co on June 10, 1864. Furloughed September 15, 1864. Did not return.

KENDRICK, John H, Pvt, H. Enlisted at Camp Holmes on April 20, 1864. Present at Appomattox.

KENDRICK, Larkin S, Pvt, F. Enlisted in Cleveland on September 17, 1861, at age 22. Gunshot wound at Fredericksburg shattering the elbow. Absent the rest of the war. Discharged March 11, 1864.

KENDRICK, William, Pvt, H. Enlisted at Camp Holmes on July 28, 1864. Deserted from Petersburg March 3, 1865. Took the oath and transferred to Sterling, Ill on public works.

KENNEDY, Jason C, Pvt, I. Enlisted in Rutherford on October 6, 1861, at age 23. Killed at Mechanicsville June 26, 1862. Son of William Kennedy.

KENNEDY, John, Pvt, I. Enlisted in Rutherford on October 6, 1861, at age 18. Accounted for each muster. Deserted August 5, 1862. Received 30 lashes in January 1863. Paroled at Newton NC April 19, 1865.

KENNEDY, Robert, Pvt, I. Enlisted in Mecklenburg on March 7, 1864. Present each muster. Paroled at Charlotte May 12, 1865.

KENNEDY, Thomas, Pvt, I. Enlisted in Rutherford on October 6, 1861, at age 30. Present every muster but one (leave). Deserted August 5, 1862. Received 30 lashes in January 1863, Present in Dec 1864.

KILPATRICK, William A, Sgt, D. Enlisted in Rowan on September 9, 1861, at age 26. Merchant. Wounded at Chancellorsville. Captured at Falling Waters and died at Point Lookout February 22, 1864.

KIMBREL, James N F, Pvt, I. Enlisted in Rutherford on October 6, 1861, at age 19. Born in Spartanburg. Enlisted with his father, Thomas. Died of disease at Goldsboro February 12, 1862.

KIMBREL, Michael A, Pvt, I. Enlisted in Rutherford on October 6, 1861, at age 24. Born in Spartanburg. Served as a nurse in Goldsboro in February 1862. Died of disease June 18, 1864.

KIMBREL, Thomas, Pvt, I. Enlisted in Rutherford on October 6, 1861, at age 49. Born in Spartanburg. Enlisted with his son, James. Discharged for disability November 15, 1861.

KIME, Wilson, Sgt, K. Enlisted in Troy NC on September 9, 1861, at age 35. Present every muster but October 1864, (on leave). Captured at Sutherland Station. Confined at Point Lookout until June 28, 1865.

KING, Ezekiel, Pvt, G. Enlisted in Charlotte on February 1, 1863, at age 37. Deserted June 1863, to January 1864. Returned and was present each 1864, muster. Present at Appomattox.

KING, Thomas J, Pvt, G. Enlisted in Charlotte on Sept 30, 1861, at age 18. Deserted March 28, 1863, returned by July 1863. Present to Nov 1864. Wounded once. Paroled at Lynchburg April 13, 1865.

KING, Wilkie J, Pvt, I. Enlisted in Rutherford on October 6, 1861, at age 37. Died of disease at Hamilton, NC March 27, 1862.

KISER, Andrew H, Pvt, C. Enlisted at Camp Vance on May 12, 1864. Hospitalized in October 1864. No record of return to service.

KISER, E, Pvt, E. Enlisted in Raleigh on August 6, 1862. Resident of Lincoln County. Deserted at Petersburg January 29, 1865. Took the oath and had transportation furnished to Newbern, NC.

KISER, George, Pvt, E. Enlisted in Gaston, NC on March 5, 1863, at age 36. Gaston County resident. Died May 9, 1863 of wounds received at Chancellorsville.

KISER, Hiram, Pvt, E. Enlisted at Camp Holmes on December 3, 1863. Resident of Gaston County. Present each muster of enlistment except one (sick). Captured at Southside Railroad. Confined at Hart's Island until June 6, 1865.

KISER, Jacob, Pvt, E. Enlisted after December 1864, at age 24. Gaston County resident. Captured at Hatchers Run March 31, 1865. Confined at Hart's Island until June 28, 1865.

KISER, John, Pvt, E. Enlisted in Gaston, NC on March 5, 1863, at age 30. Wounded at Chancellorsville and the Wilderness. Accounted for each muster. Present at Appomattox.

KISER, Robert G, Pvt, H. Enlisted in Shelby on October 1, 1861, at age 16. Born Gaston NC. Deserted April 1863. Arrested and confined until September 1863. Captured at Turkey Hill June 13, 1864. Joined the US Army, 1st U.S. Volunteers at Point Lookout. Mustered out at Fort Leavenworth November 27, 1865.

KISER, Zimri, Pvt, E. Enlisted in Gaston, NC on March 5, 1863, at age 36. Gaston County resident. Sick on two musters, present all the rest. Wounded in June of 1864. Present at Appomattox.

KISTLER, Henry, Pvt, E. Enlisted in Lincolnton on September 11, 1861, at age 25. Died July 29, 1862, of disease at Richmond.

KISTLER, Theo H, Ensg, D. Enlisted in Rowan on September 9, 1861, at age 20. Wounded at Second Manassas and Brandy Station. Accounted for on every muster. Recognized by Col. Lowrance for skill, good bearing, and gallant conduct and promoted to Ensign. Color bearer. Wounded in the abdomen at Jericho Mills and sent by train to Richmond but died on the way. Was buried in Rowan County. Son of Catherine Kistler.
KOONCE, George W, Pvt, A. Enlisted in Ashe Co on August 10, 1861, at age 35. Discharged for disability December 8, 1862.
KOONCE, Hamilton, Sgt, A. Enlisted in Ashe Co on August 10, 1861, at age 18. Promoted to Sgt. Wounded at Chancellorsville and Gettysburg. Captured at North Anna. Exchanged from Point Lookout February 14, 1865.
KOONCE, John, Pvt, A. Enlisted in Orange CH on February 20, 1864. Present each muster of his enlistment. Present at Appomattox.
KOONE, George W, Sgt, C. Enlisted in Rutherford on September 2, 1861, at age 20. Wounded in 1862. Badge of Distinction at Chancellorsville. Received a gunshot wound to the chin at Chancellorsville. Captured at Gettysburg. Died at Point Lookout February 6, 1864.
KOONE, Noah, Pvt, C. Enlisted at Camp Vance on Sept 22, 1863. Captured Petersburg March 25, 1865. Died Pt Lookout May 26, 1865.
KURF, Jacob R, Cpl, D. Enlisted in Rowan on September 9, 1861, at age 19. Accounted for every muster. Wounded at Fredericksburg. Deserted at Petersburg February 16, 1865. Took the oath and was transported to White Co, Ill on public works.
LACKEY, Columbus, Pvt, H. Enlisted at Camp Holmes on April 10, 1864. Died of Typhoid June 1, 1864, in a hospital in Richmond.
LACKEY, Dixon, Pvt, H. Enlisted at Camp Holmes on April 20, 1864. Hospitalized in Danville, VA in May 1864, for wounds. Listed sick or wounded each muster of enlistment.
LANCASTER, Duraspus D, Pvt, I. Enlisted in Rutherford on October 6, 1861, at age 30. Transferred to the 16th NC May 1862. Later died of wound received at Chancellorsville.
LANKFORD, Elberry M, Pvt, B. Enlisted at Camp Holmes on May 27, 1864. Hospitalized in Danville April 3, 1865 for a fever.
LASSITER, Harrison, Pvt, K. Enlisted in Troy NC on September 9, 1861, at age 19. Died at Goldsboro March 10, 1862.
LASSITER, William, Pvt, K. Enlisted in Troy NC on September 9, 1861, at age 21. Died of disease November 26, 1861.
LATHAM, Harvey, Pvt, K. Enlisted in Troy NC on September 9, 1861, at age 26. Deserted September 12, 1862 and did not return to the regiment. Paroled at Troy, NC May 22, 1865.

LATTIMORE, Franklin, Pvt, F. Enlisted at Camp Holmes on April 20, 1864. Brother of James Lattimore. Present each muster of enlistment. Captured at Petersburg April 2, 1865. Confined at Point Lookout until June 29, 1865.

LATTIMORE, James H, Pvt, F. Enlisted in Cleveland on October 5, 1861, at age 20. Teamster. Brother of Frank Lattimore. Held the colors to rally the regiment at the Wilderness and was shot through the shoulder. Returned by October 1864. Present at Appomattox.

LATTIMORE, Jesse R, Pvt, F. Enlisted in Cleveland on October 5, 1861, at age 19. Present on each muster. Present at Appomattox.

LATTIMORE, Thomas D, 2Lt, F. Enlisted as a private in Cleveland on October 5, 1861, at age 17. Promoted to 2nd Lt. July 25, 1862. Present each muster, leave granted Feb 1865. Present at Appomattox.

LAWING, John M, Surgeon. Enlisted in Charlotte on September 30, 1861, at age 25. Assistant Surgeon, Transferred Nov 21, 1861.

LAWING, John M, Cpl, G. Enlisted in Charlotte on September 30, 1861, at age 20. Listed AWOL from November 1863, to September 1864. Died of disease September 25, 1864.

LAWING, John Scott, Pvt, G. Enlisted in Charlotte on September 30, 1861, at age 20. Accounted for on each muster. Wounded in Seven Days battles, Gettysburg, and May 1864. Present at Appomattox.

LAWRENCE, Francis C, Pvt, C. Enlisted in Rutherford on September 2, 1861, at age 17. Died of disease at Hamilton March 20, 1862.

LAWS, James, Pvt, H. Enlisted at Camp Vance on April 20, 1864. Wounded May or June 1864. Listed AWOL October 1864.

LEACH, Archibald A, Sgt, K. Enlisted in Troy NC on September 9, 1861, at age 49. Blacksmith. Died at home of disease March 5, 1863. Deborah Leach widow.

LEACH, Edwin, Pvt, K. Enlisted in Troy NC on September 9, 1861, at age 42. Fell out at Fairfax about September 1, 1862. Listed as died of disease, date unknown.

LEATHERMAN, Jonas, Pvt, E. Enlisted in Lincolnton on September 11, 1861, at age 20. Died of disease October 15, 1862.

LEAZER, William A, Pvt, D. Enlisted in Rowan on September 9, 1861. Listed as deserted December 30, 1862 but was hospitalized at the time. Hospitalized in Huguenot Springs Feb 1863, no record after that.

LEDBETTER, John W, Pvt, C. Enlisted in Rutherford on September 2, 1861, at age 27. Captured at Falling Waters, died at Point Lookout February 28, 1864.

LEDBETTER, William O, Pvt, C. Enlisted in Rutherford on September 2, 1861, at age 21. Died May 24, 1863, of wounds received at Chancellorsville.

LEDWELL, Elwood, Pvt, K. Enlisted in Troy NC on September 9, 1861, at age 40. Discharged in October 1862, due to conscription law.
LEE, Aaron B, Pvt, F. Enlisted in Cleveland on September 17, 1861, at age 19. Captured and paroled at Chancellorsville. Accounted for each muster. Died of Typhoid September 30, 1864.
LEE, Aaron O, Pvt, F. Enlisted in Cleveland on Sept 17, 1861, at age 18. Died of disease at Guinea Station Jan 27, 1863. Son of George Lee.
LEE, John H, Pvt, F. Enlisted in Cleveland on September 17, 1861, at age 24. Captured and paroled at Chancellorsville. On duty each muster but one (sick). Ambulance driver. Deserted Petersburg March of 1865.
LEE, John J, Pvt, F. Enlisted in Cleveland on Sept 17, 1861, at age 23. Died of disease at High Point, NC Nov 26, 1861. Son of George Lee.
LEE, Timmons G, Pvt, F. Enlisted at Camp Holmes on April 10, 1864. Wounded May 1864. Captured at Petersburg March 25, 1865. Released from Point Lookout June 28, 1865.
LEE, William Capers, Pvt, F. Enlisted in Cleveland on November 15, 1863. Deserted at Petersburg February 26, 1865. Took the oath and was transported to Oil City, Pa on public works.
LEE, William Crook, Pvt, F. Enlisted in Cleveland on September 17, 1861, at age 20. Captured at Falling Waters. Exchanged from Point Lookout March 17, 1864. Returned to duty. Deserted at Petersburg February 26, 1865. Took oath and was transported to Oil City, Pa.
LEMASTER, John, Pvt, E. Enlisted in Lincolnton on September 11, 1861, at age 18. Wounded at Gaines's Mill. Wounded and captured at Gettysburg. Treated at Chester, PA and transferred to Pt Lookout. Paroled, at Camp Lee Richmond Feb 18, 1865.
LEONARD, Alpheus, Pvt, D. Enlisted at Camp Holmes on October 23, 1864. Deserted at Petersburg January 8, 1865. Took oath and was transported to Hendricks County, Indiana.
LEVENTHORPE, Collet, Colonel. Rutherford County resident. Elected on October 25, 1861. Physician. Formerly of the British Army. Transferred to 16th NC April 1862.
LEWIS, William, Lt, K. Enlisted in Troy NC on September 9, 1861, at age 37. Trader. Failed reelection and was discharged April 18, 1862.
LINEBARGER, John F, Pvt, I and G. Enlisted in Gaston, NC on March 5, 1863, at age 24. Shoemaker. Present every muster but one (sick). Wounded at Chancellorsville. Present to December 1864.
LINGERFELT, David, Pvt, E. Enlisted in Lincolnton on September 11, 1861, at age 23. Died of pneumonia Jan 16, 1862, at Raleigh.
LITTLETON, Hiram, Pvt, K. Enlisted in Troy NC on March 5, 1863, at age 36. Accounted for every muster of enlistment. Captured at Petersburg March 25, 1865. Confined at Point Lookout.

LOFLIN, James G, Pvt, K. Enlisted around November 5, 1864. Captured and paroled at Burkesville Junction April 1865.
LOFLIN, M C, Pvt, K. Enlisted at Camp Holmes on July 21, 1864. Wounded and in a hospital August 27, 1864. No records after that.
LOFTIS, W M, Pvt, D. Enlisted at Camp Vance on March 24, 1864. Killed in action May 5, 1864.
LONDON, Andrew J, Pvt, F. Enlisted in Cleveland on September 17, 1861, at age 29. Extra duty as a blacksmith. Present every muster but one (leave). Present at Appomattox.
LONDON, Henry, Pvt, C. Enlisted in Rutherford on September 2, 1861, at age 28. Wounded at least once. Accounted for each muster. Present at Appomattox.
LONDON, John Jefferson, Pvt, F. Enlisted in Cleveland on September 17, 1861, at age 18. Severe Gunshot wound to the hand during the Seven Days. Died Dec 26, 1862, of wounds received at Fredericksburg.
LONDON, John N, Pvt, F. Enlisted in Cleveland on September 17, 1861, at age 18. Accounted for every muster. Captured at Petersburg April 2, 1865. Released from Point Lookout June 28, 1865.
LONG, Eli C, Sgt, A. Enlisted in Ashe Co on August 10, 1861, at age 26. Leg wound in the Seven Days' battles. Died May 6, 1863, of wounds received at Chancellorsville.
LONG, Franklin, 2Lt, A. Enlisted as a Sgt. in Ashe Co on August 10, 1861, at age 20. Promoted to 2Lt. Was killed Sept 1, 1862, at Ox Hill.
LONG, Harrison H, Sgt, A. Enlisted in Ashe Co on October 10, 1861, at age 20. Present or on detached service in hospitals each muster. Present in October 1864.
LONG, Henry H, Pvt, E. Enlisted in Raleigh on July 22, 1864. Present at Appomattox.
LONG, Hiram W, Pvt, A. Enlisted in Ashe Co on August 10, 1861, at age 31. Deserted June 27, 1862, to March 1863. Returned and was transferred to Gen. Bragg's Army by Col. Lowrance in April 1863.
LONG, Levi, Pvt, A. Enlisted in Ashe Co on August 10, 1861, at age 20. Gunshot wound to the side at Ox Hill. Did not return from wounded furlough and dropped as a deserter February 8, 1864.
LONG, Martin, Pvt, A. Enlisted in Ashe Co on August 10, 1861, at age 23. Died of disease at Goldsboro March 1, 1862.
LONG, N J, Pvt, H. Enlisted at Camp Holmes on April 20, 1864. Deserted at Petersburg March 18, 1865. Took oath and transferred to Philadelphia.
LONG, Robert, Pvt, E. Enlisted in Lincolnton on September 11, 1861, at age 25. Miller. Wounded in Seven Days battles. Discharged for disability November 22, 1862.

LONG, Robert L, Pvt, H. Enlisted at Camp Stokes on October 26, 1864. Present in November 1864.
LONG, Wilborn, Pvt, A. Enlisted in Ashe Co on August 10, 1861, at age 19. Died in July 1862.
LONG, William, Pvt, H. Enlisted in Shelby on Oct 1, 1861, at age 19. Wounded at Gaines's Mill. Discharged for disability March 18, 1863.
LONG, William M, Pvt, H. Enlisted in Shelby on October 1, 1861, at age 22. Captured at Falling Waters. Confined at Point Lookout. Joined US service May 1, 1864, 1st U.S. Volunteers. Served as a baker and company cook. Mustered out November 27, 1865, at Ft. Leavenworth.
LONGSTON, W P, Pvt, I. Enlisted after December 1864. Captured and paroled at Athens, GA May 8, 1865.
LOOKADOO, George W, Cpl, B. Enlisted in Rutherford on September 2, 1861, at age 29. Died November 3, 1862, of wounds received at Ox Hill. Widow Julia Ann Lookadoo.
LOOKADOO, John, Pvt, B. Enlisted in Rutherford on September 2, 1861, at age 23. Born in McDowell NC. Died September 2, 1862, of disease, Son of George Lookadoo.
LOUDER, Daniel R, Pvt, D. Enlisted in Rowan on September 9, 1861, at age 18. Born Stanley, NC. Was wounded at Ox Hill. Absent the remainder of the war. Retired to the Invalid Corps November 1864. Paroled at Salisbury May 18, 1865.
LOVELACE, Daniel, Pvt, B. Enlisted in Rutherford on September 2, 1861, at age 28. Discharged due to disability February 12, 1863.
LOVETT, Timothy, Pvt, I. Enlisted at Camp Vance on May 7, 1864. Furloughed for sickness July 22, 1864. No further records.
LOWRANCE, Franklin A, Sgt, D. Enlisted in High Point on November 29, 1861, at age 18. Promoted to Sgt. Killed in action at Chancellorsville. Son of John A Lowrance.
LOWRANCE, James C, Pvt, D. Enlisted in Rowan on September 9, 1861, at age 20. Detached to the Pioneer Corps. On duty each muster. Present at Appomattox.
LOWRANCE, Samuel N, Pvt, B. Joined the regiment in Petersburg on December 25, 1864, at age 23. Brother of Col. William L. J. Lowrance. Transferred from the 56th NC. Died at Petersburg on January 2, 1865.
LOWRANCE, William B, Cpt, K. Joined the regiment February 20, 1864. Transferred from 46th NC, Adjunct, Captain in command of Company K October 14, 1864. Present at Appomattox.
LOWRANCE, William L J, Colonel. Enlisted as a lieutenant in Company D in Rowan on September 9, 1861, at age 25. Teacher. Promoted to Colonel September 7, 1862, to replace Col. Riddick. Led the brigade at Gettysburg after July 1st. Led the brigade on multiple

occasions. Granted a leave in February 1865. In the hospital in Mobile Alabama at war's end.

LUCAS, Henderson, 1Sgt, G. Enlisted in Charlotte on September 30, 1861, at age 18. Born Wake, NC. Adjunct of 11th NC April 22, 1862 under Col. Leventhorpe. Died of wounds received at Gettysburg.

LUCAS, James A, Pvt, B. Enlisted in Cleveland on February 28, 1863, at age 38. Killed at Chancellorsville. Widow Nancy Lucas.

LUCAS, P D, Pvt, H. Enlisted at Camp Holmes on April 20, 1864. Listed AWOL May/June 1864. Listed as POW July/Aug but no POW records found.

LUTZ, John W, Pvt, F. Enlisted in Cleveland on September 17, 1861, at age 23. Teamster. Accounted for each muster. Captured at Gettysburg. Confined at Ft. Delaware. Released June 7, 1865.

LYALL, Alfred, Pvt, A. Enlisted in Ashe Co on August 10, 1861, at age 19. Wounded in 1862. Discharged January 12, 1864.

LYALL, William, Cpl, A. Enlisted in Ashe Co on August 10, 1861, at age 19. Captured at Gaines's Mill. Exchanged from Ft. Delaware August 5, 1862. Wounded at Richmond in June 1864, right arm amputated June 22, 1864. Discharged February 22, 1865.

LYNCH, Ahijah Oliver, Pvt, C. Enlisted in Rutherford on September 2, 1861, at age 22. Wounded at Gaines's Mill and Ox Hill. Captured at Falling Waters. Confined at Point Lookout and Elmira. Released from Elmira March 10, 1865.

LYNCH, Cebun S, Pvt, C. Enl after Dec 1864. Present at Appomattox.

LYNCH, Humphrey P, Cpl, C. Enlisted in Rutherford on September 2, 1861, at age 24. Accounted for every muster. Wounded June 16, 1864. Returned to duty and was Present at Appomattox.

LYNCH, Robert, Pvt, G. Enlisted in Ashe Co on July 16, 1864. Deserted at Petersburg December 8, 1864. Took the oath and was transported to Indianapolis.

MACON, Calvin, Pvt, K. Enlisted in Troy, NC on September 9, 1861, at age 20. Accounted for each muster of enlistment. Wounded at Chancellorsville. Transferred to the 28th NC March 12, 1864.

MACON, William R, Cpl, K. Enlisted in Troy, NC on September 9, 1861, at age 23. Died July 18, 1862, at Scottsville VA of wounds received at Mechanicsville. Son of John Macon.

MAHUGH, Max, Pvt, H. Enlisted on March 26, 1863, at age 38. Killed at Chancellorsville.

MARTIN, Bartlett Y, 1Lt, A. Enlisted in Ashe Co on August 10, 1861, at age 33. Wounded and captured at Gettysburg. Confined at Johnson's Island, David's Island, and Point Lookout. Exchanged March 14, 1865.

MARTIN, Charles S, Pvt, E. Enlisted in Lincolnton on September 11, 1861, at age 18. Captured at Gaines's Mill, exchanged at Ft. Columbus,

NY August 5, 1862. Wounded at Chancellorsville. Captured at the Wilderness. Confined at Elmira until May 19, 1865.

MARTIN, Christopher G, Pvt, F. Enlisted in Cleveland on Sept 17, 1861, at age 27. Died May 8, 1863, of wds received at Chancellorsville.

MARTIN, J Stanhope, Pvt, D. Enlisted in Rowan on September 9, 1861, at age 18. Wounded Aug 1863. Disability discharge Dec 9, 1863.

MARTIN, James, Pvt, I. Enlisted in Rutherford on February 13, 1864. Died of disease March 27, 1864.

MARTIN, John J, Pvt, F. Enlisted in Cleveland on September 17, 1861, at age 28. Accounted for every muster. Wounded at Chancellorsville. Granted a furlough and did not return.

MARTIN, John L, Pvt, K. Enlisted in Troy on September 9, 1861, at age 26. Died of disease August 31, 1862. Son of Norman Martin.

MARTIN, W Y M, Pvt, H. Enlisted in Shelby on October 1, 1861, at age 33. Died of disease July 5, 1862. Married to Martha Martin.

MARTIN, William, Pvt, I. Enlisted in Rutherford on January 2, 1862, at age 33. Miller. Discharged in 1862. Reenlisted after December 1864. Wounded and captured at Petersburg March 25, 1865. Released from Point Lookout June 28, 1865.

MARTIN, William Jr, Pvt, I. Enlisted in Rutherford on October 6, 1861, at age 49. Wounded in the face and chin in the Seven Days' battles. Discharged for disability August 1, 1862.

MASON, Lawson, Pvt, E. Enlisted at Camp Vance on August 21, 1864. Present in November 1864. No records after that.

MAUNEY, Jacob L, Pvt, E. Enlisted in Lincolnton on September 11, 1861, at age 19. Died of wounds recd at Shepherdstown, date unknown.

MAYS, Orson, Sgt, I. Enlisted in Rutherford on February 1, 1862, at age 24. Captured at Gettysburg, Confined at Point Lookout. Exchanged November 15, 1864, at Venus Point on the Savannah River.

MCARTHUR, John B, Pvt, C. Enl in Rutherford on Sept 2, 1861, at age 19. Died at home of disease April 4, 1863. Son of W L McArthur.

MCARTHUR, Thomas R, Pvt, C. Enlisted at Camp Vance on May 11, 1864. Captured/Paroled at Burkesville Junction, VA April 1865.

MCBRAYER, Lorenzo N, Sgt, C. Enlisted in Rutherford on September 2, 1861, at age 23. Died June 2, 1863, of wound received at Chancellorsville, leg amputated.

MCCALL, Alexander, Pvt, G. Enlisted in Charlotte on September 30, 1861, at age 31. Captured at Gaines's Mill. Exchanged from Ft. Columbus August 5, 1862. Captured at Falling Waters and exchanged from Point Lookout February 24, 1865.

MCCALL, Ezekiel W, Pvt, D. Enlisted at Camp Vance on April 11, 1864. Present each muster of enlistment. Present at Appomattox.

MCCALL, James H, Pvt, G. Enlisted in Charlotte on Sept 30, 1861, at age 20. Present each muster but two (sick). Wounded at Gettysburg. Captured at Hatchers Run. Confined at Pt Lookout until June 29, 1865.
MCCALL, William C, Pvt, C. Enlisted at Camp Vance on May 25, 1864. Gunshot wound to the right arm at Petersburg June 22, 1864. Present in December 1864, with no records after that.
MCCALLUM, Calvin, Pvt, K. Enlisted after December 1864. Captured at Hatchers Run, arrived at Point Lookout under an assumed name or assumed one to get exchanged.
MCCLURD, James C, Pvt, F. Enlisted around July 1864. Accidentally killed near Petersburg July 22, 1864, while attempting to remove an unexploded shell from the line.
MCCORD, William C, 1Sgt, G. Enlisted as a private in Charlotte on September 30, 1861, at age 26. Present every muster but one (sick). Promoted to 1Sgt Sept 1, 1863. Wounded 2nd Manassas. Captured at Petersburg March 25, 1865. Released from Pt Lookout June 29, 1865.
MCCORMACK, George, Pvt, D. Enlisted at Camp Holmes on September 28, 1864. Paroled at Salisbury, NC May 24, 1865.
MCCRARY, William, Pvt, A. Enlisted after December 1864. Captured at Petersburg March 25, 1865. Released at Pt Lookout June 29, 1865.
MCDANIEL, James C, Pvt, B. Enlisted at Camp Holmes on July 1, 1864. Died of typhoid November 17, 1864.
MCDANIEL, James M, Pvt, B. Enlisted in Rutherford on September 2, 1861, at age 31. From Oak Springs NC. Captured at Gettysburg. Exchanged from Point Lookout February 18, 1865, with a detachment of paroled prisoners at Camp Lee in Richmond.
MCDANIEL, Joseph J, Pvt, B. Enlisted at Camp Vance on September 26, 1863. Present at Appomattox.
MCDOWELL, John L, Lt Co, I. Enlisted in Rutherford on October 6, 1861, at age 32. Elected Cpt. April 18, 1862 later promoted to Lt. Colonel. Dropped for prolonged AWOL, resigned commission Dec 1862. Reenlisted as a private and later promoted to Commissary Sgt. and served the remainder of the war. Present at Appomattox.
MCFADDEN, John L, Pvt, C. Enlisted at Camp Vance on May 9, 1864, at age 18. Wounded and captured at Petersburg June 23, 1864. Right leg amputated. Died of wounds July 21, 1864. Buried at Arlington. Son of Cynthia McFadden.
MCFALLS, T C, Pvt, I. Enlisted in Rutherford on March 16, 1864. Died of Typhoid June 24, 1864.
MCGEE, James T, Cpl, G. Enlisted in Charlotte on September 30, 1861, at age 20. Born Gaston, NC. Died of disease July 7, 1862. Son of Robert S McGee.

MCGEE, Joseph B, Major. Enlisted as a Sgt. in Charlotte on September 30, 1861, at age 32. Born Gaston, NC. Promoted to Major. Resigned December 13, 1862, for non-battle related health problems.
MCGEE, Thomas T, Pvt, G. Enlisted in Richmond on May 31, 1862, at age 26. Present each muster of enlistment. Present at Appomattox.
MCGINNIS, Nathan, 2Lt, F. Enlisted in Cleveland on September 17, 1861, at age 28. Born Gaston, NC. Present every muster but one (on leave). Promoted to 2Lt. June 28, 1863. Commanded F and C as of Feb 25, 1863. Served on extra duty as QM. Present at Appomattox.
MCGLAMERY, J, Pvt, H. Enlisted at Camp Holmes on April 20, 1864. Discharge was granted September 13, 1864.
MCHAHEY, Thaddeus C, Pvt, G. Enlisted in Charlotte on January 4, 1862, at age 22. Present on each muster. Present at Appomattox.
MCINNES, Allen M, Pvt, K. Enlisted in Troy on September 9, 1861, at age 22. Wounded at Mechanicsville. Killed at Gettysburg. Son of Neil McInnes.
MCKINNEY, John C, Pvt, B. Enlisted in Cleveland on February 26, 1863, at age 39. Died of Typhoid in Lexington, VA June 19, 1863.
MCKINNEY, Joseph, Pvt, I. Enlisted at Camp Vance on May 6, 1864. Discharged was granted October 13, 1864.
MCKINNEY, William A, 2Lt, I. Enlisted in Rutherford on October 6, 1861, at age 41. Failed reelection and was discharged April 18, 1862.
MCLAUGHLIN, Eli C, Pvt, D. Enlisted in Rowan on September 9, 1861, at age 28. Merchant. On duty each muster. Wounded once. Worked in the Quartermaster dept. Forage master/commissary clerk. Paroled at Salisbury May 24, 1865.
MCLAUGHLIN, John H, Pvt, D. Enlisted in Rowan on September 9, 1861, at age 30. Present every muster but one (leave). Wounded once. Present at Appomattox.
MCLAUGHLIN, Samuel W, Pvt, D. Enlisted in Rowan on September 9, 1861, at age 39. Discharged Dec 7, 1862, due to conscription law.
MCLENNON, John, Pvt, K. Enlisted in Montgomery on September 9, 1861, at age 49. 6'4" tall. Clerk of the Court. Disability discharge granted in July 1862.
MCLEOD, Archibald N, Pvt, K. Enlisted at Camp Holmes on October 31, 1863. Killed in action May 5, 1864, at the Wilderness.
MCLEOD, Martin J, Pvt, K. Enlisted in Troy on September 9, 1861, at age 21. Shoemaker and provost guard. Accounted for each muster. Captured at Burkesville Junction April 6, 1865. Released from Point Lookout June 6, 1865.
MCLEOD, Nevin C, 2Lt, K. Enlisted in Troy on September 9, 1861, at age 25. Enlisted with his brother Norman. Gunshot wound right leg at Gettysburg. Killed in action May 25, 1864.

MCLEOD, Norman J, 1Sgt, K. Enlisted in Troy on September 9, 1861, at age 22. Enlisted with his brother Nevin. Killed in action at Gettysburg. Son of Alex McLeod.
MCNEELY, Burgess W, Pvt., D. Age 31. Transferred from the 5th NC on March 1, 1865. No further record.
MCNEELY, Carmi K, Cpt, D. Enlisted in Rowan on September 9, 1861, at age 25. Resident of Deep Well, NC. Captured at Falling Waters. POW at Johnsons Island OH, Released June 11, 1865.
MCNEELY, James A, Pvt, D. Enlisted in Massaponax on May 15, 1862, at age 29. Teamster. Accounted for each muster to Dec 1864.
MCNEELY, James K, Sgt, D. Enlisted in Rowan on September 9, 1861, at age 32. Wounded at Frayser's Farm. Discharged in December 1862. Returned to service by February of 1863. Present every muster but one (leave). Killed in action August 25, 1864, at Ream's Station.
MCNEELY, John R, Pvt, D. Enlisted in Rowan on September 9, 1861, at age 24. Killed at Gaines's Mill. Son of Reul McNeely.
MCNEILLY, Alexander D, Pvt, F. Enlisted at Camp Holmes on April 20, 1864. Captured at Petersburg March 25, 1865. Confined at Point Lookout until June 29, 1865.
MCNEILLY, Robert W, Pvt, F. Enlisted at Camp Holmes on April 20, 1864, at age 37. Wounded in 1864. Retired to Invalid corps December 7, 1864. Paroled at Salisbury May 20, 1865.
MCNEILLY, William D, Pvt, F. Enlisted at Camp Holmes on April 20, 1864. Captured at Petersburg March 25, 1865. Confined at Point Lookout until June 29, 1865.
MCOLFEE, J M, Lt, D. Enlisted after December 1864. Captured in the hospital in Richmond April 3, 1865. Took the oath at Jackson Hospital in Richmond September 5, 1865.
MCPHAUL, Daniel, Pvt, G. Enlisted at Camp Holmes on April 29, 1864. Absent sick since April 1864, no further records.
MCRAE, James L, Pvt, K. Enlisted at Camp Gregg on March 28, 1863, at age 32. Teacher. Ordinance clerk. Captured June 22, 1864, at Petersburg. Confined at Point Lookout. Joined US Army 4th USV October 17, 1864. Served as a Company Clerk, Commissary, and Hospital Steward. Mustered out at Fort Leavenworth July 2, 1866.
MCRAE, Robert, Pvt, K. Enlisted in Troy on September 9, 1861, at age 41. Died April 11, 1862, at College Hospital in Goldsboro.
MCSWAIN, George, Pvt, H. Enlisted in Shelby on October 1, 1861, at age 35. Executed for desertion January 9, 1864.
MCSWAIN, S O, Pvt, H. Enlisted in Shelby on March 18, 1864. AWOL from September 1864. No record of return.

MCSWAIN, William, Pvt, B. Enlisted in Raleigh on April 10, 1864. Wounded in May or June of 1864. Captured at Burkeville Junction April 4, 1865. Confined at Point Lookout until June 29, 1865.

MEANS, George W, Pvt, G. Enlisted in Charlotte on September 30, 1861, at age 22. Enlisted with his brother James. Died at Goldsboro of disease March 15, 1862. Son of William Means.

MEANS, James K Polk, Pvt, G. Enlisted in Charlotte on September 30, 1861, at age 17. Enlisted with his brother George. Killed at Gaines's Mill. Son of William Means.

MEDLIN, James, Pvt, D. Enlisted at Camp Holmes on October 1, 1864. Deserted at Petersburg January 8, 1865. Took the oath and was sent to Indianapolis, Indiana on public works.

MEDLIN, Miles W, Pvt, H. Enlisted at Camp Holmes on September 11, 1864. Resident of Union Co, NC. Captured at Petersburg March 25, 1865. Confined at Point Lookout until June 29, 1865.

MELTON, Barnabas, Pvt, B. Enlisted in High Point on October 19, 1861, at age 20. Died at Goldsboro March 14, 1862.

MELTON, Joseph, Pvt, C. Enlisted at Camp Vance on May 18, 1864. Present up to November 1864.

MELTON, Reuben, Pvt, B. Enlisted in Rutherford on September 2, 1861, at age 30. Died of Variola (Small Pox) January 24, 1863.

METCALF, Andrew D, Pvt, E. Enlisted in Gaston, NC on March 5, 1863, at age 37. Gaston County resident. Wounded at Gettysburg. Deserted from the hospital. Returned and was captured at Hanover Junction May 24, 1864. Confined at Pt Lookout until Feb 13, 1865.

MILLER, D Walter, Pvt, H. Enlisted in Cleveland on February 28, 1863, at age 37. Captured at Falling Waters. Confined at Old Capital Prison until exchange November 18, 1863. Returned to duty and was captured at Garret Station April 2, 1865. Confined at Point Lookout and transferred to Harts Island where he was released June 17, 1865.

MILLER, E A, Pvt, H. Enlisted at Camp Holmes on April 20, 1864. Captured at the Wilderness. Exchanged at Point Lookout September 18, 1864. Was hospitalized following release. A 30-day furlough was granted. No record of return to duty.

MILLER, Eli H, Major. Enlisted in Cleveland on September 17, 1861, at age 24. Teacher. Enlisted as a Sgt. in company F. Brother of Regimental Surgeon John F. Miller. Elected Major April 18, 1862. Killed in action at Ox Hill. Son of W J Miller.

MILLER, Francis M, Pvt, D. Enlisted in Rowan on September 9, 1861, at age 23. Born Cabarrus NC. Worked as a cooper (barrel maker). Died July 31, 1862, of wounds received during the Seven Days battles. Son of John Miller.

MILLER, Ibsom A, Pvt, D. Enlisted in Rowan on September 9, 1861, at age 21. Killed at Gettysburg. Son of John Miller.

MILLER, James A, Pvt, C. Enlisted at Camp Mangum on December 8, 1861. Furloughed in December of 1862, to raise a company. Appointed Lt of Co K 50th NC.

MILLER, James C, Sgt, A. Enlisted in Ashe Co on August 10, 1861, at age 18. Courier. Accounted for every muster with one AWOL. Wounded and captured at Ox Hill. Confined at Old Capital and exchanged March 29, 1863. Present at Appomattox.

MILLER, James F, Pvt, D. Enlisted in Rowan on September 9, 1861, at age 25. Born Cabarrus NC, Wounded May 1864. Captured in the hospital April 3, 1865. Paroled April 23, 1865. Remained in the hospital until at least May 28, 1865.

MILLER, John F, Surgeon. Enlisted on May 17, 1862. Surgeon. Present each muster. Transferred to Richmond in September 1864. Paroled at Goldsboro May 12, 1865.

MILLER, Jonathan B, Pvt, A. Enlisted in Ashe Co on August 10, 1861, at age 32. Wounded in 1862. Hospitalized in May 1863. Present in Dec 1863. Furloughed and did not return. Dropped as a deserter.

MILLER, Loveless A, Pvt, K. Enlisted in Troy on September 9, 1861, at age 20. Died January 27, 1862, at home in Montgomery County.

MILLER, Martin P, Cpl, C. Enlisted in Rutherford on September 2, 1861, at age 30. Painter. Died August 14, 1862, of wounds received at Frayser's Farm. Son of Caleb Miller.

MILLER, Michael D, Pvt, A. Enlisted in Ashe Co on August 10, 1861, at age 51. Wounded and captured at Ox Hill. Confined at Old Capital and exchanged March 29, 1863. Hospitalized after release. Discharged April 18, 1863.

MILLER, Troy, Pvt, A. Enlisted in Ashe Co on August 10, 1861, at age 21. Born in Wilkes County NC. Disability discharge July 15, 1862. Reenlisted March 19, 1864. Was absent sick after August 9, 1864.

MILLER, Weldon H, Sgt, C. Enlisted at Camp Mangum on December 8, 1861, at age 23. Appointed "Right Guide of Regiment." Killed in action at Mechanicsville.

MILLIGAN, Hiram P, Pvt, F. Enlisted at Camp Holmes on April 20, 1864. Killed in action at Ream's Station.

MILLS, George C, 1Lt, K. Enlisted on August 23, 1864. Present at Appomattox.

MILLS, William T, Pvt, G. Enlisted in High Point on October 31, 1861, at age 19. Carpenter. Born in Pickens, SC. Court Martialed once for being drunk on post. Transf to 1st SC Volunteers May 16, 1862.

MILSAPS Peter P, Pvt, K. Enl after Dec 1864. Present at Appomattox.

MINTS, John C, Pvt, I. Enlisted in Rutherford on October 6, 1861. Gunshot wound in the stomach at Chancellorsville. Light duty as a Guard at Charlotte through 1864.
MINTS, John W, Pvt, B. Enlisted in Rutherford on September 2, 1861, at age 23. Captured September 12, 1862, at Fredericksburg. Confined at Fort Delaware. Paroled October 2, 1862 and exchanged November 10, 1862. Deserted May 2, 1863.
MINTS, Thomas J, Pvt, I. Enlisted in Rutherford on October 6, 1861, at age 24. Gunshot wound to the hand at Chancellorsville. Light duty at Staunton. Retired to Invalid Corp December 21, 1864.
MITCHELL, Henderson G, Pvt, C. Enlisted in Orange CH on January 11, 1864, at age 18. Present in February 1865. No record after that.
MITCHELL, J, Pvt, I. Enlisted after December 1864. Captured and paroled at Athens, GA May 8, 1865.
MITCHELL, Thomas E, Sgt, C. Enlisted in Rutherford on July 18, 1863, at age 25. Wounded June 22, 1864. Promoted to Sgt. September 1, 1864. Hospitalized in December 1864. No further records.
MITTAG, William McK, 2Lt, H. Enlisted as a private in Shelby on October 1, 1861, at age 27. Merchant. Promoted to 2Lt. Born Lancaster SC. Present every muster but one (leave). Captured at Gaines's Mill. Exchanged at Fort Columbus, NY. Present at Appomattox.
MODE, George W, Pvt, F. Enlisted in Cleveland on September 17, 1861, at age 22. Died of disease at Hamilton, NC March 18, 1862. Married to Rebecca Mode.
MODE, William M, Pvt, I. Enlisted in Rutherford on February 13, 1864. Retired to the Invalid Corps December 21, 1864.
MOONEY, Emanuel, Pvt, E. Enlisted in Gaston, NC on March 5, 1863, at age 37. Gaston County resident. Present every muster but one (sick). Bayonet wound at Chancellorsville (per pension records). Gunshot wound to the shoulder May 1864. Returned and was captured at Southside Railroad. Confined at Hart's Island, NY until June 6, 1865.
MOONEY, Isaac, Pvt, F. Enlisted in Cleveland on September 17, 1861, at age 20. Gunshot wound to the right thigh at Chancellorsville. Returned by December 1863. Present for the remainder of the war. Present at Appomattox.
MOONEY, Manuel L, Pvt, E. Enlisted in Lincolnton on August 31, 1861, at age 19. Died Sept 18, 1862, of wounds received at Sharpsburg.
MOONEY, O.V., Pvt, H. Enlisted in Shelby on October 1, 1861, at age 27. Wounded at an unknown date. Present on each muster. Paroled at Salisbury June 24, 1865.
MOOR, J. P., Pvt, C. Enlisted around December 19, 1864. Paroled at Athens, GA May 8, 1865.

MOORE, Jeremiah John, Pvt, K. Enlisted in Troy on September 9, 1861, at age 25. Discharged in November 1861. Reenlisted in October 1862. Wounded and captured at Gettysburg, exchanged August 17, 1863. Absent the rest of the war. Paroled at Troy NC May 23, 1865.
MOORE, Joab, Pvt, E. Enlisted in Lincolnton on September 11, 1861, at age 17. Killed in action at Mechanicsville.
MOORE, John, Pvt, K. Enlisted at Camp Holmes on June 1, 1864. Deserted June 15, 1864. Paroled at Troy, NC.
MOORE, John A, Pvt, B. Enlisted in Rutherford on September 2, 1861, at age 25. Gunshot wound to the hand at Chancellorsville. Listed as deserted but returned. Was captured at North Anna. Exchanged from Point Lookout March 14, 1865.
MOORE, Ross J, Pvt, H. Enlisted in Shelby on Aug 1, 1862, at age 18. Captured at Gettysburg. Died of Typhoid at Ft Delaware Aug 13, 1863.
MOORE, William, Pvt, H. Enlisted in Shelby on October 1, 1861, at age 29. Born in York, SC. Killed at Gettysburg July 1, 1863.
MORGAN, Alexander C, Pvt, K. Enlisted in Troy on March 5, 1863, at age 36. Deserted May 1863 returned December 1863. AWOL through 1864. Paroled at Troy NC May 23, 1865.
MORGAN, Anderson, Pvt, K. Enlisted in Troy on March 5, 1863, at age 38. AWOL most of enlistment. Paroled at Troy, NC May 22, 1865.
MORGAN, Eli S, Pvt, K. Enl after Dec 1864. Captured at Hatchers Run March 30, 1865. Died April 25, 1865 of pneumonia at Pt Lookout.
MORGAN, Joseph H, Pvt, K. Enlisted in Troy on September 2, 1861, at age 21. Present all musters but two (leaves). Deserted at Petersburg March 7, 1865. Took the oath and was transported to Philadelphia
MORGAN, Miles W, Pvt, K. Enlisted in Orange CH on April 2, 1864. Present every muster of enlistment. Deserted at Petersburg March 7, 1865. Took oath and transported to Philadelphia on public works.
MORGAN, Spencer, Pvt, K. Enlisted at Camp Holmes on March 25, 1863. Captured at Chancellorsville. Exchanged May 10, 1863. Present in November 1864. No further records.
MORRIS, Henry W, Pvt, K. Enlisted in Troy on September 9, 1861, at age 22. Died of disease December 4, 1861.
MORRIS, Lewis W, Pvt, H. Enlisted in Shelby on October 1, 1861, at age 18. Died in Richmond of Typhoid fever September 2, 1862.
MORRIS, Richard T, Pvt, H. Enlisted in Charleston SC on January 1863, at age 26. Transferred in from the 5th SC in 1862. Accounted for every muster. Wounded at Gettysburg. Present at Appomattox.
MORRIS, William D, Pvt, K and D. Enlisted in Troy on September 9, 1861, at age 22. Captured at Falling Waters. Exchanged from Point Lookout March 3, 1864. Returned in October 1864. Transferred to Company D February 1865. Paroled at Farmville, VA April 11, 1865.

MORROW, David G, Pvt, I. Enlisted in Rutherford on December 28, 1861, at age 37. Discharged by mistake December 8, 1862. Ordered back per conscription law but did not return.

MORROW, Elbert G, Pvt, I. Enlisted in Rutherford on October 6, 1861, at age 17. Discharged by conscription law December 8, 1862.

MORROW, George W, Pvt, I. Enlisted in Rutherford on October 6, 1861, at age 34. Granted a leave of absence March 20, 1862. Did not return and was listed as a deserted.

MORROW, James R, Cpl, I. Enlisted in Rutherford on October 6, 1861, at age 19. Wounded at Ox Hill, Chancellorsville, and Gettysburg. Captured at Gettysburg, Died at Point Lookout September 1, 1864.

MOSLEY, George W, Pvt, D. Enlisted in Rowan on September 9, 1861, at age 27. Born in Brunswick, VA. Deserted to the enemy September 8, 1862, near Frederick City Maryland.

MOSS, Henry S, Pvt, F. Enlisted in Cleveland on September 17, 1861, at age 16. Discharged October 10, 1862, due to age and a head wound received at an unspecified date.

MOSS, Rufus G, Pvt, H. Enlisted in Petersburg on August 20, 1864. Deserted at Petersburg February 16, 1865. Took the oath and was transported to Philadelphia on public works.

MOSS, W Van, Pvt, H. Enlisted in Shelby on October 1, 1861, at age 18. Born in York, SC. Discharged for disability December 22, 1862.

MUNN, Calvin D, Pvt, K. Enlisted in Raleigh on August 17, 1862. Absent sick from September 17, 1864. No further records.

MUNN, David A, Pvt, K. Enlisted in Troy on Sept 9, 1861, at age 20. Right leg amputated above the knee from a wound received at Gaines's Mill. Discharged Sept 28, 1862. Applied for artificial leg in 1864.

MUNN, T D, Pvt, K. Enlisted after December of 1864. Captured at Petersburg April 2, 1865. Died at Hart's Island April 27, 1865.

MURCHISON, Calvin J, Pvt, K. Enlisted in Troy on September 9, 1861, at age 20. Present every muster but one (leave). Wounded at Chancellorsville. Accidentally shot on October 6, 1864, while coming off picket duty in the dark by a member of 13th NC. Died around 4:00 the next morning.

MYERS, William R, Cpt, G. Enlisted in Charlotte on September 30, 1861, at age 43. Lawyer. Failed reelection, discharged April 18, 1862.

NANNEY, Drury D, Pvt, C. Enlisted in Rutherford on September 2, 1861, at age 17. Present every muster except one (sick). Present in February 1865. No records after that.

NANNEY, Elbert, Pvt, C. Enlisted in Rutherford on September 2, 1861, at age 19. Died of March 18, 1862, of disease at Hamilton, NC.

NANNEY, Isaiah, Pvt, C. Enlisted at Camp Vance on May 7, 1864. Hospitalized in September 1864, 30-day furlough granted.

NANNEY, James, Pvt, C. Enlisted in High Point on October 26, 1861, at age 55. From Guilford Co, NC, Discharged January 8, 1862.
NANNEY, James A, Pvt, C. Enlisted in Rutherford on September 2, 1861, at age 19. Died January 28, 1862, at Raleigh from Typhoid.
NANNEY, Nicholas, Pvt, C. Enlisted in Rutherford on September 2, 1861, at age 24. Hospital Nurse in Raleigh July 1863. Disability discharge in February 1864.
NANNEY, Rial, Pvt, D. Enlisted in Rowan on September 9, 1861, at age 36. Mechanic. Died of disease January 19, 1862.
NEAL, John B, Pvt, I. Enlisted in Rutherford on October 6, 1861, at age 41. Born in Union, SC. Died in Raleigh of disease Jan 25, 1862.
NEEL, G C, Pvt, G. Enlisted after December 1864. Captured at Hatchers Run. Confined at Point Lookout until June 29, 1865.
NELON, William "Willie", Pvt, C. Enlisted in Rutherford on September 2, 1861, at age 18. Captured at Falling Waters. Died at Point Lookout February 1864.
NESBIT, Adam R, Cpt, E. Enlisted in Lincolnton on September 11, 1861, at age 26. Born Lancaster SC. Merchant. Enlisted as First Sgt, promoted to Sgt. Maj. January 18, 1862. Captain/Asst. Commissary. Discharged around April 1863.
NEWTON, Benjamin O, Pvt, F. Enlisted at Camp Holmes on April 20, 1864, at age 40. Gunshot wound to the leg and hand August 25, 1864. Two fingers amputated. Treated for gangrene. Disability discharge granted January 25, 1865.
NEWTON, E, Pvt, H. Enlisted at Camp Holmes on April 20, 1864. Died of disease in Jackson Hospital in Richmond July 21, 1864. Son of W R Newton.
NEWTON, John A, Pvt, F. Enlisted in Cleveland on September 17, 1861, at age 18. Wounded and captured at Gettysburg. Left leg amputated. Confined at Decamp Hospital David's Island, NY and Fort Wood, Bedloe's Island NY Harbor. Exchanged March 7, 1864. Retired to Invalid Corps. Applied for an artificial limb.
NEWTON, Soloman A, Pvt, F. Enlisted in Cleveland on September 17, 1861, at age 20. Carpenter. Died October 19, 1862, of wounds received at Gaines's Mill. Married to Mary Newton.
NICHOLSON, John, Pvt, G. Enlisted in Charlotte on September 30, 1861, at age 18. Transferred to Co I 37th NC January 1, 1863.
NIX, Francis Marion, Pvt, C. Enlisted at Camp Vance on March 30, 1864. Present in November 1864. No records after that.
NOAH, Jacob, Pvt, K. Enlisted in Troy on September 9, 1861, at age 20. Died of disease June 18, 1862. Son of Nancy Noah.
NORMAN, Presley, Pvt, F. Enlisted in Cleveland on Sept 17, 1861, at age 22. Wounded at Gainess Mill. Captured at Falling Waters, confined

at Point Lookout until March 3, 1864. Returned to duty. Deserted at Petersburg March 7, 1865. Took oath and was sent to Sterling Ill.
NORMAN, Wilson, Pvt, F. Enlisted in Cleveland on September 17, 1861, at age 29. Died May 10, 1863, of wounds received at Chancellorsville.
NORMENT, George W, Lt. Colonel. Enlisted in Charlotte on September 30, 1861, at age 27 as a Lt in Company G. Wounded at Gaines's Mill and Gettysburg. Promoted to Lt Col March 1865. Recommended by Colonel Lowrance after Captains Wood and Hoyle waived seniority. Led the regiment to Appomattox.
NORTON, William, Pvt, I. Enlisted at Camp Vance on March 7, 1864. Captured in Hospital at Richmond April 3, 1865. Transported to Pt Lookout on the Hosp Transport Thomas Powell. Rel June 26, 1865.
O'DELL, George W, Pvt, G. Enlisted in Charlotte on Sept 30, 1861, at age 20. Born Henry County, VA, transf to 42nd Va March 11, 1863.
O'DELL, Joseph C, Pvt, G. Enlisted in Charlotte on September 30, 1861, at age 19. Born Henry County, VA, Died at Camp Mangum, Raleigh January 13, 1862.
OLLIS, A S, Pvt, C. Enlisted at Camp Vance on April 25, 1864. **AWOL from May 31, 1864. No record of return to duty.**
OSBORNE, Calvin, Pvt, A. Enlisted in Ashe Co on August 10, 1861, at age 27. Wounded at least once. Captured at Falling Waters. POW at Pt Lookout. Exchanged March 17, 1864. Deserted April 22, 1864.
OSBORNE, Ephraim, Pvt, A. Enlisted in Ashe Co on August 10, 1861, at age 21. Deserted August 8, 1862.
OSBORNE, Jonathan, Pvt, A. Enlisted in Ashe Co on August 1, 1861, at age 37. Deserted some time in 1862
OSBORNE, Washington, Pvt, A. Enlisted in Ashe Co on August 10, 1861, at age 27. Died of Typhoid August 16, 1862.
OSBORNE, Zadoc, Pvt, A. Enlisted at Camp Gregg on March 29, 1863, at age 34. Conscript. Deserted after April 1863.
OVERBY, James B, Pvt, H. Enlisted in Shelby on October 1, 1861, at age 32. Captured at Falling Waters, exchanged October 30, 1864. No record of return to duty.
OVERCASH, George M, Cpl, D. Enlisted in Rowan on September 9, 1861, at age 18. Present every muster but two (sick and AWOL). Wounded at Gettysburg. Present in December 1864.
OVERCASH, Hampton J, Pvt, D. Enlisted in Rowan on Sept 9, 1861, at age 21. Mechanic. Present on ever muster. Present to October 1864.
OVERCASH, Henry W, Pvt, D. Enlisted in Rowan on September 9, 1861, at age 23. Laurel Branch NC. Court-martial for desertion in 1862. but returned to duty. Present most of 1863-64. Deserted at Petersburg Sept 18, 1864. Took oath and was transported to Philadelphia.

OVERCASH, Hiram F, Pvt, D. Enlisted in Rowan on Sept 9, 1861, at age 20. Died of disease July 11, 1862. Son of Christopher Overcash.

OVERCASH, Joel J, Pvt, D. Enlisted in Rowan on September 9, 1861, at age 29. Died at High Point of disease August 28, 1862.

OVERCASH, John J, Pvt, E. Per pension application of his widow, Milcha D. Overcash, enlisted April 1863. Died in a hospital on an unknown date.

OVERCASH, Reuben A, Cpl, D. Enlisted in Rowan on Sept 9, 1861, at age 19. Accounted for every muster. Died of disease March 6, 1864.

OVERCASH, Silas S, Pvt, D. Enlisted in Rowan on September 9, 1861, at age 20. Died of disease August 25, 1862.

OWENS, Andrew, Pvt, B. Enlisted in Rutherford on Sept 2, 1861, at age 25. Died of wounds recd at Frayser's Farm. Judith Owens widow.

OWENS, Joseph D, Pvt, I. Enlisted at Camp Vance on May 13, 1864. Died in the hospital in Richmond July 20, 1864. Cause unknown.

OWENS, Willis, Pvt, B. Enlisted in Rutherford on September 2, 1861, at age 15. Discharged due to conscription law December 6, 1862.

OWENS, J, Pvt, K. Enlisted at Camp Holmes on May 21, 1864. Deserted June 15, 1864.

PADGETT, Marcus D, Pvt, I. Enlisted in Goldsboro on April 12, 1862, at age 24. Transferred to the 16th NC Infantry May 30, 1862.

PARKER, Benjamin C, Pvt, D. Enlisted in Rowan on September 9, 1861, at age 42. Mechanic and shoemaker. Disability discharge May 19, 1862. Paroled at Salisbury May 23, 1865.

PARKER, David W, Pvt, B. Enlisted after December 1864. Captured in the hospital in Richmond April 3, 1865. Died April 14, 1865.

PARKER, Enoch, Pvt, H. Enlisted at Camp Holmes on April 20, 1864. Deserted at Petersburg Sept 12, 1864. Was transported to Cincinnati.

PARKER, James B, Cpl, D. Enlisted in Rowan on September 9, 1861, at age 39. Discharged Dec 8, 1862. Paroled at Salisbury June 14, 1865.

PARKS, George W, Pvt, G. Enlisted in Charlotte on September 30, 1861, at age 24. Painter. Wounded and captured at Gettysburg, detailed to stay with the wounded. Exchanged September 8, 1863. Captured at Hanover Junction May 24, 1864 and confined at Point Lookout and Elmira. Released May 17, 1865.

PARKS, John P, 1Lt, D. Enlisted in Rowan on September 9, 1861, at age 27. Merchant. Elected 1Lt April 18, 1862. Killed in action at Frayser's Farm. Son of Hugh Parks.

PARRISH, Pinkney, Pvt, A. Enlisted in Ashe Co on August 10, 1861, at age 40. Wounded at the Seven Days battles and Sharpsburg. Discharged December 7, 1862.

PARRISH, William T, Pvt, A. Enlisted at Camp Holmes on August 10, 1864. Present in December 1864. No further record.

PASCHAL, John H, Pvt, A. Enlisted at Camp Holmes on June 17, 1864. Captured at Petersburg March 25, 1865. Confined at Point Lookout until June 16, 1865.
PASOUR, Levi W, Pvt, E. Enlisted in Gaston, NC on March 1, 1863, at age 38. Killed in action at Chancellorsville.
PATERSON, Jeremiah, Pvt, B. Enlisted at Camp Holmes on May 8, 1864. Deserted from Petersburg June 18, 1864. Took the oath at Bermuda Hundred VA. Sent to Henry Co, Ind.
PATRICK, William, Pvt, A. Enlisted in Ashe Co on August 10, 1861, at age 20. Gunshot wound to the left arm at Gettysburg. Ordered return to duty August 6, 1863. Listed as deserted August 27, 1863. Died in the hospital in Richmond November 10, 1863, of pneumonia and typhoid.
PATTERSON, James, Pvt, I. Enlisted at Camp Vance on October 1, 1863. AWOL each muster of enlistment. Dropped from the rolls September 1, 1864. Returned and deserted at Petersburg January 8, 1865. Took oath and was transported to Indianapolis, Ind.
PATTERSON, William G, Pvt, F. Enlisted in Cleveland on September 17, 1861, at age 38. Born in Spartanburg SC. Discharged by mistake in December 1862 but did not return.
PEACOCK, George N, Pvt, D. Enlisted at Camp Holmes on August 27, 1864. Present at Appomattox.
PEACOCK, John B, Pvt, D. Enlisted after December of 1864. Captured at Hatchers Run. Confined at Pt Lookout until June 16, 1865.
PEELER, Andrew, Pvt, F. Enlisted in Cleveland on September 17, 1861, at age 25. Teamster in the Quartermaster Department. Accounted for on every muster. Present at Appomattox.
PEELER, David C, Pvt, F. Enlisted in Cleveland on February 28, 1863, at age 19. Wounded at Chancellorsville, returned to duty by December of 1863. Was captured at Petersburg April 2, 1865. Released from Point Lookout. June 16, 1865.
PEELER, David H, Lt, F. Enlisted in Cleveland on January 1862, at age 37. Tanner. Married to Mary Ann Robinson. Failed reelection and was discharged April 18, 1862.
PEELER, Doctor D, Pvt, F. Enlisted in Cleveland on August 19, 1863, at age 18. Present every muster of enlistment. Present at Appomattox.
PEELER, John H, Pvt, F. Enlisted in Cleveland on February 28, 1863, at age 35. Captured at Falling Waters, released from Point Lookout and joined US Service January 26, 1864. Served in the 1st US Volunteers. Worked as a herder and was sent to Ft. Union in Montana in August 1865. Mustered out at Ft. Leavenworth November 27, 1865.
PENDERGRASS, Emil O, Pvt, D. Enlisted at Camp Holmes on September 29, 1864. Transferred to Co K 5th NC February 25, 1865.

PENDLETON, Lemuel, Pvt, E. Enlisted in Lincolnton on September 11, 1861, at age 24. Pioneer. Killed at Fredericksburg Dec 13, 1862.
PENNINGTON, Andrew, Pvt, A. Enlisted in Ashe Co on August 10, 1861, at age 29. Deserted August 27, 1863.
PERKINS, Daniel, Pvt, E. Enlisted in Lincolnton on September 11, 1861, at age 18. Killed in action at Gaines's Mill.
PERKINS, Elisha, Pvt, E. Enlisted in Lincolnton on September 11, 1861, at age 28. Shoemaker. Died of disease September 6, 1862.
PERRY, Henry R, Pvt, A. Enlisted in Ashe Co on August 10, 1861, at age 43. AWOL since November 8, 1862. Dropped from the rolls.
PERRY, William, Pvt, A. Enlisted in Ashe Co on August 10, 1861, at age 23. Died July 16, 1862, of wounds received June 1862, Pyaemia, caused by a gunshot wound to the knee. Married to Mundy Perry.
PETERSON, John, Pvt, E. Enlisted at Camp Vance on August 21, 1864. Resident of Yancey County. Deserted at Petersburg Sept 16, 1864 and surrendered to the Yankees. Was sent to Cleveland OH. Had wanted to go to Tennessee where he had three sons in Federal Army.
PETERSON, Joshua, Pvt, E. Enlisted at Camp Vance on August 21, 1862. Yancey County resident. Deserted at Petersburg January 8, 1865. Took oath at City Point.
PETHEL, Levi, Pvt, D. Enlisted in Rowan on September 9, 1861, at age 41. Merchant/carpenter. Discharged by conscript law Dec 8, 1862.
PETTY, Jefferson G, Pvt, F. Enlisted in Cleveland on February 28, 1863, at age 30. Killed in action at Chancellorsville.
PETTY, John, Pvt, A. Enlisted in Ashe Co on August 10, 1861, at age 19. Born Yadkin, NC. Deserted July 30, 1862.
PETTY, Moses P, Pvt, F. Enlisted in Cleveland on September 17, 1861, at age 22. Wounded at Ox Hill. Severely wounded and captured at Gettysburg. Confined at Point Lookout until October 30, 1864.
PHILBECK, Benjamin E, Pvt, B. Enlisted in Rutherford on September 2, 1861, at age 21. Died July 6, 1862, in Richmond, cause unknown. Son of John Philbeck.
PHILBECK, Benjamin F, Pvt, F. Enlisted in Cleveland on September 17, 1861, at age 18. Died in Richmond July 12, 1862, of wounds received at Frayser's Farm. Son of John Philbeck.
PHILBECK, John P, Sgt, B. Enlisted in Rutherford on September 2, 1861, at age 24. Gunshot wound in the knee at Chancellorsville. Placed on light duty for the remainder of the war. Present to October 1864.
PHILBECK, Thomas F, Pvt, B. Enlisted in Rutherford on September 2, 1861, at age 17. Accounted for every muster. Captured at Petersburg March 25, 1865. Confined at Point Lookout until June 16, 1865.

PHILBECK, William A "Billy", Pvt, B. Enlisted in Rutherford on Sept 2, 1861, at age 21. Sharpshooter. Present every muster. Wounded April 2, 1865 and captured. Escaped from the hospital prior to release.
PHILBERT, B A, Pvt, Enlisted after December 1864. Paroled May 15, 1865, by Col DM Evans 20 NY Cavalry.
PHILBRICK, T, Pvt, D. Enl after Dec 1864. Captured in the hospital at Richmond April 3, 1865. At Jackson Hospital May 28, 1865.
PHILLIPS, Hilmon, Pvt, I. Enlisted in Rutherford on October 6, 1861, at age 27. Teamster. Present every muster. Present to February 1865.
PHILLIPS, Jesse J, Pvt, G. Enlisted in Charlotte on September 30, 1861, at age 26. Killed at Second Manassas. Son of Gordon B Phillips.
PHILLIPS, Lawson, Pvt, I. Enlisted in Rutherford on October 6, 1861, at age 34. Discharged by mistake December 8, 1862. Did not return.
PHILLIPS, Thomas P, 2Lt, I. Enlisted as a corporal in Rutherford on October 6, 1861, at age 17. Born Spartanburg SC. Promoted to 2Lt July 24, 1862. Commanded I and K companies in July 1864, and A Company in May 1864. Surrendered at Appomattox.
PICKEREL, John H, Pvt, G. Enlisted in Charlotte on September 30, 1861, at age 25. Wounded in the Seven Days battles and detached as a hospital guard at Gordonsville, VA. While there was permitted to go home Patrick Co, VA. Paroled at Gordonsville June 23, 1865.
PICKLER, David, Pvt, D. Enlisted in High Point on October 18, 1861, at age 18. Died July 11, 1862, of gunshot wound in the side.
PINSON, George W, Pvt, B. Enlisted in Cleveland on Feb 26, 1863, at age 27. Captured at Falling Waters. Died at Pt Lookout Oct 1863.
PLASTER, William L, Pvt, D. Enlisted in Mechanicsville on June 14, 1862. Killed at Ox Hill. From the Laurel Branch area of Rowan Co.
PLESS, Soloman, Cpl, A. Enlisted at Camp Holmes on August 27, 1864. Present at Appomattox.
PLONK, John J, Pvt, F. Enlisted at Camp Holmes on October 19, 1864, at age 39. Disability discharged at High Point in 1861. Reenlisted in 1864. Captured in the hospital in Richmond with a gunshot wound in the right thigh. Took the oath at City Point June 30, 1865.
PLUS, F E, Pvt, K. Paroled at Salisbury May 23, 1865.
POE, George, Pvt, A. Enlisted in Ashe Co on Aug 10, 1861, at age 16. Died March 9, 1862, at Goldsboro. Son of John Poe and brother of James Poe.
POE, James M, Pvt, A. Enlisted in Ashe Co on Aug 10, 1861, at age 19. Died of wounds Sept 4, 1862. Son of John Poe and brother of George Poe.
POE, Matthias, Pvt, A. Enlisted in Ashe Co on August 10, 1861, at age 19. Wounded in 1862, did not return from furlough. Listed as a deserter February 1864.

POE, William, Pvt, A. Enlisted in Ashe Co on August 10, 1861. Discharged due to age, under 18.
POOL, Jonathan, Pvt, K. Enlisted in Troy on September 9, 1861, at age 21. Died July 6, 1862, of wounds received at Gaines's Mill.
PORTER, James M, Pvt, E. Enlisted in Lincolnton on September 11, 1861, at age 46. Carpenter. Born in Mecklenburg, Disability discharge granted Nov 18, 1861. Later served in the 4th NC Senior Reserves.
POWELL, Andrew Jackson, Pvt, F. Enlisted in Cleveland on September 17, 1861, at age 22. Captured at Gettysburg. Died of pyaemia (blood poisoning) at David's Island, NY Harbor Aug 2, 1863.
POWELL, Thomas, Pvt, D. Enlisted after October 1864. Deserted at Petersburg Sept 5, 1864. Took oath and was sent to Philadelphia.
PRESNEL, James, Pvt, C. Enlisted at Camp Vance on May 25, 1864. Wounded August 25, 1864. Deserted at Petersburg February 21, 1865, with John Presnal. Took the oath and was transported to Baltimore.
PRESNEL, John C, Pvt, C. Enlisted at Camp Vance on May 11, 1864. Deserted at Petersburg February 21, 1865, with James Presnel. Took the oath and was transported to Baltimore.
PRICE, Drury D, Cpl, F. Enlisted in Cleveland on September 17, 1861, at age 22. Fifer. Present every muster but one for sickness. Wounded at Mechanicsville. Present at Appomattox. Drowned on the way home at the Catawba River on April 25, 1865.
PRICE, Linville, Pvt, A. Enlisted in Ashe Co on August 10, 1861, at age 21. Deserted July 30, 1862. Imprisoned at Castle Thunder in November 1864. Member of the Heroes of America.
PRICE, Ransom M, Pvt, B. Enlisted at Camp Mangum on September 2, 1861, at age 27. Leg amputated. Died July 5, 1862, of wounds received in the Seven Days battles. Son of Robert Price.
PRICE, Robert J, Pvt, E. Enlisted in Lincolnton on September 11, 1861, at age 27. Carriage maker. Present every muster but one (detached duty). Extra duty as a wheelwright and carpenter. Deserted at Petersburg March 8, 1865. Took the oath and was sent to Philadelphia.
PRICE, Spencer L, Pvt, B. Enlisted in Rutherford on September 2, 1861, at age 38. Died July 5, 1862. Widow Sarah Price.
PROCTOR, Alex G, Pvt, E. Enlisted in Lincolnton on August 31, 1861, at age 19. Accounted for every muster. Present to Nov 1864.
PROCTOR, James A, Pvt, E and G. Enlisted in Lincolnton on September 11, 1861, at age 33. Disability discharge granted in July 1862, due to asthma. Reenlisted March 12, 1863. Captured at Falling Waters. Paroled at Elmira October 11, 1864. Hospitalized in Richmond February 13, 1865. Sent to Cherryville, NC.
PRUITT, John W, Pvt, A. Enlisted in Ashe Co on August 10, 1861, at age 24. Resident of Allegheny County, NC. Wounded furlough granted

September 1862, to August 1863. Deserted April 1864. Took the oath at Charleston, WV in February 1865, and sent north.

PRUITT, Nathan, Pvt, G. Enlisted at Camp Vance on August 22, 1864. Hospitalized October 17, 1864, in a comatose condition from typhoid. Furloughed. Paroled at Salisbury.

PUCKETT, James H, Pvt, G. Enlisted in Charlotte on September 30, 1861, at age 22. Born in Pittsylvania, VA. Wounded December 13, 1862. Died February 12, 1863. Son of Elizabeth Puckett.

PUTNAM, Devany, Cpl, E. Enlisted in Lincolnton on August 31, 1861, at age 27. Came from the 12th NC in exchange for John M Collins April 1863. Accounted for each muster. Present at Appomattox.

PUTNAM, John L, Pvt, H. Enlisted in Shelby on October 1, 1861, at age 19. Captured at Falling Waters. Confined at Point Lookout and Elmira. Exchanged October 29, 1864. No further records.

PUTNAM, Leroy, Pvt, H. Enlisted in Shelby on October 1, 1861, at age 29. Killed at Gaines's Mill. Margaret Putnam widow.

PUTNAM, P G Sr., Pvt, H. Enlisted in Cleveland on Feb 28, 1863, at age 39. Captured at Falling Waters. Died at Pt Lookout Aug 18, 1864.

PUTNAM, Perry G Jr., Pvt, H. Enlisted in Orange CH on April 18, 1864. Captured at Petersburg March 25, 1865. Held at Point Lookout until June 16, 1865.

PUTNAM, R K, Pvt, H. Enlisted in Shelby on October 1, 1861, at age 19. Substitute, transferred to 15th NC Infantry September 1, 1862.

PUTNAM, Samuel S, Pvt, F. Enlisted after December 1864. Present at Appomattox.

PUTNAM, Wade H, Pvt, H. Enlisted in Shelby on October 1, 1861, at age 18. Killed at Frayser's Farm. Son of Elizabeth Putnam.

QUEEN, Berry, Pvt, E. Enlisted in Lincolnton on September 11, 1861, at age 23. Married to Julia Queen. Teamster. Present every muster of enlistment. Killed in action at the Wilderness May 5, 1864.

QUEEN, Joshua A, Pvt, E. Enlisted in Lincolnton on September 11, 1861, at age 26. Teamster. Present every muster but one (sick). Wounded at Frayser's Farm. Present to December 1864.

QUEEN, Washington, Pvt, E. Enlisted in Lincolnton on September 11, 1861, at age 21. Died of disease December 4, 1861.

RABB, William, Pvt, E. Enlisted at Camp Holmes on April 16, 1864. Gunshot wound to the hand June 1864. No record after that.

RADFORD, Shadrack, Pvt, C. Enlisted in Rutherford on September 2, 1861, at age 23. AWOL March 2, 1862. Joined another regiment without permission.

RAINES, Stephen, Pvt, I. Enlisted in Rutherford on Oct 6, 1861, at age 47. Disability discharge July 15, 1862, for a non-battle related illness.

RAY, David B, Pvt, D. Enlisted at Camp Gregg on April 4, 1863. Died June 1, 1863, of wounds received at Chancellorsville; Gunshot wound compound fracture of the thigh.

RAY, David M, Pvt, I. Enl. at Camp Vance on May 25, 1864. Captured at Petersburg March 25, 1865. Held at Pt Lookout until June 19, 1865.

RAY, Hugh, Pvt, D. Enlisted at Camp Gregg on April 4, 1863, at age 42. Died of Typhoid June 29, 1863.

RAY, Joseph A, Pvt, D. Enlisted at Camp Gregg on April 4, 1863, at age 26. Wounded and captured at Gettysburg. Leg was amputated. Died at Harts Island NY July 31, 1863.

REEP, Jesse, Pvt, E. Enlisted in Lincolnton on September 11, 1861, at age 19. Accounted for every muster. Wounded in the hip at Chancellorsville. Present at Appomattox.

REEP, Laban, Pvt, E. Enlisted at Camp Holmes on April 6, 1864. Died of wounds June 11, 1864.

REEVES, Brantley A, Pvt, K. Enlisted in Troy on September 9, 1861, at age 21. Died of disease September 30, 1862. Son of Harris Reeves.

REEVES, Elijah M, Sgt, K. Enlisted in Troy on September 9, 1861, at age 20. Present every muster but one sick leave. Promoted to Sgt. July 4, 1863. Was paroled at Farmville, VA April 11, 1865.

REEVES, Franklin E, Pvt, K. Enlisted in Troy on September 9, 1861, at age 19. Captured and paroled at Sharpsburg. Gunshot wound to the left foot at Chancellorsville. Did not return. Disability discharge granted February 11, 1865.

REEVES, James C, Cpl. K. Enlisted in Troy on September 9, 1861, at age 22. Present every muster but one sick leave. Captured at Fredericksburg and exchanged. Died of Gunshot wound to the hip November 20, 1864.

REINEHARDT, Daniel, Pvt, E. Enlisted in Lincolnton on September 11, 1861, at age 26. Received a leg wound at Chancellorsville. Absent remainder of the war.

REVEL, E H, Pvt, H. Enlisted in Shelby on October 1, 1861, at age 19. Born Nash, NC. Present every muster but one leave. Wounded Sept 1862, at Harper's Ferry. Deserted at Petersburg February 6, 1865. Was transported to Bond Co, Ill for public works.

REVEL, Henry B, Pvt, H. Enlisted in Shelby on Oct 1, 1861, at age 18. Born in Nash, NC. Captured at Falling Waters. Confined at Pt Lookout. Joined 1st U.S. Volunteers January 22, 1864. Deserted at Ft. Snelling MN and mustered out Oct 1, 1865. Charges dropped in 1928.

REVEL, Robert Hammond, Pvt, H. Enlisted in Shelby on Feb 28, 1864. Died of Rubella June 18, 1864.

REVEL, Robert R, Pvt, H. Enlisted in Shelby on October 1, 1861, at age 30. Born Chester SC, carriage maker. Listed as deserted April 20, 1863. In arrest in October 1864. No record after that.

REYNOLDS, Elijah, Pvt, K. Enlisted in Troy on September 9, 1861, at age 23. Captured at Falling Waters. Exchanged from Point Lookout September 1864. No further record.

REYNOLDS, Matthew, Pvt, E. Enlisted in Lincolnton on September 11, 1861, at age 18. Wounded and captured at Gettysburg. Confined at Fort Delaware and Point Lookout. Exchanged at Venus Point on the Savannah River November 15, 1864. Captured in Jackson Hospital in Richmond April 3, 1865. Confined at Libby Prison, transferred to Newport News. Released on oath June 30, 1865.

RHODES, David, 2Lt, E. Enlisted in Lincolnton on September 11, 1861, at age 30. Killed in action at Gaines's Mill. Record notes "A faithful, courteous, and attentive officer".

RHYNE, Caleb, Pvt, E. Enlisted in Gaston, NC on March 5, 1863, at age 38. Captured at the Wilderness. Confined at Point Lookout until September 18, 1864. Hospitalized for scorbutus. Was granted a 60-day furlough. No further record.

RICHARDS, Alexander, Pvt, E. Enlisted in Lincolnton on September 11, 1861, at age 22. Disability discharge granted February 1862. Reenlisted April 20, 1864. Was captured at Hanover Junction May 24, 1864. Confined at Point Lookout until March 14, 1865.

RICHARDS, John S, Surgeon. Enlisted in Orange CH on June 15, 1862. Assistant Surgeon until October 1863.

RICHARDSON, Allen, Pvt, A. Enlisted in Ashe Co on Aug 10, 1861, at age 31. Gunshot wd left arm at Gaines's Mill. Deserted July 1863.

RICHARDSON, David, Pvt, K. Enlisted in Troy on September 9, 1861, at age 17. Present every muster. Killed in action August 5, 1864.

RICHARDSON, James, Pvt, A. Enlisted in Ashe Co on August 10, 1861, at age 23. Present every muster but one (leave). Wounded once. Captured at Hatchers Run. Confined at Pt Lookout until June 17, 1865.

RICHARDSON, James G Jr, Sgt, A. Enlisted in Ashe Co on August 10, 1861, at age 17. Present every muster of enlistment. Died June 1, 1863, of wounds received at Chancellorsville.

RICHARDSON, John, Pvt, A. Enlisted in Ashe Co on August 10, 1861, at age 18. Captured at Gettysburg. Confined at Point Lookout until April 27, 1864. No record after that.

RICHARDSON, Joseph B, Pvt, A. Enlisted at Camp Holmes on July 25, 1864. Captured at Hatchers Run. Confined at Point Lookout until June 17, 1865.

RICHARDSON, Joshua, Cpl, A. Enlisted in Ashe Co on August 10, 1861, at age 19. Accounted for every muster. Wounded at Ream's

Station. Left arm amputated on the field by surgeon Miller. Discharged December 28, 1864.

RICHARDSON, Richard, Pvt, A. Enlisted in Ashe Co on August 10, 1861, at age 29. Died March 10, 1862, of disease at Goldsboro.

RICKERT, Henry H, Sgt. Major. Enlisted as a private in Company D in Rowan on Sept 9, 1861, at age 21. Born Iredell, NC. Present every muster. Promoted to Sgt. Major July 1, 1863. Present at Appomattox.

RIDDICK, James W, Adjunct. Enlisted at Camp Gregg on June 1, 1862. Captain, Adjutant. Wounded at Gettysburg while serving on General Scales' staff. Recognized for bravery in Scales' official report. Transferred to another command November 2, 1863.

RIDDICK, Richard H, Colonel. Commissioned April 5, 1862, at age 36. Had served under General Longstreet at First Manassas. Wounded at Mechanicsville and Gaines's Mill. Died September 11, 1862, of wounds received at Ox Hill.

RIED, David V, Pvt, E. Enlisted at Camp Mangum on January 3, 1862, at age 28. Teamster. Accounted for every muster with one AWOL. Deserted, returned April 15, 1862. Pardoned on condition he would serve until his company was discharged. Wounded in the ankle, arm, left hip, and left hand at Gaines's Mill. Present at Appomattox.

RIED, George W, Pvt, K. Enlisted at Camp Holmes on June 30, 1864. Present at Appomattox.

RIED, Robert, Pvt, H. Enlisted in Shelby on October 1, 1861, at age 45. Born Chester, SC, discharged September 26, 1862.

RIED, Robert S, 2Lt, G. Enlisted in Charlotte on September 30, 1861, at age 33. Enlisted as a private and promoted to Lieutenant. Died of wounds July 9, 1862.

RIED, William R, Pvt, H. Enlisted in Shelby on Oct 1, 1861, at age 22. Died of disease at Farmville, VA July 22, 1862. Son of Robert Ried.

ROBBINS, Elisha, Sgt, I. Enlisted in Rutherford on October 6, 1861, at age 23. Wounded at Chancellorsville and awarded the Badge of Distinction. Present every muster but one (AWOL). Reduced to private, promoted again to Sgt. Captured at Petersburg March 25, 1865. Confined at Point Lookout until June 19, 1865.

ROBBINS, Jackson, Cpl, I. Enlisted in Rutherford on October 6, 1861, at age 33. Killed at Gettysburg. Elizabeth Robbins widow.

ROBBINS, James E, Pvt, B. Enlisted in Rutherford on September 2, 1861, at age 17. Died of disease December 7, 1863.

ROBBINS, John, Pvt, I. Enlisted at Camp Vance on May 13, 1864. Present in November 1864. No records after that.

ROBERTS, John A, Cpt, H. Enlisted as a lieutenant in Shelby on October 1, 1861, at age 29. Justice of the Peace and Mail Contractor for

Cleveland County. Present every muster but one (sick). Promoted to Captain. Present at Appomattox.

ROBERTS, John W, Pvt, H. Enlisted in Shelby on October 1, 1861, at age 25. Gunshot wound left hand Chancellorsville. Served as a guard in Charlotte for the remainder of the war.

ROBERTS, Luther, Cpl, H. Enlisted in Shelby on October 1, 1861, at age 19. Killed in action at Gaines's Mill. Son of Henderson and Margaret Camp Roberts and brother of Sidney and Perry Roberts.

ROBERTS, Perry Martin, Pvt, H. Enlisted in Shelby on October 1, 1861, at age 18. Killed in action at Chancellorsville. Brother of Luther and Sidney Roberts

ROBERTS, Sidney R, Pvt, H. Enlisted in Shelby on October 1, 1861, at age 18. Died of typhoid fever August 10, 1862. Son of Henderson Roberts and brother of Luther and Perry Roberts.

ROBERTS, Thomas H, Pvt, H. Enlisted in Shelby on October 1, 1861, at age 18. Died August 4, 1862, of a gunshot wound to the abdomen received at Frayser's Farm. Son of Morris Roberts.

ROBERTS, Walter R, Pvt, B. Enlisted in Raleigh on April 10, 1864. Captured at Sutherland Station. Confined at Harts Island, NY Harbor until June 19, 1865.

ROBERTS, William, Pvt, B. Resident of Cleveland County. Enlisted after December of 1864. Captured at Southside Railroad. Confined at Harts Island, NY Harbor until June 17, 1865.

ROBERTS, William G B, Pvt, C and H. Enlisted in Rutherford on September 2, 1861, at age 30. Millwright. Transferred to Company H January 11, 1862. Died of disease February 19, 1862.

ROBERTSON, Alfred, Pvt, C. Enlisted in Rutherford on September 2, 1861, at age 23. Absent sick since August 1862, dropped from the rolls.

ROBERTSON, William B, Pvt, I. Enlisted at Camp Vance on May 25, 1864. Granted a 60-day furlough in Dec 1864. No record of return.

ROBINSON, George W, Pvt, E. Enlisted at Camp Mangum on January 3, 1862, at age 19. A tinner by trade. Present every muster of enlistment. Wounded at 2nd Manassas and Fredericksburg. Died August 2, 1864, of unknown cause.

ROBINSON, J N, Pvt, H. Enlisted at Camp Holmes on April 10, 1864. Present to November 1864.

ROBINSON, Thomas, Pvt, C. Enlisted at Camp Vance on May 13, 1864. AWOL from October 6, 1864.

RODDEN, James J, Pvt, G. Enlisted in Charlotte on September 30, 1861, at age 33. Severely wounded in the Seven Days Battles. Detailed as a shoemaker and hospital guard. Granted a 30-day furlough in December 1864. No record of return.

RODGERS, William, Pvt, H. Enlisted in Shelby on October 1, 1861, at age 26. Died of Typhoid July 5, 1862. Mary Rogers widow.

ROGERS, William, Pvt, B. Enlisted in Rutherford on September 2, 1861, at age 20. Died of Small Pox Feb 1, 1863. Son of Sarah Rogers.

ROLLINS, Dock O, Pvt, I. Enlisted in Shelby on August 22, 1864. Deserted at Petersburg March 8, 1865. Took the oath and was transported to Chattanooga, TN.

ROLLINS, Drury D, Pvt, I. Enlisted at Camp Vance on June 16, 1864. Deserted at Petersburg March 8, 1865. Took the oath and was transported to Chattanooga, TN.

ROLLINS, John P, Pvt, B, and I. Enlisted at Camp Holmes on April 10, 1864. Deserted at Petersburg March 8, 1865. Took the oath and was transported to Chattanooga, TN.

ROLLINS, Lawson, Pvt, I. Enlisted at Camp Holmes on May 27, 1864. Deserted at Petersburg March 8, 1865. Took the oath and was transported to Chattanooga, TN.

ROOPE, John, Pvt, A. Enlisted in Ashe Co on August 10, 1861, at age 25. Present every muster with one AWOL. Teamster in the division commissary train. Present at Appomattox.

ROPER, David, Pvt, I. Enlisted in Hanover, VA on May 24, 1864. Suffered from Edema in the leg following Typhoid. Furloughed for 60 days in February 1865. No further records.

ROSHICH, George W, Pvt, G. Enlisted in Richmond on May 30, 1862, at age 32. Accounted every muster of enlistment. Hospitalized in June 1863, for poisoning from vaccination. Present at Appomattox.

ROYAL, Franklin, Pvt, A. Enlisted at Camp Holmes on November 4, 1863. Deserted February 8, 1864.

ROYAL, John, Pvt, A. Enlisted at Camp Holmes on November 4, 1863. Deserted February 8, 1864.

RUDD, J L, Pvt, B. Resident of Caswell, NC. Enlisted after December 1864. Captured Southerland Station April 2, 1865. Confined at Harts Island, NY until June 19, 1865.

RUDD, Thomas S, Pvt, B. Enlisted at Camp Holmes on September 20, 1864. Resident of Caswell, NC. Captured Southerland Station April 2, 1865. Confined at Harts Island, NY until released June 19, 1865.

RUPPE, Samuel, Pvt, I. Enlisted in Cleveland on Feb 26, 1863, at age 37. Wounded at Chancellorsville. Disability discharge in Nov 1863.

RUPPE, Thomas M, Pvt, F. Enlisted around November 5, 1864, at age 20. Wounded and captured at Petersburg March 25, 1865. Treated aboard the USA Steamer Connecticut and Lincoln General Hospital. Released June 12, 1865.

RUSH, Martin, Pvt, K. Enlisted in Troy on September 9, 1861, at age 18. Accounted for every muster. Wounded at Gaines's Mill and again

May or June 1864. Captured at Petersburg March 25, 1865. Confined at Point Lookout until May 14, 1865.

RUSSELL, Eli, Pvt, K. Enlisted in Troy on March 5, 1863, at age 27. Captured at Falling Waters. Died at Point Lookout December 27, 1863.

RUSSELL, Elijah A, Pvt, K. Enlisted at Camp Mangum on December 25, 1861, at age 23. Gunshot wound to the right knee at Gaines's Mill. Disability discharge granted August 22, 1863.

RUSSELL, J W, Pvt, K. Enlisted after December 1864. Hospitalized in Farmville April 6, 1865. Paroled at Lynchburg April 15, 1865.

RUSSELL, Leonard F, Pvt, K. Enlisted in Troy on March 5, 1863, at age 38. Resident of Gwinn Hill in Montgomery Co. Accounted for every muster of enlistment. Captured at Petersburg March 25, 1865. Confined at Point Lookout until June 17, 1865.

RUSSELL, Wiley W, Pvt, K. Enlisted in Troy on September 9, 1861, at age 37. Discharged December 9, 1862, due to age.

RUSSELL, William F, Pvt, K. Enlisted in Troy on March 5, 1863, at age 20. Gunshot wound to the right thigh at Chancellorsville. Returned to duty and was present through 1864. Deserted at Petersburg March 19, 1865. Took the oath and was transported to Pittsburgh.

RUSSELL, William M, Pvt, K. Enlisted in Troy on March 5, 1863, at age 37. Present to December 1864.

RUTLEDGE, B J, Pvt, E. Enlisted after December 1864. Davie County resident. Captured at Hatchers Run. Confined at Hart's Island, NY Harbor until June 20, 1865.

SADBERRY, James, Cpl, K. Enlisted in Troy on September 9, 1861, at age 21. Present every muster. Died at Winder Hospital of wounds and measles/rubella June 12, 1864.

SAINTSING, Willie, Pvt, A. Enlisted around December 19, 1864. Resident of Davidson County, NC. Deserted at Petersburg December 26, 1864. Took oath was transported to Springfield, Ill.

SANDERS, Allen J, Pvt, Enlisted after December 1864. Cleveland County resident. Deserted at Petersburg January 23, 1865. Took the oath and was transported to New York City.

SANDERS, Andrew E, Pvt, K. Enlisted in Troy on March 5, 1863, at age 18. Disability discharge granted May 28, 1863.

SANDERS, Elijah W, Sgt, K. Enlisted in Troy on September 9, 1861, at age 25. Accounted for on every muster. Wounded at Mechanicsville. Gunshot wound to the right thigh at Gettysburg. Deserted at Petersburg March 7, 1865. Took the oath and was sent to Philadelphia.

SANDERS, Elisha C, Pvt, K. Enlisted in Troy on March 5, 1863, at age 25. Captured at Gettysburg. Died at Ft Delaware August 24, 1863, of general debility.

SANDERS, James M, Cpl, K. Enlisted in Troy on September 9, 1861, at age 21. Died of disease August 22, 1862. Son of Henry Sanders.
SANDERS, Jesse A, 1Lt, K. Enlisted in Troy on September 9, 1861, at age 27. Deputy Sherriff and postmaster. Exempt from Conscript Act. Resigned July 30, 1862, due to health reasons.
SANE, Daniel, Pvt, E. Enlisted in Lincolnton on September 11, 1861, at age 21. Died of disease December 10, 1861.
SANE, Elijah, Pvt, C. Enlisted in Rutherford on September 2, 1861, at age 25. Deserted, dropped from the rolls August 11, 1863.
SANE, Jacob, Jr, Sgt, E. Enlisted in Lincolnton on September 11, 1861, at age 22. Captured at Falling Waters and confined at Point Lookout. Exchanged March 3, 1864. Returned. Was captured again at the Southside Railroad. Confined at Hart's Island until June 19, 1865.
SANE, Jacob, Sr, Pvt, E. Enlisted in Lincolnton on September 11, 1861, at age 33. Married to Barbara Sane. Died of disease Aug 8, 1862.
SANFORD, James O, Pvt, G. Enlisted in Charlotte on September 30, 1861, at age 18. AWOL from June through October 1864 was satisfactorily explained. Was captured at Petersburg April 2, 1865. Confined at Harts Island until June 17, 1865.
SANFORD, John M, Pvt, G. Enlisted in Charlotte on September 30, 1861, at age 19. Present every muster but one (sick). Wounded in Seven Days battles and Gettysburg. Died May 16, 1864, of a gunshot wound to the head received May 5, 1864, at the Wilderness.
SARRAT, Tilman, Cpl, H. Enlisted in Shelby on October 1, 1861, at age 28. Accounted for every muster. Died May 14, 1864, of wounds.
SARVICE, S T, Pvt, H. Enlisted on September 11, 1864. Gaston County resident. Captured in a hospital in Richmond. Was hospitalized for Typhoid. Transferred to the USA General Hospital at Pt Lookout on the Hospital Transport Thomas Powell. Released June 28, 1865.
SCISM, James F, Pvt, H. Enlisted in Shelby on October 1, 1861, at age 23. Carpenter. Division cattle driver and striker for blacksmiths. On duty every muster. Gunshot wound at the Seven Days battles (Gaines's Mill). Returned to duty. Present at Appomattox.
SCISM, William, Pvt, H. Enlisted at Camp Holmes on April 20, 1864, at age 23. Initially rejected by mustering officer in 1861. Enlisted April of 1864. Died of Typhoid June 11, 1864.
SCOGGINS, James W, Pvt, C. Enlisted in Rutherford on September 2, 1861, at age 19. Present or accounted for every muster. Deserted at Petersburg March 8, 1865. Took oath and was sent to Chattanooga, TN.
SCOGGINS, John L, Pvt, B. Enlisted in Rutherford on September 2, 1861, at age 16. Discharged due to age November 11, 1862.

SCOGGINS, William M, Pvt, C. Enlisted at Camp Holmes on September 25, 1864. Deserted at Petersburg March 8, 1865. Took oath and was sent to Chattanooga, TN.

SCOTT, William A, Pvt, G. Enlisted on May 30, 1862, at age 22. Killed in action at Frayser's Farm. Son of Nancy Scott.

SECHLER, John F, Pvt, D. Enlisted in Rowan on September 9, 1861, at age 40. Died July 28, 1862, of wounds received in one of the Seven Days battles. Son of Henry Sechler.

SELF, Lemuel S, Cpl, F. Enlisted in Cleveland on September 17, 1861, at age 22. Accounted for every muster. Captured at the Battle of North Anna May 23, 1864. Died of disease at Pt Lookout Oct 3, 1864.

SELF, Moses, Pvt, H. Enlisted in Gaston, NC on March 5, 1863, at age 38. Gaston County resident. Died May 9, 1863, of wounds received at Chancellorsville.

SELF, William, Pvt, F. Enlisted in Cleveland on September 17, 1861, at age 20. Died March 4, 1862, of disease at Williamston, NC.

SELLERS, Jacob, Pvt, F. Enlisted in High Point on Oct 24, 1861, at age 32. Killed in action at Gaines's Mill. Son of Anna Mary Sellers.

SENTER, Jonas, Pvt, E. Enlisted at Camp Holmes on December 3, 1863. Gaston County resident. Present each muster of his enlistment but one (sick). Captured at Southside Railroad. Confined at Hart's Island, NY Harbor until June 18, 1865.

SERCEY, Henry, Pvt, C. Enlisted at Camp Vance on May 12, 1864. Absent sick each muster of enlistment. Died August 8, 1864, in Richmond of an unknown cause.

SHARP, James W, Pvt, A. Enlisted at Camp Vance on September 1, 1863. Deserted July 1864 but returned to duty. Was captured at Petersburg April 3, 1865, Confined at Harts Island, NY. Died of Typhoid and Pneumonia June 20, 1865.

SHAW, Green B, Pvt, K. Enlisted in Troy on Sept 9, 1861, at age 39. Drummer. Died Dec 11, 1861, of disease. Married to Sarah Shaw.

SHEETS, Calvin, Pvt, A. Enlisted in Ashe Co on August 10, 1861, at age 19. Died of disease February 3, 1862.

SHEETS, Daniel, Pvt, A. Enl. in Ashe Co Aug 10, 1861, at age 21. Died of wounds May 10, 1863.

SHEETS, Harvey, Pvt, A. Enlisted in Ashe Co on August 10, 1861, at age 22. deserted August 27, 1863, Listed AWOL or Deserted three times. Wounded at least once. Deserted Oct 3, 1864. No further record.

SHEETS, Henry, Pvt, A. Enlisted in Ashe Co on August 10, 1861, at age 19. Deserted August 27, 1863, returned, captured at Weldon RR Aug 25, 1864. Released on oath from Harts Island, NY Dec 5, 1864.

SHEETS, Jesse B, Sgt, A. Enlisted in Ashe Co on August 10, 1861, at age 35. Died of wounds July 19, 1862.

SHEHAN, James F, Pvt, I. Enlisted in Rutherford on October 6, 1861, at age 21. Born in Burke NC. Blacksmith. Wounded at Ox Hill. Captured at North Anna May 23, 1864. Exchanged from Point Lookout March 14, 1865. Did not return to the regiment.

SHELBY, James L, Sgt, G. Enlisted in Charlotte on Sept 30, 1861, at age 30. Was killed at Frayser's Farm. Married to Henrietta Shelby.

SHEPHARD, Calvin, Pvt, A. Enlisted in Ashe Co on December 4, 1861, at age 22. Born in Wilkes, NC. Died of disease July 15, 1862.

SHEPHARD, George W, Pvt, A. Enlisted at Camp Vance on March 9, 1864. Captured at Petersburg April 2, 1865. Confined at Harts Island, NY until June 17, 1865.

SHEPHARD, John F, Pvt, A. Enlisted in Ashe Co on August 10, 1861, at age 43. Born in Wilkes, NC. AWOL August 1862, to March 1864. Discharged in January 1865, due to age and health.

SHEPHARD, John W, Pvt, A. Enlisted in Ashe Co on Aug 10, 1861, at age 30. Born in Wilkes, NC. Disability discharge June 10, 1862.

SHIELDS, Alexander M, Sgt, H. Enlisted in Shelby on October 1, 1861, at age 26. Carriage maker. Listed AWOL from January 1864, on.

SHIELDS, Joseph W, Pvt, H. Enlisted in Shelby on October 1, 1861, at age 28. Carriage maker. Born McDowell NC. Hospital ward master. Killed in action at Chancellorsville. Married to Elizabeth Shields.

SHIELDS, Robert H, Pvt, F. Enlisted in Cleveland on September 11, 1861, at age 23. Blacksmith. Born in Buncombe NC. Killed in action at Gaines's Mill. Married to Mary Shields

SHOEMAKER, Calvin, Pvt, A. Enlisted in Ashe Co on August 10, 1861, at age 32. Wounded in Seven Days Battles, 3 fingers amputated. Listed as AWOL the rest of the war.

SHOFFNER, Martin, Major. Enlisted in High Point on October 25, 1861. Drillmaster, AAG for the regiment. Resigned January 25, 1862, for personal reasons.

SHOTWELL, Alexander H, 2Lt, C. Enlisted in Rutherford on September 2, 1861, at age 22. Rallied the regiment at Frayser's Farm and was mortally wounded. Sent to a private home in the country three days before he died July 10, 1862.

SHUFORD, A B, Pvt, B. Enlisted around November 5, 1864. Cleveland County resident. Captured at Southside Railroad. Confined at Harts Island, NY Harbor until June 17, 1865.

SHUFORD, Carter, Pvt, D. Enlisted at Camp Vance on March 22, 1864. Absent due to wounds since June 22, 1864. No further records.

SHUFORD, Pinkney H, 2Lt, F. Enlisted in Cleveland on September 17, 1861, at age 31. Born Catawba NC. Enlisted with his brother, Thomas. Suffered from "White Swelling" of the ankle from boyhood. Resigned due to disability July 24, 1862.

SHUFORD, Thomas S, Sgt, F. Enlisted in Cleveland on September 17, 1861, at age 23. Carpenter. Drum Major. He enlisted with his brother, Pinkney. Badge of Distinction at Chancellorsville where he was killed in action. Son of Ephraim Suford.

SHULL, Charles D, Pvt, E. Enlisted in Lincolnton on September 11, 1861, at age 18. Enlisted with his father and brother, Pearson and Phillip. Accounted for every muster. Wounded at Gaines's Mill. Captured at the Wilderness. Confined at Pt Lookout, Elmira. Exchanged Oct 29, 1864. Died in Lynchburg after exchange.

SHULL, Pearson, Pvt, E. Enlisted in Lincolnton on September 11, 1861, at age 52. Enlisted with his sons Charles and Phillip. Was Discharged due to age and disability October 26, 1861.

SHULL, Phillip A, Pvt, E. Enlisted in Lincolnton on September 11, 1861, at age 21. Blacksmith. Enlisted with his father and brother, Pearson and Charles. Wounded at Second Manassas, returned to duty. Captured at Hatchers Run. Held at Pt Lookout until June 19, 1865.

SHYTLE, Esley, Pvt, C. Enlisted in Rutherford on September 2, 1861, at age 19. Accounted for every muster. Captured at Hanover Junction on May 24, 1864. Was Confined at Point Lookout until June 3, 1865.

SHYTLE, Jeremiah, Pvt, C. Enlisted in Rutherford on September 2, 1861, at age 28. Captured at Falling Waters. Confined at Point Lookout until February 24, 1865.

SHYTLE, Martin L, Pvt, C. Enl in Rutherford on Sept 2, 1861, at age 23. Teamster. Died May 21, 1863, of wounds recd at Chancellorsville.

SHYTLE, Philip, Pvt, C. Enlisted in Rutherford on September 2, 1861, at age 53. Discharged February 2, 1863, at Camp Gregg due to age.

SICELOFF, Phillip, Pvt, B. Enlisted at Camp Vance on September 26, 1864. Davidson County resident. Captured at Hatchers Run. Confined at Harts Island, NY Harbor until June 19, 1865.

SIMMONS, Asbury, 2Lt, I. Enlisted in Rutherford on October 6, 1861, at age 39. Born in Edgecombe, NC. Failed reelection and was discharged April 18, 1862.

SIMMONS, Elisha T, Cpl, I. Enlisted in Rutherford on October 6, 1861, at age 32. Died of Typhoid at Richmond Aug 17, 1862. Wife Mary Simmons.

SIMMONS, James O, Cpt, I. Enlisted in Rutherford on October 6, 1861, at age 34. Failed reelection and was discharged April 18, 1862.

SIMMONS, Moses W, Pvt, I. Enlisted in Rutherford on October 6, 1861, at age 36. Merchant. Served as a wagon master. Discharge by mistake December 8, 1864 but did not return to duty.

SIMS, Doctor L, Pvt, C. Enlisted in Rutherford on September 2, 1861, at age 27. Discharged for medical reasons April 21, 1863.

SISK, John, Pvt, C. Enlisted in Rutherford on September 2, 1861, at age 24. Died at Raleigh of Pneumonia January 15, 1862.
SIZEMORE, George W, Pvt, B. Enlisted at Camp Holmes on May 9, 1864. Captured at Petersburg June 22, 1864. Exchanged from Point Lookout September 18, 1864. Hospitalized following exchange. Granted a 30-day furlough. No record of return.
SLOAN, Joseph J, Sgt. Mgr, D. Enlisted as a private in Rowan on Sept. 9, 1861, at age 25. First Sgt. Oct. 25, 1861 but reduced to private around Feb. 1862. Disability discharged June 10, 1862.
SLOOP, Edward, Cpl, D. Enlisted in Rowan on September 9, 1861, at age 34. Died of disease July 30, 1862. Married to Mary Sloop.
SLOOP, Phillip A, Sgt, D. Enlisted in Rowan on September 9, 1861, at age 21. Student. Present every muster but one (due to a severe wound at Chancellorsville). Returned to duty and was present at Appomattox.
SLUDER, James, Pvt, K. Enlisted at Camp Holmes on December 14, 1863. Absent sick on most musters of his enlistment. Paroled at Greensboro, NC May 16, 1865.
SMART, Oliver P, Pvt, B. Enlisted in Rutherford on September 2, 1861, at age 21. Disability discharge granted January 8, 1862.
SMART, William B, Pvt, B. Enlisted in Rutherford on Sept 2, 1861, at age 24. Died of wounds recd at Chancellorsville. Left leg amputated.
SMITH, Decator S, Pvt, I. Enlisted around December 19, 1864. Present at Appomattox.
SMITH, Dillard, Pvt, I. Enlisted in Rutherford on October 6, 1861, at age 23. Died of disease June 30, 1863.
SMITH, Isaac, Pvt, K. Enlisted in Troy on September 9, 1861, at age 21. Present every muster but one (sick). Wounded at Ox Hill. Captured at Southside Railroad. Held at Harts Island until June 17, 1865.
SMITH, John T, Pvt, I. Enlisted in Rutherford on October 6, 1861, at age 34. Died of disease December 11, 1861.
SMITH, Joseph C, Sgt, I. Enlisted in Rutherford on October 6, 1861, at age 23. Record states he was "a good soldier." Transferred to the CS Navy April 5, 1864.
SMITH, Nathan, Pvt, K. Enlisted in Troy on September 9, 1861, at age 30. Died July 6, 1862, of a gunshot wound to the shoulder received at Gaines's Mill. Married to Jemeniah Smith.
SMITH, Robert, Pvt, H. Enlisted in Shelby on October 1, 1861, at age 28. Born in Gaston NC. Was captured at Falling Waters. Exchanged from Point Lookout March 6, 1864. Returned to the regiment and was present at Appomattox.
SMITH, William B, Pvt, I. Enlisted in Rutherford on October 6, 1861, at age 40. Listed as deserted from May 1862, to October 1863.

Returned and was wounded and captured at the Wilderness. Treated for a wound in the abdomen. Listed Missing in Action, died of his wound.

SMITH, William F, Pvt, G. Enlisted at Camp Holmes on April 27, 1864. Present at Appomattox.

SNOTHERLY, William, Sgt, K. Enlisted after December 1864. Captured at Petersburg March 25, 1865. Confined at Point Lookout until June 19, 1865.

SORRELLS, Silas P, Pvt, C. Enlisted in High Point on November 13, 1861, at age 22. Silas was listed on detached service as a teamster in 1863, but had died in November of 1862, in Winchester. Regiment had not heard from him since October 1862.

SORRELLS, William W, Pvt, C. Enlisted in Rutherford on September 2, 1861, at age 29. Accounted for every muster with one AWOL. Promoted to Corporal. Captured at Brandy Station August 1, 1863. Exchanged from Point Lookout April 27, 1864. Reduced to private for straggling. Captured at Petersburg April 2, 1865. Confined at Harts Island until June 17, 1865.

SOUTH, James F, Pvt, A. Enlisted in Ashe Co on August 10, 1861, at age 26. Born in Grayson, VA. Accounted for every muster with one AWOL. Received a gunshot wound in September 1862. Suffered a concussion from a shell at Gettysburg. Deserted at Petersburg March 18, 1865. Took the oath and was transported to Knoxville, TN.

SOUTHER, T M, Pvt, B. Enlisted at Camp Holmes on May 5, 1864. Deserted near Petersburg June 21, 1864. No further records.

SPARKS, Caleb L, Cpl, B. Enlisted in Rutherford on September 2, 1861, at age 18. AWOL December 1862, and December 1863. Received a gunshot wound to the leg at Chancellorsville. Captured at Petersburg March 25, 1865. Held at Pt Lookout until June 20, 1865.

SPARKS, John L, Pvt, B. Enlisted in Rutherford on September 2, 1861, at age 20. Died January 21, 1862, of disease at Goldsboro. Married to Mary Sparks.

SPARKS, Joseph, Pvt, I. Enlisted at Camp Vance on May 6, 1864. Received a gunshot wound around June 23, 1864. Was captured at Petersburg April 2, 1865. Held at Pt Lookout until June 4, 1865.

SPARKS, Joshua, Pvt, D. Enlisted at Camp Holmes on Aug 27, 1864. Deserted from Petersburg Jan 23, 1865. Took the oath at City Point.

SPARKS, William A, Pvt, B. Enlisted after December of 1864. Present at Appomattox.

SPARROW, Cyrus P, Pvt, F. Enlisted in Cleveland on September 17, 1861, at age 17. Died August 11, 1862, of wounds received at Gaines's Mill. Died of a secondary hemorrhage caused by a compound fracture below the neck. Son of H W Sparrow.

SPARROW, Thomas A, Pvt, F. Enlisted in Cleveland on September 17, 1861, at age 24. Disability discharge granted February 1, 1862.

SPENCER, Jesse S, Cpt, K. Enlisted in Troy on September 9, 1861, at age 26. Resigned June 21, 1862, for health reasons. Clerk of the Court for Montgomery County. Claimed exemption from Conscription.

SPIVEY, Mark A, Pvt, K. Enlisted in Troy on September 9, 1861, at age 20. Deserted in May of 1862.

SPLAWN, James T, Pvt, I. Enlisted in Rutherford on October 6, 1861, at age 24. Transferred to Co D 16th NC May 30, 1862.

SPURLIN, Isaac, Pvt, H. Enlisted in Shelby on October 1, 1861, at age 24. Transferred to Co C 15th NC October 1, 1862.

STALKER, Noah, Pvt, B. Enlisted at Camp Holmes on July 17, 1864. Resident of Randolph Co, NC. Captured at Southerland Station and was confined at Harts Island, NY Harbor until June 18, 1865.

STALKER, Thomas, Pvt, B. Enlisted at Camp Holmes on July 17, 1864. Died before March 1865. Unknown cause and date.

STAMEY, John T, 1Sgt, E. Enlisted as a private in Lincolnton on September 11, 1861, at age 21. Son of Nelly Stamey. Elected 1Sgt April 18, 1862. Killed in action at Shepherdstown September 18, 1862.

STAMPER, Hiram T, 1Sgt, A. Enlisted in Ashe Co on August 10, 1861, at age 35. Discharged by mistake in 1862. Returned. Was present until captured at North Anna May 24, 1864. Held at Point Lookout. Exchanged at Venus Point on the Savannah River Nov 15, 1864.

STEADMAN, James T, Pvt, I. Enlisted in Rutherford on October 6, 1861, at age 18. Born in Spartanburg, SC. Present every muster but one (sick). Wounded at Seven Days and Gettysburg. Present to Dec 1864.

STEADMAN, John R, Pvt, I. Enlisted in Rutherford on October 6, 1861, at age 15. Born Spartanburg SC. Son of E J Steadman. Wounded at Shepherdstown. Died of wounds, exact date unknown.

STEADMAN, Perry, Pvt, I. Enlisted in Rutherford on October 6, 1861, at age 26. Polk County resident. Deserted from Lynchburg on June 12, 1863. Returned around October of 1864, under Gov. Vance's proclamation. Captured at Petersburg March 25, 1865. Confined at Point Lookout until June 20, 1865.

STEADMAN, Townsend, Pvt, C. Enlisted in Rutherford on September 2, 1861, at age 31. Disability discharge granted July 16, 1862.

STEEL, Robert J, Pvt, K. Enlisted at Camp Holmes on July 26, 1864. Montgomery County resident. Captured at Petersburg April 3, 1865. Confined at Harts Island, NY until June 17, 1865.

STEPHENS, Asa Berry, Pvt, G. Enlisted in Charlotte on September 30, 1861, at age 24. Died of disease at Hamilton, NC March 27, 1862.

STEPHENS, John, Pvt, A. Enlisted in Ashe Co on Aug 10, 1861, at age 36. Died of disease May 10, 1862.

STEPHENS, Richard T, Pvt, G. Enlisted in Charlotte on September 30, 1861, at age 20. Born in Chesterfield SC. Burke County resident. Gunshot wound in the arm at Seven Days. Head wound from a shell at Fredericksburg. AWOL from November 2, 1863, to August 19, 1864. Wounded August 25, 1864. Deserted at Petersburg March 26, 1865. Took oath and was sent to Columbus, OH on public works. Escaped and was arrested and confined at Wheeling, WV April 1, 1865.

STIREWALT, Jacob Frank, Pvt, D. Enlisted in Rowan on September 9, 1861, at age 22. Mechanic, teamster. Present or on detached duty every muster. Captured at Petersburg March 25, 1865. Confined at Point Lookout until June 20, 1865.

STIRGILL, William, Pvt, A. Enlisted in Ashe Co on August 10, 1861, at age 23. Died of disease at Staunton, VA December 26, 1862.

STRICKLAND, Marion B, Pvt, I. Enlisted in Rutherford on October 6, 1861, at age 24. Wounded at Sharpsburg. Died sometime after April 1864. E E Strickland widow.

STROUD, Thomas J, Sgt, B. Enlisted in Rutherford on September 2, 1861, at age 24. Born Chester, SC. Wounded at Fredericksburg, and Chancellorsville. Listed as a deserter May 2, 1863. Did not return after wounds. Hospitalized July 1863. Paroled at Lynchburg April 1865.

STROUP, Daniel M, Pvt, F. Enlisted in Cleveland on November 9, 1861, at age 18. Born in Gaston NC. Died July 5, 1862, of wounds received at Gaines's Mill. Son of Christopher Stroup.

STROUP, Miles A, Pvt, F. Enlisted in Goldsboro on January 28, 1862. Wounded and captured at Gettysburg. Exchanged from David's Island NY September 16, 1863. Returned to the regiment by February 1864. Was present at Appomattox.

SUGGS, Nathaniel S, Pvt, K. Enlisted in Troy on September 9, 1861, at age 19. Died of disease December 18, 1861.

SULLIVAN, Harden, Pvt, A. Enlisted in Ashe Co on August 10, 1861, at age 32. Born in Davidson, NC. Died of disease August 1, 1862.

SUMMERVILLE, Robert, Pvt, G. Enlisted in November 1864. Present at Appomattox.

SUTTLE, George M, Sgt, I. Enlisted in Rutherford on October 6, 1861, at age 34. Discharged by mistake Dec 8, 1862 but did not return.

SUTTLE, Phillip, Pvt, I. Enlisted in Rutherford on Oct 6, 1861, at age 21. Present each muster. Died at Lynchburg June 5, 1863, of Typhoid.

SUTTON, Elias, Pvt, I. Enlisted at Camp Vance on October 15, 1863. Died December 7, 1863, of Typhoid fever. Married to Mary Sutton.

SUTTON, William, Pvt, I. Enlisted in Rutherford on October 6, 1861, age 28. Accounted for every muster. Wounded at 2nd Manassas. Captured at Southside RR. Held at Harts Island until June 17, 1865.

SWAFFORD, William, Pvt, F. Enlisted in Cleveland on September 17, 1861, at age 42. Discharged August 14, 1862, for age and health.
SWEENEY, Edward C, Pvt. Deserted at Petersburg July 29, 1864. Held at Bermuda Hundred. Release date unknown.
SWEEZY, George J, Pvt, B. Enlisted in Rutherford on September 2, 1861, at age 33. Killed in action at Ox Hill.
SWIM, James A, Pvt, I. Enlisted at Camp Vance on May 24, 1864. Deserted around October 1864.
TALBERT, Calvin R, Pvt, K. Enlisted in Troy on September 9, 1861, at age 23. Died of Typhoid in Lynchburg, VA September 24, 1862.
TALBERT, James C, Pvt, K. Enlisted in Troy on March 5, 1863, at age 37. Montgomery County resident. Accounted for every muster with one AWOL. Wounded in May 1864. Captured at Petersburg March 25, 1865. Confined at Pt Lookout until June 21, 1865.
TALBERT, Mark T, Pvt, K. Enlisted in Troy on September 9, 1861, at age 20. Present every muster. Was hospitalized during Gettysburg campaign and sent to work on the Richmond fortifications. Returned to the regiment. Captured Petersburg March 25, 1865. Confined at Point Lookout until May 14, 1865.
TALBERT, Miles, Pvt, K. Enlisted in Raleigh on September 17, 1863, at age 18. Wounded in April or May of 1864. Returned by November of 1864. No record after December 1864.
TALLENT, Samuel, Pvt, E. Enlisted in Lincolnton on September 11, 1861, at age 25. Born in Burke NC. Captured at Gaines's Mill. Held at Fort Columbus until August 5, 1862. Died of disease January 11, 1863.
TALLMAN, M, Pvt, K. Montgomery County resident. Enlisted after December 1864. 6'3" tall. Captured at Sutherland Station. Confined at Harts Island until June 17, 1865.
TANNER, Belton O, Pvt, C. Enlisted in Rutherford on September 2, 1861, at age 18. Killed in action at Gaines's Mill. Son of W A Tanner.
TATE, Gamewell, Pvt, I. Enlisted in Rutherford on October 6, 1861, at age 18. Disability discharge granted November 15, 1861.
TATE, Hiram G, Pvt, I. Enlisted in Rutherford on Oct 6, 1861, at age 27. Deserted after April 1863.
TAYLOR, Alexander, Pvt, A. Enlisted in Goldsboro on April 10, 1862, at age 38. Deserted in August 2, 1862. Arrested in Dublin, VA and confined. Released and returned to duty November 15, 1863. Captured at Hanover Junction May 24, 1864. Confined at Point Lookout until March 14, 1865. No record of return.
TAYLOR, David M, 1Sgt, E. Enlisted as a private in Lincolnton on September 11, 1861, at age 25. Carpenter. Promoted to 1Sgt October 1862. Accounted for every muster. Badge of Distinction at

Chancellorsville. Captured at the Wilderness. Confined at Point Lookout and Elmira until July 3, 1865.

TAYLOR, George P, Pvt, E. Enlisted at Camp Holmes on April 20, 1864. Married to Martha Taylor. Died Aug 4, 1864, unknown cause.

TAYLOR, James, Pvt, I. Enlisted in Rutherford on October 6, 1861, at age 25. Deserted August 15, 1862. Returned to duty by April 1863. Was killed in action July 1st at Gettysburg. Married to Sarah Taylor.

TAYLOR, James M, Sgt, C. Enlisted in Rutherford on September 2, 1861, at age 25. Promoted to Sgt. February 1, 1862, to replace J. L. Gray. Transferred to the 62nd NC July 11, 1862 and promoted to Lieutenant. Later was paroled at Athens, GA May 8, 1865.

TAYLOR, Jason J, Cpl, C. Enlisted in Bunker Hill VA on October 1862. Present or absent sick every muster of his enlistment. Furlough granted in December 1864, due to sickness. No record he returned.

TAYLOR, Jonathan C, Pvt, C. Enlisted in Rutherford on September 2, 1861, at age 21. Died at Raleigh of Typhoid January 28, 1862.

TAYLOR, Oliver P, Pvt, C. Enlisted at Camp Vance on May 9, 1864. Rutherford County resident. Provost Guard. Captured at Petersburg April 2, 1865. Held at Harts Island, NY Harbor until June 17, 1865.

TAYLOR, Robert A, Pvt, E. Enlisted in Lincolnton on September 11, 1861, at age 21. Blacksmith. Was captured at Chancellorsville and paroled at Old Capitol prison May 19, 1863. Returned to the regiment and was killed in action at Falling Waters. Son of David M Taylor.

TAYLOR, Thomas G, Pvt, E. Enlisted in Lincolnton on September 11, 1861, at age 18. Died of disease December of 1862.

TAYLOR, Wesley, Pvt, A. Enlisted in Ashe Co on August 10, 1861, at age 18. Sent to the hospital in Winchester around October 1862. Was believed to have died around that time.

TAYLOR, Wiley, Pvt, A. Enlisted in Ashe Co on August 10, 1861, at age 32. Captured at Gettysburg and was confined at Point Lookout. Exchanged February 18, 1865 and was assigned to a detachment of paroled prisoners at Camp Lee in Richmond. No further records.

TAYLOR, Wilson, Pvt, K. Enlisted at Camp Holmes on May 21, 1864. Absent with wounds each muster of enlistment.

TERRES, James C, Pvt, G. Enlisted in Charlotte on September 30, 1861, at age 24. Born in Philadelphia, PA. Carpenter. Wounded at Chancellorsville. Detailed as train guard and Quarter Master dept. in Charlotte starting October 26, 1863, for the remainder of the war. Paroled at Charlotte. May 11, 1865. Accounted for every muster.

THOMAS, John, Pvt, K. Enlisted in Troy on September 9, 1861, at age 26. Court martialed for AWOL March 17, 1863 and returned to the regiment. Deserted August 14, 1863, near Orange, VA and was arrested. Executed September 26, 1863.

THOMPSON, Calvin, Pvt, A. Enlisted in Ashe Co on August 10, 1861, at age 33. Listed as a deserter July 28, 1862, to March 24, 1863. Returned and deserted June 17, 1863. No record of a return after that.
THOMPSON, David A, Sgt, K. Enlisted in Troy on September 9, 1861, at age 31. Captured at Falling Waters. Confined at Point Lookout. Released on Oath April 12, 1864. Did not.
THOMPSON, George W, Pvt, D. Enlisted at Camp Vance on March 30, 1864. Present each muster of enlistment. Present at Appomattox.
THOMPSON, Sanders, Pvt, A. Enlisted in Ashe Co on August 10, 1861, at age 31. Deserted July 30, 1862. Returned around March of 1864 and received a GSW to the leg in May 1864. Furloughed due to the wound and did not return.
TIDDY, James, 1Lt, E. Enlisted at Camp Gregg on December 1, 1862, at age 21. Marble mason. Was born in England. Served as Drill Master. Wounded and captured at Gettysburg. Right foot amputated. Confined at David's Island, NY. Transferred to Point Lookout. Exchanged April 27, 1864. Retired to the Invalid Corps October 26, 1864.
TODD, Charles B, Sgt. Major. Enlisted as a private in company G in Charlotte on September 30, 1861, at age 21. Badge of Distinction at Chancellorsville. Promoted to Sgt. Major September 1863. Accounted for every muster. Present at Appomattox.
TODD, David S, Pvt, G. Enlisted in Charlotte on May 12, 1864. Present at Appomattox.
TODD, George C, Cpl, G. Enlisted in Charlotte on Sept 30, 1861, at age 20. Accounted for every muster. Wounded at Chancellorsville, one finger amputated. Wounded again May 1864. Captured at Petersburg March 25, 1865. Held at Pt Lookout until June 21, 1865.
TODD, George N, Sgt, G. Enlisted in Charlotte on September 30, 1861, at age 20. Wounded around June 7, 1863. Returned in 1864. Present to November 1864, with no further record. Listed as present or absent wounded on every muster.
TODD, Green Van Buren, Sgt, G. Enlisted in Charlotte on September 30, 1861, at age 25. Son of Samuel and Harriett Todd. Severely wounded at the Wilderness, leg, arm, and thigh, and was captured. Is believed to have died around May 6th in a Federal field hospital. Was Married to Sarah Cathey Todd in 1859.
TODD, James A, Cpl, G. Enlisted in Charlotte on September 30, 1861, at age 38. Killed at Gaines's Mill. Married to Jane Todd.
TODD, James C, Cpt, G. Enlisted in Charlotte on September 30, 1861, at age 22. Present every muster but one (on leave). Married Hanna Louise Todd on December 31, 1863. Present at Appomattox.
TODD, John W S, Pvt, G. Enlisted in Charlotte on January 1, 1864. Present throughout 1864. Present at Appomattox.

TODD, John L, Sgt, G. Enlisted in Charlotte on September 30, 1861, at age 41. Discharged due to age December 8, 1862.
TODD, John L, Pvt, G. Enlisted in Rappahannock on May 12, 1862, at age 21. Severely wounded and captured at Gettysburg. Died at Fort Delaware October 8, 1863. Son of Lawrence Todd.
TODD, Lawson N, Pvt, G. Enlisted in Charlotte on July 18, 1864. Present at Appomattox.
TOLBERT, William A, Pvt, K. Enlisted in Troy on September 9, 1861, at age 24. Died at Hamilton of disease March 8, 1862.
TOMS, James F, Pvt, C. Enlisted in Rutherford on Sept 2, 1861, at age 21. Enlisted with his brother John. Killed in action at Chancellorsville.
TOMS, John C, Pvt, C. Enlisted in Rutherford on September 2, 1861, at age 19. Enlisted with his brother, James. Died July 27, 1862, of wounds received in the Seven Days battles.
TONGUE, Willis, Pvt, E. Captured by Gen. Phillip Sheridan's cavalry August 20, 1864. Possible deserter. Was sent to Ft. Delaware but did not get there. Possibly escaped in route. Fate unknown.
TORRENCE, Samuel H, Sgt, D. Enlisted in Rowan on September 9, 1861, at age 28. Died August 30, 1863, of wounds received near Culpepper Courthouse. Married to Elizabeth Torrence.
TORRENCE, Thomas O, Pvt, F. Enlisted in Cleveland on September 17, 1861, at age 17. Died at Richmond of disease August 27, 1862.
TOWERY, Bartlett, Pvt, F. Enlisted at Camp Holmes on April 20, 1864. Multiple hospitalizations during enlistment. Suffered from Scurvy in September 1864. Captured at Sutherland Station. Died of pneumonia at Point Lookout May 14, 1865.
TOWERY, Joseph, Pvt, F. Enlisted at Camp Holmes on April 20, 1864. Absent sick most of his enlistment. Accidentally killed July 22, 1864, at Petersburg attempting to remove an unexploded shell.
TOWRY, Aaron M, Pvt, C. Enlisted in Rutherford on September 2, 1861, at age 21. Died of disease at High Point, NC November 15, 1861.
TURNER, Drury, Pvt, F, H. Enlisted May 15, 1863, at age 47. Cleveland County resident. Accounted for every muster of enlistment. Transferred to Co H. Hospitalized in Danville, VA April 5, 1865.
TURNER, John M, Cpl, F. Enlisted in Cleveland on September 17, 1861, at age 29. Accounted for every muster. Gunshot wound to the abdomen September 27, 1864, at Petersburg. Died two days later. Married to Sarah Turner.
TURNER, William A, Pvt, F. Enlisted in Cleveland Feb. 28, 1863, at age 37. Wd at Chancellorsville. Sent to Guinea Station. Fate unknown.
TURNER, William H, Pvt, F. Enlisted in Cleveland on September 17, 1861, at age 22. Captured at Falling Waters. Confined at Point Lookout. Exchanged at City Point March 16, 1864. No further record.

TWITTY, Francis L, Major. Enlisted in Rutherford on September 2, 1861, at age 21. Enlisted as a Lt. in Company C. Wounded twice including Gettysburg. Promoted to Major at Gettysburg July 1, 1863. Died suddenly September 10, 1864, at Petersburg. Cause unknown.
TWITTY, Theophilus B, Hosp Steward. Enlisted at Camp Gregg on April 1, 1863. Served as a Hospital Steward. Present every muster of enlistment but one (sick). Present at Appomattox.
TWITTY, William L, Pvt, C. Enlisted in Rutherford on September 2, 1861, at age 26. School teacher, disability discharge July 22, 1862.
UPCHURCH, Daniel, Pvt, I. Enlisted in Rutherford on February 13, 1864. Captured at North Anna. Listed as MIA since May 23, 1864. Died as a POW at Pt Lookout June 14, 1864.
VANDYKE, Joshua, Pvt, F. Enlisted at Camp Holmes on October 19, 1864. Present at Appomattox.
VAUGHN, James A, Pvt, F. Enlisted in Cleveland on Feb 28, 1863, at age 37. Died of disease at Guinea Station, VA April 18, 1863.
VAUGHN, William L, Pvt, F. Enlisted at Camp Holmes on April 20, 1864. Captured at Southside Railroad. Died of Typhoid as POW at Harts Island, NY June 17, 1865.
VIRES, Amos L, Pvt, A. Enlisted in Guinea Stat on May 22, 1862, at age 20. Wounded once, date unknown. Deserted September 18, 1862.
VIRES, William M, Pvt, A. Enlisted in Ashe Co on November 19, 1861, at age 19. Listed as AWOL following furlough granted after being wounded (date unknown). Dropped as a deserter Sept 1, 1863.
VOILS, John J, Pvt, D. Enlisted in Rowan on Sept 9, 1861, at age 33. Died of disease July 28, 1862. Married to Esther Voils. Father of three.
WACASTER, Levi, Pvt, E. Enlisted at Camp Mangum on December 7, 1861, at age 28. Gaston County resident. Discharged in 1862. Reenlisted in March of 1863. Was wounded at Gettysburg and captured at Williamsport due to being unable to be transported further. Hospitalized in Chester, PA and then confined at Point Lookout. Exchanged February 24, 1865. Died in Richmond March 7, 1865.
WAGONER, James, Pvt, A. Enlisted at Camp Holmes on November 4, 1863. Deserted February 8, 1864. Returned and was present to November 1864. No record after that.
WAGONER, John H, Pvt, A. Enlisted in Ashe Co on August 10, 1861, at age 27. Gunshot wound to the ankle at Gaines's Mill. Listed AWOL from August 5, 1862, to April 17, 1863. Present in April of 1863 and dropped as a deserter on the next muster.
WAGONER, Peter F, Pvt, B. Enlisted after December 1864. Rowan County resident. Captured at Amelia Springs April 4, 1865, on the march to Appomattox. Confined at Point Lookout until June 22, 1865.

WALDROP, Theron D, Pvt, C. Enlisted at Camp Vance on May 18, 1864. Captured at Amelia Courthouse April 3, 1865. Died as a POW at Point Lookout May 28, 1865.

WALKER, George W, Pvt, K. Enlisted in Troy on March 5, 1863, at age 39. Present every muster of his enlistment. Wounded at Petersburg March 25, 1865, shot in the left thigh. Captured in the hospital at Richmond. Transferred to Point Lookout aboard the steamer *Mary Powell*. Was released June 26, 1865.

WALKER, James T, Pvt, I. Enlisted in Rutherford on October 6, 1861, at age 22. Born in Polk NC. Died Dr. Gray's residence Warrington, VA October 1, 1862.

WALKER, John, Pvt, K. Enlisted at Camp Holmes on December 1, 1863, at age 18. Present every muster. Present at Appomattox.

WALKER, John B, Pvt, B. Enlisted at Camp Vance on July 17, 1864. Transferred to Co K 55th NC December 22, 1864.

WALKER, William, Pvt, K. Enlisted in Troy on March 5, 1863, at age 37. Present until April 1864. Listed AWOL final two musters of 1864. Paroled at Salisbury May 24, 1865.

WALLACE, Alonzo G, Pvt, C. Enlisted in Rutherford Sept 2, 1861, at age 16. Was killed at Gaines's Mill. Son of William O Wallace.

WALLACE, James M, Pvt, K. Enlisted at Camp Holmes on August 29, 1864. Montgomery County resident. Captured at Sutherland Station. Confined at Harts Island, NY Harbor until June 19, 1865.

WALLEN, Elisha, Pvt, I. Enlisted at Camp Vance on May 25, 1864. Captured at Petersburg June 22, 1864. Confined at Point Lookout and Elmira. Stated he wanted to take the oath and Join Col. Smith's Union regiment in Tennessee. Died of pneumonia at Elmira October 22, 1864.

WALLS, Henry H, Pvt, B. Enlisted in Rutherford on Sept2, 1861, at age 20. Killed in action at Chancellorsville. Son of Kinchin Walls.

WALTERS, J G, Pvt, G. Enlisted at Camp Holmes on August 10, 1864. Captured at Petersburg Oct 8, 1864. Held at Dutch Gap "at work under fire of the enemy" and later sent to Pt Lookout. Exchanged Feb 18, 1865. Sent to Camp Lee in Richmond. Was given a furlough.

WARE, B H, Pvt, H. Enlisted in Shelby on October 1, 1861, at age 35. Killed in action July 1, 1862. Married to Elizabeth Ware.

WARE, Robert H, Pvt, H. Enlisted at Camp Holmes on April 10, 1864. Present at Appomattox.

WARE, T A, Pvt, H. Enlisted at Camp Holmes on February 26, 1863, at age 26. Captured at Falling Waters. Confined at Point Lookout. Was released on oath March 14, 1864.

WARE, William, Pvt, H. Enlisted at Camp Holmes on June 1, 1864. Present at Appomattox.

WARLICK, Pinkney H, Pvt, F. Enlisted in Cleveland on April 15, 1863, at age 31. Pioneer. Present every muster until December of 1864.
WARLICK, Simpson W, Pvt, F. Enlisted in Cleveland on April 15, 1863, at age 30. AWOL Nov. 1863 returned Sept. 1864. Deserted at Petersburg Feb 26, 1865. Took the oath and was sent to Oil City, Pa.
WARREN, Emory E, Pvt, F. Enl in Orange CH on Aug 14, 1862, at age 18. Captured at Falling Waters. Died at Pt Lookout Sept. 7, 1863.
WARREN, H M, Pvt, H. Enlisted in Goldsboro on January 16, 1862, at age 20. Born in Cleveland County. Accounted for every muster. Captured at Southside RR Held at Harts Island until June 17, 1865.
WARREN, John, Pvt, E. Enlisted at Camp Vance on August 21, 1864. Buncombe County resident. Captured at Southside Railroad. Confined at Hart's Island, NY Harbor until June 18, 1865.
WATERS, Abraham G, Cpt, F. Enlisted in Cleveland Sept. 17, 1861, at age. Lawyer. Born in Spartanburg. Was killed at Gaines's Mill.
WATKINS, Jonas B, 1Sgt, I. Enlisted in Rutherford on October 6, 1861, at age 23. Died of disease in Richmond July 7, 1862. Son of Phillip Watkins.
WATKINS, Kindred C, Pvt, I. Enlisted in Rutherford on October 6, 1861, at age 35. Discharge by mistake Dec 8 1862, and did not return.
WEAVER, Alfred K, 1Lt, C. Enlisted in Rutherford on September 2, 1861, at age 25. Bayonet wound in hand in one of the Seven Days battles. Resigned his commission February 21, 1863.
WEAVER, Berry "Benjamin", Pvt, B. Enlisted in Rutherford on September 2, 1861, at age 16. Discharged due to age Nov 11, 1862.
WEAVER, James D, Pvt, C. Enlisted in High Point on October 25, 1861, at age 23. Leave granted in May 1863 and did not return.
WEAVER, John M, Pvt, D. Enlisted in Rowan on September 9, 1861, at age 42. Born in Cabarrus NC. Discharged Dec 8, 1862, due to age.
WEAVER, Joseph, Pvt, H. Enlisted in Cleveland on February 26, 1863, at age 18. Accounted for each muster. Wounded at Gettysburg. Died June 24, 1864, of Typhoid.
WEAVER, Thomas C, Pvt, C. Enl at High Point on Dec 1, 1861, at age 21. Gunshot wound to the thigh at Chancellorsville. Did not return.
WEBB, A J, 1Sgt, H. Enlisted in Shelby on October 1, 1861, at age 22. Promoted to First Sgt. April 1, 1863. MIA at Gettysburg. Probably killed in action.
WEBB, Daniel, Pvt, I. Enlisted in Rutherford on October 6, 1861, at age 23. Went home from High Point on sick furlough, did not return.
WEBB, Gilbert, Pvt, C. Enlisted in Rutherford on Sept 2, 1861, at age 43. Died of disease at Goldsboro Jan 26, 1862. Wife Mary Webb.,
WEBB, Patillo P, Pvt, C. Enlisted in Rutherford on September 2, 1861, at age 17. Discharged November 9, 1862, due to age.

WEBB, William H, Pvt, B. Enlisted in Rutherford on Sept. 2, 1861, at age 21. Died April 4, 1862, at Goldsboro. Son of Cinderella Webb.

WEBSTER, Daniel, Pvt, H. Enlisted at Camp Holmes on April 10, 1864. Hospitalized in May 1864, with Rubella. No record of return.

WEEKS, William, Pvt, C. Enlisted in Rutherford on September 2, 1861, at age 30. Leg amputated from a wound received at Chancellorsville. Did not return to duty.

WELLMAN, John F, Pvt, F. Enlisted in Cleveland on September 17, 1861, at age 19. Died at Goldsboro of disease February 2, 1862. Married to Huldah Wellman.

WELLS, A, Pvt, B. Enlisted after December 1864. Paroled at Charlotte May 3, 1865.

WELLS, Andrew J, Pvt, B. Enlisted in Rutherford on September 2, 1861, at age 28. Died of disease in Danville, VA August 24, 1862. Married to Rebecca Wells.

WELLS, Francis M, Pvt, H. Enlisted at Camp Holmes on April 10, 1864. AWOL from September 1864.

WELLS, Jesse R, Pvt, C and B. Joined at Camp Holmes on May 7, 1864. Wounded July 6, 1864. In the hospital August 10, 1864, no further record.

WELLS, Woody B, Pvt, B. Enlisted in Rutherford on September 2, 1861, at age 19. Accounted for on every muster. In a hospital in Farmville July 1, 1863, sent to the fortifications at Richmond July 8. Wounded June 1864. Captured at Hatchers Run. Confined at Point Lookout until June 21, 1865.

WESSON, James D, 1Sgt, H. Enlisted in Shelby on October 1, 1861, at age 18. Present every muster but one due to a wound in May of 1864. Captured at Gaines's Mill. Exchanged from Ft. Columbus August 5, 1862. Promoted to First Sgt. February 1, 1864. Present at Appomattox.

WESSON, William C, Cpl, H. Enlisted in Shelby on October 1, 1861, at age 35. Captured at Falling Waters. Confined at Elmira. Exchanged March 14, 1865 and hospitalized for Small Pox. Died in Richmond March 24, 1865.

WHETSTINE, David, Pvt, E. Enlisted at Lincolnton on September 11, 1861, at age 58. Musician. Shoemaker. Discharge May 13, 1862 for age, and disability.

WHISNANT, Adam, Pvt, F. Enlisted in Cleveland on September 17, 1861, at age 26. Captured at Falling Waters, confined at Point Lookout. Exchanged March 3, 1864. Returned and was present at Appomattox.

WHITE, Albert Green, Pvt, B. Enlisted in Rutherford on September 2, 1861, at age 16. Died of disease June 2, 1862. Son of James White.

WHITE, Asbury, Pvt, I. Enlisted at Camp Vance on June 1, 1863. Deserted June of 1864, and returned Oct 20, 1864, by Gov. Vance's proclamation. Present to Dec 1864. Paroled at Salisbury in 1865.
WHITE, Henry L, Pvt, I. Enlisted at Camp Vance on September 2, 1864. Paroled at Salisbury in 1865.
WHITE, Hiram J, Pvt, B. Enlisted in Rutherford on September 2, 1861, at age 18. Captured at Brandy Station and confined at Point Lookout. Joined the First U.S. Volunteers. Went to Kansas and took part in the Blizzard March in 1866 at Ft. Fletcher. Honorably discharged May 10, 1866 at Fort Leavenworth.
WHITE, James G, Pvt, F. Enlisted in Cleveland on September 17, 1861, at age 23. Died of disease at Goldsboro February 13, 1862.
WHITE, John, Pvt, F. Enlisted in Cleveland on September 17, 1861, at age 18. Born in Floyd, VA. Killed in action at Gaines's Mill.
WHITE, Thomas H, Pvt, E. Enlisted in Raleigh on May 1, 1864. Gaston County resident. Wounded in the right temple at the Wilderness. Returned to duty. Captured at Petersburg April 2, 1865. Was confined at Point Lookout until June 21, 1865.
WHITE, William, Pvt, I. Enlisted in Rutherford on October 6, 1861, at age 25. Born in Spartanburg. Absent for sickness each muster except for present in December of 1863. Disability discharge Jan 14, 1864.
WHITE, William D, Pvt, D. Enlisted in Rowan on September 9, 1861, at age 22. Born in Cabarrus NC. Killed in action at Gaines's Mill.
WHITE, William V, 1Sgt, F. Enlisted in Cleveland on September 17, 1861, at age 23. Promoted to 1st Sgt in 1862. Wounded at Chancellorsville. Captured at Gettysburg and sent to Point Lookout. Exchanged March 17, 1864. Returned to duty and was present at Appomattox.
WHITESIDE, Aaron W, Pvt, C. Enlisted in Rutherford on September 2, 1861, at age 19. Killed in action at Ox Hill.
WHITESIDE, James W, Pvt, C. Enlisted in Rutherford on September 2, 1861, at age 17. Grassy Knob, Polk Co NC. Listed AWOL following sick furlough, did not return. Dropped as a deserter Sept 10, 1863.
WHITESIDE, Jonathan E, Pvt, C. Enlisted in Rutherford on Sept 2, 1861, at age 17. Died of disease at Goldsboro Feb 13, 1862.
WHITESIDE, Jonathan L, Pvt, C and B. Enlisted in Rutherford on September 2, 1861, at age 39. Discharged in December 1862. Reenlisted May 1864. Served in companies C and B. Wounded at Petersburg March 25, 1865, leg amputated. Captured in the hospital. Transferred to Point Lookout aboard the steamer Mary Powell. Released June 26, 1865.

WHITESIDE, Joseph U, Pvt, C. Enlisted in Rutherford on September 2, 1861, at age 24. Appointed Color bearer of regiment November 8, 1861. Died of wounds received at Ox Hill, exact date unknown.
WHITESIDE, Noah H P, Sgt, C. Enlisted in Rutherford on September 2, 1861, at age 21. Wagon master. Present every muster but one AWOL. Present at Appomattox.
WHITMIRE, George W, Pvt, D. Enlisted at Camp Vance on March 23, 1864. Discharged due to disability September 18, 1864.
WILES, Elbert J, Pvt, A. Enlisted in Ashe Co on August 10, 1861, at age 19. Accounted for every muster but on (AWOL). Wounded at Fredericksburg. Present at Appomattox.
WILKERSON, James, Pvt, C. Enlisted in Rutherford on September 2, 1861, at age 26. Pioneer corps. Killed in action at Chancellorsville. Son of William Wilkerson.
WILKIE, Lorenzo T, 2Lt, C. Enl as a private in Rutherford on Sept. 2, 1861, at age 24. Promoted to Sgt and then 2Lt after Chancellorsville. Present every muster until wounded at Ream's Station, gunshot wound to the lower left lung. Granted a 40-day furlough. No record of return.
WILKINS, Franklin H, Sgt, H. Enlisted in Shelby on Oct 1, 1861, at age 28. Born in York SC. Accounted for every muster. Died after Oct 1864, exact date and cause unknown. Married to Jane Wilkins.
WILKINS, William T, 2Lt, C. Joined the regiment on April 15, 1863. Transferred from the 16th NC. Wounded July 1863, left thigh, wounded again in June 1864. Present at Appomattox.
WILKINS, William W, Pvt, H. Enlisted in Shelby on October 1, 1861, at age 24. Wounded in left leg in the Seven Days battles. Listed absent sick/AWOL since July 1863.
WILLIAMS, Bodisco, Asst Surgeon. Assigned to the regiment March 15, 1864, at Petersburg. Present at Appomattox.
WILLIAMS, David C, Pvt, A. Enlisted in Ashe Co on August 10, 1861, at age 23. AWOL most of his enlistment. Captured at Hatchers Run. Confined at Point Lookout until June 21, 1865.
WILLIAMS, Doctor F, Pvt, F. Enlisted in Cleveland on February 28, 1863, at age 38. Wounded Chancellorsville. Present every muster until he was wounded around July of 1864. Wounded February 1865, at Petersburg with a gunshot wound to the face. No record of return.
WILLIAMS, Fielding, Pvt, A. Enlisted in Ashe Co on August 10, 1861, at age 18. Captured/paroled at Warrenton September 30, 1862. Died at Warrenton October 30, 1862.
WILLIAMS, Govan, Pvt, H. Enlisted in Shelby on October 1, 1861, at age 28. Captured at Gaines's Mill, Confined at Ft. Columbus. Exchanged August 5, 1862. Deserted after exchange. Arrested and sentenced to 5 years confinement at Salisbury.

WILLIAMS, Hartwell S, Sgt, E. Enlisted in Lincolnton on September 11, 1861, at age 28. Elected Sgt. April 18, 1862. Died of Typhoid fever in Lynchburg August 25, 1862.

WILLIAMS, Harvey C, Pvt, C. Enlisted in Lincolnton on September 2, 1861, at age 20. Died of disease at Camp Mangum Dec 22, 1861.

WILLIAMS, Hugh, Pvt, H. Enlisted in Shelby on October 1, 1861, at age 26. Musician. Died at home of a fever November 9, 1862. Married to Catherine Williams.

WILLIAMS, Jesse L, Pvt, K. Enlisted in Troy on September 9, 1861, at age 29. Transferred to another regiment February 1862.

WILLIAMS, John B, Pvt, A. Enlisted in Ashe Co on August 10, 1861, at age 22. Captured at Falling Waters. Died of small pox at Point Lookout August 15, 1864.

WILLIAMS, John H, Pvt, B. Enlisted in Rutherford on September 2, 1861, at age 33. Captured on reconnaissance to Winchester December 2, 1862, and paroled. Died of Small Pox December 22, 1862.

WILLIAMS, John L, Pvt, C. Enlisted in Rutherford on Sept 2, 1861, at age 21. Wounded in June 1862. Transf to the 16th NC May 1863.

WILLIAMS, John M, Pvt, F. Enlisted in Berryville VA on November 10, 1862, at age 47. Enrolled as a substitute. Wounded at Chancellorsville. Wounded again July/August of 1864. Captured at Petersburg April 3, 1865. Held at Harts Island until June 17, 1865.

WILLIAMS, John W, Pvt, H. Enlisted at Camp Holmes on April 10, 1864. Present at Appomattox.

WILLIAMS, Joseph, Pvt, D. Enlisted after December 1864. Captured at Hatchers Run, held at Harts Island, NY Harbor until June 18, 1865.

WILLIAMS, Lawson M, Pvt, F. Enlisted in Cleveland on February 28, 1863, at age 18. Captured at Gettysburg. Confined Point Lookout. Exchanged March 14, 1865 and returned to duty. Gunshot wound in the face about March 27, 1865, at Petersburg. Captured in the hospital. Turned over to Provost Marshall May 5, 1865.

WILLIAMS, Robert, Pvt, E. Enlisted in Lincolnton on September 11, 1861, at age 46. Discharged due to disability May 13, 1862.

WILLIAMS, Upshur, Pvt, K. Enlisted in Troy on September 9, 1861, at age 24. Transferred to another regiment February 1862.

WILLIAMS, William H, Pvt, F. Enlisted in Cleveland on September 17, 1861, at age 19. Provost Guard. Drummer. Present every muster but one (leave). Captured at Petersburg April 2, 1865. Confined at Point Lookout until June 22, 1865.

WILLIAMS, William W, Pvt, F. Enlisted in Cleveland on February 28, 1863, at age 37. Wounded at Chancellorsville. Absent remainder of war until transferred to light duty in Charlotte in late 1864.

WILLIFORD, James T, Pvt, D. Enlisted in Rowan on September 9, 1861, at age 20. Wounded at Chancellorsville and in November 1863. Worked as a nurse and provost guard. Found fit for duty in October 1864 and returned. Captured at Amelia CH April 5, 1865. Confined at Point Lookout until June 30, 1865.
WILLIFORD, John A, Pvt, D. Enlisted in Rowan Sept 9, 1861, at age 52. Born in South Hampton, VA. Disability discharge July 23, 1862.
WILLIS, Henry J, Pvt, F. Enlisted in Cleveland on September 17, 1861, at age 16. Discharged due to age Oct 9, 1862.
WILLIS, Joseph G, Pvt, F. Enlisted in Cleveland on February 28, 1863, at age 36. Present every muster but one (sick). Captured at Petersburg March 25, 1865. Held at Point Lookout until June 22, 1865.
WILLIS, Joseph S, Pvt, F. Enlisted in Cleveland on Sept 17, 1861, at age 20. Wounded at Frayser's Farm. Returned late 1863. Captured at Petersburg April 2, 1865. Held at Pt Lookout until June 22, 1865.
WILSON, David A, Pvt, F. Enlisted in Cleveland on September 17, 1861, at age 26. Killed in action at Gaines's Mill.
WILSON, Green B, Pvt, B. Enlisted in Rutherford on September 2, 1861, at age 18. Discharged due to disability July 13, 1862.
WILSON, James F, 3Lt, H. Enlisted in Shelby on October 1, 1861, at age 32. Died of disease July 11, 1862. "A good officer."
WILSON, James M, Sgt, B. Enlisted in Rutherford on September 2, 1861, at age 28. Blacksmith. Present every muster but one (leave). Wounded at 2nd Manassas. Was killed May 5, 1864, at the Wilderness.
WILSON, John, Pvt, B. Enlisted in Rutherford on September 2, 1861, at age 23. Died of wounds July 15, 1864.
WILSON, John J, Pvt, C. Enlisted in Rutherford on September 2, 1861, at age 18. Accounted for every muster. Present January 1865.
WILSON, Joseph, Pvt, I. Enlisted in Rutherford on October 6, 1861, at age 17. Born in Spartanburg. Disability discharge Nov 25, 1861.
WILSON, Joseph W, Sgt, C. Enlisted in Rutherford on September 2, 1861, at age 24. From Webb's Ford. Accounted for on every muster. Wounded once, date unknown. Present at Appomattox.
WILSON, Perry R, Pvt, C. Enlisted in High Point on November 15, 1861, at age 30. Died of disease March 27, 1862. Son of Susan Wilson.
WILSON, Stephen N, Cpt, A. Enlisted in Ashe Co on August 10, 1861, at age 45. Resigned August 30, 1862, due to age and declining health. Felt he stood in the way of another officer's promotion.
WILSON, Street, Pvt, B. Enlisted in Rutherford on September 2, 1861, at age 20. Wounded at Frayser's Farm. Died at Guinea Station February 21, 1863, of unknown cause. Son of R H Wilson.

WINN, Wallace, Pvt, B. Enlisted in Cleveland on February 26, 1863, at age 37. Conscript. Badge of Distinction at Chancellorsville. On detached duty from December 1863, until discharged August 2, 1864.
WISE, Daniel, Sgt, E. Enlisted in Lincolnton on September 11, 1861, at age 26. Killed in Action at Gaines's Mill.
WISE, Lawson, Pvt, E. Enlisted in Lincolnton on September 11, 1861, at age 23. Carriage maker. Present each muster of enlistment. Wounded at Chancellorsville. Transferred to the CS Navy in April 1864.
WITHERS, Marcus L, Pvt, E. Enlisted in Lincolnton on September 11, 1861, at age 21. Captured at Gettysburg and held at Fort Delaware and Point Lookout. Exchanged at Boulware's Wharf Feb 18, 1865.
WITHROW, Adolphus C, Pvt, B. Enlisted in Rutherford on September 2, 1861, at age 18. Slight wound (hand) at Mechanicsville. Died of disease in Richmond Dec 25, 1862. Son of James Withrow.
WOMACH, John, Pvt, B. Enlisted in Rutherford on September 2, 1861, at age 17. Captured and paroled at Chancellorsville. Captured at Falling Waters and sent to Point Lookout. Exchanged May 3, 1864. Returned and transferred to the 56th NC March 2, 1865.
WOOD, James, Cpt, I. Enlisted in Rutherford on October 6, 1861, at age 29. Born Spartanburg. Elected captain April 18, 1862. Wounded at Gettysburg (shell right hand, head, and neck). Returned and was present the remaining musters. Present at Appomattox.
WOOD, Marcus, Pvt, I. Enlisted in Rutherford on June 1, 1862. Present every muster until captured at North Anna. Confined at Point Lookout. Exchanged October 11, 1864, at Cox's Wharf. Hospitalized in Richmond and died October 29, 1864. Son of John Wood.
WOOD, Thompson J, Pvt, I. Enlisted in Rutherford on October 6, 1861, at age 18. Wounded at Chancellorsville and Gettysburg. Present every muster but one (sick). Was captured at Sutherland Station and sent to Pt Lookout. Arrived under an assumed name or assumed one after arrival to be exchanged. Date of release not recorded.
WOODIE, Bryant, 2Lt, A. Enlisted in Ashe Co on August 10, 1861, at age 24. Enlisted as a private. Promoted to 2Lt after Chancellorsville. Wounded at unknown date. Died of disease November 18, 1862.
WOODIE, Calvin, Pvt, A. Enlisted in Ashe Co on August 10, 1861, at age 28. Deserted twice, captured the second time at Orange Courthouse January 4, 1864. Sentenced to death but escaped the guardhouse and surrendered to Federal troops. Treated for frostbitten feet and Variola. Released on oath to Philadelphia, Pa.
WOODIE, George W, 2Lt, A. Enlisted in Ashe Co on August 10, 1861,, at age 33. Gunshot wound July 1st at Gettysburg (fractured skull). Gunshot wound May 5, 1864, at the Wilderness, (right foot). Accounted for on every muster. Retired to invalid corps Nov 15, 1864.

WOODIE, Henry B, Pvt, A. Enlisted at Camp Vance on March 19, 1864. Captured at Hanover Junction May 24, 1864. Died at Point Lookout June 22, 1864, of Gastro Enteritis.
WOODIE, James, Sgt, A. Enlisted in Ashe Co on August 10, 1861,, at age 21. Killed in action at Frayser's Farm.
WOODIE, Logens, Pvt, A. Enlisted in Ashe Co on August 10, 1861, at age 26. Wounded at Chancellorsville. Died of disease in Richmond November 18, 1863.
WOODIE, Nelson C, Cpt, A. Enlisted in Ashe Co on August 10, 1861, at age 29. Son of James and Margaret Woodie. Promoted to Captain Sept 1, 1862. Wounded at Fredericksburg (most of the lower jaw removed due to gunshot wound). Died June 9, 1863 from the wound.
WOODIE, Talton, Pvt, A. Enlisted at Camp Holmes on October 1, 1863. Present each muster of enlistment through November 1864.
WOODSIDE, John C, Pvt, D. Enlisted in Rowan on September 9, 1861, at age 18. Ambulance driver. Present or on detached duty every muster. Present at Appomattox.
WORTMAN, J, Pvt, H. Enlisted at Camp Holmes on April 20, 1864. Killed in action June 13, 1864, near Petersburg.
WRIGHT, Berry, Pvt, F. Enlisted in Cleveland on May 17, 1862, at age 19. Killed in action at Gaines's Mill. Son of Sarah Wright.
WRIGHT, Francis, Pvt, F. Enlisted in Cleveland on April 1, 1864. Red hair. Captured at Southside Railroad and sent to Harts Island, NY Harbor. Released June 18, 1865.
WRIGHT, George, Pvt, F. Enlisted in Cleveland on Sept 17, 1861, at age 22. Accidentally shot in Sept 1862. Discharged Oct 25, 1862.
WRIGHT, George W, Pvt, B. Enlisted at Camp Holmes on Sept 20, 1864. Captured in the hospital in Richmond April 3, 1865. Transferred to a hospital in Newport News, VA. Died of disease May 23, 1865.
WRIGHT, Jacob A, Cpl, B. Enlisted in Rutherford on September 2, 1861, at age 29. Died August 7, 1862. Married to Elizabeth Wright.
WRIGHT, Nathan, Pvt, B. Enlisted in Rutherford on September 2, 1861, at age 30. Died of Typhoid at in Gordonsville, VA Dec 11, 1862.
WRIGHT, Newton, Pvt, F. Enlisted in Cleveland on September 17, 1861, at age 34. Detailed as a nurse in 1863-64. Returned to the regiment after October 1864. Present at Appomattox.
WRIGHT, Noah, Pvt, F. Enlisted in Cleveland on January 15, 1864. Resident of Pierceville, NC. Hospitalized May 28, 1864, for a gunshot wound to the forehead. Recovered and was present at Appomattox.
WRIGHT, Noah J, Pvt, H. Enlisted at Camp Holmes on April 20, 1864. Worked as a provost guard in Dec 1864, due to a heart condition.

WRIGHT, Perry, Pvt, F. Enlisted in Massaponax May 17, 1862, at age 19. Captured at Falling Waters and sent to Pt Lookout. Exchanged March 18, 1864. Returned and wounded May 1864. Absent thereafter.
WRIGHT, Richard, Pvt, E. Enlisted around November 5, 1864. Captured at the Southside RR. Held at Hart's Island until June 18, 1865.
WRIGHT, Sidney, Pvt, F. Enlisted in Cleveland on April 1, 1864. Wounded June 23, 1864, at Jerusalem Plank Road. Deserted at Petersburg February 26, 1865. Was transported to Oil City, Pa.
WRIGHT, William B, Pvt, B. Enlisted in Rutherford on September 2, 1861, at age 33. Died July 1, 1862, of wounds received at Gaines's Mill. Married to Sally Wright.
WRIGHT, William H, Pvt, F. Enlisted in Cleveland on September 17, 1861, at age 20. Wounded at either Mechanicsville or Gaines's Mill. Present every muster but one (leave). Captured at Southside Railroad. Confined at Harts Island until June 18, 1865.
WRIGHT, Willis G, Pvt, K. Enlisted in Troy on Sept 9, 1861, at age 19. Died of disease Nov 27, 1861.
WRISTON, Charles W, Sgt, G. Enlisted in Charlotte on Sept. 30, 1861, at age 21. Brick mason. Present each muster but one (leave). Promoted to Sgt in Sept 1863. Was killed May 21, 1864.
WYATT, James E, Cpl, I. Enlisted in Rutherford on October 6, 1861, at age 19. Born Union SC. Accounted for on every muster. Present in November 1864. No records after that.
YANCY, John G, Pvt, C. Enlisted in Rutherford on April 25, 1864. Captured at North Anna. Held at Point Lookout until June 12, 1865.
YARBOROUGH, Daniel, Pvt, K. Enlisted in Troy on March 5, 1863, at age 37. Accounted for every muster of enlistment. Captured at Southside Railroad. Confined at Harts Island until June 17, 1865.
YELTON, George W, Pvt, B. Enlisted in High Point on October 19, 1861, at age 19. Died of disease at Goldsboro February 23, 1862.
YODER, John F, Sgt, E. Enlisted in Lincolnton on Sept 11, 1861, at age 19. 6'3" tall. Present every muster but one (leave). Gunshot wound to the right leg July 16, 1863. Wounded around April 4, 1865.
YOUNG, John D, Cpt, C. Enlisted at Camp Gregg March 6, 1863. Served as Colonel Lowrance's Aide at Gettysburg. Commanded Scales' Sharpshooter Battalion. Present at Appomattox.
ZIMMERMAN, David, Pvt, B. Enlisted at Camp Vance on September 26, 1864. Resident of Davidson County. Captured at Southside Railroad. Confined at Harts Island, NY Harbor until June 19, 1865.

Summary of Musters
34th North Carolina Infantry

Muster	Total Last Muster	Added Since Last Muster	Dropped Since Last Muster	Deaths Since Last Muster
Jan/Feb 62	915	39	71	49
Mar/Apr 62	883	6	57	37
Jan/Feb 63	832	45	339	202
Mar/Apr 63	538	100	22	10
Jul/Aug 63	616	14	101	70
Sep/Oct 63	529	8	18	11
Nov/Dec 63	519	23	20	8
Jan/Feb 64	522	14	40	9
Mar/Apr 64	496	86	19	4
May/Jun 64	563	96	43	32
Jul/Aug 64	616	72	40	26
Sep/Oct 64	648	64	43	12

Muster	Total	Present	AWOL	Sick/Wd	POW	Oth Abs
Jan/Feb 62	883	743	3	79	0	58
Mar/Apr 62	832	708	10	102	0	12
Jan/Feb 63	538	372	58	66	2	40
Mar/Apr 63	616	507	43	38	0	28
Jul/Aug 63	529	199	50	158	95	27
Sep/Oct 63	519	246	52	110	83	28
Nov/Dec 63	522	310	40	60	79	33
Jan/Feb 64	496	290	25	41	64	76
Mar/Apr 64	563	403	18	43	57	42
May/Jun 64	616	266	28	189	97	36
Jul/Aug 64	648	310	29	172	86	51
Sep/Oct 64	669	390	32	127	75	45

Index

All CAPS indicates the subject is in the roster.

1

13th Missouri Cavalry, 301
16th NC, 18, 37, 44, 60, 65, 83, 138, 151
1st South Carolina, 33, 51
1st USV, 295

2

22nd NC, 101, 124, 138
22nd. Virginia, 38
2nd Arkansas, 38, 60

3

38th NC, 33, 38, 45, 60, 138, 142, 147, 151, 191
3rd Louisiana Battalion, 33

4

45th Georgia, 33
49th Georgia, 33
4th USV, 297

5

5th New York, 51

7

7th North Carolina, 51, 60

A

Abernathy, 19, 309
    Hiram, 19, 32, 115, 128, 130, 146
    John, 146
    Thomas, 57

ABERNATHY, 309
Abshear
    William, 191
ABSHER, 309
Adams
    Harvey, 290
ADAMS, 309
ADKINS, 309
Aikin, 309
AIKIN, 309
ALCORN, 309
ALEXANDER, 309
Allen, 310, 371, 387, 391
    Clark, 20
    Perry, 295, 299
ALLEN, 310
ALLEY, 310
ALLIS, 310
ALLISON, 310
Ambler
    John, 103
Amelia Courthouse, 265
American Fur Company, 298
Anders, 310, 311
    Meridith, 17
ANDERS, 310, 311
Anderson, 34, 61, 330, 342, 376
    Joseph, 33, 34, 44
ANDERSON, 311
ANTHONY, 311
Appomattox, 269
Appomattox River, 261, 268, 270
Archer
    James, 44
ARMSTRONG, 311
Army of Northern Virginia, 39, 65, 103, 112, 157, 271, 279
ARNETT, 311
ASBURY, 311
ASHBURN, 311

Ashe County, 12, 13, 16, 17, 52, 56, 73, 85, 96, 106, 114, 118, 129, 149, 182, 188, 191, 230, 237
Ashland, 315
Athens Georgia, 285
ATKINSON, 311
Atwell, 11, 18, 311, 314
   Burrett, 67
ATWELL, 311
ATWOOD, 311
Austin
   Edwin, 16
AUSTIN, 312
Avery
   Vincent, 102
AVERY, 312
AXION, 312

B

BABER, 312
Badge of Distinction for bravery at Chancellorsville, 130
BAGWELL, 312
BAILEY, 312
BAILIFF, 312
BAIN, 312
Baker
   George, 73
BAKER, 312
BALTON, 312
Banks
   Nathan, 36
BANNARD, 312
Bare, 17
   Wiley, 188, 189, 191
BARE, 313
BAREFIELD, 313
BARLOW, 313
BARNETT, 313
BARNHARDT, 313, 314
BARNWELL, 314
Barr
   Richard, 47, 116, 122, 196
BARR, 314
Barrett
   James, 96
BARRETT, 314
Basinger
   James, 12, 68, 96
Battery No. 45, 233
Battery Number 45, 230
Battle of Ox Ford, 212
Battle of Williamsport, 170
BATTON, 314
Baxter, 19
BAXTER, 314
Beam, 17, 19, 314, 315
   Martin, 101
   Peter, 30, 36
   William, 101, 167, 183
BEAM, 314, 315
Beaman
   Andrew, 117
   John, 117, 125
BEAMAN, 315
Beamon
   Andrew, 125
BEAN, 315
BEATY, 315
Beaver Dam, 41, 45
Beaver Dam Creek, 41, 45
Bedford, 17
   Joseph, 85
   Seth, 205
BEDFORD, 315
BEDWELL, 315
BELL, 315
Bellfield Station, 238
BENNETT, 315
Bennick
   Augustus, 112
BENNICK, 316
BERRYHILL, 316
BESS, 316
Biggerstaff
   Joseph, 285
BISHOP, 316
Black
   John, 233
BLACK, 316
Blackburn

James, 209
BLACKBURN, 316
BLAKE, 317
Blankenship
   Washington, 214, 225
BLANKENSHIP, 317
Blanton
   George, 116
   James, 287
BLANTON, 317
Bliss barn, 143, 147
Boatswain's Creek, 50, 52
BOGGS, 317
BOLIN, 317
BORDERS,, 318
BORVIG, 318
BOSTIUN, 318
Botts
   John, 67
BOTTS, 318
Bourquin
   Fred, 289
BOURQUIN, 318
BOWEN, 318
Bowers
   William, 222
BOWERS, 318
BOWMAN, 318
Boyd
   Alexander, 231
BOYD, 318
Bradley
   William, 63
BRADLEY, 318
BRAY, 319
Brewer
   Hiram, 231
   William, 91
BREWER, 319
Bridges, 17
   Wilson, 215
BRIDGES, 319, 320
BRILES, 320
Bristoe Station, 186
BROADWAY, 320
Brooks, 320

BROOKS, 320
BROTHERTON, 320
Brown
   John, 289
   William, 35, 295, 296, 298
BROWN, 320, 321
Bryant, 321, 412
BRYANT, 321
BUMGARDNER, 321
Bunker Hill, 99, 100, 178
Burgess, 372
BURGESS, 321
BURLISON, 321
BURNET, 321
Burnside
   Ambrose, 28, 94
BURR, 321
BURROUGHS, 321
Byers
   Joseph, 17, 32, 146, 183, 247
BYERS, 321

C

Callicott, 21, 273
   Charles and Claiborne, 130
   Henry and John, 130
CALLICOTT, 322
Camp, 288
   John, 285
   John and Joseph, 172
   Joseph, 20, 116, 146, 184
   Joshua, 32
   Tyrell, 122
CAMP, 322
Camp Fisher, 23
Camp Gregg, 108, 111
Camp Holmes, 197
Camp Mangum, 27
CAMPBELL, 322, 323
CANIPE, 323
Capps
   James, 234
CAPPS, 323
Captured April 2, 1865, 260

Captured at the Battle of Brandy
    Station August 1, 1863, 178
Captured at the Battle of Ox Ford,
    212
Captured May 8, 1865, at Athens,
    GA, 285
CARGAL, 323
Carpenter
    Benjamin, 151
    Noah, 286
CARPENTER, 323, 324
CARRIER, 324
CARROLL, 324
CARSON, 324
CARTER, 324
CASS, 324
CASTELOW, 324
Castle Thunder, 237
Casualties at the Battle of Falling
    Waters, 176
Casualties from the Battle of
    Chancellorsville, 127
Casualties from the Battle of
    Frayser's Farm, 62
Casualties from the Battle of
    Fredericksburg, 106
Casualties from the Battle of
    Gaines's Mill, 54
Casualties from the Battle of
    Gettysburg, 154
Casualties from the Battle of
    Jerusalem Plank Road, 221
Casualties from the Battle of North
    Anna, 211
Casualties from the Battle of Ox
    Hill, 85
Casualties from the Battle of
    Ream's Station, 229
Casualties from the Battle of The
    Wilderness, 205
Casualties from the Battles at
    Petersburg - March 25, 1865,
    253
Catawba River, 287
Cathey, 19, 324, 402
    Lt Alexander, 90, 141, 146, 156,
        165, 171, 240

Lt. Alexander, 32
Pvt Alexander, 202
CATHEY, 324
CAUBLE, 324
CAUDILL, 325
CAVIN, 325
CAVINESS, 325
Cedar Mountain, 73
Chamberlain
    Joshua, 143
CHAMPION, 325
Chancellorsville, 119, 127, 130
CHANCY, 325
Chandler
    Eli, 16
CHANDLER, 325
CHAPMAN, 325
Charleston, 324, 355, 376, 385
Childers, 19
CHILDERS, 325
Chimborazo Hospital, 99
Clark
    Adam, 133
    George, 131, 141
    Henry, 27
CLARK, 325, 326
CLARKE, 326
CLARY, 326
Clay
    Henry, 184
CLAY, 326
CLAYTON, 326
Cleveland County, 13, 17, 19, 36, 52,
    56, 83, 96, 106, 117, 143, 157, 183,
    256, 291, 295
Cleveland Guards, 24
CLIFTEN, 326
CLODFELTER, 326
COBB, 326
Cochran
    David, 21
COCHRAN, 326
COCKRAN, 326
CODY, 326
COFFMAN, 327
Coggin, 21

William, 220
COGGIN, 327
COLBERT, 327
COLLINS, 327
COLLUMS, 327
COMPTON, 327
Conner
   William, 265
CONNER, 327
Conscription Act, 32, 68, 100
COOK, 327, 328
COONE, 328
COOPER, 328
COPPLE, 328
Corn
   Ezekiel, 296
CORN, 328
CORRIHER, 328
COSAND, 328
COSTNER, 328
Cottage Home, 131, 284
Cotton, 113
   Burwell, 30, 68, 107, 113, 125, 171, 175, 178, 179, 182, 186, 220
COTTON, 329
COVIN, 329
COWAN, 329
Coward, 20
Cowen, 329
   Robert, 61
Cox, 17, 412
   Hiram, 16, 32
   Hiram and David, 129
   William, 87
COX, 329
Cranford
   Eli, 216
   Joel, 125
   Leonard, 203
CRANFORD, 329
CRAVER, 329
Crawford
   John, 131
CRAWFORD, 330
Crescent City, 241
Cresswell
   Anderson, 19
Creswell
   Anderson, 32
CRESWELL, 330
CRISP, 330
CROMPSON, 330
CROTTS, 330
CROW, 330
Crowder
   Robert, 83, 160
CROWDER, 330
Crumpler
   Thomas, 12
Crytz
   William, 2
CRYTZ, 331
Cunningham's Crossroads, 167
Cypress Hill Cemetery, 289

D

Daily
   Joel, 17
DAILY, 331
Dakota, 300
Dancy
   Alpheus, 99
   Mary, 100
DANCY, 331
Davenport
   John, 39
DAVENPORT, 331
Daves
   Elijah, 169
DAVES, 331
David's Island, 183
Davidson College, 11, 89
Davis
   Champ, 37
   Micah, 18, 68, 146
   Simon, 122, 293
   Tilman, 115
   William, 25
DAVIS, 331, 332
DEAN, 332
DEATON, 332

DECK, 332
Dellinger, 20
   Frederick, 69, 245, 286
   Henry, 133
   Jacob, 90, 198, 245, 281
   Michael, 282
   Samuel, 254, 289
DELLINGER, 332, 333
Dennis, 333
   John, 82
DENNIS, 333
DEPRIEST, 333
Devil's Den, 143, 158
Dickerson, 333
   Marcus O, 18, 21, 180
   Robert, 18
DICKERSON, 333
DICKSON, 333
Dillworth
   John, 297
DILWORTH, 333
Dimmock Line, 258
DIXON, 333
Dobbins, 17, 334
   A J, 250
   Felix, 290
   Jesse, 75
   John, 250
DOBBINS, 333, 334
DOGGETT, 334
DOTY, 334
DOUGLAS, 334
DOWELL, 334
DOWNS, 335
DUNN, 335
DURHAM, 335
Dycus
   Ancil, 208, 225, 245, 249, 254, 273, 287
DYCUS, 335
DYER, 335

E

EADES, 335
Eaker, 19, 335
   Abraham, 296, 298
EAKER, 335, 336
EARLEY, 336
Earls, 20
EARLS, 336
EARLY, 336
Eaton
   Henry, 85
EATON, 336, 337
Edgecombe, 395
EDMISTON, 337
EDMOND, 337
Edwards, 337
   John, 17, 30
   John N, 17
   William, 17, 90
EDWARDS, 337
Elam, 337
   George, 19, 56
ELAM, 337
ELKINS, 337
Eller, 11
   Green, 12
ELLER, 337
Ellerson, 356
Ellerson's Mill, 46
Elliott, 21, 338, 352, 356
   Hugh, 104
   James, 291
   Virgil, 104, 291
ELLIOTT, 338
Ellis
   John, 12, 14, 27
   Sgt John, 224
ELLIS, 339
Elmira, 289
Emmitsburg Road, 148, 150
England
   Robert, 85
ENGLAND, 339
Erwin
   James, 22, 112
ERWIN, 339
Etters
   Pinkney, 76
ETTERS, 339

Ewing
  John, 115
EWING, 339

F

Falling Waters, 168, 173, 176
FALLS, 339
Farmville, 268
Fayetteville, 13
FELMENT, 339
FERRIS, 339
FINGER, 339
Fisher
  Charles, 23
FISHER, 339
FISMIRE, 340
FLACK, 340
Flat Rock Seven, 288
FLINN, 340
Floyd Rifles, 6, 19, 24, 56, 146, 160, 199, 200, 218, 274, 277, 308
FORBUSH, 340
Ford's Theatre, 286
Forest City, 17
FORESTER, 340
Fort Berthold, 298, 299
Fort Delaware, 184, 185, 241, 288
Fort Fletcher, 301
Fort Leavenworth, 298
Fort McHenry, 184
Fort Pulaski, 242
Fort Rice, 296, 298
Fort Ridgley, 300
Fort Snelling, 300
Fort Stedman, 251
Fort Sumpter, 14
Fort Union, 298
Fortenberry
  Robert, 19
FORTENBERY, 340
Forts Gregg and Whitworth, 259
Foster
  Alfred, 233
  George, 11
FOSTER, 340, 341

FOWLER, 341
FOX, 341
FRANCIS, 341
FRANKLIN, 341
Frayser's Farm, 59, 264
Frazer, Montana, 298
FRAZIER, 341
Fredericksburg, 34, 104, 106, 132
Freeland
  James, 30, 107
FREELAND, 341
FREEMAN, 341
FREEZE, 341
French
  Cpl. George, 284
FRIDAY, 342
FRONEBERGER, 342
FRY, 342
Fulbright
  George, 166
FULBRIGHT, 342
FULENVILLER, 342

G

Gaines's Mill, 49, 51, 117, 130, 213
Galvanized Yankees, 192
Gannt
  Able, 19
Gantt, 19, 342
  William, 209
GANTT, 342
GARDNER, 342
GARREN, 342
GARVY, 342
Gaston County, 117, 131, 181
GATIS, 342
General Order No. 9, 271
GENTLE, 343
GETTYS, 343
Gettysburg, 136, 158
GIBBONS, 343
GIBBS, 343
GILBERT, 343
GILL, 343
Gillon

Monroe, 68, 176, 224
GILLON, 343
Gilmer
    John, 13
GINGERY, 343
Glendale, 59
GLOVER, 343
GOINGS, 343
Gold, 343
GOLD, 343
Goldsboro, 28, 29, 31
Goode
    George, 224
    John, 20
GOODE, 344
GOODNIGHT, 344
GOODSON, 344
Gordon
    George T, 108, 119, 124, 131, 140, 141, 145, 153, 157, 187, 221, 232
GORDON, 344
GRAGG, 344
Graham
    John, 18
GRAHAM, 344
Grant
    Ulyssess, 196
GRANT, 344
GRAY, 344
Green, 156, 310, 337, 345, 393, 402, 407, 411
GREEN, 344, 345
GREENHILL, 345
Gregg
    Maxcy, 44, 48, 51, 81, 105, 108
GRICE, 345
GRIFFIN, 345
GRIGG, 345
GRUBBS, 345
Guest
    William, 257
GUEST, 345
GUY, 345
GYERE, 345

H

HAGE, 345
Hagerstown, 172
HALES, 345
HALL, 345, 346
Haltom, 346
    Joseph, 116
    Thomas, 21, 147
HALTOM, 346
HAMBY, 346
Hamilton, 29, 311, 313, 324, 336, 350, 362, 363, 364, 375, 377, 398, 403
HAMILTON, 346
Hammarskold
    Charles J, 19, 32, 52, 58, 61, 66, 264
HAMMARSKOLD, 346
Hammond General Hospital, 290, 339
Hamrick, 17, 347
    Charles, 190
    Doctor "Doc", 17
    E, 107
HAMRICK, 346, 347
HANNAH, 347
Hanover Courthouse, 36, 37
HANSEL, 347
HARDESTER, 347
Hardin, 347, 348
    John, 107, 250
HARDIN, 347, 348
HARGROVES, 348
HARMON, 348
Harper's Ferry, 91, 96
Harrelson
    William, 88
HARRELSON, 348
Harrill, 17, 315, 348
    David, 17, 244
    Drury, 47
    James, 304
    William, 17
HARRILL, 348
HARRIS, 348, 349
Harrison
    James, 290

HARRISON, 349
HART, 349
Hart's Island, 184, 288, 289
Hartness
   Miles, 296
HARTNESS, 349
Hartzog
   Able, 163
HARTZOG, 349
HARVEL, 349
HASSELL, 349
Hatcher's Run, 256
HATLEY, 350
HAWKINS, 350
HAYES, 350
HAYNES, 350
Hays
   Samuel, 222
HAYS, 350
Hazelwood
   Asa, 197, 211, 225
HAZELWOOD, 350
HEARN, 350
HEAVNER, 350, 351
HEDGEPETH, 351
HELMS, 351
Henderson
   James, 107, 233
HENDERSON, 351
Henderson County, 296
HENDRICK, 351
Henry Hill, 82
HENSDALE, 351
HENSLEY, 351
HENSON, 352
Herbst Woods, 138
Heroes of America, 119, 237
Herr Ridge, 137
Hester, 20
HESTER, 352
Heth
   Henry, 174, 202
HIATT, 352
HICKS, 352
Higgins
   Mills, 141, 159

HIGGINS, 352
High Bridge, 268
High Point, 12, 15, 21, 23, 25, 272
Hill
   A P, 258
   A. P., 38, 40, 41, 42, 60, 91
   John F, 18
HINSHAW, 353
Hipp
   John, 209
HIPP, 353
HODGE, 353
Hodgins
   John, 12
HODGINS, 353
Hoey, 20
   Samuel, 19, 90, 115, 194
HOEY, 353
Hogan
   Joseph, 247
HOGAN, 353, 354
Hogue
   Jacob, 57
HOGUE, 354
HOLAWAY, 354
Holden
   William, 181, 194
HOLIFIELD, 354
Holland
   F M, 215
HOLLAND, 354
HOLLY, 354
Home Guards, 235
Home Guardsmen, 118
HONEYCUT, 354
HOOVER, 354, 355
Hopper, 355
   Romulas, 63
   Romulus, 217
HOPPER, 355
Hornet's Nest, 24
Hospital Steward, 116
Hospital Transport Thomas Powell, 265
Houck
   William, 11, 18, 21, 22, 32

HOUCK, 355
HOUSE, 355
Houser
   Emanuel, 198
Hovis
   George, 254
   Malachi, 151, 157
HOVIS, 355
Howard
   Oliver O, 121
HOWELL, 355, 356
Hoyle, 19, 314, 356, 379
   Benjamin, 56, 274
   David, 19, 57, 146, 274, 292, 308
   Henry, 274
   Jonas, 286
   Martin, 218, 274
   Maxwell, 274, 292
HOYLE, 356
HUDGINS, 356
Hudson
   Wilborn, 106
HUDSON, 356, 357
HUFFSTETER, 357
HUGHES, 357
HULL, 357
HULLENDER, 357
HULLET, 357
HUMPHRIES, 357
HUNTER, 357
Huntley
   George, 24, 27, 28, 35, 65, 71, 75, 120, 131, 141
HUNTLEY, 357
Huntly
   George, 131
Huntsinger, 357
HUNTSINGER, 357
Hurley, 21
   Alfred, 52
   Armistead, 117, 125
   Willis, 29
HURLEY, 357, 358
HUSS, 358
Hutchison
   Scott, 104, 150, 291

HUTCHISON, 358
HUTSON, 358
Hyman
   Joseph, 249

I

Imboden
   John, 166
Iredell County, 18
IRVIN, 358

J

Jackson
   Anna, 284
   Jackson, 131
   Stonewall, 36, 41, 49, 72, 75, 92, 120, 122
JACKSON, 358
James
   Robert, 290
JAMES, 358
Jamison
   Milas, 196
JAMISON, 359
Jarrett
   Samuel, 209
JARRETT, 359
JARRIL, 359
Jenkins, 20
   Henry, 147, 179
   John, 185
JENKINS, 359
JENNINGS, 359
Jericho Mills, 210
Jerusalem Plank Road, 219
JOHNSON, 359
Johnson's Island, 184, 288
Johnston, 312, 317
   Joseph, 34
JOHNSTON, 359, 360
JOLLY, 360
Jones
   William, 190
JONES, 360

Jones's Farm, 233
Jordan
   Hurley, 20
JORDAN, 360
JUSTICE, 360

K

KANADY, 360
KANE, 360
KANEDY, 360
KEETER, 360, 361
Keever
   Alex, 251
   George, 18
KEEVER, 361
KELLY, 361
Kendrick
   Larkin, 28, 107
KENDRICK, 361
Kennedy, 361
   John and Thomas, 111
   Joseph, 288
KENNEDY, 361
Killed in Action at Mechanicsville, 47
KILPATRICK, 361
KIMBREL, 361, 362
Kimbrell, 20
Kime
   Wilson, 216
KIME, 362
King
   Thomas, 115
KING, 362
King's Mountain, 7
King's Mountain Military Academy, 20
Kiser
   Robert, 215, 295, 298
   Zimri, 224
KISER, 362
Kistler
   Theo, 178, 211
KISTLER, 362, 363
Koonce
   Hamilton, 182
KOONCE, 363
KOONE, 363
KURF, 363

L

LACKEY, 363
LANCASTER, 363
LANKFORD, 363
LASSITER, 363
Latham
   Harvey, 91
LATHAM, 363
Lattimore, 19, 364
   Franklin, 200, 203, 274
   James, 200, 203, 274
   Jesse, 143, 274
   Thomas, 151
   Thomas D, 6, 25, 29, 32, 36, 46, 54, 68, 74, 95, 141, 146, 170, 175, 197, 259, 269, 274, 279
LATTIMORE, 364
Laurel Springs Guards, 16, 17, 85, 104, 110, 118, 129, 146, 182, 217, 263, 276
Lawing
   John, 22, 25
LAWING, 364
LAWRENCE, 364
LAWS, 364
Leach
   Edwin, 83
LEACH, 364
LEATHERMAN, 364
LEAZER, 364
LEDBETTER, 364
LEDWELL, 365
Lee
   Robert E, 34, 37, 39, 45, 53, 89, 106, 120, 132, 135, 219, 267, 271
   William Capers, 250
   William Crook, 250
LEE, 365
LEMASTER, 365

LEONARD, 365
Leventhorpe, 368
   Collett, 21, 23, 27, 31, 64, 137, 166, 168, 235
LEVENTHORPE, 365
LEWIS, 365
Light Division, 38, 41, 42, 48, 53, 54, 94, 96, 97, 104, 108, 123, 132
Lincoln
   President Abraham, 12, 14, 235, 286
Lincoln County, 9, 18, 85, 96, 102, 106, 115, 117, 131, 151, 163, 166, 175, 177, 181, 264, 284, 298
Lincolnton, 31, 58, 66, 67, 283, 284, 286
LINEBARGER, 365
LINGERFELT, 365
Little Big Horn National Cemetery, 297
Little Round Top, 143
LITTLETON, 365
LOFLIN, 366
LOFTIS, 366
London
   John, 106
LONDON, 366
Long
   Franklin, 85
   William, 295, 296, 298
LONG, 366, 367
LONGSTON, 367
Longstreet, 388
   James, 42, 53, 58, 75, 81, 158, 185, 204, 267, 269
Lookadoo
   George, 294
LOOKADOO, 367
LOUDER, 367
LOVELACE, 367
LOVETT, 367
Lowrance
   Samuel, 248
   William L J, 11, 18, 89, 90, 103, 115, 119, 140, 144, 148, 149, 152, 173, 186, 210, 248, 305, 308
LOWRANCE, 367
Lucas
   Henderson, 19, 31, 137, 166, 168
LUCAS, 368
Lutz
   John, 19, 288
LUTZ, 368
LYALL, 368
LYNCH, 368

M

MACON, 368
Mahone
   William, 219
MAHUGH, 368
Malvern Hill, 62
Martin, 309, 311, 315, 322, 336, 340, 345, 354, 356, 366, 369, 371, 374, 389, 390, 394, 395
   Barlett, 184
   Bartlett, 90, 110, 146
   Charles, 76, 97, 112, 134, 157, 206, 289
MARTIN, 368, 369
Marye's Heights, 105
MASON, 369
Matthews
   Washington, 299
MAUNEY, 369
MAYS, 369
MCARTHUR, 369
MCBRAYER, 369
MCCALL, 369, 370
McCallum
   Calvin, 290
MCCALLUM, 370
McClellan, 136
   George, 34
McClurd
   James, 224
MCCLURD, 370
MCCORD, 370
MCCORMACK, 370

MCCRARY, 370
MCDANIEL, 370
McDowell, 352, 367, 394
   Irwin, 34
   John, 32, 90, 119, 131, 274
MCDOWELL, 370
McFadden
   John, 225
MCFADDEN, 370
MCFALLS, 370
Mcgee, 19
McGee, 370
   Joseph, 32, 71, 90
MCGEE, 370, 371
McGinnis
   Nathan, 57
MCGINNIS, 371
MCGLAMERY, 371
MCHAHEY, 371
McIlwain Hill, 255
McInnes, 371
McIntire
   David, 142, 153
McKinney
   William, 20
MCKINNEY, 371
McLaughlin, 11, 18
MCLAUGHLIN, 371
McLeod
   Nevin, 141
   Norman, 141
MCLEOD, 371, 372
McMillan Woods, 143
McNeely, 11, 18, 288, 372
   Carmi, 11, 90, 146, 175, 184
MCNEELY, 372
MCNEILLY, 372
MCOLFEE, 372
McPherson's Ridge, 139
McRae, 299
   James, 299
MCRAE, 372
McSwain
   George, 188, 189
MCSWAIN, 372, 373
Meade
   George, 257
Means, 373
MEANS, 373
Mechanicsville, 41, 45, 96, 324, 348, 355, 358, 361, 368, 371, 374, 376, 383, 384, 388, 391, 412, 414
Mecklenburg Boys, 19, 76, 87, 146, 222, 278
Mecklenburg County, 7, 19, 76, 166, 205, 209
MEDLIN, 373
MELTON, 373
METCALF, 373
Miller, 11, 348, 354, 366, 369, 373, 374, 388
   Eli, 19, 32, 67, 71, 84
   Francis, 18
   James and Michael, 85
   John, 21, 22, 24, 25, 85, 109, 182, 188, 230
   Troy, 196
MILLER, 373, 374
MILLIGAN, 374
MILLS, 374
MILSAPS, 374
Mine Run, 187
Minnesota, 300
MINTS, 375
Miranda, 11
MITCHELL, 375
Mittag
   William, 115
MITTAG, 375
MODE, 375
Montana, 298
Montgomery Boys, 52, 147, 273, 279
Montgomery County, 13, 20, 29, 30, 83, 91, 106, 111, 113, 114, 116, 117, 130, 141, 186, 192, 193, 220, 224, 231, 234, 247, 273, 299
Monument Station, 301
Mooney
   Manual, 96
MOONEY, 375
MOOR, 375
Moore

Ross, 184
MOORE, 376
Morgan
   Clay, 125
MORGAN, 376
Morris, 389
MORRIS, 376
Morrow, 20
MORROW, 377
MOSLEY, 377
MOSS, 377
Munn
   David, 56
   T. D., 289
MUNN, 377
Murchison
   Calvin, 234
MURCHISON, 377
Mutiny, 103
Myers
   William, 19, 32
MYERS, 377

N

Nanney
   James, 18
NANNEY, 377, 378
NEAL, 378
NEEL, 378
NELON, 378
NESBIT, 378
Newton, 361, 378, 413
   Benjamin, 230
   John, 56, 157, 171
   Solomon, 67
NEWTON, 378
NICHOLSON, 378
NIX, 378
NOAH, 378
Norman, 369, 371, 372
NORMAN, 378, 379
Norment
   George, 19, 90, 115, 146, 249
NORMENT, 379

North Carolina's secession convention, 15
Norton
   William, 265

O

Oakland Guards, 11, 18, 99, 146, 277
O'DELL, 379
Oil City, PA, 250
Old Capital Prison, 184
OLLIS, 379
Osborne
   Ephraim, 73
OSBORNE, 379
outliers in Montgomery, 113
OVERBY, 379
Overcash, 11, 18, 380
   Henry, 231
OVERCASH, 379, 380
Owens, 380
   Bill, 113, 193
OWENS, 380
Ox Hill, 83, 85, 86

P

PADGETT, 380
Palmer
   William, 283
Parish
   Pinkney, 96
Parker
   Enoch, 231
PARKER, 380
Parks, 380
   George, 166
   John, 12, 18, 61
PARKS, 380
Parrish
   Pinkney, 104, 106
PARRISH, 380
PASCHAL, 381
Pasour
   Franklin, 153
PASOUR, 381

PATERSON, 381
PATRICK, 381
Patterson
   Jeremiah, 234
PATTERSON, 381
Peace meetings, 181
Peach Orchard, 143
PEACOCK, 381
Peebles's Farm, 233
Peeler
   David, 19
   John, 296, 298
PEELER, 381
Pender, 44, 72
   William D, 37, 42, 44, 45, 48, 50, 56, 61, 65, 70, 73, 78, 80, 90, 124, 138, 143, 178
PENDERGRASS, 381
Pendleton
   Lemuel, 106
PENDLETON, 382
PENNINGTON, 382
PERKINS, 382
Perry
   Henry, 103
   William, 67
PERRY, 382
Peterson
   John, 232
PETERSON, 382
Pethel
   Levi, 103
PETHEL, 382
Pettigrew
   J Johnson, 145, 174
Petty
   Moses, 171
PETTY, 382
Philbeck, 382
   William, 262
PHILBECK, 382, 383
PHILBERT, 383
Phillips
   Thomas, 68, 131, 147
PHILLIPS, 383
PICKEREL, 383

Pickett
   George, 109, 145
PICKLER, 383
Pig War, 108
PINSON, 383
PLESS, 383
PLONK, 383
PLUS, 383
Poe, 17, 383
POE, 383, 384
Point Lookout, 184, 192, 225, 290
Pond's Creek Station, 301
POOL, 384
Pope
   John, 71
PORTER, 384
Powell
   Andrew, 184
   Thomas, 223
POWELL, 384
Presnel
   James, 250
   John, 250
PRESNEL, 384
Price
   Drury, 287
   Jesse, 118
   Linville, 118, 237, 263
   Robert, 251
PRICE, 384
PROCTOR, 384
PRUITT, 384, 385
PUCKETT, 385
Putnam, 327, 385
PUTNAM, 385

Q

Queen, 385
QUEEN, 385

R

RABB, 385
RADFORD, 385
RAINES, 385

Raleigh, 27, 311, 317, 319, 322, 323, 325, 329, 332, 334, 336, 338, 339, 345, 347, 348, 353, 354, 362, 365, 366, 373, 377, 378, 379, 389, 396, 400, 401, 408
RAY, 386
Ream's Station, 227
Red Strings, 119
REEP, 386
Reeves, 21, 386
   James, 216, 220
REEVES, 386
REINEHARDT, 386
Revel, 20
   E H, 96
   Henry, 172, 295, 296, 300
REVEL, 386, 387
REYNOLDS, 387
Rhodes
   David, 19, 56, 57
RHODES, 387
RHYNE, 387
Richards
   Alexander, 196
RICHARDS, 387
Richardson
   David, 224
   Joshua, 230
RICHARDSON, 387, 388
Richmond, 34, 37
Rickert
   Henry, 142
RICKERT, 388
Riddick, 367
   James, 140, 142
   Richard, 31, 40, 46, 50, 56, 65, 71, 79, 81, 84, 86, 89
RIDDICK, 388
Riddle's Shop, 215
Ried, 388
   Robert, 32
RIED, 388
Ripley, 45
Roanoke River, 29
Robbins, 388
   Elisha, 38

ROBBINS, 388
Roberts, 20, 389
   John, 20, 116, 146
ROBERTS, 388, 389
ROBERTSON, 389
ROBINSON, 389
RODDEN, 389
RODGERS, 390
ROGERS, 390
Rollins
   Dock, 251
ROLLINS, 390
ROOPE, 390
ROPER, 390
ROSHICH, 390
Rough and Readys, 19, 217, 278, 282
Rowan County, 11, 12, 18, 22, 25, 31, 67, 96, 99, 100, 175, 187, 211, 231, 237, 283
ROYAL, 390
RUDD, 390
RUPPE, 390
Rush
   Martin, 13
RUSH, 390
RUSSELL, 391
Rutherford Band, 20, 38, 147, 278
Rutherford County, 7, 13, 17, 18, 20, 21, 22, 31, 37, 47, 60, 63, 65, 85, 101, 111, 116, 122, 126, 131, 141, 170, 205, 206, 230, 234, 251, 284, 285, 290, 303
Rutherford Rebels, 18, 24, 141, 146, 159, 180, 277
Rutherfordton, 21, 284
RUTLEDGE, 391

S

SADBERRY, 391
Sailor's Creek, 267
SAINTSING, 391
Salisbury, 11, 12, 23, 119, 283, 287
Sand Creek Massacre, 301
Sanders, 392, 402
   Elijah, 184

Jesse, 21
SANDERS, 391, 392
Sandy Run Yellow Jackets, 17, 24, 85,
   101, 146, 183, 244, 262, 276, 293,
   294, 300, 304
Sane, 19
SANE, 392
Sanford
   John, 205
SANFORD, 392
SARRAT, 392
Sarvice
   S T, 265
SARVICE, 392
Scales
   Alfred, 98, 135, 140, 157, 182, 188,
      201, 209, 232, 238, 249
SCISM, 392
Scoggins
   James, 251
   William, 251
SCOGGINS, 392, 393
SCOTT, 393
SECHLER, 393
Second Battle of Brandy Station, 178
Seine-hauling, 239
SELF, 393
Sellers, 393
Seminary Ridge, 138, 140
SENTER, 393
SERCEY, 393
Seven Days, 63
Seven Pines, 37
Shady Grove Rangers, 2, 18, 88, 133,
   134, 277, 281
SHARP, 393
Sharpe
   James, 288, 289
Sharpsburg, 96
Sharpshooter, 194, 227
SHAW, 393
Sheets, 17
SHEETS, 393
Shehan
   James, 20
SHEHAN, 394

Shelby, 66, 189, 289, 299, 300
SHEPHARD, 394
Sheridan
   Phillip, 259
Shields, 20, 394
   Robert, 19
SHIELDS, 394
Shoemaker, 317, 325, 365, 371, 382,
   407
   Calvin, 56
SHOEMAKER, 394
Shoffner
   Martin, 22, 32
SHOFFNER, 394
Shotwell
   Alexander, 18, 60, 61, 67
SHOTWELL, 394
Shufford
   Pinkney, 19, 66
Shuford
   Thomas, 130
SHUFORD, 394, 395
Shull, 19
SHULL, 395
SHYTLE, 395
SICELOFF, 395
Simmons, 20, 32, 395
   Asbury, 20
   James, 20
   Moses, 20
SIMMONS, 395
SIMS, 395
Sioux, 298
SISK, 396
Sitting Bull, 297
SIZEMORE, 396
Sloan
   Joseph, 22
SLOAN, 396
SLOOP, 396
SLUDER, 396
SMART, 396
Smith
   Richard, 284
   William, 206
SMITH, 396, 397

SNOTHERLY, 397
Sorrells
　Silas, 18
SORRELLS, 397
South
　James, 149
SOUTH, 397
SOUTHER, 397
Southside Railroad, 256, 259
Sparks
　Caleb, 122
SPARKS, 397
Sparrow, 397
　Cyrus, 67
SPARROW, 397, 398
Spencer
　Jesse, 13, 21
SPENCER, 398
SPIVEY, 398
SPLAWN, 398
Spotswood Hotel, 232
Spotsylvania Court House, 210
SPURLIN, 398
STALKER, 398
Stamey
　John, 96
STAMEY, 398
Stamper
　Hiram, 104
STAMPER, 398
Stampler
　Hiram, 183
Steadman, 20, 398
　Perry, 232
STEADMAN, 398
Steamer Mary Powell, 265
Stephens
　Richard, 229
STEPHENS, 398, 399
Stephenson
　Richard, 107
Stirewalt
　Frank, 12
STIREWALT, 399
STIRGILL, 399
Stokes County, 197

Stoneman
　George, 283
Stoneman's Raid, 283
STRICKLAND, 399
STROUD, 399
Stroup, 399
STROUP, 399
Stroupe, 9, 35
SUGGS, 399
SULLIVAN, 399
SUMMERVILLE, 399
Sutherland Station, 256, 259
SUTTLE, 399
SUTTON, 399
SWAFFORD, 400
SWEENEY, 400
SWEEZY, 400
SWIM, 400

T

TALBERT, 400
TALLENT, 400
TALLMAN, 400
TANNER, 400
TATE, 400
Tax-in-Kind, 117
Taylor
　James, 286
　Robert, 175
TAYLOR, 400, 401
TERRES, 401
The 34th North Carolina Infantry - Surrendered at Appomattox, 276
The Blizzard March, 302
the Wagoner's Battle, 170
The Wilderness, 119
Thomas
　John, 186
THOMAS, 401
THOMPSON, 402
Tiddy
　James, 108, 115, 151, 165, 171
TIDDY, 402
Todd, 19, 402, 403
　George, 209

Green, 206
James, 146
TODD, 402, 403
TOLBERT, 403
TOMS, 403
TONGUE, 403
TORRENCE, 403
Totopotomony Creek, 213
TOWERY, 403
Towry
  Aaron, 25
  Jack, 224
TOWRY, 403
Trimble
  Isaac, 144
Turkey Hill, 214
Turner
  Drury, 133
TURNER, 403
Twitty, 152
  Francis, 18, 142, 146
  Theophilas, 165
  Theophilus, 116
TWITTY, 404

U

U. S. 3rd Maryland Cavalry, 185
Underground Railroad, 119
Unionist, 13, 14, 16, 117
UPCHURCH, 404

V

Vance, 194
  Governor, 68, 101, 125, 181, 194, 232
  Zebulan, 14
VANDYKE, 404
Vaughn
  William, 289
VAUGHN, 404
VIRES, 404
VOILS, 404

W

Wacaster
  Levi, 151, 157, 177
WACASTER, 404
WAGONER, 404
WALDROP, 405
Walker
  George, 265
WALKER, 405
Wallace, 405, 412
WALLACE, 405
WALLEN, 405
Walls
  Henry, 126
WALLS, 405
WALTERS, 405
Ware, 405
  B H, 63
WARE, 405
Warlick
  Simpson, 250
WARLICK, 406
Warren
  Gouverneur, 210
WARREN, 406
Waters
  Abraham, 19, 52, 56
Watkins
  Jonas, 20
WATKINS, 406
Weaver
  Alfred, 18
WEAVER, 406
Webb
  A J, 154
  Gilbert, 28
WEBB, 406, 407
WEBSTER, 407
WEEKS, 407
WELLMAN, 407
WELLS, 407
Wesson, 20
  William, 104
WESSON, 407
Wheat Field, 143

WHETSTINE, 407
WHISNANT, 407
White
  Albert, 300
  Asbury, 232
  Hiram, 296, 300, 303
  Thomas, 207
WHITE, 407, 408
Whiteside
  Jonathan, 254, 265
WHITESIDE, 408, 409
WHITMIRE, 409
Wilcox
  Cadmus, 181, 202, 219, 259
Wilderness, 201
WILES, 409
WILKERSON, 409
Wilkie
  Lorenzo, 18, 230
WILKIE, 409
Wilkins
  William, 167
WILKINS, 409
Williams
  Bodisco, 196
  Lawson, 256
WILLIAMS, 409, 410
Williamsport, 168
Williford
  James, 187, 290
  John, 11
WILLIFORD, 411
Willis, 329, 348, 358, 380, 403, 414
WILLIS, 411
Wilson
  James, 20
  Jim, 17
  Stephen, 16, 30, 71
WILSON, 411
Winn
  Wallace, 131
WINN, 412
WISE, 412
WITHERS, 412
Withrow, 412

WITHROW, 412
WOMACH, 412
Wood
  James, 146, 197
  John, 157
  Thompson, 290
WOOD, 412
Woodie, 413
  Calvin, 188
  Nelson, 16, 90, 104, 106
WOODIE, 412, 413
Woods
  James, 167
WOODSIDE, 413
Woody
  George, 146
Wortman
  J, 215
WORTMAN, 413
Wright, 19, 413, 414
  Sidney, 250
WRIGHT, 413, 414
Wriston
  Charles, 209
WRISTON, 414
WYATT, 414

Y

YANCY, 414
YARBOROUGH, 414
YELTON, 414
YODER, 414
Young
  John, 140, 142, 146, 174, 195, 239, 255
YOUNG, 414

Z

ZIMMERMAN, 414
Zouaves, 206

Bibliography

Alexander, Edward S. 2015. *Dawn of Victory, Breadthrough at Petersburg March 25 - April 2, 1865*. 1st. El Dorado Hills, California: Savas Beatie LLC.

Archives, The National. 1960. "Compiled Service Records of Confederate Soldiers Who Served in Organizations From North Carolina." Washington DC: The National Archives and Record Service, General Services Administration.

Auman, William T. 2014. *Civil War in the North Carolina Quaker Belt*. 1st. Jefferson, NC: McFarland & Company, Inc.

Beitzell, Edwin W. 1983. *Point Lookout Prison Camp for Confederates*. 5th. Leonardtown, Maryland: St. Mary's County Historical Society.

Brown, Dee. 1963. *The Galvanized Yankees*. 2nd. Urbana, Ill: Bison Book.

Bynum, Victoria E. 2010. *The Long Shadow of the Civil War*. First. Chapel Hill: The University of North Carolina Press.

Calkins, Chris M. 2008, 2011. *The Appomattox Campaign March 29 - April 9, 1865*. 2nd. Lynchburg: Schroeder Publications.

Carolina, State Library of North Carolina and State Archives of North. n.d. *North Carolina Digital Collections*. Accessed February 25, 2017. http://digital.ncdcr.gov/cdm/compoundobject/collection/p15012coll8/id/681/rec/20.

Carpenter, Robert C. 2016. *Gaston County, North Carolina, In The Civil Ward*. First. Jefferson, NC: McFarland & Company, Inc.

Census, The United States. 1860. "The 1860 United States Census." North Carolina: The United States Census.

Center, North Carolina Digital Heritage. 2017. *North Carolina Newspapers*. Accessed June 28, 2017. http://newspapers.digitalnc.org.

Chalafant, William Y. 1989. *Cheyennes and Horse Soldiers*. 2nd. Norman, OK: Red River Books.

Coddington, Edwin B. 1968. *The Gettysburg Campaign - A Study in Command*. 3rd. New York: Charles Scribner's Sons.

Crawford, Martin. 2001. *Ashe County's Civil War-Community and Society in the Appalachien South*. 1st. Charlottesville: The University Press of Virginia.

Dowdey, Clifford. 1960. *Lee's Last Campaign*. New York: Skyhorse Publishing.

—. 1978. *The Seven Days*. The Fairfax Press.

Dunlop, William S. 2012. *Lee's Sharpshooters*. 2nd. Forgotten Books.

Elliott, James C. n.d. "The Southern Soldier Boy." James C. Elliott - Post war writing.

Ernsberger, Don. 2008. *Also for Glory*.

Evans, Capt. Thomas C. 2017. *The Siege of Petersburg Online*. Accessed June 23, 2017. http://www.beyondthecrater.com/resources/np/1864-np/sep-64-np/np-18640908-raleigh-confederate-scales-brigade.

Foley, J Timothy Cole and Bradley R. 2007. *Collett Leventhorpe The English Confederate*. Jefferson, NC: McFarland and Company Inc, Publishers.

Gaines, Dr. J. M. 1899. *Sick and Wounded Confederate Soldiers at Hagerstown and Williamsport*. Accessed April 30, 2018. http://www.csa-dixie.com/csa/prisoners/t71.htm.

Girvan, Jeffrey M. 2010. *Deliver us From This Cruel War, The Civil War Letters of Lieutenant Joseph J. Hoyle, 55th North Carolina Infantry*. 1st. Jefferson, North Carolina: McFarland & Company, Inc. Publishers.

Hartley, Chris J. 2010. *Stoneman's Raid 1865*. 1st. Winston-Salem, NC: John F. Blair.

Hassler, William W. 1965. *One of Lee's Best Men The Civil War Letters of General William Dorsey Pender.* The University of North Carolina Press.

Hassler, William Woods. 1957. *A. P. Hill Lee's Forgotten General.* 2nd. Chapel Hill: The University of North Carolina Press.

Hess, Earl J. 2009. *In The Trenches At Petersburg-Field Fortifications and Confederate Defeat.* 1st. Chapel Hill: University of North Carolina Press.

Jones, Stephen Collis. 1920. *Full Text of "The Hamrick generations, being a genealogy of the Hamrick Family.* Accessed June 20, 2017. https://archive.org/details/hamrickgeneratio00jone.

Krick, Robert K. 2007. *Civil War Weather in Virginia.* Tuscaloosa: The University of Alabama Press.

Lattimore, Thomas D *T.D.*". 1901. "34th North Carolina Infantry." Shelby, NC: Lattimore.

Longacre, Edward G. 2001. *General William Dorsey Pender, A Military Biography.* 1st. Conshohocken, PA: Combined Publishing.

Longstreet, General James. 1992. *From Manassas to Appomattox.* 2nd, Introduction by Jeffrey D. Wert 1991. New York: Da Capo Press, Inc. a subsidiary of Plenum Publishing Corporation.

Lonn, Ella. 1940. *Foreigners In The Confederacy.* 3rd. Chapel Hill: The University of North Carolina Press.

Martin, Clifford R. n.d. "Grandfather, CSA."

McNeely, Carmi K. 1907. "Remeninces, "A Tale of the Civil War as Told by C. K. McNeely Co. D 34th North Carolina."

McPherson, James M. 1997. *For Cause and Comrades.* New York: Oxford University Press.

Norris, Joseph. 2017. *South Tried to End the War at St. Mary's.* Accessed October 5, 2018. http://www.thebaynet.com/articles/0617/south-tried-to-end-civil-war-in-st-marys.html.

Patterson, Gerard A. 2001. *From Blue to Gray The Life of Confederate Generral Cadmus M. Wilcox.* 1st. Mechanicsburg: Stack[pole Books.

Perry, Aldo S. 2012. *Civil War Courts-Martial of North Carolina Troops.* 1st. Jefferson, NC: McFarland & Company, Inc. Publishers.

Randolph W. Kirkland, Jr. 2002. *Dark Hours - South Carolina Soldiers, Sailors, and Citizens Who Were Held in Federal Prisons during the war for Southern Independance 1861-1865.* First. Charleston, SC: The South Carolina Historical Society.

Ray, Fred L. 2006. *Shock Troops of the Confederacy.* 1st. Asheville: CFS Press.

Rhea, Gordon C. 2000. *To The North Anna River.* 2nd. Baton Rouge: Louisiana State University Press.

Robertson, James I., Jr. 1992. *General A. P. Hill The Story of a Confederate Warrior.* First Civil War Library Edition. New York, NY: Vintage Books, a divison of Random House, Inc.

___ .1987. *General A. P. Hill, The Story of a Confederate Warrior.* 2nd. New York: Vintage Civil War Library, Vintage Books, A Division of Random House Inc.

Scandinavian Confederates. Accessed June 15, 2017. http://www.borgerkrigen.info/ScandinavianConfederates/swedish.

Sears, Stephen W. 1996. *Chancellorsville.* New York: Mariner Books.

Siniard, Diane. 2007. *Military Obituaries September and October 1862.* Accessed January 15, 2017. http://www.nccivilwar.lostsoulsgeneology.com/obits.

Speer, Lonnie R. 1997. *Portals to Hell - Military Prisons of the Civil War.* 1st. Mechcnicsburg, PA: Stackpole Books.

Stokes, Karen. 2013. *The Immortal 600, Surviving Civil War Charleston and Savannah.* First. Charleston, SC: The History Press.

Taylor, Michael W. 1994. *The Cry is War, War, War.* Dayton, OH: Morningside House Inc.

Thornburg, Kitty. 1913. *Dallas County, North Carolina: A Brief History.* Charleston, SC: The History Press.

Tisdale, Jean. 1997. *Dear Companion.* Spindale, NC: Kaleidoscope Publishers.

Trotter, William R. 1988. *Bushwhakers! The Civil War in North Carolina The Mountains.* First. Winston-Salem, NC: John F Blair.

Trotter, William R. 1988. *Silk Flags and Cold Steel.* Winston-Salem: John F. Bliar.

Trout, Robert J. 2011. *After Gettysburg - Cavalry Operations in the Eastern Theater July 14, 1863 to December 31, 1863.* Hamilton: Eagle Editions Ltd.

Trudeau, Noah Andre. 2002. *Gettysburg A Testing of Courage.* 2nd. New York: Harper Collins Publishers Inc.

Tucker, Phillip Thomas. 2016. *Pickett's Charge - A New Look at Gettysburg's Final Attack.* New York: Skyhorse Publishing.

Gettysburg at 150: The Story of Pickett's Charge. Accessed April 17, 2017. http://rare.us/uncategorized/gettysburg-at-150-the-story-of-picketts-charge/.

Wert, Jeffry D. 2011. *A Glorious Army.* New York: Simon & Schuster.

Wiley, Bell Irvin. 1970. *The Life of Johnny Reb - The Common Soldier of the Confederacy.* Baton Rouge: Louisiana State University Press.

William W. Hassler, Jr. 1970. *Crisis at the Crossroads: The First Day at Gettysburg.* 1st. University: University of Alabama Press.

Wills, Brian Steel. 2013. *Confederate General William Dorsey Pender, The Hope of Glory.* 1st. Baton Rouge: Louisiana State University Press.

Winik, Jay. 2001. *April 1865 The Month That Saved America.* First. New York: HarperCollins Publisers Inc.

Wittenberg, Eric J., J. David Petruzzi, and Michael F. Nugent. 2008. *One Continuous Fight.* 1. New York, NY: Savas Beatie LLC.

United States Government, War of the Rebellion: Serial. 1862. *Report of Brigadier General William D Pender.* The Ohio State University: eHistory.OSU.EDU/books/official-records.

About The Author

Donald E. Hazelwood lives in West Virginia with his wife and two daughters on a farm that has been in the same family for generations. He holds a BA in Accounting and has worked in various roles in banking for the past twenty-four years. He currently works in compliance and fraud investigation for a local financial institution. His study of the 34th North Carolina was inspired by his principal Civil War ancestor who died while serving in the 34th.

Tom Perry's Laurel Hill Publishing

LHP

Thomas D. "Tom" Perry
4443 Ararat Highway
P O Box 11
Ararat VA 24053

276-692-5300
laurelhillpub@gmail.com
https://squareup.com/store/laurel-hill-publishing-llc

This book was published by agreement with Tom Perry's Laurel Hill Publishing.

Tom Perry's books are available at the links listed below.

Autographed copies available at https://squareup.com/store/laurel-hill-publishing-llc
and
Available Tom Perry's Author Page on Amazon at https://www.amazon.com/-/e/B002F4UJGEA

Copyright 2019 Donald E. Hazelwood

ISBN: 9781792037207

Book Design Copyright 2019 Tom Perry's Laurel Hill Publishing

Made in the USA
Middletown, DE
05 October 2023